by names and images

BRINGING THE GOLDEN DAWN TO LIFE

PEREGRIN WILDOAK

SKYLIGHT PRESS

First published in Great Britain in 2012 by Skylight Press,
210 Brooklyn Road, Cheltenham, Glos GL51 8EA

Designed and typeset by Rebsie Fairholm
Publishers: Daniel Staniforth and Gareth Knight

www.skylightpress.co.uk

Printed and bound in Great Britain by Lightning Source, Milton Keynes.
Text typeset in Minion Pro. Titles set in HoneyBee, a font by Laura Worthington.
Symbols set in Segno Pro and Adobe Hebrew.

British Library Cataloguing in Publication Data.
A catalogue record for this book is available from the British Library.

ISBN 978-1-908011-50-3

Dedicated to

G.H. Fr D.H.
and
Morgan

For their wisdom, guidance and presence.

Acknowledgements

This book is the fruit of years of learning and sharing with many people and much generous support. In particular I would like to thank: Gareth, Rebsie and Daniel at Skylight Press for giving new life to this old work; Gareth Knight for his kind words, wisdom and examples of good quality esoteric writing; everyone at the OLC, especially GH Fr SV and VH Fr II, for the initiations and Sr SEC and VH. Sr LP for the ongoing study; Srs LiC, SA and EH for helping in the first Order; Celia for numerous engaging emails; all the members, past and present, of the Golden Dawn Society of Western Australia for so many things, magical and personal; the members of the Cauldron of Change, Tikkun and the Fires of Azrael; Fay for the initial proofreading; Patrick Zalewski for answering all my questions; my parents, Cliff and Geraldine for the welcoming back; my son Robin for simply being him and the gaming breaks; and above all, for just about everything already mentioned and far, far more, my beloved one, Morgan.

TABLE OF CONTENTS

DIAGRAMS AND TABLES

Diagram List

Table List

APPROACHING THE GOLDEN DAWN

HE Golden Dawn in one form or another continues to be one of the main expressions of the Western magical tradition. Despite its age, pompous Victorian form, sexist language and dense original texts, it is still flourishing in today's 'grab-it and run' spiritual era. Regardless of pronouncements (some of them nearly a century old) from some magicians that the GD was useful in its day, but is now obsolete, the tradition continues to be a living, growing one. And like it or not, its techniques, rituals, magical approach and energy are still being siphoned off by Neo-Pagans and others whose practices fall short when it comes to delivering consistent results at the subtler and higher levels.

Why does the Golden Dawn continue to be such a spiritual force today? Because it works and will continue to work even if the unlikely occurs and one day humanity does 'enter' that mythical Age of Aquarius where suddenly we will all shift our consciousness and evil will lessen its grip on the world. I have known feminist witches grit their teeth and use the GD Rose-Cross and its 'name of Jesus', simply because they know it will provide the healing and protection they need. I have seen many instances of New Age Wiccans and others using techniques taken or derived from the GD and believing them to be 'traditional' Craft material. Indeed the GD permeates the entire contemporary magical and Neo-Pagan movement.

This sheer utility of the Golden Dawn has led to it being spiritually strip-mined in recent years, its magical rituals and practices ripped from the bedrock of tradition where they grew and were nurtured. Not that there is really anything wrong with this per se. The Golden Dawn, like the entire Western magical tradition, has and will survive these explorations and its mined products are certainly useful to some.

However, if we wish to experience the full transforming power of the Golden Dawn we need to approach it on its own ground. We need to cease to focus on the utility of the GD, cease asking ourselves 'what can I get' from the rituals and techniques and open ourselves to the tradition as a whole. We need to approach the GD on equal terms, seeking not only for it to serve our spiritual ends, but also be truly open and willing to serve its spiritual ends. These spiritual ends are the same as those of any legitimate spiritual tradition – the awakening of humanity, the healing of the world and the restoration of divinity within the daily lives of us all.

If we take our magical spirituality seriously we have to be open to this 'calling'. The Golden Dawn, like all authentic Western traditions derives its magic from inner realm Beings. These Beings have put in place, monitor and maintain a stream of spiritual blessing that may be brought into our lives and into the world by the rituals and practices of the tradition. This has not been done for our amusement or solitary spiritual unfoldment. Nor has it been done so that we may better our material lives, develop psychic powers or test our magical prowess in 'astral battles'. These Beings have created the Golden Dawn for one purpose only and that is to further the unfoldment of the One Being of All. The Golden Dawn is one of many invitations by God to seek our active participation in a joint venture to heal the world, or as some Christian traditions put it, to affect the divinization of the Earth.

If we are not willing to engage in this project; if we do not wish to surrender ourselves to Goddess or if we are unable to allow ourselves to be an agent for healing and change in the physical, real flesh and blood world, then our Golden Dawn magic will be less than fully transformational. All the great religions, spiritual systems and teachers agree on this one point; God calls us to be active in the world, to change it and restore justice. The Golden Dawn is one way of helping us to achieve these ends, one that is effective and beautiful, coherent and personal.

Some contemporary magicians would disagree with some of my statements here, and that is fine. Ultimately however, we need to look at where we wish to be, what spiritual energies we wish to align ourselves with. The contemporary magical community with its ever present lies regarding magical succession, ego-boosted adepts, 'magical battles' and many dysfunctional leaders may not be where we wish to head. I believe that many of these problems occur in the magical community because of an endemic failure to approach our magic with surrender, openness and an understanding of service.

MOTIVATION FOR MAGIC

The key here of course is the motivation that we bring to our magic. Why are we seeking to practice or study Golden Dawn magic? There is no right or wrong answer, but we do need to be honest with ourselves as we begin to engage with any form of spirituality, let alone magic. There is a wonderful discussion on this theme in *Psychology and the Spiritual Traditions* between Scottish author R.J. Stewart and Ngakpa Chögyam, a lama from the Nyingma lineage of Buddhism. Ngakpa points out clearly that a drive to be 'alternative' or to 'drop out' are unsuitable reasons for entering a spiritual journey. He also raises the issue of the search for personal and psychological healing through spirituality:

> '...I feel that it's very important that people look at their own personal pain in a 'non-esoteric' manner before they shroud their own neurosis in the cloak of arcane mysteries. The intrinsic Mystery of Being is mysterious enough without filtering our involvement with its methods of Realisation through the web of belligerent potty training.' (p.33)

It is necessary to own and face our inner pain and damage before embarking upon deep magical work. In the contemporary Western world there seems to be very few of us who have escaped without some form of childhood or adolescent scar. Some of us may be better off seeking counselling or therapy rather than engaging with magic. Israel Regardie, the person who first published the Golden Dawn magical tradition, was very clear in his view that every magician should undergo therapy before *any* deep magic is attempted. And while of course we need to ensure the therapy we choose will be effective and transformational the key to its success lies within us, our honesty and willingness to look at ourselves. Regardie also was clear on the forms of therapy he considered effective, recommending only body-focused forms of therapy such as those inspired by the work of Wilhelm Reich. We will cover the need for inclusion of the body within magic later, but at this stage it is important to note that we need to choose both our therapist and our magical groups (if any) with conscious care and deliberation.

Whatever motivation we bring to magic and the Golden Dawn will manifest. If our hidden motives are for personal glory and the need to feel special, we will find that quite quickly we are selected for membership to an elite astral club, receive an important 'mission' from an inner realm being or discover a string of really powerful magical past-lives. If our motivation is to fuel our paranoia that we have been hard done to in life, we will find ourselves victims of astral attack. If we harbour unconscious wishes to be controlled and dominated we will speedily find the right group, leader or temple to do just that.

All this occurs because the realm where the majority of our magic first takes place is what is traditionally called 'the astral light'. This light is flexible, malleable, and it will take the form of the consciousness and unconsciousness we take to it. We will find all we are secretly looking for and none of it may exist outside of our own spheres and minds. We will cover the ramifications and workings of the astral light more in the first chapter.

Fortunately if we come to magic with a deep, open surrender and a desire to work in partnership with the Divine we will find opportunities occur to do just this. Our intentions and desires here stem from a realm of consciousness that is traditionally 'higher' than the astral light and thus contamination and illusion are less likely to occur. It is therefore extremely important for us to be honest about our magical motivations and also our willingness to surrender to the Divine. The Golden Dawn tradition is quite clear in its understanding that if we are unable or unwilling to surrender to our Sacred One(s), then we will only go so far in our spiritual unfoldment and service to the world. One of the original versions of the 'application for initiation' form used by the GD has the following piece of information for the prospective member or candidate:

'Belief in a Supreme Being, or Beings, is indispensable. In addition, the Candidate, if not a Christian, should at least be prepared to take an interest in Christian Symbolism.' (Gilbert, R.A. (1986) *The Golden Dawn Companion: a guide to the history, structure and workings of the Hermetic Order of the Golden Dawn.* p.45. Aquarian, Wellingborough.)

I take the word 'belief' here to mean something more than a cursory nod at a concept of God, but rather an active relationship with the Divine, and this was clarified in some of the later Orders stemming from the Golden Dawn. We also find within the closing section of the Neophyte ceremony, the first initiation and entry point into the Golden Dawn, this piece of advice:

'To this end let me first earnestly recommend you never to forget due honour and reverence to the Lord of the Universe, for as the whole is greater than its parts, so is He far greater than we, who are but as sparks derived from that unsupportable Light which is in Him.'

This I believe is an essential part of the way the Golden Dawn tradition works. We need to have an ongoing, active relationship with our Sacred One(s) and we need to surrender to them and their power and wisdom. True, we can certainly practice the Golden Dawn rituals without such a quality, and yes we will generate 'magical power'. But because we are not open on the core level of our being, the place where God and human commune, the rituals will not transform us fully. The result of this lack of openness and full transformation can be seen in both the history of the original Orders and the contemporary magical community – tales of woe and deception, lies and paranoia, abuse and madness. Without surrendering to the divine, such things are inevitable, and without a personal surrender on your behalf, you will at best be limited in unfoldment and at worst become intimate with a psychiatric disorder not of your choice.

PRACTICAL MAGIC OR SORCERY

Magic is one of those unfortunate words that have a number of different meanings and which elicit even more reactions when spoken about. The Golden Dawn quite clearly views magic as a process of linking with the Divine and the natural forces of the universe. There are few indications in the GD texts that suggest this tradition may be utilised to create changes in our personal lives, better jobs, new lovers and so forth. This form of magic falls into the realm of what many people would call practical magic or sorcery. If you are seeking instruction in this type of magic, you will not find it here.

Rather than degenerate into a 'high' magic (that which is not for the self) is better than 'low' magic (that which is for the self) discussion I want to point out something that is seldom mentioned in these discussions: most readers of books such as this actually do not need any help from magic. In a world where twenty thousand people will die from poverty and starvation each day, any Westerner who can afford to buy a book on magic is to be counted as rich beyond measure. To use our magical blessings, which stem ultimately from Goddess, to increase our station in life rather than to balance out the stakes a little for those who are literally starving to death and have nothing, says something for our personal magical motivation. And in this vein, the profusion of spell-craft manuals and coffee table books bristling with all forms of sorcery says a lot for the general motivation of the esoteric and New Age communities today.

However, the fact is that there are many competent writers and teachers who present Golden Dawn derived rituals and techniques as tools for bettering our personal and material lives. Israel Regardie himself detailed one such approach in his *Art of True Healing* essay and recounts how he used such magic to 'set himself up' financially upon his retirement. Each of us must decide for ourselves on the validity or otherwise of attempts to magically address material concerns. In his commentary to Dion Fortune's *The Circuit of Force*, English magician and author Gareth Knight examines the idea of using magical techniques to affect our personal, material lives and comes to these conclusions:

'There has always been a certain amount of controversy as to how far such techniques should be used, not as means for spiritual regeneration but almost as spells for changing circumstances. Affecting the material world by psychic means is however, not so simple as it may seem, and requires more than knowledge of a few names to chant and coloured symbols to imagine. … For most of us however, we only think seriously of food or sex or money when it becomes a problem, which is to say when we feel we are not getting our share. When we find ourselves in that situation then I regret to say that meditational visualisations are really not the best way to remedy the lack. This is simply a way of trying to avoid rendering to Caesar the things that are Caesar's. We are here in a physical condition in a physical world and while in that state we have to abide by the laws appropriate to it.' (Fortune, Dion and Knight, Gareth, (1998) *The Circuit of Force: Occult Dynamics of the Etheric Vehicle*, p.188-9. Thoth Publications, Loughborough.)

BRINGING THE GOLDEN DAWN TO LIFE

I have written this book to share the inner processes of the Golden Dawn tradition, which while not being clearly explained in other works are the heart and soul of it all. In recent years there have been small attempts by various authors to share what I call 'inner workings' of the rituals and techniques of the Golden Dawn – the required visualisation, movements of energy, focus, breath and dynamics that empower each and every ritual. Foremost amongst these authors is John Michael Greer and I heartily recommend his books listed in the bibliography.

However, there is still a pronounced tendency for magical authors to detail the words and actions of a ritual without explaining completely the required inner work on the microcosmic consciousness to make it as transformational as it possibly can be. This book then fills a gap in that it examines the core Golden Dawn rituals and practices and provides in exact detail the required inner work needed to empower these rituals so they become potent agents for change and partnership with God.

The original Golden Dawn texts had very little information in them regarding the inner workings required and the transmission of this knowledge was often undertaken orally. Consequently much of this information has become lost or scattered and there has arisen any number of variants. I do not claim that the suggestions given in this book are in any sense 'true' or 'secret'. Nor do I claim that they stem in an unbroken line from the 'original' Golden Dawn. None of this matters. What is important is that they work and will bring our Golden Dawn practice into the fullness it requires for the full and effective transformation it offers. Most of the inner workings and ideas offered here stem from a combination of my own analysis, knowledge from inner realm teachers, and information and sharing with a number of experienced GD magicians.

CRITICISMS OF THE GOLDEN DAWN

Nothing is perfect, especially a Western magical tradition that was created anew in a secular culture robbed of its mystery traditions centuries ago. The Golden Dawn tradition therefore has a number of problems, which are being slowly addressed and changed in today's magical communities. We cannot ignore these problems and must face them head on if we are to engage in the most effective magic and transformation possible. Without engaging in a full critique of the Golden Dawn, which has been effectively done elsewhere from a number of viewpoints, I do wish to focus on three main areas that need attention: the feminine, spiritual advancement and the body.

CHRISTIAN PATRIARCHY OR HIDDEN GODDESS?

Within the Golden Dawn corpus there are repeated mentions to 'God' and 'The Lord of the Universe'. This however should not be taken as an indication of Christian monotheism; the terminology is poetic and can be replaced by other equally poetic inspirations without detracting from the transformational power of the tradition. Though most of the early Golden Dawn members were, due to the nature of the society of the day, Christians, the order itself was not Christian. Throughout the ceremonies and rituals a great many non-Christian deities are invoked, but not formally worshipped. Similarly Christ, or His essence, was often invoked but not worshipped. This is not an attitude of simple religious tolerance and ecumenicalism, but rather a profound realisation of the mystic truth behind various religious forms. This is a hallmark of the type of magic and spirituality found within the Golden Dawn and its inner order. It can easily be seen in the following quote from the 'Fourth Knowledge Lecture':

> 'In true religion there is no sect. Therefore take heed that thou blaspheme not the name by which another knoweth his God. For if thou doest this thing in Jupiter thou will blaspheme YHVH (Jehovah): and in Osiris, YEHESUAH (Jesus).'

The Golden Dawn is also often criticized for being inherently patriarchal and authoritarian. On the surface and in much of the organisation, this is true. But we must remember when the Order, that is, the outward form *not the magic itself*, was formulated. For a spiritual system founded in the late 1800s, the Golden Dawn was remarkably progressive. Men and Women were admitted on equal terms, an unheard of innovation, as were the followers of any religion whatsoever, not simply Christianity. The members were not restricted in any way in their personal beliefs or morals. The leaders of the Order insisted on this, though many sought to have them impose rules for exclusion on the grounds of 'sexual immorality', that is homosexuality. MacGregor Mathers, one of the founders of the GD was himself was a staunch supporter of Women's rights and anti-vivisection, and may have helped Anna Kingsford work political magic against vivisectionists. He wrote in his introduction to *The Kabbalah Unveiled*:

> ' ...The translators of the bible have carefully crowded out of existence and smothered up every reference to the fact that Deity is both masculine and feminine ... Now we hear much of the Father and the Son, but we hear nothing of the Mother in the ordinary religions of the day.'

In recent years the lack of explicit recognition within the Golden Dawn of the Goddess or 'the feminine face of God' has begun to be addressed. However, there is still a long, long way to go. Of course the One Being of All has no gender or any other human attribute in the way we understand them. However, the terminology and world-view used by any spiritual system needs to reflect honour and respect to all its adherents. Because of the societal and Masonic environment it sprung from, the original

Golden Dawn failed to do this. Mary K. Greer in her monumental and inspiring *Women of the Golden Dawn* has shown up the sexist, petty-minded and unconscious reactions from male magicians to their female counterparts the world over. If we do not take care, we can, in our own practice, unconsciously reproduce this damaging ideology.

One of the ways to avoid this is to look at the GD rituals and theory in a different light. For instance the names of many of the traditional Archangels invoked and worked with in the GD contain the suffix 'el'. This is normally translated as 'God' and thus we think of Raphael, for example, as the Healer of God. However, the root word 'el' or 'al' actually and literally means 'the One' or 'All' and is found in many Semitic names of the divine such as **Al**lah, **El**ohim etc. Thus Rapahel becomes the healer of the One Being of All. This small but crucial re-framing allows us to be more aware of our tradition and gives space for the Goddess to arise from its core, where She has always been. (Throughout this book I use the terms 'God', 'Goddess', 'the One' and 'the One Being' inter-changeably).

Now to say that the Goddess has always been at the core of the Golden Dawn is, I confess, a mite provocative and will be seen in some quarters as a complete misunderstanding on my behalf. However, the core of the Golden Dawn is in essence divinity itself, the One Being. Some of us may call this Being God or Christ since that is how they know Him. Others may call Her Isis, since that is how we know Her. Ultimately we recognize that our knowing is small and dependant upon our own experience, religion and culture. In owning this limitation we realise that we can never actually know this Being and are quite comfortable in our own attempts to name it and in other attempts that give it a different name and a different form, but the same essential qualities. The essential qualities that emanate from the divinity at the heart of the Golden Dawn exactly match those of the Goddess as She is envisioned today: compassionate, protective, powerful, nurturing, radical, transformational to self and society, personal and direct.

Spiritual Advancement or Personal Unfoldment?

We should also keep in mind that the Golden Dawn grade system of 'advancement' through ceremonial initiation should not be taken literally. It is an artificial construct and not a statement of truth. Essentially, it does not imply that a fourth degree Philosophus is 'better' or more 'advanced' than a first degree Zelator. It merely shows that a Philosophus is working in a different magical area than a Zelator, that is, with the element of Fire rather than the element of Earth.

The whole notion and misunderstanding of 'spiritual advancement' has been one of the more distressing and damaging ideas within the Western magical traditions. It has been used to justify, often unconsciously, some pretty narrow and nasty actions by so called adepts. At its core it robs us of the awareness of the incredible divinity and sacredness within each and every person. Of course as we continue in our practice and surrender to the One Being we do change, we do transform radically and utterly, but this is more of the nature of an unfoldment rather than advancement. The key difference here is that advancement is a measurement of progress against an external yard-stick of some sort; some pre-defined qualities and ideas that can never be useful to everyone. Unfoldment on the other hand reflects the ongoing expansion and transformation of ourselves into being more ourselves and is not a measure of any kind where we may fail to meet the grade.

The concept of unfolding is mentioned first in the Golden Dawn as part of the Neophyte Ceremony. It can best be illustrated in two ways, one traditional and the other very modern. The first is by looking at the form of a solid cube. It has six sides, joining one another. This may be said to be our enfolded earthy state, the state of 'the natural man' as the Golden Dawn (drawing on St Paul) puts it, and indeed the cube is one of the symbols of the material plane. However, if we take the cube apart, unfold it, and lay it out as in diagram 1, then we find we have the shape of the Calvary Cross. This is our unfolded state of being, related through its Christian symbolism to the sphere of the consciousness of the 'Higher Self' or 'Higher and Divine Genius'.

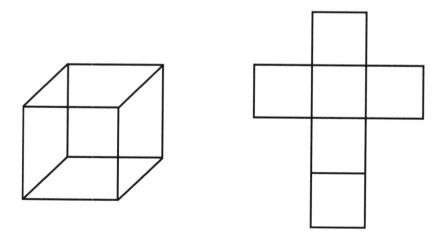

Diagram 1a: Cube   1b: Cube Unfolded into Six Squared Calvary

As useful and as profound as this metaphor is, I much prefer the following one first used in connection with my professional work providing information to counsellors of torture survivors. This uses a modern science toy, the Hoberman Sphere. This in essence is an expanding sphere formed of interlaced struts or connections as shown in the pictures below (if you can get hold of one of these things and actually play with it yourself this will make far more sense). If we take this structure as being ourselves, then in its enclosed or enfolded state (diagram 2a) it represents us as we are before spiritual awakening. We may also see each strut as some aspect of our essential self. In this state the struts are obscured and crowded in, just as for most of us our divinity and creativity, our deep love and power are obscured. In the centre of all, totally obscured is what we may consider as Higher and Divine Genius. The whole enclosed sphere as we see it from the outside may be considered as our lower self, our personality self hiding the presence of our Higher and Divine Genius within.

As we practice our tradition and spirituality the sphere slowly expands. It does this as our Higher and Divine Genius is awakened and grows larger in its influence, expanding and refining the various struts of our personality self. This is why spiritual change is always so disruptive to the concept of self – the self is actually being stretched and changed and transformed. The more our Higher and Divine Genius or deeper self comes into operation, the more we grow.

Notice now that in diagram 2b all of the struts are free and clear of each other, which is a metaphor for the opening out and owning of all parts of our beings, the creative and destructive. Please note also the *gaps* between the struts which indicate that these component aspects of our

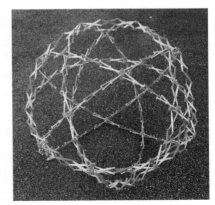

Diagram 2a:
Enfolded Sphere of the Self

Diagram 2b:
Unfolded Sphere of the Self

personality, while still being there, are no longer as important to us as they once were. This shows that in our unfoldment we become who we are, but expanded and freer to make choices. We never lose any aspect of our selves, they simply become part of a more fulfilled and harmonious whole. The more we unfold, the larger the 'gaps' in our personality selves become. And it is through these 'gaps' that the deeper self or Higher and Divine Genius can shine out to the world, helping to change and heal the injustice within it.

THE BODY WITHIN MAGIC

One of the most dangerous and problematic lacks within the original Golden Dawn tradition was its failure to fully include the body. Of course, when we perform ritual we move the body in various ways, but none of them are designed to fully open our consciousness to the divinity of the body and its place in our spiritual unfoldment. In recent years there has been much work done in the magical community to remedy this problem and I strongly recommend that you take up this idea also. Integrating the practice of yoga into our magical work is one obvious approach. For a more western option I refer you to several other authors who have performed this task far better than I can. Any of these approaches, provided you follow the instructions given by the authors carefully, will make up for this problem in the Golden Dawn.

The exercises known as 'the Five Rites' from Donald Michael Kraig's *Modern Magick* are an excellent idea for daily performance.

Israel Regardie in his *Twelve Steps to Spiritual Enlightenment* gives some wonderful relaxation and tension reduction exercises.

These exercises by Regardie are expanded into a full course of 'emptying out' bodily based spiritual exercises in C.S. Hyatt's *Undoing Yourself with Energised Meditation and Other Devices*. They are further re-stated and re-worked once more in Hyatt's *Secrets of Western Tantra*.

USING THIS BOOK

I have written this book for both the newcomer and experienced magician alike. Because of this it is not laid out in a series of steps or lessons, though it does follow a general sequence of easy through to harder processes. Magical and spiritual unfoldment is by its very nature a personal thing, and where we can draw many general principles they can never be applied universally. Also to be borne in mind is the value of general life and spiritual experience we all have. A middle aged parent or person in long-term partnership possesses skills and self awareness a brilliant and enthusiastic youth cannot begin to understand. This is what we bring to our spirituality and magic, this is what makes us unique beings and what will make our spiritual unfoldment unique also. There is then little point in arranging this book in such a way that will suit, at best, only a few of its readers.

Experienced magicians or those simply interested in using Golden Dawn rituals piecemeal may use this book as a reference point. All of the major rituals of the tradition, together with their inner work have been listed in the table of contents. Students of other traditions or those interested in the ideas of the Golden Dawn may like to follow the book in order as it gives a good overall rationale behind the GD tradition of magic, how and why it works. Readers wishing to follow a full Golden Dawn approach to their magical and spiritual unfoldment are advised to read the entire book through at least once before undertaking any practical work. Next re-read the Golden Dawn magical curriculum in Chapter Nine. Once you are clear on what you are going to do, and why, you may begin magical practice. For anyone embracing the Golden Dawn in this way, it is also essential you obtain either of the two Regardie compilations *The Golden Dawn* or *The Complete Golden Dawn System of Magic*. Several other books on particular aspects of the tradition not elucidated by Regardie are also recommended from time to time. As a magical system the GD is deep and vast; it has a lot to accomplish. Do not be put off by the complexity of some of the more 'advanced' rituals you read here. Take your time, read them but focus on the introductory rituals and slowly grow your knowledge and spiritual skill.

If we approach the Golden Dawn with our deepest and clearest motivation, if we surrender to its core, which is God; if we work its rituals on the inner and the outer realms and if we are willing to change the tradition where required, then we will find it to be one of the greatest gifts of our lives. I fell in love with the Golden Dawn long before I fell in love with another human being, and like any first love we have had a wonderful journey together. I hope that the fruits of this journey, which I offer here, will be of use and help to all. Any and all grace and wisdom belong to my teachers and guides; mistakes and omissions are my own.

THE GOLDEN DAWN TRADITION OF MAGIC

*A*s a magical tradition the Golden Dawn seeks to give to the magician tools so that she may transform her own consciousness at will. This is a risky undertaking since in any creative project we make mistakes before we get it right. And whereas we may bemoan a ruined canvas or sigh at the waste of wood in an unbalanced table, a mistake in transforming our own minds may lead to far more dire results. This is why the magical arts are traditionally considered dangerous, as too are the Tantric arts in the East. In each case the magician or tantrist is boldly stepping out with her own mind as the canvas and paints with which to create a new person.

Traditionally these dangers are minimised by two important factors. Firstly, by surrender to and partnership with our Sacred One(s), no matter what religion or spiritual tradition we belong to. Such an attitude of surrender and good relationship may be found in traditional Christianity, Judaism, Islam and some of the Neo-Pagan religions. Without this attitude of surrender and partnership with our Sacred One(s), embarking upon Golden Dawn magic is a highly dangerous venture. Ego-inflation and delusion are sure to result. If your personal understanding and approach to the Sacred is not one of surrender and good relationship, leave the Golden Dawn well and truly alone.

The second traditional safeguard is a structured approach to the task of transformation, one that is rooted in tradition, one that is slow and careful and one that is supported by inner realm Beings who have often been there before us and who have achieved what we are seeking. Specifically in the context of this book, this means designing a careful and insightful long term approach to our magic, one that will ensure unfoldment balanced by the need for stability and safety. Such an approach is outlined in Chapter Nine.

Tradition of course has its own problems, but without such a structured approach to magical transformation offered by a tradition we may find ourselves in deep water indeed. This is one of the great strengths of the Golden Dawn – it offers to each and every one of us a complete and structured coherent approach to our transformation, and today we need not belong to any Order to partake of this invitation. Obviously group work will help many people in their unfoldment, but for others it may do little either way and for some it may actually hinder their growth. This is especially the case with the high level of dysfunction in the magical community at present.

The Golden Dawn tradition of magic is unique in both its complexity and simplicity. It has often been said that this tradition is only for the scholarly, the intellectual, the elite, the intelligentsia or the upper class. Historically this was indeed true. Sadly today, despite many changes in attitudes and the public availability of the core Golden Dawn texts, it is still largely true. However, in its clearer forms and expressions, devoid of ancient clutter and ideology, the Golden Dawn can take our breath away with its sheer and simple beauty. The whole of its magic rests upon these simple words:

'By names and images are all powers awakened and re-awakened.'

'Colours are not symbols of forces but are the forces themselves.'

Please do not be fooled by this statement, nor gloss over what has just been said – literally the entire power of the Golden Dawn rests upon the principles embedded within these two sayings. The power and blessings of the magic may stem from the inner realms and those Beings who inhabit those realms, but for us to link to those realms and Beings we need to use and understand the principles here.

DIVINE NAMES

The power of names is an ancient belief occurring in most cultures throughout the world. It was historically believed that possession of somebody's true name would enable a person to have power over him or her. There are many myths and stories concerned with this belief, one of the best known being that of the Egyptian deities Isis and Ra. In this myth the Great Goddess Isis tricks the sun god Ra into revealing His true name so that She may have power over him. She does this by covertly poisoning Ra and then refusing to supply the antidote until His name is revealed. It is this belief in the power of names that caused, and still causes, many magicians to keep secret their magical names from all but trusted colleagues.

Another important magical belief is that 'the name itself is the thing itself'. That is, the name of a Goddess or God *is* the Goddess or God. This idea is very prevalent in most religions, and is where the idea of blasphemy stems from. Also implicit here is the awareness that the emotional and spiritual resonance that a name creates within us is determined, at least in part, by its usage. If we often hear a sacred name being used in an abusive or defamatory manner, we will begin to associate that name with the energy with which it is uttered. On the other hand if a name is only ever used in a very precise and sacred context, when we come to speak the name we will find it draws strength from the way we have heard it used.

A corollary to this belief of the name and the named being one, is that by uttering the true name of a Goddess or God (the true pronunciation or vibration) you will also bring the force of that deity into action. This shows that through the use of a divine name, the named (a God), the name and the namer (the magician) become One. It is this belief that is at the core of the Golden Dawn's use of divine names and is why the use of divine names is one of the key and most highly potent aspects of the Golden Dawn.

ANCIENT HEBREW AS MAGICAL LANGUAGE

Most of the names used by the Golden Dawn 'to awaken and re-awaken' forces are ancient Hebrew. This language is used simply because it is the historical language of the Qabalah, a mystical system used heavily in Western magic for many centuries. In Qabalistic cosmology the 22 letters of the Hebrew alphabet are more than just letters. They are also symbols and keys to the inner forces of the universe.

Qabalistic practice involves the frequent meditation upon these 22 letters, the repetition of which eventually 'builds' the letters within the psyche and subtle bodies of the magician. This does two main things. Firstly, it divides the psyche of the magician into a number of well defined areas, each being symbolised and keyed to one of the Hebrew letters. This is in effect an ordering of the chaotic nature of the mind into an artificial system so that certain aspects of the psyche may be called upon at will and others ignored. So, for example the magician will meditate upon the letter Mem, which means 'Water' and a whole host of correspondences to it, which we will look at later. The area of the self of the magician that is 'invoked', called forth, stirred into being by meditation upon this letter is now symbolised and placed under the control of the letter. Thus the utterance of each of the letters will therefore release a certain defined force from the psyche of the individual. Whenever the letter 'Mem' is used, specific qualities are able to be drawn forth from the magician. These will be different to the force provoked by another letter, Shin, corresponding to Fire, for example.

The letters then become 'keys' or activation symbols for the different emotional and spiritual energies within us, which are subjective in nature. However, since these letters are from a long tradition and have, many believe, a sacred origin, meditation upon them also links us to the cosmic forces of the universe they symbolize. This second aspect would not occur if we decided to key our various emotional and spiritual energies to a frivolous or arbitrary set of symbols. We could certainly select or invent a number of different symbols or sounds and they would function just as well as keys for our own subjective psyches as the Hebrew letters, but they would not link us to any coherent cosmic force.

Within Golden Dawn practice when a letter or divine word is used it first awakens our own subjective energies. These subjective energies are then directed exteriorly from us into the universe, where it activates the universal, objective force also associated with that letter or name. This objective, universal force is then called into the temple or being of the magician. This will help to clarify and balance the subjective force within us and deepen our links to the objective force. More importantly however, it will also strengthen our partnership with the objective forces of the universe. As we work with all the Hebrew letters in this way we deepen our partnership with the divine within all aspects of our being.

If you wish to practice Golden Dawn magic fully you will, at some point, need to learn the form, sound, meaning and numerical value of each of the Hebrew letters. There are many good and not so good books out that there that go into incredible complexity regarding the profundities of the Hebrew alphabet. These do not need to be studied unless you wish to delve deeper into the tradition. The magical curriculum in Chapter Nine gives suggestions for when to begin learning the Hebrew alphabet and the various symbols associated with it. The table below shows the alphabet and its English equivalent. Please note that Hebrew runs from right to left not left to right like our English and European alphabets. Also, five of the letters have a different form and numerical value when they occur at the end of a word. Their power and meaning stay the same.

Table 1: The Hebrew Alphabet

Letter	Name	Power	Value	Meaning
א	Aleph	A	1	Ox
ב	Beth	B, V	2	House
ג	Gimel	G, Gh	3	Camel
ד	Daleth	D, Dh	4	Door
ה	Heh	H	5	Window
ו	Vau	O,V,W	6	Pin or Hook
ז	Zayin	Z	7	Sword or Armour
ח	Chet	Ch	8	Fence or Enclosure
ט	Teth	T	9	Snake
י	Yod	I, Y	10	Hand
כ	Kaph	K, Kh	20	Fist
ל	Lamed	L	30	Ox Goad
מ	Mem	M	40	Water
נ	Nun	N	50	Fish
ס	Samech	S	60	Tent Prop
ע	Ayin	Aa, Ngh	70	Eye
פ	Peh	P, Ph	80	Mouth
צ	Tzaddi	Tz	90	Fishhook
ק	Qoph	Q	100	Ear or back of head
ר	Resh	R	200	Head
ש	Shin	S, Sh	300	Tooth
ת	Tau	T, Th	400	Cross
Finals				
ך	Kaph	K, Kh	500	Fist
ם	Mem	M	600	Water
ן	Nun	N	700	Fish
ף	Peh	P, Ph	800	Mouth
ץ	Tzaddi	Tz	900	Fishhook

Visualisation Within Magic

The second part of the first quote mentioned above concerning the use of images to 'awaken and re-awaken' forces, refers to visualisation. So much has been written about visualisation, how it works and its benefits that there is little point repeating it here. It is now an (almost) generally accepted fact that energised (enthusiastic) visualisation can cause change within both the psychological and spiritual aspects of our beings. The Golden Dawn utilises these visualisation techniques considerably to produce changes in consciousness and spiritual awakening. It is important here to make a distinction between idle imaginations and directed, willed visualisation, which uses the power of the imagination to effect changes. The power of imagination should never be underestimated and in many ways magic is the use of imagination, nothing more. There are many good works that show this well, and an equal number of pithy sayings that attempt to convey it all succinctly. From the magical point of view one of the best is *Magic and the Western Mind*, in which Gareth Knight states:

'[magic] is the science and art of the human imagination, and as long as we have imagination, we shall have magic. The right use of the imagination can bring many deep and lasting benefits, and might even prove a key to our survival'. (*Magic and the Western Mind*, Gareth Knight (1991). Llewellyn, St Paul.)

This 'right use' of the imagination is one of the keys to the way the Golden Dawn works with visualisation. There are two main differences in the traditional use of visualisation by the Golden Dawn and the approach found in much of the New Age community. Firstly, there is a clear understanding that visualisation means being able to see in the inner realm. Many newer approaches have it that if a vision, object, scene or symbol are 'felt' but not seen it is still visualisation or the equivalent. This view is not shared by the Golden Dawn and where it states that things need to be seen, they need to be *seen*. This is because the inner sight works within a particular aspect of the inner realms, and it is the visual aspect that creates the forms within this realm.

Secondly, the Golden Dawn visualisations are often performed upon symbols which are considered to be 'keys' to certain inner states of consciousness, like the Hebrew letters mentioned above. Some of the more complex GD visualisations are also designed to build up certain images that allow the contacting of astral or inner realm forces and Beings. These astral Beings use the images we create by building up a visualisation as a form in which to inhabit, thereby allowing communication between us and them. That is, these Beings are in themselves formless and consist solely of consciousness. They require forms built by magicians to inhabit so they can become operative in the inner realms most easily perceived by humanity. At the end of this chapter you will find some simple exercises designed to develop your visualisation.

Regardless of the rationale behind the GD use of visualisation however, nearly all make heavy use of colour, which brings us to the second quote. That certain colours produce certain 'moods' is also now a generally (and Western scientifically) accepted fact. Various groups of people such as artists, storytellers, psychologists and interior decorators have always made use of this knowledge. The GD uses colour to change the magician's consciousness, and this explains the heavy use of the different coloured robes, banners, mantles and equipment within the tradition. The GD also makes use of what it poetically terms 'the flashing colours', that is a colour and its spectrum opposite on a colour wheel, bright red and emerald green being one example. By using both colours alternately on a magical item, the colours do indeed seem to 'flash' and this can have a very profound effect upon our consciousness. This flashing is also useful in that it is a mode of attracting astral or inner realm force and energy, very much like a vortex.

There is also a philosophical consideration here – that of force and counter-force. The GD maintains that balance and equilibrium are essential for the unfolding of a deeper level of consciousness and the use of a colour and its opposite reflects this belief, both forces being present in a state of balance. The colours are always seen in GD magic as also being a force by themselves, that is, they have inherent properties regardless of whether they are perceived by a human magician or not.

The Golden Dawn went to considerable lengths to develop a system of colour correspondences to the various spheres of the Qabalah (which we will consider later). This is truly one of the greatest innovations of the Golden Dawn, previous magical colouring schemes being less complex and complete. In part this may be because before the 19th century the average person would not have had access to the range of paints and pigments needed to paint and create the various symbols and tools in the complex colours used in the Golden Dawn. The complexity and creativity of the colour schema within the GD was most likely an innovation of Moina Mathers, wife of one of the founders and a trained artist.

Much of this colour system has been retained and utilised by other traditions. Other aspects have been and are being revised by various

Orders and individuals, some of which claim to have the 'one true' system. Of course, this is all nonsense and we must come to a place where we can choose for ourselves which variant on a theme we prefer. To say that one scheme is valid for everyone and the rest false is rather akin to saying the way one singer sings Amazing Grace is the one true way and all the other versions are false. In this book I use the version of the GD colour scales published by Israel Regardie in his classic *The Golden Dawn*. You will find other versions listed in other books, the most complete and sensible being *The Magical Tarot of the Golden Dawn* by Pat and Chris Zalewski. At this stage I have listed the colours you need to memorise, at some point in your magical development, in Table Two. The Zodiacal and other attributions are given here for the sake of convenience and will be referred to in later chapters.

Table 2: Golden Dawn Colours

Sphere or Power	Colour	Attribution
Elemental Principles		
Air △	Yellow	
Fire △	Red	
Water ▽	Blue	
Earth ▽	Olive Green or Black	
Spheres on the Tree		
Kether	White	Air
Chokmah	Grey	Fire / the Zodiac
Binah	Black	Water / Saturn
Chesed	Blue	Water / Jupiter
Geburah	Red	Fire / Mars
Tiphareth	Yellow	Air / the Sun
Netzach	Green	Fire / Venus
Hod	Orange	Water / Mercury
Yesod	Purple	Air / the Moon
Malkuth	Olive Green	Earth / the World

Sphere or Power	Colour	Attribution
Hebrew Letters and the Paths on the Tree		
Aleph א	Pale yellow	Reflection of Air
Beth ב	Yellow	Reflection of Mercury
Gimel ג	Blue	Reflection of the Moon
Daleth ד	Green	Reflection of Venus
Heh ה	Red	Reflection of Aries
Vau ו	Red-Orange	Reflection of Taurus
Zayin ז	Amber	Reflection of Gemini
Cheth ח	Orange	Reflection of Cancer
Teth ט	Yellow	Reflection of Leo
Yod י	Yellow-Green	Reflection of Virgo
Kaph כ	Violet	Reflection of Jupiter
Lamed ל	Green	Reflection of Libra
Mem מ	Deep Blue	Reflection of Water
Nun נ	Green-Blue	Reflection of Scorpio
Samech ס	Blue	Reflection of Sagittarius
Ayin ע	Indigo	Reflection of Capricorn
Peh פ	Red	Reflection of Mars
Tzaddi צ	Violet	Reflection of Aquarius
Qoph ק	Crimson	Reflection of Pisces
Resh ר	Orange	Reflection of the Sun
Shin ש	Red	Reflection of Fire
Tau ת	Indigo	Reflection of Saturn
Planets		
Saturn ♄	Black and Indigo	
Jupiter ♃	Blue and Violet	
Mars ♂	Red	
Sun ☉	Yellow and Orange	
Venus ♀	Green	
Mercury ☿	Orange and Yellow	
Moon ☽	Purple and Blue	

FORMS OF GOLDEN DAWN MAGIC

The Golden Dawn tradition has numerous processes designed to achieve the exaltation of consciousness from the ordinary to the divine. All of the processes may be classed under eight headings, though this is my own classification and not traditional. Other folk may disagree with this classification, but in any case it makes understanding a complex tradition easier. It is rather like the old joke, 'how do you eat an elephant? – one bite at a time'. The headings are:

Purification, which is the removal of unwanted energies from the magician's mind and subtle bodies as well as from physical areas such as temple spaces. We will cover this in depth in Chapter Two.

Meditation, which within the Golden Dawn is the art of stilling the mind, often using the breath, to focus upon only one thought, idea, symbol, sacred phrase etc. We will examine this in Chapter Three, along with divination.

Divination, which is the art of using little exercised powers of the mind to ascertain the hidden aspects, motivations and forces operating within ourselves and the world. As with meditation we will cover this topic in Chapter Three, though not in depth. Golden Dawn divination has been exhaustively detailed in other books, far better than I can do justice to the subject.

Aura Control, which may also be considered a sub-class of invocation, involves techniques that charge the subtle bodies or aura of the magician with non-physical energies. It also involves modifying the channels within the subtle bodies that move and transfer energy. We will examine the theory and practice of aura control in Chapter Four.

Invocation, which is the art of calling forth specific non-physical energies and Beings into a temple space or other physical environment such as a talisman. This topic is covered in depth in Chapters Five and Six.

Otherworld Contacts is a term for a variety of methods whereby we may connect with or move our conscious into various non-physical astral or inner realms. By doing this we may also come into contact with an assortment of Beings who reside in these realms. This thorny issue is the subject of Chapter Seven, where we will examine its theory, practice and the required safeguards of the techniques involved.

Evocation is an advanced technique in which a non-physical being is directed to manifest to varying degrees within a prescribed area within a temple, most often within a triangular figure. A cursory examination of this vast and very advanced technique is given in Chapter Eight.

Initiation in the Golden Dawn tradition is a complex set of ceremonial actions designed to cause spiritual change in the person being initiated. We briefly examine Golden Dawn initiation in Chapter Nine and examine how solo magicians may obtain the same benefit, through individual spiritual work, as a temple initiation. Finally, in Chapter Ten we give a series of techniques to connect us with the Golden Dawn tradition itself.

GOLDEN DAWN RITUAL SPIRITUALITY

Often these processes are combined within a ritual structure, a series of physical and verbal actions that embody and enact a spiritual and energetic purpose or mystery. Within any Golden Dawn ritual structure we will find what may be called 'inner workings', the inward visualisations, manipulations of energy and consciousness that enliven the ritual and make it a spiritual rather than dramatic event. Ritual and ceremony within the Golden Dawn is never performed for its own sake, but rather as a means of producing transformation in ourselves and the universe.

Ritual, unlike other spiritual practices, relies heavily on the use of the body and material tools; we move around the temple, we speak, we sprinkle with water and inscribe symbols in the air with wands or hands. This heavy use of the physical dimension is a double-edged sword. On one hand since we are using our bodies and engaging our senses in spiritual practice, the transformation that may result can be far deeper than through less embodied spiritual pursuits. On the other hand it is all too easy to let ourselves be taken with the form of the ritual, the sound of our own (or another's) voice, the beauty of the robes and props, the importance of correct action and perfect wording. When this occurs our rituals and practices cease to have inner and spiritual meaning and effects. As in all things magical, with ritual and ceremonial practice we walk along a razor edge, and it is only our own conscious awareness and inner motivation that will keep us moving rather than falling.

Another problem with Golden Dawn ritual spirituality is the possibility of energetic and astral intoxication. The astral and etheric energies channelled or created by many Golden Dawn ceremonies and techniques can be quite intense. Many people enjoy the feeling that results when we interact with these energies and will often describe rituals in terms of their level of energy or power, judging those with high levels of energy as 'good', and those with low levels, as 'bad'. While it is very true that we can get 'high' from Golden Dawn ceremonies and practices, this is not their intention. There is a large difference between the spiritual bliss reported by mystics the world over and the astral highs of modern magical junkies. This difference lies in the transformation a practice produces; whether it changes the magician and unfolds her service to the One Being further, or whether it bombards her astral body with excess energy, causing a temporary alteration of consciousness.

What makes the difference between these two states is how 'earthed' or 'grounded' we are, that is how well we continue to function in this regular everyday world during ritual, as well as within the subtle inner worlds of energy, symbol and meaning. By remaining focused in this world as well as in the inner realms, we are able to 'earth' the spiritual blessings and forces of our rituals into this world and our daily lives, transforming ourselves and others. Without earthing these blessings and powers, the transformation they offer can never be fully realised. When we engage in ritual in this fashion our experience may be less 'high' and intense. However, it will have more effects and positive outcomes. We do not need to be 'blown away' by a ceremony for it to be effective. One of the West's most potentially transforming ceremonies, the Christian Eucharist, is performed in an environment where the priest is still fully in this world, able to deliver sermons and read church notices.

The Golden Dawn tradition attempts to achieve this earthing process via a number of means. For example, in the original Orders the only ritual initially performed for quite some time was the Lesser Ritual of the Pentagram, which focused solely on the Earth element. These days newcomers often practice far more complex and less earthed rituals quite early on, which may feed the tendency to become less grounded; a tendency that is quite common among those attracted to Western magic. Overcoming this tendency is important and is the reason why the Lesser Ritual of the Pentagram is essential daily work for both the newcomer and the more practiced Golden Dawn magician. When engaging with the rituals and practices described in this book please stay focused and grounded throughout. Do not follow any interior sensations or visions and be honest about any desire you may have to get a 'buzz' from the processes, particularly the Middle Pillar exercise. Look at these desires, examine them closely and see where they are coming from. If they are not part of your higher motivations to unfold and to serve the One, discard them as best you can.

THE QABALAH

To fully understand these various processes and rituals there needs to be an overarching framework that connects them, a single unifying view that can place them alongside each other. In the Golden Dawn this is traditionally provided by an understanding of the Qabalah. There are by now hundreds of books on Qabalah, most of which can help with this. However the book that still stands heads and shoulders above many others is Gareth Knight's *A Practical Guide to Qabalistic Symbolism*. This is essential reading and in many ways supplements the published Golden Dawn corpus found in Regardie's *The Golden Dawn*. Other useful works are listed in the bibliography.

For now, and to practice all the techniques in this book you only need to have a simple understanding of the Qabalah, which I have included below. However, I am aware that there are limitations in my elucidation of the Qabalah, so please obtain and read other material. I have added to the overview of the Qabalah a section on the subtle bodies and corresponding inner planes or realms, as this approach has been found useful elsewhere. Direct use of this information belongs in chapter four, aura control, but without an understanding of what parts of ourselves are being affected by what rituals, we will not understand the Golden Dawn magic described here.

The Qabalah is an esoteric, or traditionally hidden, form of teaching and philosophy, derived from the Judaic tradition, which lends itself to many practical uses. The word itself is Hebrew, deriving from the root 'QBL' which means 'to receive' and 'to reveal', and refers firstly to esoteric philosophy received orally, and secondly to that philosophy having the potential to reveal the secrets of the Universe and our own being. The Qabalah is one of the foundation stones of the Western Mystery Tradition, and the Golden Dawn made extensive use of its more practical aspects. The origins of the Qabalah are too complex to deal with here but it is necessary to point out however, that the Qabalah utilised by the GD is not the traditional Hebrew Qabalah, but rather a post-Renaissance adaptation generally known as the Hermetic or Christian Qabalah.

The Qabalah today is normally classed as follows:

1. Oral Qabalah
2. Dogmatic Qabalah (sometimes called written Qabalah)
3. Literal Qabalah
4. Practical Qabalah

The first does not concern us here, since it refers to secret oral instruction that either no longer exists or is still secret. Much of the oral Qabalah utilised in the original GD and its predecessors can now be placed in one of the other categories, since it has been written and published.

Dogmatic Qabalah consists largely of medieval treatises on the Qabalah, the most important being the *Sepher Yetzira* and the *Sepher Zohar* (Book of Formation and Book of Splendour). In the *Sepher Yetzira* there are many correspondences attributed to the 22 letters of the Hebrew alphabet, some of which were incorporated into the Golden Dawn. For example the letter Aleph (silent or A) is said to correspond to the element of Air, the letter Beth (B or V) to the planet Mercury etc. This practice of forming correspondences to the letters was greatly expanded by the Golden Dawn, and forms the underlying matrix for many of its rituals. An example of a list of correspondences for Kether, one of the Sephiroth, or emanations of God, is included at the end of this section. A complete list of Correspondences used within Golden Dawn Qabalah may be found in such works as *777* by Aleister Crowley and *The Living Qabalah* by Will Parfitt.

Literal Qabalah is comprised of three techniques, **Notariqon**, **Temurah** and **Gematria**, designed to decode information hidden within particular Jewish texts, words or phrases. It was utilised by the Golden Dawn in a few contexts, such as the formation of certain symbols to be used on talismans. It is also utilised in conjunction with meditation. For example, each letter of the Hebrew alphabet is also a number. So, Aleph is one, Beth is two etc as shown in Table One. A key principle of Gematria is that words with the same numeration are linked or equivalent to one another. The classic example of this is the Hebrew word Achad, 'one' or 'unity'. Its total numeration is 13, the same as Abah, 'love'. Thus we see that love is unity and unity is love, and the Qabalist would further meditate on the resonance between these words. This seems easy, but the meditation is harder when we have words like ShD, 'green' and RDQ, 'white' both having the same numeration (304) and thus equivalent. Prolonged meditation and contemplation on why these two words have the same essence will move us way beyond logic and thought and into a deeper consciousness. The aim here is the process of doing such meditation rather than the outcomes we obtain from them.

Practical Qabalah was the area that was most prevalent in the GD. It refers to practical exercises such as the use of Tarot, invocation and meditations, based upon the ideas taken largely from the Dogmatic and then Oral, but now written, Qabalah. Much of this form of Qabalah is found within the ceremonial initiations and the meditations included in Regardie's *The Golden Dawn*.

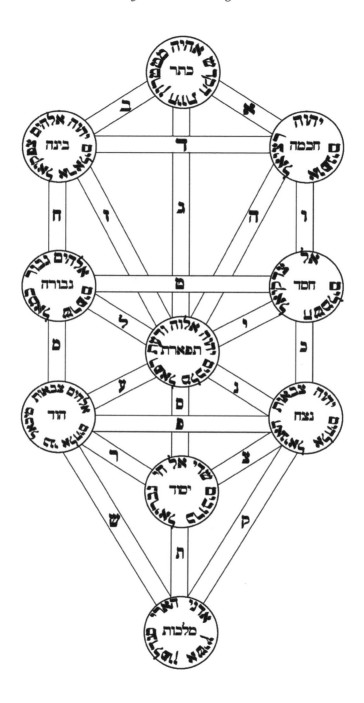

Diagram 3a: The Tree of Life with Hebrew Names

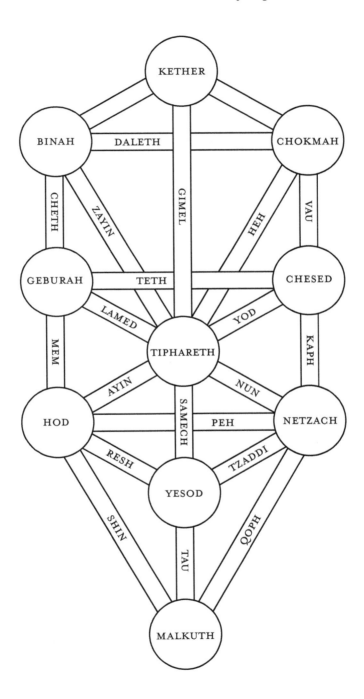

Diagram 3b: The Tree of Life with Hebrew Names in English

THE TREE OF LIFE

Interpenetrating and binding all forms of Qabalah together is a diagram known as the Tree of Life, as shown on page 40-41. The Tree is an entire cosmology unto itself, a construct or symbol that depicts the workings, structure and inner reality of the human being and also the Universe. The tree is comprised of ten spheres called Sephiroth (literally: 'shining' or 'brightness') and 22 paths connecting the spheres in a particular pattern, to which are attributed the 22 letters of the Hebrew Alphabet and many other things. The ten Sephiroth in order show the creation of the Universe from the unknowable First Source down to the physical reality of our world. It also shows the way 'back' to the First Source.

This at first glance is a very structured, even hierarchal view of the universe. It is important here to remember that it is only one way of looking at things, and there are many others. As we come to know the Tree more fully we find that hierarchy, in the sense of any single sphere being 'better' than another, falls away and each sphere is known as equally holy, each mirroring the One. Also, no method of describing the universe *is* the universe itself, but merely a map and in the words of Korbyzi, 'the map is not the territory'. This is a crucial point to remember in our magic as far too many magicians get caught up into believing their maps are 'real' or 'true' and the way the universe actually 'is'. This is simply not the case, and I have listed a number of books in the bibliography that expand on this theme with great clarity and humour. The danger of believing the maps we use is what Aleister Crowley had in mind when he penned this warning in his introduction to *Liber O*:

> 'In this book it is spoken of the Sephiroth and the paths, of spirits and conjurations, of Gods, Spheres, planes and many other things which may or may not exist. It is immaterial whether they exist or not. By doing certain things certain results follow. Students are most earnestly warned against attributing objective reality or philosophical validity to any of them.'

Looking at the diagram of the Tree on page 40, we see that the ten Sephiroth form three Pillars – the Pillar of Mercy on the right, the Pillar of Severity on the left and the Pillar of Equilibrium in the centre. These pillars symbolise the two opposing forces of the Universe and the hidden or third reconciling force. This force is at the same time both of the opposites and something beyond both. It is to this state that the GD magician aspires – to be beyond the opposites of the dual manifested

Universe. This can be said to be constantly living in the paradox that transcends apparent irreconcilable forces, ideas or points of view.

Each of the Sephiroth can be seen as being stages in the creation of the Universe, and relate to a certain state of consciousness within the magician. In conjunction with the Hermetic understanding of correspondence – every force in the universe is resonant with a number of other forces and physical objects, Qabalists also assign stones, colours, herbs, scents, trees etc to each of the Sephiroth and paths. Use of these physical objects in the right way is understood to be able to invoke the force it corresponds to. By utilizing the various correspondences to those Sephiroth, such as the vibration of the Divine names attributed to them, and burning the appropriate herbs etc, the magician can change her consciousness accordingly. This has tremendous importance in exploring the inner realms of the unconscious of the magician and in practical magic.

Qabalistic knowledge is vast and complex. It is also living and changing. The descriptions here and below are only suggestions and there would undoubtedly be some magicians who would say things differently. The aim of the Qabalah however is to build your own Tree of Life, that is to create within your own subtle bodies and mind your own personal and individual Tree. This will broadly speaking be the same as the traditional Tree, but will also reflect your own unique characteristics and spiritual unfoldment. Please use these notes as the first springboard of many to start creating your own Tree. As part of this process you will need to read and actively engage with several good books on the Qabalah. Suggestions are listed in the bibliography. If you have any inkling of following the Golden Dawn tradition or using its magical processes you should start doing this as soon as possible.

THE SEPHIROTH UPON THE TREE OF LIFE

These can be seen to be emanations of the Divine or Goddess. The word emanation is used here to convey a sense of opening and expansion from potential. We can see this within a seed or a bulb. There is no flower within the seed or bulb, but when planted and nurtured the flower will emanate from the seed. The difference here though is that these emanations, or Sephiroth, are continually emanating the power, beauty and force of Goddess, always and at all times. This seed metaphor is poetically accurate also in that we are to grow the Tree within us.

1. Kether (כ ת ר KThR)

This first Sephira is the concentration of the 'limitless light' of the unmanifest that exists beyond the Universe and all consciousness. This light focuses down and concentrates into a single point which is Kether, the ultimate Godhead, the source of all that exists. Kether is unity and completion, the returning to our oneness with Goddess. The word itself means 'Crown', referring to the crown of the Tree of Life. This title reflects the understanding that everything stems from Kether, just as everything in feudal society stemmed from the King or Queen. There is also a connection here with the crown centre or energy point, the position of Kether within our bodies. And just as the crown centre, and the physical crown of the Queen, are beyond the physical body, so too Kether is, in its fullness, beyond our comprehension. The fact that Kether is positioned just outside of the body also indicates that the energy and divine powers we contact there are objective. To fully understand Kether requires our reunion with Goddess and thus losing ourselves and our comprehension, which is a faculty of mind, not of union.

On a personal level Kether is the divinity within us that leads to Unity with the One. Within our body Kether is above the crown of the head.

2. Chokmah (ח כ מ ה ChKMH)

Kether, in order to know itself, to begin the expansion of the Universe, creates or extrudes from within it a 'double' of itself, which then becomes Chokmah. Chokmah means wisdom and has connection with the Holy Spirit. Originally seen as a feminine force, most Qabalists see Chokmah these days as the archetypal, primal driving force of the universe, and thus as male. It is the raw essence of what becomes force when manifested further down the tree. Chokmah cannot be fully understood without its opposite, Binah, described below. Chokmah is the impetus that begins the process of manifestation, Kether being the unified state. Therefore within Chokmah is all the blueprints or the divine plan, of the universe and of Goddess, which is received from Kether. We can see here the meaning of Wisdom as referring to the wisdom of the divine plan of Goddess.

On a personal level Chokmah is the divinity within us that can be awakened by masculine, dynamic symbols and images. Within our body Chokmah is the left hand side of the brain and just outside the left area of the head.

3. Binah (בינה BINH)

In Qabalistic cosmology the universe and consciousness is created within a framework of archetypal balance. Therefore as Chokmah is formed so too is its opposite, Binah. Just as Chokmah may be seen to be the divine, primal male force, many Qabalists see Binah as the divine, primal female force. Binah takes the raw force of Chokmah and binds and constricts it, folding it back on itself to create the first understanding of form within the cosmos. This matrix or underlying pattern will be used in the process of manifestation to produce actual formations and matter. Often people see Binah as a pushing off point, a thrusting block, whereby the force of Chokmah can find its balance and guidance. The name means Understanding and refers to the understanding, which is the more concrete apprehension, of the divine plan within the wisdom of Chokmah. Typically it is said that we can be wise about abstract principles but we need a more concrete idea or situation before we understand it.

On a personal level Binah is the divinity within us that can be awakened by feminine, formative symbols and images. Within our body Binah is the right hand side of the brain and just outside the right area of the head.

4. Chesed (חסד ChSD)

From Binah there is emanated Chesed, the translation of which is Mercy. Chesed is the first Sephira with any degree of actual manifestation and as such is the 'head' Sephira of the manifest Universe. It is the force that creates, sustains and builds up the universe – the catabolic force, the growing force. It is often seen as the creative principles of the three Supernal Sephiroth, Kether, Chokmah and Binah, on a lower plane. The idea and principle of just, correct ruler-ship and leadership applies to Chesed, as it is the Sephira that takes the understood divine plan from Binah and starts applying it to manifestation, overseeing its unfoldment. Again, like any Sephira on the two pillars of extremes, Chesed needs to be considered in conjunction with its counterpart, Geburah. The translation of Chesed, Mercy, is often seen to refer to the mercy of the divine plan as it begins to unfold here for the first time in the manifest universe.

On a personal level Chesed is our deep compassion. Within our body Chesed is the left shoulder.

5. Geburah (גבורה GBURH)

The balancing point to Chesed, Mercy, is Geburah – translated as Severity. In contrast to Chesed, Geburah is the catabolic force of the universe, the power that destroys and breaks down, removing for recycling any used forms or outdated aspects of or ideas within creation. Geburah and Chesed keep each other in check, creating a balance between creation and destruction, which is needed for manifestation and life to continue and proceed. The destruction here is not negative, but is equally as important as the creation of Chesed. Severity is often seen as the opposite of Mercy, and is the power needed to destroy and remove in balance.

On a personal level Geburah is our will and power. Within our body Geburah is the right shoulder.

6. Tiphareth (תפארת ThPhARTh)

Tiphareth is the central Sephira upon the Tree of Life. It thus functions as a harmonizing and equalizing power throughout the manifest universe. All forces, apart from the manifested, physical matter are connected directly into Tiphareth via the paths on the Tree of Life. Thus Tiphareth is said to be able to balance all forces and able to represent all forces. Upon the Tree we see that this sphere is the balancing point of Geburah and Chesed and is formed by their union in balance together with the influx of the light of Kether. The Hebrew word Tiphareth means Beauty, which is the beauty of the harmony of the universe in balance.

On a personal level Tiphareth is our sense of self which has, but not is, emotions, a mind, an unconscious and a body. Within our body Tiphareth is the heart centre.

7. Netzach (נצח NTzCh)

Netzach is emanated from Tiphareth and still retains some of the qualities of Tiphareth. This is particularly seen in the planetary attributions of the Sephiroth, the Sun to Tiphareth and Venus, the morning star, the Light Bringer, to Netzach. Netzach is the sphere of the potential of manifested nature, the living Earth Herself. Netzach in our consciousness is also the love for and belonging to nature we feel intuitively. In Netzach, the numerous life-forms (within the astral realms) of the myriad forms of nature – plants, minerals and animals – are unexpressed, linked as one chain. It requires Netzach's opposite, Hod, to divide them out into separate existence. The word itself means Victory, which is the victory of the divine plan moving through and into the forms of the natural world.

On a personal level Netzach is our emotions and creative-artistic consiousness. Within our body Netzach is the left hip.

8. Hod (הוד HOD)

Hod is the counter-weight to Netzach and through its powers the many forms of the manifested universe, of the natural word, are separated and made distinct, each within its own family and place. Netzach can be considered as a rainbow, containing all the colours within one form, and Hod as the seven separate colours. Consciousness here then is concerned with the idea of separation and knowing of the self through identification of differences between the self and the other. The name Hod means Glory in Hebrew, which is seen to be the glory or splendour of the multitude of forms within Hod, all existing in harmony.

On a personal level Hod is our rational mind. Within our body Hod is the right hip.

9. Yesod (יסוד YSOD)

Yesod is produced from the Union of Hod and Netzach, with the influx of harmony from Tiphareth. It is the reconciling factor, on a lower plane, of these two spheres, just as the Tiphareth is the reconciling factor on a higher plane. Yesod can be seen as the sphere of the workings and movements that underlie and underpin the manifest universe – the subtle and constant interplay of forms emerging from the connection of Netzach and into the separateness of Hod, and vice versa. Yesod is thus in a constant state of flux and reflux, a movement back and forth, producing the astral world that underlies the physical. This is aptly summed up in the translation of the word, Foundation, referring to this sphere as the foundation that the physical universe rests upon.

On a personal level Yesod is our unconscious and subconscious. Within our body Yesod is the gential and pelvic area.

10. Malkuth (מלכות MLKUTh)

Malkuth is the condensation of Yesod, and the whole Tree of Life, into the manifest and physical universe where we live and eat and love. It is the sphere we recognise as physical reality – matter that can be touched, tasted, moved and composted. It contains all the essence and powers of the rest of the Tree of Life within it. The name means Kingdom or Queendom, and refers to physical universe being the home of Goddess as Queen of Universe.

On a personal level, Malkuth is our bodies. Within our body Malkuth is below the feet so we stand upon it.

EXAMPLES OF CORRESPONDENCES – KETHER

Hebrew Spelling:	(כתר K-Th-R)
Translation:	The Crown
Number:	1
Godname:	Eheieh איה א (AHIH)
Godname Meaning:	'To be'; or 'I will be'
Archangel:	Metratron מטטרון (MTTRVN)
Archangel Meaning:	'Throne of the One Being'
Choir of Angels:	Chaioth ha Qodesh חאית הקדש (ChAITh H QDSh)
Choir of Angels Meaning:	Holy Living Creatures
Material Expression:	Rahashith ha Gilgalim הגילגלים רהשית (RHShITh H GILGLIM)
Material Expression Meaning:	The first swirlings
Gods:	Atum, Ptah, Parabrahm, Zeus, Gaia
Mystical Number:	1
Spiritual Experience:	Union with God
Sepher Yetzira Description:	Admirable or Hidden Intelligence
Virtue:	Completion of the Great Work
Vice:	None
Titles:	The Smooth Point, the Vast Countenance, Ancient of Days, Concealed of the Concealed, The Most High, The White Head, the Primordial Point, the Crown, the Swastika

Symbolic Animal:	Swan
Symbolic Plant:	None
Precious Stone:	Diamond
Geometric Figure:	Point
Magical Tools:	None
Magical Image:	Ancient and bearded King in profile
Incense:	Almond, ambergris
Parts of the Body:	Crown of head
Tarot Cards:	The Four Aces:
Colours:	In Atziluth – Brilliance
	In Briah – Pure White Brilliance
	In Yetzira – Pure White Brilliance
	In Assiah – White flecked gold.

THE FOUR WORLDS

Another important map used within the Golden Dawn Qabalah is that of the Four Worlds. In this map the creation of the universe is seen as following a four-fold, or to use traditional and sometimes obtuse terminology, a *Tetragrammatic* process (Tetragrammaton meaning 'four lettered name'). This four-fold process or division is found within many aspects of the Golden Dawn and we will discuss it further in the next chapter when we examine the four elements. One way of looking at the four worlds is their being 'stages' of creation, from pure abstract deity to our knowable and material universe. The four worlds and their brief descriptions are most often given as:

World of **Atziluth**, Archetypal in quality. Home of Pure Deity or simply God in His various aspects.

World of **Briah**, Creative in quality. Home of the Archangels.

World of **Yetzira**, Formative in quality. Home of the Angels.

World of **Assiah**, Active in quality; Home of the Kerubim, who are expressions of the four elements, and the home of humanity and all physical beings.

This four-fold creative process can also be seen as a formula of:

Origin, **Expansion**, **Formation** and **Expression**.

This four-fold formula is sometimes a bit obtuse and hard to grasp, but without understanding it your understanding of the Four Worlds will be hampered. A good way to enhance your awareness and understanding of this process is to meditate on the keywords just given and the following geometric figures (see chapter three on meditation):

Atziluth	Origin	Point
Briah	Expansion	Line
Yetzira	Formation	Triangle
Assiah	Expression	Cube

Each of the four worlds gives rise or birth to the world following it. This can be explained graphically by the concept that each world contains its own tree of life. That is there is a full Tree in each of the four worlds, giving four trees, forty Sephiroth and 88 paths. This is shown in diagram 4. In this schema the Malkuth of the Tree in a particular world is also the Kether in the world immediately following or below it. That is, Malkuth of Atziluth is the Kether of Briah. Similarly the Malkuth of Briah is the Kether of Yetzira and the Malkuth of Yetzira is the Kether of Assiah. Thus all four Trees are joined to one another in a seamless ladder.

An alternate way of representing the Four Words is to view them as being corresponded to areas of a single Tree. The most common Hermetic Qabalah view of this process is shown in diagram 5. Both schemas are useful, though there is no doubt that the second schema is more traditional in pre-Hermetic Judaic Qabalah. The forty Sephiroth schema is more useful within the practical application of Golden Dawn magic.

Atziluth

This is the realm of pure essence, being and the primal divinity. It is the undiluted originative aspect of the One, corresponding to Kether on the Tree. To this world is corresponded the impersonal divine names or God Names that reflect aspects of the One Being operative in the lower

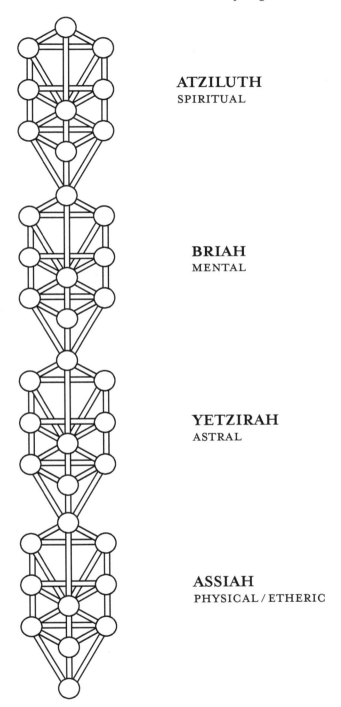

ATZILUTH
SPIRITUAL

BRIAH
MENTAL

YETZIRAH
ASTRAL

ASSIAH
PHYSICAL / ETHERIC

Diagram 4: Four Trees in One Tree

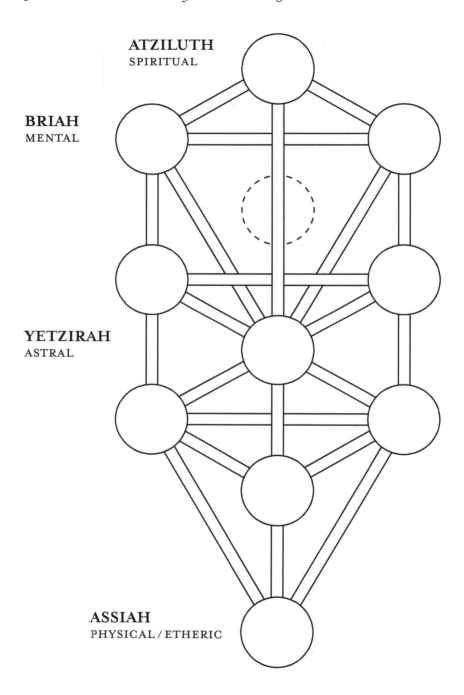

ATZILUTH
SPIRITUAL

BRIAH
MENTAL

YETZIRAH
ASTRAL

ASSIAH
PHYSICAL / ETHERIC

Diagram 5: Four Worlds of the Qabalah marked on One Tree

worlds. Using a human analogy, Atziluth is the Chief Executive Officer of a large organisation. She makes decisions that influence the organisation and those people 'below' her in the corporate ladder but is not actually involved in implementing or carrying through these decisions. Moreover, while her energy, via her decisions, may be felt by those below her, the CEO herself may remain unseen, only known by names and images within the staff newsletter. This is like the personal Atziluthic energy within us; we cannot see or recognise it directly, though we feel its presence. On a personal level, Atziluth is the spark of an abstract idea that cannot be seen or grasped, but which excites our whole being and inspires us into action.

Briah

This word is derived from the Semitic root, BRA – to beget or create. Here the force of Atziluth is expanded and the first stirrings of creation ensue. It is here that the 'plan' of the One Being is worked out and the blueprint for the created universe is constructed. In this world, Binah and Chokmah are eternally co-joined and their union produces the world of Yetzira, formation, below them. The abstract spiritual impulse of Atziluth enters the creative fecundity of Briah and is expanded into an outline, a plan or an idea. The essence of Briah, of the creative world, is expansion through polarity and interaction. Continuing our analogy, Briah is the collection of divisional or regional managers who take the abstract decisions of the CEO and create a strategy for implementing them. They interact with each other, much as Binah and Chokmah interact, and from their creative interaction comes a plan for implementing the ideas of the CEO. They too, like the Archangels attributed to this world, do not actually engage in the practical carrying out of this plan. They simply create it and administer its execution. On a personal level, Briah is the creative leap of having an abstract thought transform into knowledge of what it actually is that is required or wanted. That this leap often comes about through the sharing of our abstract thoughts and ideas (the best we can) with others indicates the interactive nature of Briah.

Yetzira

This word is derived from the Semitic root, YTzR – to form or make. The creative energy of Briah is now condensed down and utilised to achieve the divine plan. Traditionally Yetzira is thought of as the 'child' of Atziluth and Briah, and therefore has aspects of both. The spiritual impulse of Atziluth is retained, but is now formed, via the creative impulse of Briah, into a vast number of different parts or components. These myriad forms underlie the material universe and are later given material expression, through being 'clothed in matter' within Assiah. However not all of the forms are successfully birthed into Assiah and tradition suggests that the forms themselves are open to conscious human manipulation. This is why Yetzira is the realm where most magic is conducted – the magician attempting to alter and choose the Yetziratic forms and energies that will be 'real' in his life and the world. The Beings who reside in Yetzira are the Angels, who traditionally exist within a choir or an Order, not as separate Beings. In our metaphor, the Angels correspond to the large number of specialist workers who implement and actually carry out the creative plan of the Briatic managers. These workers turn the plan into reality. On a personal level, Yetzira is the doing of the work; the purchasing of the paints and the painting process itself, the composing, the studying and writing.

ASSIAH

This is the culmination of the worlds, the expression and realisation of the other three. It is our own material universe, the world of action and expression. Its inhabitants are all the myriad biological life forms and also the subtle etheric Beings, such as the shells of the dead before they move on. Assiah is the actual, flesh and blood universe. In our analogy, Assiah is whatever product is produced by workers, be that a car, a house, a presidential campaign etc. Assiah is the physical result and actualisation of the work of Yetzira. On a personal level, it is the song, the essay or the cake that we produce. Of course not all of our plans in Briah or work in Yetzira manifest in Assiah.

SUBTLE BODIES AND THE AURA

Throughout many spiritual traditions and esoteric systems there is a recurring awareness of the nature of the human being as being comprised of many levels or 'bodies' other than the physical flesh and blood body we generally know. These bodies are often called subtle bodies to distinguish them from the physical body, though in the Eastern traditions they are often called 'sheaths'. Throughout the various traditions and systems of spirituality there is no uniformity of perception of these bodies. That is, different traditions state clearly that there *are* different numbers and differing forms of these subtle bodies. In addition, where there is a common perception, that is where two or more systems agree with each other on the number and type of bodies, there is often no uniformity of classification or naming. Thus what one system calls the etheric body another system may call the astral and vice versa. All of this leads to much confusion and occasionally acrimony between adherents of the various traditions.

As you study this topic further you will find much that conflicts and much that agrees with what is said here. You need to work out for yourself your own interaction with these traditional wisdom teachings. These are simply brief notes to point the way and also to outline the schema that we will use for the purpose of this book. This is a vast field with hundreds of books written on the subject, several dealing with only one specific subtle body. While a good, sensible awareness of the subject is required within the Golden Dawn tradition, expert or comprehensive knowledge is not. Out of all the books on this topic that are written from a Western esoteric perspective the best is *The Circuit of Force* by Dion Fortune and Gareth Knight. The most sensible and intelligent introduction to this whole topic, taking in Eastern and Western approaches I have found is *The Body of Light* by John Mann and Lar Short.

SUBTLE BODIES AND LAYERS WITHIN THE AURA

Many esoteric schools and spiritual traditions worldwide hold the concept of three particular bodies that reflect certain distinct states of being and consciousness. Within each of these bodies may be layers or 'sub-bodies'. A good generic comparison would be as follows:

Tradition	1st Body	2nd Body	3rd Body
Hinduism	Physical	Subtle	Cosmic
Buddhism	Emanation	Enjoyment (Illusory)	Truth
Taoism	Physical	Soul (Energy)	Spirit/Immortal
Qabalah	Guph & Nephesch	Ruach	Neschamah, Yechidah & Chiah
Theosophy	Physical	Astral	Spiritual
Western	Physical	Astral	Higher Self

In the schema above, the first body is the physical body and the physical consciousness. This means that this body includes the instincts and primal functions and patterns of the body. So, for example if as a child we learn to feel fear whenever we see an image of a traditional Witch then the automatic body responses of fear to images of a Witch would be included in this body. Of course, these are not physical in the sense that we cannot dissect the body and find them, but they exist none the less.

The second body is what is generally understood as the astral body in the West. It is the body that may 'leave' the physical body easily, move to other realms and interact with other Beings. It is the storehouse for our emotions and feelings and thoughts also. Most traditions would say that this body functions automatically most of the time and habitually resides in the same locale as the physical body. However this body is fully under the control of the will and we can will it to, at least partially, travel away from the physical body. We all do this occasionally when we day dream and come back to ourselves after unconsciously repeating an habitual physical task. When consciousness is within the second body, even when it has been directed away from the physical body, our perceptions through this body will still be somewhat physically based. That is, we will feel and see ourselves 'travelling' to the other side of the room or other planes or realms. We will still experience some aspect of time and dimension. These may be counter to or at right angles to everyday physical experience, but they are still there.

The third body is timeless and space-less. Often there is no vision when our consciousness is centred here, no awareness of separation between ourselves and the universe, Goddess and God. It is often symbolised by light or images of unity, such as the sexual embrace of Tantric deities. Some traditions would say that this body does not exist upon birth and has to be 'built' by spiritual practices. Others say it is there, but only in potential and needs to be nurtured and purified. In either case spiritual practice is required.

THE SUBTLE BODY MODEL USED IN THIS BOOK

As said previously, many traditions would see various layers to some or all of these bodies. This ends up as a complex situation. Here we are choosing to distinguish two layers of the first body – the physical body and the etheric body. The etheric body acts as a link between the physical body and the astral body. The second body, the astral, we leave as is. With the third body we distinguish two functions or layers; the first being what we call the mental body, which is a link between the astral body and the second aspect of the third body, the spiritual body. So we have the model of:

THE PHYSICAL BODY

This is the body that Western science and medicine can heal and dissect. It can be photographed and touched. In our schema this body does not include the example given above of the instinctual reactions. This exists in the next body, the etheric. With reference to the Qabalah this body is named the Guph. It operates in the material world or the world of action, Assiah. The quintessential substance of this body is connective tissue.

ETHERIC BODY

This is the densest subtle body and the link between the physical body and the astral body. It is comprised of what energy it can draw from the Earth and sun and other sources of vital energy (ether). It interpenetrates the physical body and extends out from it, producing the classic auric egg that surrounds us. It is intimately connected with physical health and well-being, vitality etc. While there are several layers to this body, for our purposes we focus on two:

(i) The Etheric Double. This is a replica of the form of our physical body comprised entirely out of etheric energy. It interpenetrates our physical bodies, but is slightly larger, thus extending one to two inches above the surface of our skin. Every organ, every part of physical body has therefore its etheric equivalent. The etheric double is where the basis for a lot of hands on healing takes place. Healing damage and lesions to this body will often result in physical healing also.

(ii) The Etheric Aura. This is the energetic egg that is formed around our physical bodies. It can extend several feet or more from our physical bodies if we are very healthy and connected to sources of etheric energy. When people say they see auras, this is often what they see. It is often perceived as a sort of grey-blue misty energy surrounding the body. Our etheric aura is constantly moving and changing, throwing off and receiving etheric energy. Wherever we move, we leave behind minute traces of our etheric energy. Our etheric auras also collect these traces of energy. These energy forms often stick to our etheric auras, and make us feel heavy or tired. This is what occurs when moving through a crowded city street. Our etheric auras are constantly interacting with the other etheric auras and discarded etheric energy (due to the high emotion and frustration crowds create). We collect this 'alien' energy to ourselves and our etheric system then tries to accommodate it, to make it our own, much the same way as compost over time becomes Earth, though the auric shift occurs much quicker. This uses up our energy, making us tired and listless. We see then why regular purification and cleansing of our energy fields is a good idea as it removes and cleanses the etheric garbage we have picked up. In the Golden Dawn the classic method of achieving this is the Lesser Banishing Ritual of the Pentagram, discussed in the next chapter.

Many traditions say that there are numerous sub-levels to the etheric aura. We will not be working with these levels in this book. The whole etheric body, double and aura is affected by heat and cold, acids, running water, sudden change of temperature, crystals, salts, herbs, iron, garlic and onions. Etheric energy can be willed out and away from our auras and into objects or space for purposes such as consecrating items and drawing pentagrams or other symbols in the air. Etheric energy is constantly being drawn into our auras from our connection with the Earth and through the light of the sun. The Earth's etheric aura extends miles into the air, and we can still connect with it anywhere humans can live. The many examples of mystical experience and contact experienced by astronauts, living outside of the Earth's aura, are said by some people to be from receiving only solar etheric energy. With reference to the Qabalah this body can be seen as part of the Nephesch. It operates both within the material world of Assiah and the formative world of Yetzira, and may be seen to be a link between these worlds.

THE ASTRAL BODY

This is the classic astral body discussed so freely in the New Age literature. While not being inherently bound or limited by time and space, the astral body habitually interpenetrates the etheric body and aura. Thus what effects one body affects the other. For example, when undergoing body or breath-work which affects the etheric aura, it also then moves and changes the energy in the astral body. This will allow deep emotions to be stirred and released. Some people would say that the 'lower' bodies are affected by the higher bodies, but not the higher by the lower, a belief that I do agree with. When we are talking about the astral body we need to be clear we are also talking about our thoughts, ideas and memories as well as emotions. All of these are contained within the astral body.

When perceived the astral body is normally seen as auric colours surrounding a person, each colour reflecting a particular emotion, thought or energy. These colours and their correspondence to emotions and thoughts are often very individual. The colour yellow may mean one thing in your own personal auric sight, and another in mine. Often people working within the same tradition may have very similar auric sight perceptions, but that does not mean these correspondences are 'true' or set in stone. Also, our own sight is determined by our own aura since we look through our own aura when we look at another person's. The energy of our own aura determines how we see another aura, in the same way that sunglasses affect our perception of colour and shade.

Our consciousness, when willed, can affect the astral body. This may then in turn affect the etheric and then the physical bodies. This is the basis for all popular New Age healings through positive affirmations. We see here then that the links between the various bodies are important, as without two clear links, between astral and etheric and etheric and physical, there is less chance of healing on the emotional level affecting us physically. These links are cleared and strengthened by traditional Western and Golden Dawn practices that move consciousness from one body to another. Any process where you first sense and feel your physical body, then your energy, then notice your emotions and thoughts also does this.

The astral body is the seat of our everyday consciousness. Where it 'goes', we go. Thus we can daydream and 'leave our body' to some degree. That is, the astral body has withdrawn from interpenetrating our etheric auras and has moved into some inner realm. Here it is free from time and space restrictions, but will still experience some type of form and time. Indeed our astral bodies may go anywhere our consciousness can travel or conceive of. And since the astral bodies are what we ourselves believe ourselves to be most of the time, we can use our will to alter our consciousness on this level greatly. This is one of the principles which allows the imagination, as discussed earlier, to be such a powerful force in magic. Our willed and deep imagination can affect our whole astral body, its make-up, its powers, strengths and weaknesses. In this we would do well to keep in mind the words of Colonel C.R.F. Seymour, one of the greatest and most underestimated magicians of the 20th century: 'a magician is *what* he believes himself to be; a magician is *where* he believes himself to be'.

It is often said that 'astral travel' occurs in deep sleep. However, it is not willed then, nor are we conscious to a large degree of the travelling and experience. Willed withdrawal of the astral body is a trained skill. Please note clearly that here we are talking largely about the withdrawal of the emotional and intellectual areas of the personality or lower self, not the body self. This explains why astral contacts and journeys can be undertaken while the magician is able to remain seated, her body self not being fully asleep. As an aside, it also explains why on these astral journeys we may feel and know ourselves being burnt or in other ways physically affected, but not have marks to show for it. It also explains why dreams where we die do not kill us. Of course large amounts of energy contacted within the astral realm can produce effects upon the body, such as erotic dreams or the physical stigmata that occur in some mystics.

When the astral body is withdrawn from the etheric aura and travels 'elsewhere', its destination will be determined by either will or the energy within it. Magically, this principle is used in rituals where strong invocations are performed; filling the astral body with the energy of the place or sphere we wish to visit. When we then direct our astral bodies out of the etheric body, it will go to that sphere. Regardless of the type of energy within it however, with willed direction the astral body can be made to go wherever we choose, *providing we know where we are going and can conceive of the location*. With reference to the Qabalah, this body is referred to as the Ruach and operates within the formative world of Yetzira.

THE MENTAL BODY

This body, in our schema, is best thought of as a link between the astral body and the spiritual body, allowing the wisdom and consciousness of the Higher Self to be more accessible to our astral bodies, and thus our regular everyday consciousness. Here we are passing out of the realm of everyday experience and into what is often called 'higher consciousness'. Whereas we all dream, and all experience the functions of the astral body consciously through fantasy, not everyone is aware of the functions of the mental body. Indeed many traditions would say that the mental and spiritual bodies need to be developed or built and that we are not born with them.

Consequently we are talking about a subject where consensus perception and knowledge does not exist, and words are not sufficient to accurately portray this body and realm. This leads to many very convoluted works being written, full of long winded descriptions trying in vain to be 'accurate' about this body. We will try to avoid this by simply not saying very much at all. Essentially, whatever you read here is to be taken as a very rough mud map for your own experience to flesh out. Remember the map is not the territory; the menu is not the meal. Reality is just a word.

The mental body (called several other terms or ignored in other systems) functions as the vehicle of the communion of the 'lower' astral consciousness with the 'higher' spiritual consciousness. It has only the most rudimentary forms of presence and identity. When our consciousness is moved from the astral body to the mental body, we do not know ourselves as ourselves at all. There is often no distinct vision, no sounds, no words and no forms, from a mental body experience, only the sense of an expanded 'I'. To better understand this we can look at how information is accessed by the various bodies. The physical body receives information about the physical plane it moves within through sensation. The etheric body receives information about the etheric plane it moves in through energy. The astral body receives information through feelings, thoughts, and images. The mental body simply experiences direct, timeless intuition. Whenever we *know* something without thought, without emotion, without time, without any understanding of the steps of how we know it, it is our mental body functioning. Please note this is not what most people mean when they talk about having a 'feeling' about some course of action or a person or a situation. Direct intuition conveys knowledge, as if from 'nowhere'.

The mental body does not actually reside within or around the physical body. It has no shape, no form and really the term body here is just confusing. It does however have an energetic linkage and connection with the astral body through the brow energy centre. Qabalistically this is the intersection of the paths of Gimel and Daleth – see the diagram of the Tree of Life on page 41. This centre is commonly called the Third Eye and within Eastern traditions, the Ajna chakra. It is traditionally through this centre that the consciousness of the magician or mystic is transferred out of the astral body and into the mental body. This body is only ever 'seen' or perceived by gifted clairvoyants who are themselves functioning on the mental level. Typically they then need to translate their direct intuitional knowledge into astral symbology and colours. Thus published descriptions of clairvoyants describing mental bodies they have 'seen' can be very confusing and seem 'far out'. People talk about 'astral wings' and 'angelic embryos', all of which is simply an attempt to convey intuition beyond form or words. With reference to the Qabalah, the mental body is often equated with the Neschamah and operates in the creative world of Briah.

SPIRITUAL BODY

This 'body' is that part of the human being that allows complete union with the One. There is not really much to be said here. The experience of our Higher Self uniting with our consciousness in our astral body, producing a mental body experience, is really about the deepest level of spiritual experience we can meaningfully share. Beyond that experience through the spiritual body, there is simply unity and bliss. There is no 'I' to remember any experience, indeed no experience at all, since there is no 'I' to experience it and no 'other' to produce the experience. Symbols and poetry here are the only language to convey spiritual body experience. Infinity. Clear Light. Endless white light. The Void. Goddess and God in sacred sexual union. These are all glimpses of the experience. The connection to our Higher Self and spiritual body is through the crown, Kether centre of the astral body, the Sahasara centre in Eastern traditions. With reference to the Qabalah, this body is referred to as the Yechidah and operates in the divine world of Atziluth.

Throughout the rest of this book we will be referring to these bodies and planes. However, I will also refer to the various levels of consciousness and the inner realms by the traditional Qabalistic terminology. In this way you will become familiar with both and see the connections between the two systems. This will help in 'translating' and understanding other models from other traditions and authors.

POWER CENTRES OR CHAKRAS

Intrinsically connected with the subtle bodies concept is the awareness that within the various subtle bodies there exist a number of energy centres, commonly called Chakras, a Sanskrit term popularised by the Theosophical Society and subsequent movements from 1875 on. The use of this term and the Theosophical version of the seven Chakras has so influenced the contemporary Western esoteric community that it is commonly believed that these seven Chakras are *the* Chakras. It has also been assumed that awareness and work with them has been part of the Western and traditions from time immemorial. This is not the case. Like subtle bodies, there are many different perceptions and classifications of the Chakras, even within very close Eastern traditions.

Historically the methods of perception and working with the centres of power within the body as part of the Western traditions varied considerably from school to school and teacher to teacher. Here we use the most consistent contemporary understanding stemming from the Golden Dawn, where five main centres are used, not seven. We will focus quickly on this system here. If you wish to look at the correspondences between Eastern and Western systems, you cannot go past *Tantra for Westerners* by Francis King and *The Circuit of Force* by Dion Fortune and Gareth Knight. Other useful books from the Western magical perspective are: *The Middle Pillar* and *The Art of True Healing* by Israel Regardie. The most useful Western utilisation of the Eastern system is *Wheels of Life* by Anodea Judith.

FUNCTIONS OF THE CENTRES OR CHAKRAS

Various traditions, authors and teachers believe that the Chakras do a number of things. The most common functions of them are as:

◆ The intersection point between the body and consciousness.
◆ Entry and exit points to the body and subtle bodies of particular forms of energy.
◆ Entry points to the body and subtle bodies of particular forms of information and communication.
◆ The point within the body that various layers of the aura are generated from.

We will be looking at practical work with these centres and the subtle bodies in depth in chapter four. However, for now it is a good idea to get a general grasp of these concepts. As we examine the various techniques within this book we will be looking at what bodies they affect and how this is done. Therefore it is useful to quickly examine the various types of magical actions within the Western traditions and see what effects they have on which bodies. Speaking very broadly we might say that:

The Physical Body is affected by ritual, movement, postures, gestures, magical signs. All of these however, if performed correctly, will affect other bodies also.

The Etheric Body is affected by breathing exercises, chanting, vibration of divine names, incense, consecrated water, herbs, precious stones and crystals. The various magical signs, postures and gestures, if performed correctly will also affect this body, altering the channels whereby etheric energy flows within it. This body is also strongly affected by Evocation as it is the raw substance of the magician's etheric body that is part of the energy used by spirit in order to manifest.

The Astral Body is affected by visualisation, invocation, emotional intensity, otherworld contacts and astral travelling and any process that is consciously designed to affect this body via the will.

The Mental Body is affected by the presence of legitimate inner plane contacts, the power of divine names (please note this is not the simple act of vibrating the names, but rather opening to the spiritual force behind the names), Qabalistic exegesis such as Gematria, devotion and deep meditation.

The Spiritual Body is only affected by opening to the power of God or the Gods, mostly achieved through the exaltation of consciousness due to powerful devotional rituals, initiation ceremonies and pure contemplation of the divine. None of these processes however are guaranteed to affect the spiritual body each and every time, where we *can* say that vibration of divine names will affect the etheric body every time. At this level all is mystery and in many ways we wait for the grace of the Gods.

The most powerful and transformational ceremonies will utilise a number of these actions so that all the various bodies are affected. A good ceremony will engage the participants in ways that move their body in divine and magical gestures. It will require a period of breath meditations and the use of consecrated water and incense to engage the etheric body. It will certainly have a large degree of visualisation to affect the astral body. It will also invoke deities, otherworld Beings and inner plane contacts. This affects not only the astral bodies, but by the presence of these Beings and the power behind their names, the mental bodies also. Finally, it will have as a focal point a period for the contemplation of and devotion to God.

As wonderful and simple as this seems, we cannot expect to cobble together a ritual with these components and achieve instant success. Each aspect and action within a ceremony just described needs to be understood and mastered on its own ground before combining them in full ceremony. This is what the original Golden Dawn attempted to do with its knowledge lectures, meditations and magical curriculum of the Inner Order. And this is what we will achieve as we work through the various chapters and exercises within them from this book. For now, however, it is time to return to our starting place and come to grips with visualisation.

VISUALISATION EXERCISES

Please do not underestimate the importance of these types of exercises, as simple as they seem. Even though such exercises were never fully elucidated in the original Golden Dawn, without some level of mastery of the basics, our spiritual unfoldment within magical traditions will be hampered. Even if you have been practicing magic for a while, it will pay you to undertake these exercises, especially exercise six that helps us to test our visualisation.

EXERCISE ONE – VISUALISE AN ORANGE

Many systems and teachers worldwide use a form of this exercise. Relax and close your eyes. Now imagine you are holding an orange. See it clearly. Note how it looks, its skin, any blemish it may have. Notice the small details as you examine it closely. Feel it in your hands, feel its weight and texture. Imagine the smell of the orange. Do this for about five minutes. Now open your eyes and record how well the exercise went. You may like to have a real orange nearby so you can compare the real with the imagined after you have completed the exercise and see how you went. Keep repeating this exercise until you can hold the image of an orange in your mind for at least two minutes.

EXERCISE TWO – OPENING ROSE

Again, relax and close your eyes. Now imagine you are looking at a rosebud. See it clearly in your mind. Notice its colour, shape, any blemish. See the stalk of the rosebud; notice its colour and shape. Now, as if you were watching a time-lapse movie, see the rose slowly start to open. Imagine it unfolding and the leaves uncurling until it is in full bloom. Examine the entire rose closely. Once complete, let the image fade and start again. Do this continually for five minutes. Keep repeating this exercise until you can get the movement of the unfolding of the rose clear and crisp in your inner eye at will.

EXERCISE THREE – CUBE

Again, relax and close your eyes. Now imagine a transparent cube (see diagram 1). See this clearly and completely. Hold the image steady for at least a couple of minutes, then finish and open your eyes. Repeat this exercise until you can create this image in your imagination clearly and easily at will.

Exercise Four – Colour

Relax and close your eyes. Now imagine blue. See nothing but the colour blue. Keep seeing nothing but the colour blue for two minutes. Once you have achieved this, move onto changing the colour. First see blue, then after ten seconds red, then green, then purple. Keep playing with changing from one colour to another quickly until you can do this easily. You may like to use your computer or phone to record at random a list of colours separated by five to ten seconds. Record about 60 minutes of yourself reciting a random list of colours. Then for five minutes each day, play the recording and change your visualisation to whatever colour is described.

Exercise Five – Colour Cube and Rose

This combines some of the previous exercises. Using your same list or recording of random colours, see a coloured cube. Change the colour of the cube to match the colour being described. Once you have done this satisfactorily, see a coloured rose. In this case make sure the green stem of the rose remains green and only the petals change colour. Again, keep doing this until you can quickly visualise a purple rose at will.

Exercise Six – Tic Tac Toe

This exercise requires a partner. Before you start look at the grid for a tic tac toe game and number the squares from one through nine. Memorise which square corresponds to what number. Let your partner sit behind you so you cannot see them. They should have a sheet of paper with several tic tac toe grids already drawn up and numbered. Now you are ready to play. Imagine a grid before you and let your partner go first. Have them first write down and then call out their move, for example 'I place my 'X' in square number five'. In your mind see an 'X' form in square five, the rest remaining blank. Now have your go and wherever you choose to place your 'O', see it form in that square and tell your partner. She should write an 'O' in the square mentioned on her piece of paper. Continue to play this game.

You should continue your visualisation development until you can play 'inner' tic tac toe at will without any mistakes. Of course, make sure you are not simply remembering the locations of the O and the X, but are *seeing* them. Aleister Crowley used to be able to play two games of chess at once using this method, never confusing the two imagined chessboards in his head. While we need not strive to that level of attainment, we do need to be able to master these techniques up to the levels I have suggested here.

Diagram 6: Red Cross and White Triangle of the Golden Dawn

A Note on Ritual Props and Temple Space

The Golden Dawn, like most fraternal and magical lodge traditions makes heavy use of temple props, robes and a vast array of consecrated items and diagrams. For a solo magician most of these are simply redundant and for any group the effort and cost of making the items can be shared. For the work throughout this book there are only a few minimum requirements. Nor is a dedicated temple room required. Some minimal space is required for performance of various rituals, but the average home or room can accommodate this well. In several of the rituals, options on closing or finishing the ritual are given depending on whether you have a separate room or not. Please choose the correct option, not the easiest.

At some point you may wish to make and consecrate your magical items according to Golden Dawn tradition. The best reference for this process is *Making and Using Magical Tools* by Chic and Sandra Tabatha

Cicero. However please look carefully at the suggestions in that book and work out the inner workings required in the various ceremonies, as they are sometimes absent or scant. An important point to remember is that you should begin magical and spiritual practice when you are ready and not when you have the perfect set of tools. The minimum tools you will need for your exploration and unfoldment into the Golden Dawn tradition are:

♦ A plain black robe. Patterns and instructions for making robes can be found on the Internet, particularly on Wiccan websites, or in a number of books including the Ciceros' just mentioned.

♦ A small cabinet to use as an altar. This can be cleared away and used each time, or you can dedicate one to this purpose alone.

♦ A plain black cloth to cover the altar when in use.

♦ A red cross and a white triangle, the symbol of the Golden Dawn, as shown in diagram 6. These can be cut out of pasteboard, painted with a white undercoat and then painted on both sides with bright acrylic paint.

♦ A symbol or magical tool for each of the four elemental principles; Air, Fire, Water and Earth. These can be a simply rose and vase; a red votive glass jar, a cup of water; and a small plate on which is placed small pieces of bread and salt. A white candle or lamp for spirit is also required for some rituals. If you wish to follow the Golden Dawn process fully you would make an Air dagger, a Fire wand, a Water cup and an Earth pentacle along traditional lines. Full instructions for constructing these can be found in *Making and Using Magical Tools* by Chic and Sandra Tabatha Cicero. Less complete instructions are also within *The Golden Dawn* by Israel Regardie.

PURIFICATION

THE easiest way to understand what is meant by purification in the Golden Dawn context is to look for everyday life actions that mirror it. Whenever we wish to start any new project in life, from cooking dinner to starting a new relationship, it is wise to first clear the space where the new project will be performed. So we clean the kitchen or we take solitary space with ourselves before dating once again. The same principle applies to magic – purification is simply the act of clearing space, within us, without us in a temple area and within the inner realms.

Purification may therefore be defined as the clearing or releasing of unhelpful emotions, thoughts and energy from the mind, subtle bodies and inner realms. When applied solely to a person it is often called 'purification', and when applied to a physical area, such as a temple, it is often called 'clearing space' or 'cleansing'. Directed, controlled and applied purification is one of the basic building blocks we need to learn in the practice of Golden Dawn spirituality. Without it our spheres of working, whether that be our own consciousness or a temple space, will contain energies that may hinder the working in question or lessen its transformational powers.

Purification serves a number of ends.

Firstly, it helps us concentrate and focus our will and ability to visualise. This is one of the reasons that the original Golden Dawn used to instruct the newcomer in the Lesser Ritual of the Pentagram.

Secondly, it allows our minds and energy fields to be clear so that we can more accurately perceive whatever we commune with or contact in our spiritual practice, be it energy, a Goddess or another person. If we are carrying around tension, stress and negative energy, we are less likely to be able to perceive the subtle nuances of our interactions with other Beings and the universe.

Thirdly, purification clears our subtle bodies, so that the energies we connect with via these bodies can flow through us easily to the Earth. If these energies get stuck in our subtle bodies then our transformation by them is lessened, since a complete circuit from the inner realms to the material realm needs to be achieved. Without such a complete circuit, the symbolic connection of heaven to Earth through the magician, there will be no ongoing flow and interaction between the various areas of our being and their universal counterparts.

Fourthly, purification removes from our etheric body any alien etheric energy that we have collected from other people, places or situations. This alien energy will hinder our magical effectiveness as it is not under the control of our will.

Fifthly, the removal of energy blocks or hindrances within our subtle bodies means that we, and any group we work with, are safer in the magic we are performing. This is because any unhelpful emotions and energy we are carrying when we contact subtle energy are magnified by that energy. So if we enter a magical circle feeling angry or depressed, and these emotions are not cleansed, then they will get stronger and more intense as the work proceeds. Often when this occurs it is not very conscious, and the energy in the temple seems to just get very 'heavy' or 'thick' without any real reason. Conversely, if we enter a circle feeling mildly sexually attracted to a member of the group, often that attraction magnifies over time. This can be just as effective a spoiler of magic and spiritual connection as the temple feeling heavy.

Within purification we see the concept of needing to return to a clear and centred space, much like the void or Unmanifest that many magicians insist we need to re-connect with before starting any magic. The metaphor of an empty glass is useful here. If we view ourselves as an empty glass, waiting to be filled with the wine of the Goddess, then purification wipes the muck of the surface of the glass, cleaning, polishing it, so that the light may shine through and show the beauty of the wine clearly.

It is important to understand that when the Golden Dawn tradition talks about purification or purification of energy and emotions, we are not passing moral judgment on emotional states, assigning some as 'bad' and others as 'good'. All emotions are valid and need expression, but not necessarily within a magical temple. Purification is required for culturally labelled 'positive' emotions, as well as those termed 'negative'. Feeling child-like or happy and buoyant and playful is wonderful, but it too will get in the way of effective magical transformation if not cleansed. Because the Western mysteries have been hidden within the patriarchal Judeo-Christian religions, they have, in part, adopted some of the worst aspects of those traditions. This is especially true when it comes to practices like purification, where some Western mystery practitioners were historically concerned with purity and cleanliness to what now seems an unhealthy degree. The unclean culprits in these cases were often sexual desires and feelings. In our spiritual practice and groups we need to watch our cultural tendencies to presume that anger, desire, grief, fear etc are bad or negative, and must be 'washed away' or removed. These emotions are valid, and need expression.

The Golden Dawn tradition has a specific set of techniques that banish energy and unhelpful Beings within a number of different realms or worlds. Here will we focus upon just two, others being discussed under their invoking aspect in Chapter Five:

> *The Lesser Banishing Ritual of the Pentagram*
> *The Lesser Banishing Ritual of the Hexagram*

In addition there are a number of techniques of purification that occur during the initiation rituals and a few other advanced techniques that need not concern us here. Also to be noted is that each of these rituals have their invoking counterparts, the Lesser *Invoking* Ritual of the Pentagram and Hexagram. The actual difference in the rituals performance is mostly one of intention, visualisation and changes in the methods of inscribing the lineal form of the symbol. A very important aspect of the Golden Dawn methods of purification and invoking is **learning to banish before you learn to invoke**. That is, become proficient in the banishing aspect of a ritual before attempting its invoking aspect. By doing this your subtle bodies will be clear in the realms where the ritual has the most effect and the energy drawn in by the invocation will be clearer and utilised better.

THE FOUR ELEMENTAL PRINCIPLES

Before proceeding any further we now need to come to grips with the four elemental principles of Air, Fire, Water and Earth. These elemental principles are ancient descriptions of certain forces existing within the universe and human being. The terms do not refer to the physical manifestations of Fire, Water, Air and Earth. Traditionally it is taught that everything, including humanity, was comprised of a mixture of these four elements, bound together by a fifth 'element', spirit. The conception of the four elements reflects a four-fold thinking process by the Western mind that we see manifest in the four compass directions, the four seasons, the four times of day etc. Just as the whole world we know can be classified using these four modes ('house is in the North', 'it's a cold winter's night'), so too can the psyche be classified into four areas. These areas are reflections and manifestations of the great underlying principles of the universe that we label the four elemental principles. We can subdivide these categories further, like the various compass directions (South-East etc) as each element contains all the others within it. Thus within Earth there is Air of Earth, Fire of Earth, Water of Earth and Earth of Earth.

The elemental theory is that all of our conscious states can be assigned to one or more of the four elements, over which presides the spirit. In the case of human consciousness the presiding spirit is our sense of self which we find in Tiphareth on the Tree. One of the traditional first tasks of the Western magician is to analyse the various parts of her consciousness and assign them to the elements. Working with the following exercise over a period of time will do this.

THE ELEMENTAL MIRROR OF SELF

This exercise is, by now, a 'traditional' one used by many groups and teachers in a number of Western traditions. Its popularisation is due to its inclusion in the influential *What Witches Do* by Stewart Farrar (1971), who believed he was recording a traditional Witch teaching from Alex Sanders. However, it has only been in use in this form since the 1930s within certain European Hermetic schools, and it was first recorded, I believe, in Franz Bardon's *Initiation into Hermetics* (1956). It is a very useful and insightful exercise when conducted with vigour. Consciously make time and space for this exercise as part of your spiritual practice. It is not something to be rushed or handled without due care.

Take your journal and on a clean page, list all the 'good' or positive qualities of yourself. Everything you feel is useful and helpful. Be proud of what qualities you have and write them all down. Keep descriptions to one or two words only. To do this, you may like to imagine yourself as you behaved in past situations. Spend a fair bit of time, connecting and tuning into yourself. Leave no stone unturned, be totally honest with yourself. Our culture does not teach us to praise and value ourselves for who we are, only for what we've got. So go deeper than this and really tune into your positive qualities. Write them all down.

Now take a break. When you come back, list all your 'bad' or negative qualities. Again, be honest and real with yourself. Imagine how you have reacted in past events. Look over your whole life. Remember though, do not use this exercise as an opportunity for self flagellation – be honest and open with yourself but do not hate yourself. If you find feelings of hate or self-disgust start occurring, stop and take a break. Ask God or your Sacred One(s) to help you, and then continue. Again, our culture teaches that most of us are in most ways, down deep, self-focused people. Do not fall into the trap of believing this, but remain honest with yourself on those parts of your personality that are negative and do not serve you and the world.

Now take another break. You may like to finish for now and come back another time. When ready, ground and purify. Now light some incense for Air and a candle for Fire. Have near you a glass of water and some Earth or salt and bread on a small plate. Divide a page in your journal into four quarters. Label one for each of the four elements, Fire, Water, Air and Earth. Now look at your list of good points. Take each in turn and feel out which element it relates to the most. There are traditional lists below to give you pointers, but it is vitally important to make this your own mirror, and this requires you to have your own understanding. Of course, there are some broad general guidelines. A fault of going with the flow too much is unlikely to be ascribed to Earth. Most people would place it with Water.

When you have chosen an element, place a tick next to the quality in question and then rewrite it in the quarter of the page assigned to it. If you find one that is not clear, pause, breath deep, let it go. Then quickly tune into the elements before you; watch the smoke of the incense and inhale it; feel the heat of the candle, touch the Water and Earth. Now look at the word again and decide. If it is still difficult, leave it for now, and move onto the next one. Once they are all done, take a break.

Come back and repeat the process with your negative qualities but on another page. Once this is done, it is best to take a break for the night. The next morning or whenever possible, return to look at your lists. Don't read too many words. Look and see if there is any pattern to the pages. Are most of your good qualities in one or two elements? Does the element with the largest number of good qualities have the least number of bad qualities? Ask yourself these and other questions. See what you can notice about yourself. Know that when working with the elemental principles you will also be working with these aspects of your personality. It is good to repeat this exercise (without looking at the old one) quite often. Then compare the two, see how you have changed.

SOME TRADITIONAL QUALITIES ASSIGNED TO THE ELEMENTS

Fire *Positive:* activity, enthusiasm, firmness, courage, will, passion.
Negative: jealousy, hatred, vindictiveness, irascibility, anger.

Water *Positive:* modesty, fervency, compassion, tranquility, forgiveness.
       Negative: indifference, laziness, compliance, insolence, instability, frigidity.

Air   *Positive:* diligence, joy, kindness, optimism, mental dexterity, fun loving.
       Negative: frivolity, boasting, presumption, gossiping, squandering.

Earth *Positive:* responsibility, punctuality, respect, thoroughness, endurance.
       Negative: melancholy, irregularity, dullness, conscienceless, slothfulness.

An important point to remember is that the four elemental principles exist throughout the various subtle and non-physical realms of the universe. We can come to a clear understanding of this concept by looking at water. In most places on the Earth it exists as a liquid, in other environments as ice or steam but it is still the same substance, simply altered by its environment. It is the same with the four elements – the same principle exists in differing forms on different planes or realms, with the 'form' or 'pattern' the principle takes being altered by the nature of the inner realm in question. The elements exist, though very differently to how we see them in our world, within each of the ten spheres of the Tree of Life described previously.

We can now see two important aspects of the model used throughout this book – the various inner realms of the universe, the Sephiroth or spheres of the Tree of Life and the four elemental principles that exist within each of those realms. Within practical Western magic the realms are often symbolised by the seven planets and the elemental principles by the physical substances of Air, Fire, Water and Earth. We may also add to this map the connecting points or Paths between the spheres on the Tree. With these ideas in mind we can now look at the effects of the two rituals considered in this chapter.

The Lesser Ritual of the Pentagram when performed correctly will affect the whole of the Tree in Assiah apart from Malkuth of Assiah. Our entire etheric bodies will be cleansed by this ritual. It will also affect the Yetziratic realm to some degree since Malkuth of Yetzira is the Kether of Assiah. Malkuth of Yetzira will be completely cleansed by this ritual.

The Lesser Ritual of the Hexagram (generic) has its primary effects on the connecting point between Assiah and Yetzira. That is, the 32nd Path of Tau between Malkuth and Yesod.

It is also important to remember that both of these rituals, as stated previously, may be used to purify these realms (banish) as well as to invoke or bring forth the energy and blessings from these worlds. We will discuss this more in Chapter Five.

THE LESSER RITUAL OF THE PENTAGRAM (LRP)

Aleister Crowley once wrote that 'Properly understood (the LRP) is the medicine of Metals and the stone of the Wise'. Effective use of the LRP will promote incredible forces of transformation and spiritual awakening within us. Indeed it is one of the most versatile and effective rituals used by the Golden Dawn and subsequently by much of the modern pagan and magical communities. It was the first piece of ritual magic given to the Golden Dawn magician and remained the sole piece of real magic they were permitted to undertake for many years. When correctly performed, the LRP can also be used for a variety of purposes beside spiritual unfoldment, some of the most popular being to cleanse the etheric and astral atmosphere of a room and to remove any obsessing thought or idea from the mind. We can list functions of the LRP as:

1. Purifying the etheric and astral bodies.
2. Balancing the elemental make-up within the astral body and the psyche.
3. Creating a link with the Higher and Divine Genius.
4. Protecting the magician from negative energies, and placing within the astral and etheric bodies structures (the pentagrams) that will activate automatically when needed.
5. Placing within the astral body of the magician keys that will allow her easier access to the inner realms.
6. Grounding or Earthing the magician.

When performed correctly the banishing ritual will leave the magician and room feeling clean and pure, while the invocatory ritual will result in a feeling of consecration and sacredness. The ritual should be practiced in its banishing or purifying aspect for at least a month before the invocatory aspect is used. It is best to learn the ritual by heart mentally before attempting it physically.

Traditionally the LRP is to be performed at least twice each day, once banishing before sleep and once invoking upon awakening. In this it forms an excellent ritual for daily spiritual practice. This double practice is useful for two reasons. Firstly, it connects us with the Earth currents, which are alive more in the morning and less in the evening. Secondly, the banishing at night clears and balances ourselves so we may easily, as we sleep, move to the deeper realms of the inner world for guidance and re-vitalisation. The invoking in the morning strengthens what guidance we have received overnight, and balances and strengthens us for whatever the day may bring. In the evening once more, our personality self will likely be less balanced due to the events during the day, so we balance and purify ourselves with the banishing ritual. The banishing in the evening also removes any negative or unhelpful energy we have connected with during the day.

ELEMENTAL SYMBOLISM WITHIN THE LRP

One of the fundamental ideas within modern Western magic is that working with the elemental principles will allow the controlled and gradual changing of the entire conscious psyche. The LRP is only one example of such workings (though perhaps the most simple yet effective). To perform it effectively you need to know that the elements and sub-elements being banished and invoked relate directly to your own being as well as the objective realms outside of us. This should become very clear to you as you work with the Elemental Mirror of Self exercise described previously.

Apart from psychological characteristics, the four elements are assigned certain traditional attributes which may be found in any number of books and on the internet. The three most important correspondences to the elements for the effective performance of the LRP are colour, quarter and time of day:

AIR	Yellow, East, Dawn
FIRE	Red, South, Noon
WATER	Blue, West, Dusk
EARTH	Olive Green, North, Midnight

These correspondences need to be learnt before attempting the ritual.

THE VIBRATION OF DIVINE NAMES

Vibration or intonation of divine names is a traditional practice within many spiritual paths, particularly those that have their roots in the native Middle Eastern traditions, such as Judaism and Sufism. It rests on the belief and awareness that the name of a deity or being contains the blessings of that deity or being. So for example, the name of Raphael is not simply a name, but a key to the full powers and energies of the Archangel himself. Vibration is said to unlock those powers and energies from the name. In doing so they then are able to transform us. Vibration simply awakens the powers of the name we vibrate. Traditionally, a very important caution to remember is to **only ever vibrate divine names**. That is, we only ever use vibration with names whose energies we wish to awaken. Practicing vibration using common words or names is not a good idea, as there is no real way to ascertain what powers this may awaken within you. Please do not disregard this warning.

As a key part of the LRP, and most Golden Dawn rituals, certain divine names **must be** vibrated or intoned rather than simply spoken. If you are not already familiar with vibration, I suggest you purchase a recording or two listed in the bibliography and hear the technique for yourself. Alternatively there are Golden Dawn Websites on the Internet that have samples of vibration to download. In any case it is important to hear this rather than read about it. It is also important that when you vibrate, the vibrations are felt in the chest and palms. Make sure you are vibrating from your belly, not from your throat. If your throat hurts after a while of vibrating, you need to learn how to vibrate from lower down. Apart from the physical discomfort of a sore throat, vibrating in this way places a strain upon the throat centre or chakra, which we wish to avoid.

The Golden Dawn tradition also uses an advance technique by which we may vibrate the divine names. This is known as the Vibratory Formula of the Middle Pillar and we examine it in depth in Chapter Five. You do not need to practice this formula to perform the LRP effectively. When you have mastered the technique, adding it to your LRP performance will greatly enhance its transformational effects, but it is by no means essential. It is far more important to begin the LRP as soon as possible rather than wait for perfection. For convention all names to be vibrated in this book are given in **BOLD AND CAPITALS**.

INSTRUCTIONS FOR THE LESSER RITUAL OF THE PENTAGRAM

THE OPENING QABALISTIC CROSS

Stand facing the East and relax for a few minutes by deep breathing.

Place your hand (most people use their right hand) down in front of your body pointing to the Earth. Slowly raise your hand up the central line of your body and above your head.

Bring the hand slowly down to your forehead and touching it vibrate: **ATEH** (pronounced Ah-Tayh)

Lower your hand to touch the stomach, belly or genitals. Vibrate **MALKUTH** (Mal-kooth).

Touch the right shoulder, vibrate **VE-GEBURAH** (Vay-Gebv-uh-rah).

Touch the left shoulder, vibrate **VE-GEDULAH** (Vay-Ged-oo-lah).

Fold both hands on the centre of your chest, vibrate **LE-OLAM** (Ley-Ohlahm).

Bow slightly, vibrate **AMEN**. Then slowly lower your hands to rest by your sides. Then raise your head.

THE INSCRIPTION OF THE PENTAGRAMS

With your forefinger (or first two fingers) inscribe a pentagram in the air, about three feet in height; touch the centre of the pentagram and vibrate **YOD-HEH-VAU-HEH** (Yodh-Heyh-Vowh-Heyh). See diagram 7 for methods of inscription of the pentagram.

Turn to face the South. Repeat the inscription of the pentagram using the divine name **ADONAI** (Ah-Don-Aye).

Turn to face the West. Repeat the inscription of the pentagram using the divine name **EHEIEH** (Ehh-Heh-Yah).

Turn to face the North. Repeat the inscription of the pentagram using the divine name **AGLA** (Ah-Glah).

Turn back to face the East.

Diagram 7: Banishing (left) and Invoking (right) Lesser Pentagrams

The Invocation of the Four Archangels

Hold your arms out to the sides in the form of a cross and say/vibrate:

'Before me **RAPHAEL** (Rah-Feyh-El).
Behind me **GABRIEL** (Gahb-Bree-El)
On my right hand, **MICHAEL** (Mee-Cai-El).
On my left hand, **AURIEL** (Ohr-Ree-El).

For about me flame the pentagrams
And above me shines the six-rayed star.'

The Final Qabalistic Cross

Repeat the Qabalistic Cross as described above.

Full Description and Inner Work of the LRP

The Opening Qabalistic Cross

Stand facing the East in the centre of your temple or area where you work and worship.

Relax for a few minutes by deep breathing. The Golden Dawn traditionally suggested a four-fold breath – see chapter three on meditation.

Place your hand down in front of your body, so that your hand is resting over your genital area. Your palm should be to your body and your fingers pointing towards the Earth. Slowly raise your hand up the central line of your body. (Still in your rhythmic breath imagine a ray of light or your will moving from your hand into the Earth below you. Allow this to travel deep into the centre of the Earth where it connects with the Inner Light of the Earth. Draw this light up towards you as you breathe in and move your hand. See the white light from the Earth enter your body and move through your feet and fill you completely as you raise your hand above you).

Still raising your hand, move it straight above your head. Bring the hand slowly down to your forehead, and touching it vibrate: **ATEH** (pronounced Ah-Tayh). (As you raise your hand see yourself growing larger and larger until you stand on the Earth with your head among the stars. Look up and see at the end of the Universe, a limitless flashing and divine white light. This fills your vision and you know it to be the light of the One. As your physical hand rises high, the light is just able to be reached by your fingertips. Yearn for the connection of the One. Move your hand into the white light and then bring your hand down towards your head. As your hand moves down to your forehead bring down a shaft of brilliant white light. See the light coming to rest inside your head, filling your whole head. As you vibrate see the light grow brighter and stronger.

Lower your hand to touch the stomach, belly or genitals. Vibrate **MALKUTH** (Mal-kooth). (As you move your hand down, visualise a shaft of white light going down through your body to rest at the base of your feet. It is important not to stop the light where your hand stops but to continue the visualisation to just below the feet and thus filling the whole Earth. Again, when vibrating see the light grow bright and strong, like a brilliant ball of light upon which you stand).

Touch the right shoulder, vibrate **VE-GEBURAH** (Vay-Gebv-uh-rah). (With your hand bring the light to your shoulder. Again, when vibrating see the light grow bright and strong, forming a brilliant ball of light).

Touch the left shoulder, vibrate **VE-GEDULAH** (Vay-Ged-oo-lah). (As you move your hand from the right to the left shoulder see a glowing bar of white light being formed. Again, when vibrating see the light grow bright and strong, forming a brilliant ball of light).

Fold both hands on the centre of your chest, vibrate **LE-OLAM** (Ley-Ohlahm). (As you vibrate see the connecting point of light of the two shafts grow bright and strong and form a ball of light).

Bow slightly, vibrate **AMEN**. Then slowly lower your hands to rest by your sides. Then raise your head. (As you vibrate see the cross of light within you grow bright and strong. As you slowly lower your hands, see yourself returning to normal size, no longer standing upon the world with your head amongst the stars. As you return to normal size maintain the visualisation of the shaft of light connecting the crown of your head with the brilliant white light above the stars.

INSCRIPTION OF THE PENTAGRAMS

With eyes open, will and imagine that the light from your crown moves down into your heart centre. There allow it to unite with the light from the Earth already drawn into your body. Send the united light from your heart to your hand and with your forefinger (or first two fingers) inscribe the pentagram in the air as shown in diagram 7, starting at the described spots for invoking or banishing. (See the light in your hands directed out of your finger as electric blue light as you inscribe the pentagram. The pentagram should be inscribed with care and precision, though with a reasonable amount of speed. It should be fairly large, at least three feet high. See the pentagram shine before you, hanging in the air, pulsating with electric blue light).

With your finger, touch the centre of the pentagram and vibrate **YOD-HEH-VAU-HEH** (Yodh-Heyh-Vowh-Heyh). (As you vibrate imagine that the force of your voice and vibration carries the sound of the divine name to the ends of the universe in that direction. The name takes with it any unbalanced or unresolved energies of the Air qualities of your elemental self, that is your talking self; intellect, communication, logic etc.)

Keeping your hand at the same level (shoulder height) and pointed out before you, turn to face the South. (As you turn the 90 degrees to the South, see a wall of white light being formed around you).

Repeat the inscription of the pentagram with the same intent and visualisations, but using the divine name **ADONAI** (Ah-Don-Aye). (As you vibrate imagine that the force of your voice and vibration carries the sound of the divine name to the ends of the universe in that direction. The name takes with it any unbalanced or unresolved energies of the Fire qualities of your elemental self; your passion, will, drive, sexuality etc.)

Keeping your hand at the same level (shoulder height) and pointed out before you, turn to face the West. (As you turn the 90 degrees to the West, see a wall of white light being formed around you).

Repeat the inscription of the pentagram with the same intent and visualisations, but using the divine name **EHEIEH** (Ehh-Heh-Yah). (As you vibrate imagine that the force of your voice and vibration carries the sound of the divine name to the ends of the universe in that direction. The name takes with it any unbalanced or unresolved energies of the Water qualities of your elemental self; your feeling self, emotions, intuitions, instincts etc.)

Keeping your hand at the same level (shoulder height) and pointed out before you, turn to face the North. (As you turn the 90 degrees to the North, see a wall of white light being formed around you).

Repeat the inscription of the pentagram with the same intent and visualisations, but using the divine name **ALGA** (Ah-Glah). (As you vibrate imagine that the force of your voice and vibration carries the sound of the divine name to the ends of the universe in that direction. The name takes with it any unbalanced or unresolved energies of the Earth qualities of your elemental self; your body self, health, vitality, spatial knowledge etc.)

Turn back to face the East. (As you turn the 90 degrees to the East, see a wall of white light being formed around you. This will complete the circle or wall of white light around you.)

INVOCATION OF THE FOUR ARCHANGELS

Hold your arms out in the form of a cross and say/vibrate:

'Before me **RAPHAEL** (Rah-Feyh-El)'. (Visualise the archangel Raphael standing before you as a tall, elegant figure clothed in yellow with yellow and violet robes and wings outstretched, covering the whole Eastern quarter. He stands in the dawn light and you can see the sunrise behind him. From him feel the cleansing effects of a gentle breeze of Air).

'Behind me **GABRIEL** (Gahb-Bree-El)'. (Visualise Gabriel standing behind you as a tall figure clothed in bright blue and sea coloured robes with orange and blue wings outstretched, covering the whole Western quarter. She stands at the edge of a vast sea, on the horizon of which the sun is setting. Beside her is a huge waterfall. From the waterfall feel a gentle spray of cleansing Water).

'On my right hand, **MICHAEL** (Mee-Cai-El)'. (Visualise Michael standing on your right as a tall figure clothed in bright red and orange with flashes of emerald green, and red and green wings outstretched, covering the whole Southern quarter. He stands beneath a noon-day sun, bright and strong, and he is surrounded by orange and gold flames, from which you feel the warm glow of Fire).

'On my left hand, **AURIEL** (Ohr-Ree-El). (Visualise Auriel standing on your left as a tall figure clothed in clear olive green, rustic brown and russet robes with black and white wings outstretched, covering the whole Northern quarter. She stands in a glorious forest at midnight with many stars overhead. About her feet are crops and harvests of many sorts and the fruits of the land. From her you feel a sense of stability and the power of Earth).

'For about me flame the pentagrams' (Visualise all four pentagrams once more in bright electric blue around you).

'And above me shines the six-rayed star' (Visualise a golden Hexagram or six pointed star resting above your head like a crown).

THE FINAL QABALISTIC CROSS
Repeat the steps for the Opening Qabalistic Cross.

THE VISUALISATIONS WITHIN THE LRP

All the visualisations of the Archangels given above are intentionally brief. Apart from giving a basic outline it is unwise to influence the vision each magician has of the divine beings, which is necessarily personal. The images given for the LRP vary slightly from book to book, teacher to teacher and tradition to tradition. Experiment and create your own images that you find comfortable and which work for you, changing the sex of the Archangels also if you desire. The above images are based on the traditional Golden Dawn colour and time period associations with the elements. The important thing to remember in building up your own images for the Archangels is to keep them in synch with one another. That is, if you start seeing Michael with a Wand, the symbolic tool of Fire, see the other three holding appropriate tools also.

MEANING OF THE DIVINE NAMES AND WORDS WITHIN THE LRP

Every magician should be fully aware of the meaning of the words he or she uses in ritual. Below is the standard rough and ready English translation of the Hebrew used in the LRP.

Word	Hebrew	Meaning
Ateh	אתה	Thou art/thine/unto you
Malkuth	מלכות	the Kingdom
Ve-Geburah	וגבורה	and the power
Ve-Gedulah	וגדולה	and the glory
Le-Olam	לעולם	unto the ages.
Amen	אמן	A sealing word from the old Egyptian, **Amenti**, the Underworld.
Yod-Heh-Vau-Heh	יהוה	Literally, 'to be', often translated as God.
Adonai	אדני	Lord, ruler, or ruling power.
Eheieh	אהיה	'I will be'
Agla	אגלא	An acronym for the Hebrew sentence **A**teh **G**ibor **L**e-Olam **A**donai: translated roughly as 'Thou art mighty unto the ages, Lord'.
Raphael	רפאל	Healer of the One Being of All
Gabriel	גבריאל	Strength of the One Being of All
Michael	מיכצל	Like Unto the One Being of All
Auriel	אוריאל	Light of the One Being of All

(Please note that while the archangelic suffix 'el' is generally translated as 'God', it is actually gender neuter. Its original root meaning is 'unity' or 'the One'.)

Though the LRP may seem complex and difficult to learn, it is very easy once attempted. It is best at first to confine your practice to the Qabalistic Cross, perfect that and then move on to the whole ritual. Practice the words and vibrations before the ritual movements and it will all come together very quickly.

ANALYSIS OF THE LRP

The ritual has four distinct sections:

1. The Qabalistic Cross
2. The Inscription of the Pentagrams
3. The Invocation of the Four Archangels
4. The Qabalistic Cross

Looking quickly at each section in turn will show the purpose behind the ritual and how it works.

THE QABALISTIC CROSS

We will spend a bit of time on this section as in many ways it is the most crucial action within the ritual. Despite its simplicity it is also the most important ritual action within the entire Golden Dawn tradition. This is because it is the means whereby the magician connects with the guidance of the Light or the deepest connection we have with the One. This is brought into her body and then balanced throughout the whole of her by the use of the cross formula. This produces a state of balance within the energy system of the subtle bodies, clears the central channel from crown to feet and links the light of the One to the body. The entire ritual is now under the guidance of the 'higher'. This is why most Golden Dawn rituals commence with the Qabalistic Cross; it ensures our magic is in partnership with the divine, not solely from our own motivations and for our own ends.

This act of 'starting right' is an ancient practice from the Middle Eastern spiritual traditions. In Islam all chapters of the Koran begin with the word 'Bismi'allah', translated as 'we begin in the name of God (unity)'. The Hebrew equivalent is 'B'shmy', 'begin in the name and vibration of God'. This initial act dedicates the whole ritual and affirms the magician's intention to be directed and led by her connection with God. This is carried forward into the ritual by directing and using the light drawn from this connection, in union with the light of the Earth, to inscribe the Pentagrams.

Traditionally drawing up the light from within the Earth was omitted from the Qabalistic Cross. However, this I feel is simply the result of the

Earth negative ideology within the historical Western religious traditions. From a viewpoint of balance and remembering the Qabalistic saying 'Kether is in Malkuth and Malkuth is in Kether', this action is entirely appropriate. There is also a very old belief that the lights of the stars are reflected in the Earth, that there is an inner source of light within the Earth itself. This has a certain resonance with both the traditional Rosicrucian vault and the Underworld, themes explored within the work of R.J. Stewart. See his *The Underworld Initiation, EarthLight* and *The Power Within the Land.* Given all this, I feel this extra step to be a welcome innovation on the original format. However, you may wish to use the traditional version and omit this step.

Another way of understanding the concept of 'starting right' is to look at the English translations of the Hebrew. As simple and as basic as the standard translation is, we still get a sense of the humbling cosmic scope of this action: 'Unto thee be the Kingdom, the Power and the Glory, until all ages, Amen'. Here we are addressing the unnameable One Being and placing our life their hands. We give over our sense of self; our power and our Inner Light to God for all times, allowing ourselves to be guided and moved by Him, to serve His ends. This is the meaning of the Qabalistic Cross and we need to approach it each and every time with these spiritual ends in mind for it to be fully effective. Also we need to desire this connection, this linking with the Light. This is why we stretch our hands up and we can only just reach the light. It produces a state of active yearning and desiring towards the light. When doing this part of the ritual I encourage you to strongly feel your desire to link to the deeper, higher self and to serve Goddess. Channel all of this desire into your connection with the light.

We see then that the Qabalistic Cross is not simply a method of balancing energy, but properly performed it is a whole regenerative process in and by itself, one that will align all our actions to the divine. One of the most important actions within the ritual is the movement of the light from above our heads to below our feet. In terms of the Tree of Life this is a linking of Kether to Malkuth. Thus our bodies stand as a bridge between heaven and Earth, God and creation, unity and diversity, the All and the singular. By this we dedicate ourselves to the regeneration of the Earth, as shown by the light of God entering the world below our feet.

This action also sets up a polarity of force between the Kether and Malkuth centres in our subtle bodies. This polarity is one of the most important channels of force within our subtle bodies. The Qabalistic Cross clears this channel and strengthens this polarity. Through the cross bar of Geburah and Gedulah (Chesed), this polarity is then taken into a new mode or dimension, bringing forth a new polarity of the universe; constriction (severity) and expansion (mercy). This is to complement and evolve the polarity of the Unmanifest to the manifest in Kether and Malkuth respectively. This is energetically and symbolically placing the template of the creation of the Universe within us.

These two polarities are now resolved and balanced by the words **Le Olam**, 'unto all ages', showing that the union of the polarities produces infinite life. This occurs within the sphere of balance, Tiphareth within our heart centres. The whole is sealed by the ancient word **Amen**, which stems from the Semitic root AMN which means 'hidden' and refers to the deep hidden underworld within the Earth. Thus all the actions are sealed by linking to the dark within the underworld. In effect this movement of light into the underworld produces the seeds from which new life and actions in alignment with God may spring.

The Qabalistic Cross is also important in that it shows forth the whole Golden Dawn tradition, not simply in its dedication of our lives to Goddess, but also in its summation of the initiatory process within the tradition. There is a method of Qabalistic exegesis whereby the ideas and spiritual powers contained in a whole book may be summed up into a chapter, then into a paragraph, then into a sentence and then into a single word. We can see this within the Golden Dawn also. The initiatory system from Neophyte to Adeptus Minor is summed up in the Lesser Ritual of the Pentagram: the initial Qabalistic Cross is symbolic of the Neophyte initiation, the initial link to the Light. The pentagrams and the Archangel invocations are symbolic of the four elemental grades. The concluding statement and reaffirmation of the pentagrams around us, with the six rayed star above us, is symbolic of the Portal Grade. And finally, the concluding Cross is symbolic of the Adeptus Minor initiation whereby we take on the consciousness symbolised by the Calvary Cross itself.

The Qabalistic Cross in turn however condenses and sums up these meanings further: the initial yearning and movement towards the light is the Neophyte grade. The four elemental grades are shown by the four termini of the Cross: Air at the forehead, Earth at the feet, Fire at the right shoulder and Water at the left shoulder. The Portal grade of spirit is shown by the fifth unifying action of the hands over the heart and the Adeptus Minor Grade by the word 'Amen', the underworld or tomb from where we are reborn, like the Vault within the Adeptus Minor ceremony.

THE INSCRIPTION OF THE PENTAGRAMS

This draws upon several ancient and established connections with the symbol of the pentagram, those being: protection, a means of access to the inner realms, and the balance of the four elements in the human being overruled by spirit. The pentagram carries with it these currents of spiritual blessing which are used in the LRP. The particular way of inscribing the pentagram in the LRP refers to the element of Earth and our physical, everyday life and minds. The same Earth pentagram is inscribed at each of the four quarters with different names, pertaining to the sub-elements of Earth: Air of Earth, Fire of Earth, Water of Earth and Earth of Earth.

These sub-elements are cleansed and balanced by the pentagram and the divine names, which means that our whole everyday consciousness is affected and balanced. The inscription of the pentagrams also places within the etheric and astral bodies the four pentagrams in balance around us. This will not only continue the effects of the ritual within us, but the pentagrams once placed there by many repetitions will act as a protection against negative forces on these levels. The placement in the etheric body is by the actual direction of energy from the fingers and the placement in the astral body is by the visualisations.

THE INVOCATION OF THE ARCHANGELS

These invocations use traditional images and colours to invoke the Archangels who represent and channel the four elements in their pure state. These pure elemental forces will charge and re-vitalise the elemental forces within ourselves. The pentagrams first purify and balance the sub-elements of Earth within our consciousness and then the archangels bring us the pure elements from Spirit to enliven and enlarge our elemental make-up. The pure energy of the elements, even when directed and under the presidency of the Spirit, can sometimes be overwhelming, and here the Pentagrams serve another function. They act as filters that allow the influx of the pure elements to enter our being slowly over a period of time. They do this firstly on the astral level and then on the etheric.

At first the Archangels may appear as mere visualisations, but over time they will begin to actually be there. Tradition teaches us that the Archangels are real spiritual Beings. However, originating from the Creative World (Briah), they have no actual form or astral body. This is why we can vary our visualisations of them to suit our personal needs. By our visualisations we create an astral body for their presence to inhabit, so that they will come and live within our spheres when we call them.

For this to be a long term and continuous presence we need to prepare the right space and atmosphere for them. This is akin to trying to grow plants from a rainforest in Iceland – for them to survive we need to create an appropriate atmosphere, that is a greenhouse. By continued use of the LRP, our auric fields actually change into the purified and consecrated elemental atmospheres that the Archangels can live in. They will then, over time, 'move in'. When this happens, it is most noticeable and wonderful.

THE SECOND QABALISTIC CROSS

This closes and seals the ritual and indicates that all the proceedings from start to finish have been under the guidance of the light of Goddess. The final part of the final cross is the visualisation of the shaft of light from the magician's crown to the Light. This is an energetic connection, and affirmation, that helps the magician to be guided by her connection with God from then on.

THE LESSER RITUAL OF THE HEXAGRAM

This ritual was originally given to the Golden Dawn magician only when she had progressed through all of the various initiation ceremonies. It is part of a more complex set of Hexagram rituals which we will cover in Chapter Five. Unlike the Lesser Ritual of the Pentagram, the LRH was never originally designed to be used as an ongoing daily practice, though it may be used as such for a particular work or aim. It is therefore a ritual that is seldom performed around the aura or sphere of sensation, and mostly around the temple. That is, instead of simply turning to face each of the directions we move to the perimeter of the temple at that direction before inscribing the form. We then circle around the edge of the temple to the next quarter or cardinal point ready to inscribe the next form.

It is a ritual that is designed, in many ways, to consolidate the Lesser Banishing Ritual of the Pentagram, and is seldom performed without the LBRP preceding it. With reference to the Tree of Life in diagram 5, the Lesser Ritual of the Hexagram effects the 32nd path of Tau, the path that connects our world of Assiah with the astral world of Yetzira. The use of this ritual, by cleansing and consecrating this path, allows for the influx of potent astral forces to be drawn into the temple or ourselves without distortion or problems. The combination of the banishing rituals of the pentagram and the hexagram produce a strong and safe cleaning effect that is ideal as an opening for most Golden Dawn rituals. The Lesser Pentagram is first done in order to cleanse and stabilise the energies of our world, and then the channel to the inner realms is cleansed via the Lesser Hexagram. After this is done, we are then free to perform a deep and full invocation or ritual that 'brings down' or 'through' the required spiritual blessings in balance.

The LBRH is often used to prepare the space for and precede the Analysis of the Keyword, described in Chapter Five. The combination of LBRP, LBRH and Keyword is very effective and deeply transformational. Some books and Orders view the Lesser Ritual of the Hexagram as being intrinsically linked to the Analysis of the Keyword. This is not the case, though mostly the two are practiced together. The Lesser Hexagram is also often used on its own for a variety of purposes. Also some books have the Keyword performed before and after the hexagram. If we accept the understanding that the role of the LBRH is to prepare the channel for the invocation of forces so they are not distorted, then we can see that invoking with the Keyword before purifying with the LBRH is not a good idea.

ELEMENTAL ATTRIBUTIONS WITHIN THE LRH

While using the four elemental principles and the four directions, the Lesser Hexagram (and all Hexagram rituals) does so with different elemental correspondences to the directions than the Lesser Pentagram (and all the Pentagram rituals). With the LRP, the original schema was based on the qualities of the winds of Northern Europe. The hexagram rituals' correspondences are based on the allocation of the elements as they are attributed to the signs of the Wheel of the Zodiac which encircles the Earth. Comparing the two sets of correspondences we have:

Direction	Pentagram Rituals	Hexagram Rituals
East	Air	Fire (Aries)
South	Fire	Earth (Capricorn)
West	Water	Air (Libra)
North	Earth	Water (Cancer)

Even though the hexagram rituals do not work with the elements as we generally understand them, it is important to know these correspondences.

The difference in the quarter attributions of the elements means that save for experimentation or specific work, the invoking Lesser Pentagram and the invoking Lesser Hexagram should **never** be performed in the same ritual. To do so would invoke the elements, though in different states of manifestation, into the different quarters. This interaction can cause a fair degree of chaotic energy *unless expected and worked with*. This can, in advanced work, be done to experience the vibration of the elements between the quarters and between the 32nd Path of Tau and Malkuth. From this we get:

Air	Vibrating between	West and East	Manifesting towards the East
Fire	Vibrating between	East and South	Manifesting towards the South
Water	Vibrating between	North and West	Manifesting towards the West
Earth	Vibrating between	South and North	Manifesting towards the North

THE FORMS OF THE HEXAGRAM

One of the things we first notice when we look at the lineal forms to be traced in the Lesser Hexagram rituals is that they are not hexagrams at all – diagram 8. In fact they are versions of a hexagram with a displaced triangle. These forms are traditional and appear in several ancient Western magical texts, most notably *The Key of Solomon the King*. They are symbolic of the four elemental principles and we can spend much fruitful time meditating on this.

The method of tracing the forms for each direction stems from the attribution of the seven planets to the six points and centre of the hexagram forms as shown in diagram 9. The exact method for tracing is determined by the rule within all the hexagram rituals of tracing the first line from the planet in question and the second from the opposite planet, on the opposite triangle. The direction of tracing is determined by the rule of clockwise for invoking and anti-clockwise for banishing. The generic Lesser Hexagram works with the 32nd Path of Tau which is corresponded to Saturn and therefore the hexagrams we use are Saturn hexagrams. If you look at the mode of tracing in diagram 9 with reference to the attribution of Saturn (and its opposite planet of the Moon) to the points of the four forms of the hexagram you will see why the inscriptions start and finish where they do. However, please note we are not conducting a Lesser Ritual of the Hexagram of Saturn, as some authors suggest, but rather simply using that mode of drawing. There are

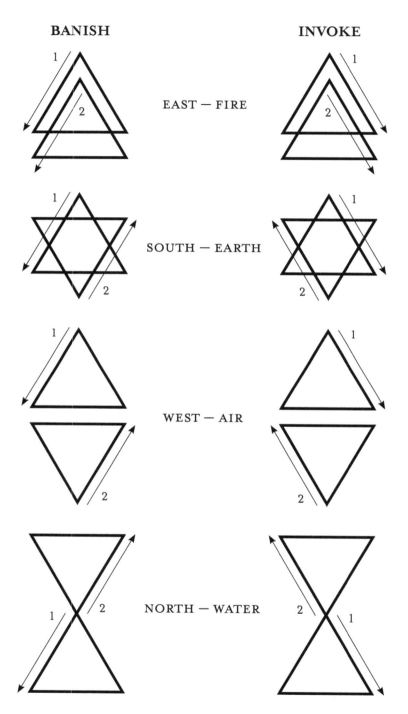

Diagram 8: Lesser Ritual of the Hexagram, Forms and Tracing

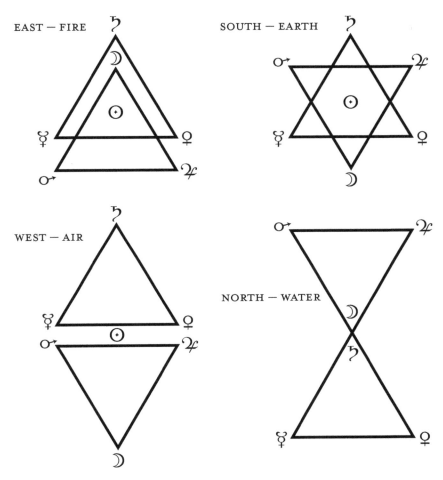

Diagram 9: Planetary Attributions of the Four Lesser Hexagram Forms

differences between the generic LRH and the Lesser Saturn Hexagram and these are discussed in Chapter Five.

Another innovation suggested by some authors is the so called 'Unicursal Hexagram'; a lineal form with six points that may be traced in a single line rather than two triangles. Despite the popularity of this approach (it saves time) there are a number of symbolic and energetic problems with it. Without going too deeply into this we can name two very important points. Firstly, the 'Unicursal Hexagram' is in fact the 'Hexangle', a lineal form used in advanced Golden Dawn angelic magic. Whereas the hexagram contains within it the energies of the seven planets, as shown in diagram 9, the Hexangle contains the energies of

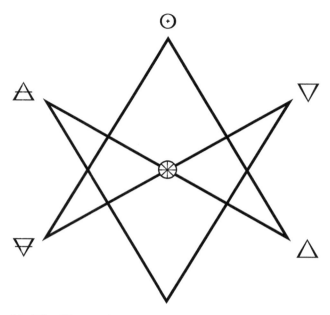

Diagram 10: The Hexangle with Elemental and Planetary Attributions

the four elements, Sun, Moon and Spirit – diagram 10. It is therefore an inappropriate form to use in planetary workings.

Another concern is that the Unicursal Hexagram ritual ignores the vital Golden Dawn principle that for different forces to be affected there needs to be different names and/or images used. So if we are seeking to affect each of the four elemental principles we need to have four differing names or images. In Lesser Pentagram we use the same form, the banishing Earth pentagram, but change the name at each quarter. In the Lesser Hexagram, we use the same name, **Ararita**, but change the forms (a procedure which, incidentally, reflects the unifying power of the name itself). The Unicursal Hexagram uses the same form and name in each quarter and is therefore is not fully effective nor as transformational. However, I am sure that some magicians would disagree, though I have yet to see a rationale behind their disagreement.

Please Note: Up until recently, many Golden Dawn books and copyists reproduced the Lesser Hexagram incorrectly. The main mistake came in the instructions for the tracing of the Water Hexagram (North), where the order is reversed. Please bear this in mind when reading elsewhere, or simply use the correct version given here. Most books these days seem to have fixed the problem, but some have not.

LESSER RITUAL OF THE HEXAGRAM INSTRUCTIONS

1. Perform the LBRP.
2. Go to the East of the Temple.
3. With either the finger or the appropriate tool inscribe the first form of the Hexagram (see diagram 8).
4. Place your hand or tool in the centre of the Hexagram and as you do so vibrate: **ARARITA.**
5. Move around to the South of the temple, keeping your hand outstretched at the same level.
6. With either the finger or the appropriate tool inscribe the second form of the Hexagram.
7. Place your hand or tool in the centre of the Hexagram and as you do so vibrate: **ARARITA.**
8. Move around to the West of the temple, keeping your hand outstretched at the same level.
9. With either the finger or the appropriate tool inscribe the third form of the Hexagram.
10. Place your hand or tool in the centre of the Hexagram and as you do so vibrate: **ARARITA.**
11. Move around to the North of the temple, keeping your hand outstretched at the same level.
12. With either the finger or the appropriate tool inscribe the fourth form of the Hexagram.
13. Place your hand or tool in the centre of the Hexagram and as you do so vibrate: **ARARITA.**
14. Move around, back to the East of the temple, keeping your hand outstretched at the same level, completing the circle of place.
15. Return to the centre of the temple and finish with a Qabalistic Cross, or continue with the rest of your ritual work.

BRIEF INNER WORKINGS OF THE LESSER RITUAL OF THE HEXAGRAM

The Qabalistic Cross is performed in exactly the same manner as in the Lesser Banishing Ritual of the Pentagram. However, an additional point may be added to help the ritual affect the 32nd Path of Tau. This is simply not to return to normal size at the conclusion of the Cross. By doing so our consciousness is more aligned with and able to affect the 32nd

Path. Some people do not need this little innovation, but beginners often find it useful. While you should no longer focus on being as large as the universe during the rest of the ritual, you should affirm that you shall remain so until completing the Qabalistic Cross at the end.

We start in the East to align ourselves with the powers of re-birth and new beginnings, dawn etc. This is the traditional starting place within the Western mystery traditions.

Direct energy out of your hand (and through your tool if using one), to inscribe the Hexagram in the air. It should be large and well formed. In this instance we use only the macrocosmic energy drawn from our Kether, crown centres and directed into the hand or tool. We do not use the combination of Kether and Earth energies, as we do in the Pentagram rituals, since the hexagram is not concerned with the Earth realms. As well as directing the energy out of our hands and tools, we also visualise the hexagram formed in the air in flashing gold light.

This is done, ideally, by using the Vibratory Formula of the Middle Pillar as detailed in Chapter Five. We can use the English letters here, **ARARITA**, or the Hebrew אראריתא – Aleph, Resh, Aleph, Resh, Yod, Tau, Aleph. If you start practicing with the English, ensure that you move as soon as possible to the Hebrew. The name is a Notariqon, or Qabalistic abbreviation for a sacred Hebrew phrase that affirms the Unity of the One throughout the universe, from beginning to ending and through the various forms of life. It is often translated as 'One is his beginning, One is his individuality, his permutation is One'. Later after you have learnt it, you may like to use the Vibratory Formula of the Middle Pillar when vibrating the Name. If so, see the letters in flashing gold light.

As you move from quarter to quarter, visualise a wall of white light surrounding the temple area.

See instructions above, changing only the form of the hexagram. Ensure you visualise the wall of white light from the North to the East, completing the circle.

Again, see the section on the Qabalistic Cross within the Lesser Ritual of the Pentagram. If you have remained extended and large from the opening Qabalistic Cross, remember this time to bring yourself back to normal size.

MEDITATION AND DIVINATION

THE WILL WITHIN MAGIC AND SPIRITUALITY

WE begin this chapter with a discussion on the will, as without control and enhancement of your will, your meditative and divinatory practices will suffer. For most of us it is only our will that keeps us going when we run, as we all do, into one of those 'dry' patches where meditation after meditation we seem to be going nowhere. A strong and conscious will is one of the keys to success in the art of magic, particularly when it comes to some of the more advanced techniques, such as dramatic invocation in Chapter Six. Note the use of the words 'strong and conscious'. When it comes to magic, a strongly developed will without a corresponding degree of self-awareness and introspection is only a little more beneficial than plain bull-headed stubbornness.

Some of the best definitions of magic used by 20th century magicians involved the conscious use of the will:

'The art of changing consciousness in accordance with will.'
– paraphrasing Dion Fortune

'The art and science of causing change in conformity with the will.'
– paraphrasing Aleister Crowley

The will may also be seen in one of the four sides of the traditional 'Magician's Pyramid' (now also called the Witches' Pyramid). The pyramid has a square base and upon the qualities provided by all four sides the magician can build her spiritual practice, her unfoldment towards the higher consciousness, symbolised by the apex of the pyramid. The four sides are normally assigned the qualities: to Know, to Will, to Dare and to Keep Silent. In modern parlance we might say something like:

To Know: we need to know what exactly it is we wish to change in our lives, our consciousness or the world. We also need to know how this change can be brought about. This requires a degree of traditional spiritual or magical knowledge and a far greater degree of self-knowledge and introspection.

To Will: we need to actually want change to occur and to choose to make it happen, living with the consequences and results (see below for expansion on this simple statement).

To Dare: we need courage to go through our obstacles to change and transformation, guided by our knowledge and will, 'feeling the fear and doing it anyway'. Our courage and daring here is required to stop our fear paralysing our wills.

To Keep Silent: We need to allow the changes to gradually grow in our beings and lives without checking on them and trying them out before ready. If we keep opening the oven door to check on it, the soufflé will never rise. So too with our beings – we need to leave the seeds of the new self, the transformed self, to rest and germinate in our psyches, trusting they will arise in time. Keeping silent also inhibits the tendency to bolster our egos by parading how much we are changing and unfolding.

Our will to transform, our desire to change, may seem simple; however from the Western esoteric tradition's perspective there are a number of points to consider:

1. We are not united beings. Walt Whitman once said: 'You say I contradict myself: very well then, I contradict myself. I am large, I contain multitudes'. We all have within our beings numerous different parts of selves, often wanting conflicting things. An alcoholic may truly desire to give up drinking because it ruins her life. However, another part of her wants to keep drinking to numb out the inner pain she feels. And yet another part, the damaged part, may simply want to cry and get angry and rage and be held. Some spiritual traditions consider we have many different selves. The esoteric psychology used within the Golden Dawn talks of the Ruach, the Will, as being somewhat disparate, each section having a natural function and desire of its own.

2. By and large, we are not conscious of the will of the various parts of our beings. As magicians and people engaged in partnership with the divine we are called upon to 'wake up' from our sleep and become conscious of what we do and why. This involves a measure of self-observation and realisation, a whole path in itself in many traditions. Once we become aware of the wills of our various selves, we can move towards *choosing consciously* how to act in a certain situation.

For example, let us suppose I am at work, working late after a hard day, the last one in the office. I am tired but still busy working when I take a break and, slightly hungry, look into the shared fridge. There I notice some fruit, some cool drink and a packet of chocolate biscuits. Unless I am balanced and whole, I may have several 'wills' happening at once. My Air, talking, rational self, who wants to finish the paper I am writing, may want to ignore the biscuits, quickly close the fridge door and get back to my work. My Earth, body self may want me to use the interruption to take a break and move away from the computer and nurture myself with the fruit. My Water, feeling self, after 10 hours of rational intensity, may wish to indulge in the emotional satisfaction the chocolate will seem to deliver. My Fire, passionate self may simply want to throw the project out the window and impulsively leave the office for dinner.

Once I know all these differing wills, I can **choose** what I do. Being conscious in our lives is one of the objectives of the Golden Dawn. I once read or heard a very interesting saying that expresses this well: 'every time a conscious act is performed, the universe is more healed'.

3. The Western Mystery tradition, particularly the Golden Dawn, is very clear that the prime aim is the unification of the disparate wills within us so that they may be in union with and serve the 'Higher Will' or 'True Will'. We need firstly to become aware of these various aspects of ourselves, then place them under the control of our conscious direction and finally unite them into a more harmonious whole. We can then form a partnership between our newly balanced and harmonious self and the deeper consciousness and will within us, what the Golden Dawn refers to as the Neschamah. This is the will, the spiritual direction, of that part of us that was never born and thus will never die. This concept of True Will has led to many discussions and ideas within the modern Western magical and Pagan communities. Much of this centres around two quotations from Aleister Crowley's channelled work, *The Book of the Law*.

'Do what thou wilt shall be the whole of the Law'

'Love is the law; love under Will.'

From my perspective, bearing in mind many people may feel differently, these quotes refer to a state of consciousness where the Higher Will is so fully embodied and lived that it influences every action and thought of the person. This comes about through a conscious partnership and opening to the Higher Will. If we were in this state, we could not want to do anything that was not in accordance with the divine will, which is 'the whole of the Law'. Environmental activist John Seed echoed this philosophy when being interviewed by Ram Dass. When asked how he made decisions on what to do next in his work, John said that he went into the forest, covered himself with leaves and merged with the forest. When he stood up, he simply did whatever he felt like doing, knowing it would be the right thing. In our terminology, John's small will united with the larger will of the forest, and thus whatever he felt like doing would serve the forest and him both.

Crowley once wrote something like 'do what thou Wilt is to say to water to find its level, bees to suck for nectar'. It refers to a state of being, rarely seen in human beings, where we are motivated and driven by the Gods themselves. To achieve, promote and foster this state of consciousness is one of the main purposes of magic and spirituality in the West. The Golden Dawn, along with most of the Western traditions, recognises that our everyday wills are in disarray and many parts of us do not wish to unite with the Divine Will. This is why we begin all practices and magic by placing our lower wills under the guidance and direction of the Higher Will through the formula of the Qabalistic Cross.

WILL AND EMPOWERMENT

The strength of our will is intimately bound up with our own sense of power. If we feel that we are powerless in our lives, if this is our inner understanding of ourselves, then we will find it hard to begin to strengthen our will. If this is the case, the first thing to do is address our own power issues. The Golden Dawn is lacking in this aspect and to remedy this I have included a Personal Empowerment Ritual, adapted from a Pagan tradition, at the end of this section. This ritual can be repeated as often as you need. Better still, analyse it, see what it is doing and how it works, and create your own ritual. Remember, increasing your sense of personal power will change your relationships with other people and indeed your whole life. Be prepared to change. For a Western spiritual approach to the issues of power and empowerment I really cannot recommend enough the works of Starhawk, particularly *Truth or Dare: Encounters with Power, Authority and Mystery*.

DEVELOPING THE WILL

While writing this section the opening scenes of the movie *Lawrence of Arabia*, starring Peter O'Toole, came to mind. Lawrence is showing off to another British officer by holding his finger in the flame of his cigarette lighter without flinching. The officer is aghast and says to Lawrence, 'Good God man, doesn't it hurt?' To which Lawrence replies, 'Of course it hurts. The trick is not to mind that it hurts'. I am still not clear whether to consider this a great act of will or the bull-headed stubbornness I spoke of earlier. While some magicians would have you believe performing such feats are required to gain 'magical power', I do not. We can develop our wills to a large degree without the need for physical injury or deprivation that may do harm. Please remember this, as you may read some very strange and sometimes extreme suggestions when you approach this topic. Choose what techniques you perform with great care.

OBSERVING YOURSELF

This is the basic 'becoming the observer' practice found in many traditions and is useful as an aid in developing our wills. It is also crucial for a continuous spiritual unfoldment. Next time you are at a party or at a friends house, withdraw your attention inward a little and watch yourself. See your reactions to people, events, clothes, music. Do not try to change anything or analyse it – simply watch your own reactions. Keep watching. Make notes when you get home. Practice this awareness as often as you can.

SELF TALK

After doing the above exercise for some time, recall the last consciously observed event. Now go back and remember it from the perspective of one of the single, un-unified and disparate selves within you. When, for example at a party, a drunk person swayed towards you, what did your body, your Earth-self, want to do? Now recall what your Water-feeling self wanted to do in the same situation. Now go through all of your selves. Repeat for several other situations. Please note, not every self within you will have a reaction to every event. In these cases those selves may be 'asleep', that is not functioning or integrated into our consciousness to any degree. This is obviously healthy in some contexts and not in others.

When all of our selves are 'asleep' at once (and we are not physically sleeping), we are what psychologists like to call 'dissociating'.

ACTION AND REACTION

Choose something small that you can change in your life. It should not have any emotional attachment or moral significance for you. For instance, do not choose that you will not eat meat if it has any sort of moral significance for you. Under no circumstance choose an action that causes you distress or tests your pain threshold. Good examples are things like: whenever you see a blue shirt you will touch your nose briefly; you will not drink from a glass, only a mug for three days; for one week you will brush your teeth in front of a mirror (if you don't already) or without a mirror (if you normally use one); you will not turn the radio on in the car for a week; you will wash only with the left (or right) hand for a week. Once you have chosen, perform a simple ritual where you perform a Lesser Banishing Ritual of the Pentagram and then ask the Sacred One(s) for aid and say out loud 'I am (name) and for the next week (or other period of time) I will...' Now close with another Qabalistic Cross. These simple ritual actions are very useful, not only for the psychological effects, but also you are stating your will and decision within a sphere that is balanced and linked to the light, and this will aid your decision.

Notice your actions and keep to your willed act. Record how often you do it, and (if there are any) how many times you forget. It is very important to record this, and keep a track of your improvement. If these examples seem too large to work with, make smaller ones to begin with. Use your own imagination to devise them. When you have developed your will and have mastered the type of examples above, you may progress into the harder exercise below.

FORGOING A PHRASE

Choose a word or phrase, such as 'Hello' or 'I'm fine' or 'you know', which you use regularly, totally unconsciously (ask your friends about this). Now decide to avoid that phrase for a week. Start by ritual as in the above example. Record your success. Ultimately, after mastering this exercise, you may like to work up to avoiding words like 'I'. Once this is fully mastered – which will take a long time, move on to trying to avoid even the concept of 'I' forming in your mind. Even a few hours of the last two, practiced astutely, can produce powerful realisations and strange states of being. So do not persist in them. Also, do not under any circumstances perform the two following exercises until you have completely mastered the earlier ones. These two exercises begin the process of surrendering to our Higher Wills, which needs to be done with care and grace. Without having first developed our ordinary wills to some degree, this surrender will be immature at best and troublesome at worst.

Random Will 1. Take 10 to 20 small index cards. Write on one side a willed action as discussed above. Leave the other side blank. Every morning shuffle the cards and choose one. Do that action or non-action for the day. Record your results.

Random Will 2. Choose a fairly common name which is not already in use amongst your friends. Use the cards above to assign a random willed act to this name. Remember this. Go about your life until you meet someone with this name or hear it mentioned, even on the TV. Then start the willed act. Record your results. The beauty of this random will exercise is that our minds do not get a chance to prepare, which really tests our will.

PERSONAL EMPOWERMENT RITUAL

Read through the ritual to get a good sense of how it will go before attempting it. Make sure all the required props are ready when you start.

1. Perform a Lesser Banishing Ritual of the Pentagram.
2. Get a bowl of water and add some salt, a teaspoon is enough. Now trace just above the surface of the water, the *banishing* pentagram form from the LBRP. Use exactly the same inner workings, but trace the pentagram over the water. In the centre of the pentagram intone **YHVH**. Now trace another pentagram and repeat for **ADNI**. Do the same for **AHIH** and **AGLA**. There is no need to invoke the Archangels. You have now effectively cleansed and consecrated the salt water.
3. Ask the One Being or your Sacred One(s) to help you in your intention to explore and strengthen your personal power.
4. Hold the bowl or chalice of salt water next to your belly. Now close your eyes gently and recall a time in your life that you have felt powerless, unable to change the situation. If it feels right, name this event aloud, while still seeing it with the inner vision. Now consciously tune into the feelings you had on this occasion. Direct

and imagine those feelings entering the water. Repeat this for two or three more times when you felt powerless.

5. Pause. Breathe deep. Now perform a Qabalistic Cross and repeat the consecration of the bowl of water as described in step two. See the divine energy and blessings of the names of God purify and transform the feelings of powerlessness that are in the water.

6. Pause. Breathe deep. Now recall an event in your life where you felt powerful, either on your own, *power from within*, or with others, *power with*. Do not choose a time when you held power over someone. Recall those events clearly. If appropriate name them aloud. Now direct all the feelings of being powerful into the water. Repeat with two or more events.

7. Pause. Breathe deep. Now perform a Qabalistic Cross. This time trace four *invoking* pentagrams over the water, using the names and full inner workings. See the divine energy and blessings of the names of God expand, strengthen and clarify your feelings of power and strength.

8. Stand up. Face East, hold the bowl out in front of you. Breathe deep, and say out loud clearly and with purpose: 'I am (name). I am powerful. I am empowered in my mind and thoughts, within all that is of Air within me. Amen.' Take a sip of the water.

9. Turn to face the South. Hold the bowl out in front of you. Breathe deep, and say out loud, clearly and with purpose: 'I am (name). I am powerful. I am empowered in my passion and my will, within all that is of Fire within me. Amen'. Take a sip of the water.

10. Turn to face the West. Hold the bowl out in front of you. Breathe deep, and say out loud, clearly and with purpose: 'I am (name). I am powerful. I am empowered in my feelings and intuition, within all that is of Water within me. Amen.' Take a sip of the water.

11. Turn to face the North. Hold the bowl out in front of you. Breathe deep, and say out loud, clearly and with purpose: 'I am (name). I am powerful. I am empowered in my body and my life, within all that is of Earth within me. Amen'. Take a sip of the water.

12. Turn back to face the East. Close your eyes and hold the bowl next to your heart. Breathe deep, and say out loud, clearly and with purpose: 'I am (name). I am powerful. I am empowered in my spirit and inner world. Amen'. Take a sip of the water.

13. Thank the One Being or your Sacred One(s) and your deeper self. Close with a final Qabalistic Cross. Dispose of the water respectfully.

MEDITATION AND DIVINATION

From the generic standpoint both of these topics have been covered excellently in many other books and articles. The Golden Dawn or Western magical approach to meditation and divination has also been covered well in recent years, so we will not go too deeply into the topic here. For meditation within a Western magical tradition I suggest the works of W. G. Gray, especially *Western Inner Workings*. For Golden Dawn and Western magical views on divination, I suggest John Michael Greer's *Earth Divination: Earth Magic: Practical Guide to Geomancy* and *The Golden Dawn Journal I: Divination*, edited by Chic and Sandra Tabatha Cicero.

MEDITATION

There are many different definitions and types of meditation and what I say here cannot be considered as definitive but only explorative and suggestive. For many people meditation is their complete spiritual path. These forms of meditation however are a far cry from the college course and adult education forms of meditation that proliferate today in the West. As useful as these types of meditation are, and many are in fact really forms of relaxation, they do not work with the same level of depth as the traditional Eastern or Western practices. Meditation is not easy and will certainly, if practiced truly, result in radical spiritual transformation.

The essence of meditation is the control of the mind. This is where the difficulty lies as we find it hard, most of us, to control our thoughts even for a few seconds. There is a story, quite likely mythic, but wonderful none the less, of Aleister Crowley demonstrating this difficulty well. When asked by a student 'what is the secret of magical power?' Crowley replied 'the secret of magical power is to meditate for a week on the secret of magical power without once thinking of this spot'. And with that Crowley leant over and tapped the woman on the shoulder. Having cunningly 'keyed in' the idea of the woman's shoulder into her mind, she would then have found it difficult to meditate on 'the secret' without the idea of her shoulder popping up at least once. However, if she *could* control her mind that well she would have indeed found the 'secret' of magical power.

The practice of meditation is the only way to really understand it. For our purposes here we may use the definition that meditation is 'the technique of stilling the mind in order to allow either a feeling of inner calmness and peacefulness or to receive inner wisdom'. If carried to its fullest extent though, meditation can lead to states of bliss, expanded consciousness and spiritual awareness. Please note the central aspect of this definition is mental mastery. Often people describe inner experiences they may have had via a guided visualisation, where their mind wanders and visions pop up willy-nilly, as 'meditating'. From most respected teachers and authors' point of view, and ours also, this is not meditation. It is still a valid inner experience and shows something, but it is not meditation.

From the perspective of the Western traditions we may like to distinguish between two broad categories of meditation. These are often called:

Passive Meditation is typically practiced through exercises designed to produce a detached awareness, a dispassionate observation of the thoughts and processes of the human psyche and environment. Often the aim of passive meditation is to continually surrender all mental activity, even the dispassionate observations, in order to arrive at a state of no-thing, no ego or 'I' awareness at all. Some people consider this form of meditation 'true meditation'.

and

Active Meditation, which focuses the concentration and awareness on a single symbol, sound, chant, ideal, idea, sacred phrase, deity etc. There are two distinct aims of active meditation. The first is to concentrate and meditate completely on the meditation object and to receive inner wisdom or a deeper intuitive understanding about that object. The second is to ignore any inner wisdom and keep meditating solely upon the object until the mind transcends itself and an ego-less, I-less awareness is produced, identical to that produced by passive meditation. This aim is summed up by the phrase 'don't stop just because Buddha appears'.

In the broader Western magical tradition both forms of meditation, active and passive are essential building blocks in our spiritual unfoldment. Passive meditation allows us to relax and return our consciousness to the void state, the primal No-Thing, the Unmanifest. It is this state of consciousness that allows us to connect with our deepest source of being. Many of the wisest modern Western magicians insist that without first returning in some way to the No-thing, magic cannot happen fully. Qabalistically this equates with the Three Veils of Negative Existence situated 'above' or 'before' Kether on the Tree of Life.

With active meditation the magician practices focusing her will and consciousness into a one pointed purpose. This skill is required for most forms of magic. It also allows us to engage with and receive a deeper understanding of the symbols, forms and words we use in our rituals and practices. The importance of meditation within the Western mystery traditions cannot be overstated. Without mastering it to some degree you will only be able to unfold so far on your path, and then no more. In nearly every extant Western tradition I have encountered, meditation is one of the first skills to be learnt. In fact some Golden Dawn groups are clear in saying that we need to meditate with all of the symbols, godforms, images and words we use in any deep magic *before* attempting that magic.

What this means is that we need to open ourselves on deep levels to the inner life of a symbol before we actively explore and energise it in ritual. This conditions our mind to be open to the higher spiritual forces and activates mental body change before astral or etheric. In this way when we begin working in the astral realm (Yetzira), we are likely to have a balanced and transformational experience since the astral is being informed, as it were, by the mental plane. That is, the deeper spiritual and creative forces of Briah, already activated by our prolonged meditation, are by our astral work and magic moved down into Yetzira. Without such an approach we often find our magic remains within the astral/Yetziratic world, where there will be plenty of movements of energy and splendid visions, but little spiritual unfoldment.

The traditional Golden Dawn system recognised this need and developed a series of structured 'grade meditations' to match their initiation ceremonies. Within recent years however, many of the Golden Dawn meditations have been dropped or understated or else replaced with more generic forms. This is unfortunate because, like much within the Golden Dawn system, the meditations are there for a reason and we need to be careful about altering it. Many commentators and authors have assumed that the meditations within the Golden Dawn were hastily thrown together bits and pieces of occult lore. This however ignores the fact that these pieces of lore were part and parcel of the broader esoteric Masonic traditions for centuries. The Golden Dawn inherited and codified these traditional practices, and they can bring just as much insight today as they have always done.

For some people meditation may be an easy skill to acquire, for others it may be harder. However, for everyone, a persistent and regular daily practice is the best way of mastering this skill. In this it is better to practice for only five minutes once a day than for half an hour on the weekend. If you are starting meditation for the first time, the following tips may be useful.

TIPS FOR MEDITATION

1. Do not expect too much too quickly. Imagine if you were being asked to learn how to ride a unicycle on a tightrope while blindfolded – you would expect to develop your skill level very slowly. It is the same with meditation, so do not be discouraged by lack of 'results'. Also do not be put off by over confident and arrogant writers on the subject. One European magician many years ago wrote that gaining complete control of our thoughts, without a single wandering idea, for ten minutes would take the 'average man' a week to accomplish with two short sessions a day. This of course is nonsense and does nothing but discourage and depress the beginner in magic and meditation. Speak to honest people who have been meditating for years and find out what it is really like.

2. Try and set aside a special room or part of a room for your practice, even a chair that is not used for anything other than meditation and magical purposes will make a large difference.

3. If possible meditate at the same time every day. Early morning is often the best time, though some people prefer just before bed.

4. Cut down on stimulants like coffee, cigarettes etc, especially an hour or two before meditating. However, do not let the fact that you have just indulged provide excuses for never starting meditation.

5. Be prepared to have an inner fight over doing the meditation practice at some stage. This is a normal and healthy occurrence and is to be expected. It does not indicate failure on your behalf, on the contrary it shows that you have succeeded in stirring up inner resistance to what, if persisted in, will result in transformation. This 'fight' may occur sooner or later, but for most of us it does occur. Again, the important thing is to note it, respect it but not to cease our meditative practice.

6. Be prepared to give up a certain amount of time watching television, lounging around, surfing the Internet etc for your meditation, magic and spirituality. Prepare and actively give this up consciously before you start on your meditation course. Again, five minutes a day is better than half an hour once a week.

7. Be realistic about your life. For example, do not expect to do an hour's meditation a day if you are caring for a baby, unless you have lots of support people. Look at your life and know that life is constantly changing. If you cannot commit to a large amount of time, then do what you can now. Do not put it off until your kids have grown up, the course is finished, work is less busy or the divorce is finalized. Again, five minutes a day will make a difference in your life right now. The same principle, of course, applies to all magical and spiritual practices.

8. Choose a posture that is comfortable for you and where your spine is straight. Use a chair and supporting cushions for the lower back if needed. Do not lie down, especially on your bed. Beds are typically for sleeping, making love, cuddling or chatting. Our minds will struggle with us more if we attempt meditation on our beds.

PRACTICE OF GOLDEN DAWN MEDITATION

This is a generic meditative framework designed to augment the spiritual and magical exercises within the Golden Dawn tradition. Other traditions may have opposing views on some of the suggestions here, and that is fine. Once you are clear of this framework, you may then add in the symbols, letters, phrase, name, idea etc you are meditating upon. This is to be included in point five.

1. Lesser Banishing Ritual of the Pentagram. This is not essential but it does help a lot. If you are new to meditation try saying out loud 'now I am going to meditate'. This simple vocalization of intention is a very sound piece of magic and will often make the practice easier and more fulfilling.

2. Sit down in your posture or chair, spine straight.

3. Relax your body. The quickest and easiest way is to take several deep breaths in, fully, from belly to top of lungs, through the nose and then sigh out, imagining and feeling your tension dropping away. If after four or five of these breaths your body is still very tense, you are too tense to meditate. Move into the body relaxation technique given at the end of this section. Come back to this point once you are fully relaxed.

4. Begin deep and rhythmic breathing, in and out through the nose. Breathe slowly and calmly. Concentrate on your breath, simply observing it moving in and out of your nose and lungs. Do this for two or three minutes, or longer if you wish. The Golden Dawn traditionally taught a four-fold breath. That is, breath in for a count of four; hold for a count of four; breath out for a count of four; hold for a count of four and return to the start of your cycle. Once your breath is full, rhythmic and deep, move on to:

5a. Passive meditation. Here simply focus on the natural breath and allow yourself to observe any thoughts, feelings and ideas. Watch them come, watch them go. If you have followed any thought – for example, if a thought of eggs arose and you started remembering the best egg sandwich you've ever had, and then you realise what you have done – do not get agitated or berate yourself. Simply pause, bring your mind back to focus on the breath and then start again. Do not worry if for your first group of practices this is all you seem to do. This is normal and healthy. Keep going.

5b. Active meditation. Bring to your inner attention, or outer focus, your meditation object. A meditation 'object' is simply the focus for the meditation; it does not have to be physical or capable of existing physically at all. For example, we may choose as our meditation object the unconditional love of Christ for all Beings. Sometimes however you may choose to have a symbol before you on a wall or on an altar rather than inwardly visualising it. If you choose this route, do remember to blink your eyes. Staring at an object without eye blinking or movement will lead to your vision of the object disappearing. This is not due to increased energy or psychic sight, but simply because the rods in the retina of our eyes can only see movement. Without any movement caused by the object moving or our eye blinking, your eyes simply cannot function as they are designed to and the vision disappears.

Now continue your breath but focus all your attention upon the meditation object. In Western magical traditions the purpose here is nearly always to gain a deeper understanding of the meditation object, not to transcend the mind. So we concentrate our focus on the object and then allow insights, ideas, energy etc to come from our **mind's interaction** with the object. When these occur do not focus upon them, let them come, note them, let them go and return to focusing upon the object. You will always 'remember' the insights if they are important at the end of the session, so do not fret about losing some vital piece of esoteric wisdom. Again, like passive meditation, if you find you have followed a train of thought, stop, relax and return to the meditation. Do the same if an intrusive thought arises.

Remember the idea here is to gain insights from our own interaction with the meditation object. These insights may often not be verbal or even capable of being put into words. This is because they exist within our Briatic level of consciousness, our mental bodies; a realm of pure consciousness. Just because you do not arrive at a new, explainable insight each session does not mean the meditation is not successful. Also we are not trying to channel wisdom or talk to inner realm Beings. An authentic inner world being will not interrupt your meditation, but they may make their presence and willingness to talk with you known, though this will seldom happen with beginners. If this does occur, note it, let it go and return to the meditation. If you have enough experience and are ready then you may like to make another session, using some of the Golden Dawn techniques, where you can engage with the otherworld being.

6. When ready, (often people set an alarm or a beeper), end the meditation. A good starting time is five or ten minutes. From there you can work upwards to half an hour or even an hour. Return your focus to yourself. Again, if you are new to meditation you may like to name out loud and touch ten parts of your body. This will effectively bring your consciousness back to normal parameters.

7. Thank your Higher and Divine Genius, your Sacred One(s) and if you used one, the meditation object itself. This is an important point, as abstract principles, geometrical forms and ideas all have a consciousness in the inner realms. It is important to express our gratitude and respect towards them and their blessings.

A BASIC RELAXATION TECHNIQUE

This technique can be practiced on its own and not as part of the meditation session. It is very useful for those periods in our lives when we are undergoing heavy stress and anxiety. There are a number of other techniques and variants to this basic technique available also. Many people find using one of the commercial relaxation CDs or tapes very useful. Use whatever suits you and works.

Lie down somewhere quiet, either on the floor or a mat, or your bed if it is firm. Place a pillow under your head and one under your knees. Your arms should either rest gently by your sides or on your stomach, it does not matter which. Be sure you get completely comfortable as you will be lying in this position for some time.

Take two or three slow deep breaths, relaxing and sighing on the out breath. Try and let your mind relax and go blank.

You will now reduce the tension in your muscles by first tensing them and then releasing the tension. You will work through your body starting from the toes and gradually working your way up your body to your face.

Begin by concentrating on your left foot. Tense all the muscles – clenching the toes and the entire foot. Hold the clench for a few seconds. Let go, and feel your toes and foot completely relaxed and floppy, relaxed and warm. This may take a few times to get used to. Keep clenching and relaxing until you get the relaxed, heavy and warm sensation in your foot. This is the deep relaxation you wish to experience over all your body.

Now move onto the calf muscles of the left leg. Tense the muscles, hold the clench and let go. Again, feel the warm heavy relaxed sensations.

Now continue with the left thigh and leg, feeling it tense and then relax and go heavy and warm. Let it sink into the floor. If the leg does not feel relaxed and heavy, lift it slightly up from the floor and then tense it until it is difficult to hold it up and tense any longer. Then let it fall gently back to the floor, relaxed and heavy.

Repeat the process for the right leg.

Now, with both legs heavy, warm and relaxed, continue the process, moving up the body. Clench and hold your buttocks tightly and then, let go. Pull up your stomach muscles, hold them tight and taut and then let them go and relax with a deep sigh. Feel your lower back and buttocks sinking into the floor. Feel the warmth spreading up your body.

Now spend a minute or two simply breathing slowly and deeply. With every out breath, sigh deeply and imagine you are sighing all the tension out and away from your body.

Now focus on your left hand, clenching it into a fist, holding the fingers very tight. Then let go and relax. Tense the muscles of your whole arm, really tight, them let them go floppy, feeling the warmth and relaxation spreading. Use the same method with your right arm. Repeat the process if the arms do not feel heavy and relaxed.

Now hunch your shoulders up towards your ears and hold for several seconds. Then let go and let them sink down to the floor, heavy and relaxed. Perform this particular movement several times, as we often have a good deal of tension built up in and around our shoulders. Now pull the shoulders up towards the ceiling, hold them there, and then relax and let them sink back down. Again, repeat this process several times.

Now focus on your whole head. Very gently move it from side to side. Do this for about thirty seconds or until you feel your neck loosens a little. Do not force your neck to turn any more than it can do easily. As you move back and forth, sigh out any tension in your neck. Now breathe deeply and slowly again for another three minutes, sighing out all tension from your neck and body.

Now move onto your face. Yawn and stretch your facial muscles in every direction. Make funny faces, screwing up your face, hold for a moment and then let go. Relax with a sigh. Now focus upon your scalp. Raise and lower your eyebrows, relaxing with a sigh on each out breath.

Your whole body will now be feeling very relaxed and warm. Take some more slow and deep breaths, knowing and saying to yourself that with every breath you are feeling more and more relaxed. Do this for a couple of minutes.

Now just lie here, in this deep relaxed state for around five minutes. When ready to move, do so slowly and carefully. Stretch and yawn and slowly get up.

MEDITATION OBJECTS IN THE WESTERN TRADITION

THE NEOPHYTE MEDITATION OF THE GOLDEN DAWN

One of the most beautiful and transformational meditations within the Golden Dawn tradition is that given within the 'First Knowledge Lecture' and generally known as the Neophyte Meditation. Two forms of this meditation have been used within the various Golden Dawn Orders over the years. Firstly, that published by Regardie in his *Golden Dawn* and another version which does not appear in the Regardie compilations but has appeared in several other Western mystery books. Both are designed to lead to the same end – to allow the magician to experience the sense of the immanence of God. I give both versions here, but really prefer the second version and have found it far more useful. The Order to which I belong uses this version exclusively.

The meditation does not limit the sense of immanence to an abstract Oneness, but rather allows it to be perceived as part of magician's own religious framework. There is a fictional account of a spiritual experience connected with this meditation in Stewart Farrar's Witchcraft novel, *The Sword of Orley*. In this novel a Witch experiences the immanence of the divine through the meditation as follows:

> '...and then for a mere diamond-point of time only the Centre was real. But the point was infinity! The Centre was the Circumference ... Frontier-less, the Goddess touched her...'

This meditation teaches us to be without a frontier, without barriers or self-definition so we may be touched by the divine. And in that touch we come to know the One and the world as the One. This meditation may be practiced by anyone and is certainly not to be confined solely to the period after the Neophyte initiation or equivalent. It can bring us spiritual blessing and insights for as long as we live. The first form of the meditation as published by Regardie is:

> 'Let the Neophyte consider a point as defined in mathematics – having position but no magnitude – and let her note the ideas to which this gives rise. Concentrating their faculties on this, as a focus, let her endeavour to realise the immanence of the Divine throughout Nature, in all her aspects.'

The origins of the second version stem back to St Bonaventure, a thirteenth century Franciscan mystic and theologian. It is to mediate and realize the following sentence:

> 'God is the circle whose centre is everywhere and whose circumference is nowhere.'

The Hebrew Letters

Another basic practice in many Western ceremonial traditions is meditation upon the letters of the Hebrew alphabet. There are a few different approaches to this and as you gain experience you can combine several at once. Start by simply visualising the shape of the letter in question in black. It is best in this instance to have a large copy of the letter close by so you may refer to it before starting the meditation. The shape and the presence of the letter is the important area for meditation here. There have been many works over the centuries on the mystical import of the Hebrew letters, but the aim here is not to read someone else's meditation results to but to gain your own. It is best to ignore such commentaries until after you are clear in your own experience. The twenty two letters are best meditated upon in the correct sequence, Aleph through Tau.

Later you may wish to add to your meditation one of the correspondences of the letter. For instance you may meditate on Aleph and the concept of 'Ox', keeping the image of the letter and the concept of 'Ox' together in your meditation. Other aspects to include here, one at a time, are: number, colour, path on the Tree of Life, Yetziratic attribution etc. We can see here there is fruit for many, many years worth of meditation on the Hebrew alphabet alone.

FURTHER SUGGESTIONS

The Elemental Symbols. The symbols of the four elemental principles are also a source for much fruitful meditation. It is best, in the Golden Dawn context, to start with meditation upon their qualities given below while holding the inner vision of their symbol shown below.

Air – Hot and Moist
Fire – Hot and Dry
Water – Cold and Moist
Earth – Cold and Dry

The Divine Names associated with the Sephiroth along with their English meanings. This is a large and profound avenue for meditation. It is best to allow yourself to be unhindered by previous translations and meanings of these names and interact with them yourself. Remember we are dealing here with eternal powers and truths, ever living divine forces and Beings, and it is unwise to pin down their meaning and revelation like a butterfly in an insect collection. Interact and form your own relationship with these names of God and you will find your own revelation.

DIVINATION

The practice of divination within the Golden Dawn tradition has nothing to do with the foretelling or working out of the future. The future is always fluid, changeable and never fixed, since as human beings we are blessed with free will and potentially conscious of all our actions. We can look at possibilities and probabilities, but all of these can change instantly when a single human being in the equation does something with consciousness, not out of repeated patterns and addictions.

From the Western magical viewpoint divination, by any means, is more concerned with the discovery, development and utilization of certain aspects of the mind normally hidden within our materialist and mechanistic culture. Often people call these aspects simply 'intuition' or label them as 'psychic powers' or 'clairvoyance' or other terms and lump them all under the same banner. There are however a few distinct and different modes of inner awareness that may be utilized in divination. By understanding what it is we are working with we will be in a much better position to choose (or not) to develop these modes of awareness. The terminology I use here is not universal, so be careful when reading other material to 'translate' terms.

For our purposes we can define three related but different modes of inner awareness; that is, perception through non-physical means: psychic awareness, intuition and inspired intuition.

Psychic Awareness

Over the last fifty years there have been literally thousands of books published and techniques devised to develop the psychic powers latent within everybody. Despite the high sales of these books and success of the courses, these powers are no more apparent within people today than previously. From many people's perspectives this is because these powers and modes of awareness are too latent, too buried within the majority of the population. In short, not everyone is psychic to any degree of usefulness and certainly not consistently. Psychic awareness appears to be a particular mode of inner awareness, often developed from an early age but also often developed following a traumatic event. Sometimes people may experience a temporary expansion of their psychic awareness and abilities following the shock from such an event, only to 'lose' them as they integrate the event more into their daily life, as they heal.

While it may be true that everyone can develop these powers to some degree, the time and effort required, which is considerable for most people, far outweighs potential benefits gained from possessing such skills. Also we must consider why we should want to be able to develop these powers – is it to unfold spiritually, to serve the One Being – or is it to bolster our egos or shore up our insecurities? The intermixing of the notion of psychic powers and spiritual unfoldment within Western magic is unfortunate and has led to some quite ridiculous notions of what makes someone 'spiritually evolved'. Reading the history of psychic research, parapsychology and occultism makes it quite clear that spectacular and unusual psychic phenomena can be produced by the most immoral, self-centred and corrupt people. There is no correlation between spiritual practice and psychic phenomena.

The Society of the Inner Light (founded by the most significant magician of the twentieth century, Dion Fortune) has this to say concerning psychic awareness: 'Psychism is simply one type of inner awareness and there are other types at least as valid and as common'. It is quite possible to practice divination and obtain good results without being 'psychic'. Often the untrained 'naturally psychic' reader may occasionally produce excellent readings, but over the long haul will prove to be more unreliable and less effective as someone trained in divination, but uses others forms of inner awareness. In the discussion below I will be assuming the reader is not psychic to any large degree. Genuinely psychic readers, who do not wish to utilise intuition and inspired intuition within their divination, will need to find advice and training elsewhere.

INTUITION

Intuition is a mode of inner awareness that is shared and used everyday by most of us. It is the 'feeling' we get that someone is lying to us, the 'hunch' we use to discover the right solutions to problems, the ability to 'know' when our child is 'up to something'. There is nothing mysterious about this form of inner awareness, we all know it, though some people choose to listen to and focus upon it more than others. We call it an inner awareness because it is not something that can be readily explained in outer terms by pointing to or describing material events.

From a magical and Qabalistic framework this form of intuition takes place within the Sephira of Yesod. On a universal level, this sphere is the foundation for the material universe we live in. On a personal level, it is the foundation for our material life and consciousness. One of the spiritual experiences or states of inner awareness, traditionally ascribed to Yesod, is that of 'the vision of the machinery of the Universe'. This is a glimpse into how things really work; an awareness of hidden connections and movements that manifest as physical change. It is like seeing the cogs and wheels inside the wind-up toy, or the HTML tags that produce a beautiful website.

When we are being 'intuitive' our consciousness is operating not only in this realm (Malkuth) but also partly within Yesod. We can thus catch the fleeting glimpse of the inner machinations of our lives and those we interact with. This is because whenever we interact with people we do so within the inner realms also. This knowledge often has no outer manifestation at the stage we catch it, and thus appears to be from 'nowhere', a gut instinct, a strong feeling. Often we are correct in our intuitions but still 'wrong' because not all the forms and ideas in Yesod actually are birthed into physical existence in Malkuth. So in one sense we are 'wrong', but in another sense we *may* still correctly perceive the flow of energy and events in Yesod – they may simply not manifest in Malkuth, the shared physical reality. This is one of the great limitations of the regular intuition.

Another major limitation is intuition which has been corrupted or distorted for some reason. This may not only be wrong but may also be embarrassing, painful or even harmful if followed. Corruption to our intuition occurs for two main reasons. Firstly, most of us when being simply intuitive very rarely get a sense of the universe outside our own beings. This is simply because on the inner realms we are very small Beings, shrivelled and enfolded due to the nature of our cultural upbringing that focuses so heavily on the outer and derides the inner. With this limited sphere of activity comes a limited perception of the inner universe beyond our own mind. Our intuitive powers then may be very good for our own lives, but limited and inaccurate beyond them. Despite this, most of us are at some stage tempted to share our intuitions about other people, and often we can be wrong. Friendships can easily be lost with such indiscriminate sharing.

The second and major cause of corrupted intuition is due to the nature of Yesod being the sphere of the unconscious and the malleable astral light, a substance whereby we will find our own unconscious wishes and ideas forming before us. Thus our intuition may be affected by our own unconscious desires and wounding. We may find own inner infantile needs being played out in our intuitions, 'knowing for sure' things that can be damaging to ourselves and others if acted upon. The only sure antidote for this possibility is self awareness, personal healing and strong integrity. The Golden Dawn and other traditions teach a variety of techniques whereby we may test our intuition and vision, and these are detailed later in Chapter Seven. However, for a person unconsciously determined to deceive themselves and others, these testing techniques may not be effective:

> 'To avoid unbalanced conditions of the astral light it is not sufficient simply to perform particular banishing formulae; what is required is the tranquillity of mind and heart that comes from stable outer life relationships and a selfless dedication.' (Gareth Knight, *The Circuit of Force*, p.183)

We therefore come back to our original premise at the start of this book, that it is only through surrender to the Divine and dedicating ourselves to its purposes and work that we may find full unfoldment and safety in magic. In the realm of intuition and for any 'received' information, this is essential. The history of Western magic is littered with the foibles of magicians who did not heed this warning, people who had visions from Beings they assumed were Gods, telling them to engage in acts that a first year psychology student would spot as stemming from their own unconscious.

Another very crucial aspect to intuition, one that is always in the awareness of those magicians sensible enough not to believe everything they feel, is that of outer plane confirmation. That is, if we perceive something intuitively on the inner plane that prompts any ideas of changes in the outer planes, there will be an outer plane manifestation of what we perceived. For example, if we perceive that a person we have just met is an advanced spiritual teacher, then there should be an outer plane manifestation of that awareness. If they do not display the traditional qualities of compassion, honesty, strength, integrity and humility, then we can easily conclude that our intuition was corrupted, perhaps by our need for a father or mother figure.

What this means is that we do not undertake material and outer action prompted solely by inner awareness. We do not attack a person, verbally through gossip or otherwise, simply because we intuit their unsavoury activities. Often, when we look at it closer we may find we are projecting, in the psychoanalytic sense, our negative qualities onto them. All of the great magicians have asked for material confirmation of received information before acting, and often received it.

The function of intuition is part and parcel of the human condition. It is however often atrophied to a remarkable degree in many people through disuse. The correct practice of any form of divination will re-awaken and strengthen it. This is one of the main reasons why the Golden Dawn tradition includes divination as part of its journey towards spiritual unfoldment. In magical work, when we are dealing with the inner realms, we need to have effective 'inner realm sense organs'. The practice of divination, forcing us to use our intuition, develops these inner organs of perception. In truth then, it is the practice of divination rather than any results we may obtain that is important within the Golden Dawn. As we practice more and more, we develop our inner perception and, if we are practicing our other spiritual techniques, we clear the areas of our unconscious that are likely to result in corrupted intuition. In the Golden Dawn it does not matter if we are 'right' or 'wrong' in our divination. It only matters that we actually practice divination.

INSPIRED INTUITION

One of the most powerful formulas of magic within the Golden Dawn tradition, the Z Formula, is the underlying framework not only for initiation and rituals of spiritual development but also for ceremonial acts of divination. This has often puzzled commentators on the Golden Dawn, since divination can be performed quite effectively in a non-ceremonial manner, with much less expenditure of time, effort and resources. Many people simply assume the Z Formula form of divination within the GD is an example of the tendency to make a simple thing complex, so as to make it seem more important or more advanced. However, careful examination of the Z Formula itself and the work of its creators or expounders show that something other than ritual for ritual's sake was going on. That something was an attempt to create a form of divination that would be based on what we call 'inspired intuition' rather than regular intuition.

As we discussed previously, intuition arises out of an awareness of the flows and changes of the astral light in Yesod. Inspired intuition however arises initially out of a 'higher' consciousness, that of Tiphareth. The astral light and the subtle movements and currents in the plastic and malleable realm of Yesod are viewed from the standpoint of Tiphareth, the place of the intrinsic sense of 'I', the state of non-ego based consciousness. This allows the perceptions of the astral realm to be seen with far more accuracy and clarity than viewing them from the Yesodic realm. Unfortunately most of us simply do not function at this level, at least in our daily lives and even during our best Tarot reading. We are all ego based at some level, all imperfect and open to delusion.

Inspired intuition does occur spontaneously in some people, but for most of us we cannot say when or how. It has been said that inspired intuition is never wrong since it stems from the Tipharetic level, the sphere of the sharing of human and God consciousness. Theoretically at this level we can gain some insight into the map or plan of God and (since according to this view, all events are planned by God) know the future as well as the past. Personally I doubt this surety and have never seen any evidence of infallible intuition within anyone, Golden Dawn Adepti included. What may be said is that inspired intuition will produce more accurate results in divination that regular, non-inspired intuition. This is why most Golden Dawn divinatory techniques invoke, utilise or move consciousness towards Tiphareth and why the Z Formula was prescribed for divination. Another important point here though, regardless of good results, is that by accessing our inspired intuition we are less likely to be deceived or deluded by the subconscious and unconscious elements of our own psyche, resident in our personal Yesod.

GOLDEN DAWN DIVINATION

This section does not go into all the nuts and bolts instructions of how divination is performed within the Golden Dawn tradition – ample instructions for this can be found in *The Golden Dawn* by Regardie and elsewhere. Here I wish to outline some of the underlying frameworks, concepts and practices that rest behind all forms of Golden Dawn divination. The inner practices and suggestions given here can be readily fitted into the various methods given in other books.

All of the Golden Dawn methods of divination were originally designed to be worked through inspired intuition, by magicians who have connected with the Tipharethic level of Yetzira, and placed their own ego aside for the time being. I would venture to say here also that such an exaltation of consciousness is one of the main purposes for divination within the Western mystery traditions. The accuracy of the Tarot spread predicting the next three months of our love life or career prospects pales into insignificance next to the potential of connecting with the Higher consciousness within us. That said, a great many Golden Dawn magicians do practice divination with results and accuracy in mind, and those who have published on this subject should certainly be read in conjunction with the notes here.

One of the essential keys in the practice of any form of divination is that to be right we need to be open to being wrong. Just like learning any new craft or skill, we need to expect that our first efforts will be less than satisfactory. We also need to accept our limitations and realise that despite our best efforts we are not going to get it right all of the time, even if we have been practicing for twenty or more years. By accepting that we will fail at times, we relax, do not try so hard try and force results. Since divination draws on our intuition and hopefully inspired intuition, it is by its very nature 'beyond' our logical thought processes and the perceived laws of the universe; in essence it is a mystery to our mundane consciousness. We should try and develop openness to that mystery, a relaxed state of aligning ourselves to it, not seeking to force it to occur via will. Trying desperately to succeed, or being afraid of failure, is a sure way to stem that openness and dispel our relaxation.

The following simple exercise should be undertaken in the spirit of experimentation, not seeking to be right (or wrong). In fact it is best not to calculate rates of accuracy until a least a month of daily practice has gone by.

Firstly, cleanse your auric sphere with an LBRP. Relax. Using an ordinary pack of playing cards, shuffle and cut the deck. Now take one card, face down and try to perceive its suit. At this point some people may be wondering how to 'perceive' this – if you have no inner perception, which most of us will not at this stage, just guess from nowhere. In your journal write the suit down. Turn over the card and record if you are right or wrong. Move onto the next card. Repeat for a total of ten cards then end the session. The key to this practice is to notice the inner sensations and feelings you have when seeking to be open to the perception of the suit. The more you focus inwardly on what passes through your mind and emotions at this point, the greater the success you will have – success here being awareness of your inner processes more than the accuracy of your guesses.

Keep repeating this exercise at least once a day for a month. Then tally your results. Now perform it for another month and tally the results (by this stage it is best to use a new deck to eliminate the possibility of unconscious 'fraud' by perceiving slight variations on the backs of the cards). Eventually you will notice some change in your perceptions. This form of exercise is designed to help develop your intuition. To develop our inspired intuition requires an ability to focus upon and access our regular intuition, and exercises such as these, boring as they may seem, are essential building blocks.

THE TAROT

'Practical work with the archetypes of the Tarot is essentially a matter of using the imagination' – Gareth Knight, Western magician and author.

Since my own divination work has been confined mostly to Tarot I will focus on that modality here. Readers interested in Astrology or Geomancy, the other two forms of divination utilized heavily within the Golden Dawn, may like to consult the work listed in the bibliography.

If we are seeking to develop our inspired intuition for use within divination, one of the best ways is to use as our method of divination a system of spiritual lore that is harmonious and complete within itself. By utilizing, linking to and befriending such a system we can open ourselves to rich sources of spiritual potency and transformation – even as we practice divination. However, the key here is to befriend our divination tool or system, to grow into a good relationship with it, spending time in its presence pondering over its mysteries – simply because they are there – not trying to get anything from it. One such spiritual system is the Tarot, a card set which, like a good magician, acts on all levels – as a simple card game, as a map of the astral or inner realms and as a bridge or gateway for universal powers to enter this world and vice versa. I won't go into the history of and Western magical utilisation of the Tarot here; that has been done very well in other works listed in the bibliography.

Within the Golden Dawn the Tarot is often referred to as 'the book T' and has a great angel associated with it – HRU, who is said to be 'set over the operation of the Secret Wisdom'. HRU is also invoked in the Consecration of the Vault ceremony, the ritual that empowers the main place of magical work for members of the tradition who are linked to the Tipharethic energies and blessings. During this invocation HRU is asked to:

'…increase the spiritual perception of the members (of the Order) and enable them to rise beyond the lower self-hood which is nothing unto that highest Self-hood which is in God, the vast One.' (Parentheses added).

We see here a direct reference to moving to the Tipharetic level of consciousness, the 'highest self-hood' which in terms of the Tarot, the other main area governed by HRU, is the use of the inspired intuition. It is for this reason that the Golden Dawn method of Tarot divination begins first with an invocation to and request for assistance from HRU. By invoking her we are aided in our movement of consciousness from Yesod to Tiphareth, from intuition to inspired intuition.

One of the more curious aspects concerning the angel HRU is that in the original documents her/his name is often written as H.R.U. as if the letters of the name are abbreviations. The Qabalistic approach of the Golden Dawn often incorporated many levels of meaning from a single name. For example a Gnostic name of God, IAO, was seen to also represent the synthesis of the Egyptian deities Isis Apophis and Osiris. There has to my knowledge been little public discussion applying this method to the name of HRU and my own inner teachings reveal that the letters can be viewed as *implying* the title Humanitas Regina Universalus – the Queen of the Universal Human. This once again shows the Tipharetic connection, Tiphareth being that state of consciousness that rules over the lower four Sephiroth of daily consciousness and life. The 'Universal Human' aspect of the name shows that HRU, through the unification of consciousness in Tiphareth, holds the secret wisdom of all the manifestations of the basic nature and being of all humanity. She can thus guide all people to the 'highest Self-hood' and also give insights, through Tarot divination, into the motivations and hidden aspects of all who seek her wisdom.

Before outlaying a simple approach to inviting and working with (as opposed to using) HRU in a Tarot divination, it is best to address an oft repeated magical misunderstanding. A common belief among magicians is that non-human persons, such as angels, can be compelled to take part in magical actions due to the divine nature of human will. In this worldview angels and other beings are seen almost as mechanical processes. The traditional magical approach is very different from this, and all who seek to compel Angels will ultimately fail as the only state that 'compels' or moves Angels towards a course of action is deep humility and a desire to serve.

Before attempting a Tarot divination it is important to stress again that we need to develop a relationship with the Tarot and our own particular deck of cards. In the original Golden Dawn this was accomplished – at least in theory – very simply; everyone had to make their own deck based on the Golden Dawn images and colour system. In practice of course this rarely occurred and people used commercial decks for divination and perhaps painted the Major Arcana cards alone. Today most magicians (myself included) have succumbed to the ready availability of decks and simply purchased one. However if we are wishing to use our decks in conjunction with our Golden Dawn spirituality, we need to make sure our deck is based on the traditional 78 card Qabalistic framework. Decks such as the Golden Dawn deck, the New Golden Dawn Ritual Tarot, the Waite-Rider, the Gareth Knight, the Aquarian, Morgan-Greer and the Crowley Thoth are all wonderful decks suited to this purpose.

If we have not created or designed our own deck, we need to fully link ourselves with it. This means linking to both the etheric and astral components of the physical deck in front of us and the inner mysteries and structures that make up the real purpose of any Tarot deck. This is best accomplished by learning to know deeply and love your deck. Apart from reading some of the by now extensive literature on the Tarot, some suggestions that may help you do this are listed here.

WORKING WITH THE TAROT

Active Meditation: Choose a card as a meditation object for your active meditation as described earlier this chapter. It is best to start with the Major Arcana or trumps and work from the Fool through to the Universe

(World). After this proceed with the sixteen Court Cards and then the forty Pip or numbered cards.

Colouring the Cards: Make or photocopy black and white outline images of the cards and then colour them yourself in a meditative space. Be conscious of the colours used. What changes in the energy and spiritual qualities of the cards would a major colour change bring?

Dreaming the Cards: Simply contemplate a card before you go to sleep. Read a little about it, ponder it, stare at it, feel the qualities. Then place it under your pillow as you sleep, consciously placing it within your etheric and astral bodies. Notice any dreams. Work through the complete deck, a card a night for 78 nights, following the pattern outlined above.

Building the Cards Into Your Mind: Choose a card and study it for several minutes, trying to remember its image as much as possible. Turn the card over. Now draw each symbol that you remember and list as much as you know about these symbols – both what you have read and what you sense or ponder deeply. Do the same with the colours on the card and the patterns in space the symbols make – do three symbols form a triangle? Are all the light colours in one area of the card? What do these things mean? Once complete, turn the card over and see what symbols, colours or patterns you missed. Again work through Trumps, Court Cards and then Pip cards.

TAROT DIVINATION WITH HRU, THE ANGEL OF THE SECRET WISDOM

This is a basic formula for a Tarot divination working with HRU, the Great Angel. Please fill in the particulars according to your own needs, following the same basic pattern of: purification, extension of consciousness, invocation of HRU, linking of currents.

Purification: perform an LBRP or at least a Qabalistic Cross.

Extension of Consciousness: At the end of the Qabalistic Cross, hold your cards in your hands. Imagine that your consciousness now extends to the level of Tiphareth of Yetzira, while still also functioning fully in this plane. This is a process that can only be achieved fully through a lot of practice and awareness of the Qabalah. Remember the original Golden Dawn member practicing tarot divination would have undergone the transformational and powerful Adeptus Minor initiation and be linked to this level of consciousness. For our purposes here we can achieve the same ends via the quick and directed inward use of imagination and consciousness change.

We have all practiced this extension of consciousness to some degree through the Qabalistic Cross, where we see ourselves growing larger and larger but remain standing on and connected to the Earth. In this advanced technique we do not cease to grow when our hands reach towards the infinite white light, which we may equate to the Ain Soph Aur of Assiah and the 32nd Path of Yetzira. We continue to extend our consciousness and move through the white light and as we do so we extend our consciousness through the 32nd Path. We then arrive at Yesod of Yetzira, which inwardly we see as glowing violet light. Once we see ourselves as entering this violet light, which is infinite in extent, we inwardly vibrate the divine name of Yesod, **Shaddai el Chai**. Since this name brings forth the Briatic blessings of Yesod, or Yesod in Briah, it will solidify and stabilise our consciousness in Yesod within Yetzira. However, as soon as we experience this stabilization, we continue to extend our consciousness and visualise ourselves leaving the glowing violet light of Yesod and entering a path of bright blue light. This is the path of Samech in Yetzira. Again, inwardly we intone the name **Samech** as we extend our consciousness along this path. We continue to do this until we sense a change of consciousness and energy.

Next we see the light change to brilliant yellow-gold light, which we move our consciousness into. Inwardly we vibrate the divine name of Tiphareth, **YHVH Eloah Va-Daath**. This will solidify and stabilise our consciousness within this realm. Once we have practiced this technique, we will find such an extension of consciousness can be achieved quickly and easily. Note the operative word here is extension – you should still be functioning fully in the flesh and blood world of Assiah.

Invocation of HRU: holding the cards in one hand, cover them with the palm of the other hand. Reconnect with the sense of part of your consciousness being in Tiphareth of Yetzira. Now inwardly connect with HRU by inwardly vibrating his name three times into the sphere of Tiphareth. Three inward vibrations should be enough to establish a connection with HRU. Do not expect great lights or cosmic visions. I have never seen HRU and never expect to. I have however received her assistance and wisdom in countless tarot readings and other spiritual endeavours. Be open to the subtlety of his presence. Once you have a sense of HRU's presence, ask for her aid by speaking outwardly the following words – which should be also spoken inwardly:

'Great Angel **HRU**, who is set over the operations of the Secret Wisd
ask for your aid to see with clarity the hidden forces and the hidden I
(here name the person you are doing the reading for, or simply 'mys
so that with this wisdom, balance and harmony may prevail. I ask th
the name of the One Being (or Goddess or God etc). Amen'.

Remove your hand from above the deck. You are now ready to commen
the reading. During the entire reading you should maintain your conta
with the great angel HRU by inwardly intoning his name and conscious
being open to his presence from time to time. It is also good to maintai
the extension of consciousness to Tiphareth by inwardly intoning YHVI
Eloah Va-Daath occasionally. As the reading proceeds you shoulc
attempt to receive the inspired intuition and information from HRU. Dc
not connect with or try to engage on an emotional level with the person
you are reading for. HRU, as the angel of the Tarot, will be connecting
with the person at the higher level of Tiphareth, where the distortion of
the lower four Sephiroth are not present. What should be occurring is the
formation of a triangle from you to HRU and from HRU to the person
whose cards are being read. This exists at the deeper level of Tiphareth.
Information will be gathered by HRU from the person whose cards are
being read and transferred to you for the reading. Again do not expect
HRU to whisper in your ear. She will simply inspire, clarify and direct
your reading.

    This method of working with HRU can be applied to any card spread.
If at any time during the reading you are stuck and not clear as to the
meaning of a card, you can pause, place your hand over the card and
inwardly intone HRU once again. This reconnection normally shifts
any sense of being stuck and helps the reading to flow. At the end of the
reading, after the cards are gathered up, with sincere gratitude inwardly
and outwardly thank HRU:

'Great Angel **HRU**, who is set over the operations of the Secret Wisdom,
thank you for the wisdom and guidance you have given tonight. Amen'.

Consciously and carefully return the extension of your consciousness to
normal by reversing the inward imagination from Tiphareth, through
Samech, Yesod, the 32nd Path, the infinite white light. Then perform a
Qabalistic Cross to end the session and return to normal consciousness
in a balanced fashion.

ɔm, I
fe of
ɔlf ')
s in

ːe
ːt
ɿ

AURA CONTROL

ɪpter we examine in more depth the concept of subtle bodies
to in chapter one. Specifically we will look at methods by
ve can consciously choose to adapt, modify and transform our
ubtle bodies and thereby, as magical theory posits, our life also.
ɪ these changes we are then, hopefully, fashioning ourselves as
ɪnd clearer tools for the will of God or our Sacred One(s). At this
we need to spend some time reviewing the section on subtle bodies
ɪapter One, even if we feel we have a pretty decent handle on the
ect already.

We may distinguish two classes of aura control, the first designed
improve the aura and the second to invoke or invite specific, divine
ɪrce into the aura. Often the two are combined within one operation,
ɪut we may see the first as a re-organization of already existing energies
into a more balanced and harmonious whole and the second as an
introduction of desired energies and qualities. The first type of aura
control, that of balancing and harmonising, is readily accomplished
through methods and practices already discussed; controlled breath,
bathing in Epsom salts, relaxation and meditation. The second form is
that most utilised by the Golden Dawn tradition and the form largely
discussed here.

One of the principles of auric work in the Western traditions is that
change in the subtle bodies will produce change in consciousness and
vice versa. By the methodical introduction and grafting of new spiritual
qualities into our auras, we will provoke the corresponding mental and
emotional qualities from within ourselves. At least in theory. In practice
effective change of consciousness requires more than this mechanistic
approach, not the least being a true and clear desire for change and
transformation based on selfless motives. Such a motivation activates
the higher levels of our mental body, the Neschamah in Golden Dawn
terminology, and thus establishes the framework for effective change that

is based on what our Higher and Divine Genius requires not what we feel we 'need' or desire.

Aura control is one of the mainstays of Western spirituality and we can find examples of it dating back thousands of years through to the present. Often techniques and practices within religious traditions work with the same principles we will be examining here, but do not overtly refer to the aura or subtle bodies or energy centres. An example of this is the famous meditation on the Sacred Heart of Jesus, which when effectively practiced sets up a rapport between the heart (Tiphareth) centre of the meditator and the blessings of Christ as expressed through a symbol of His undaunted compassion. Through this rapport the meditator will, over time, align the area of her consciousness connected with the heart – love, compassion, emotional tone, and service – with that of Christ Himself. She will then become more like Christ – at least in this aspect of Her life.

Within the original Golden Dawn corpus very little of direct and practical relevance was written on this topic. Many GD magicians, when confronted with a need to understand the aura and subtle bodies, were left to fend for themselves, and introduced concepts and frameworks on the subtle bodies carried over from Theosophy. The resulting mish-mash of ideas and traditions has resulted in much partial understanding by magicians and authors alike. In recent years however there have been a number of good books produced on this topic. By far the most useful is *The Circuit of Force* by Dion Fortune and Gareth Knight. This book is an expanded version of a series of articles Dion Fortune wrote on this topic in the latter years of her life and together with Gareth Knight's wise commentary there is much direct and real wisdom to be found within its pages.

The importance placed on aura control by the Golden Dawn is shown by the inclusion of the Qabalistic Cross (which directly manipulates the aura) as a preface of nearly all rituals and practices. The very first action we undertake, it balances our auric sphere and also introduces the non-ego based energy of the Light into it. We also seek to inwardly graft a link between our own sphere and that of the Earth beneath us and the Higher above us, through the feet and crown centres respectively. However, the main forms of direct aura control within the traditional Golden Dawn framework were left for the Inner Order magician – someone who had previously balanced their elemental nature to some degree and had a direct connection to their higher or deeper nature. These days members of all grades practice aura control, in the form of the popular Middle Pillar exercise. However, the original idea of keeping such practices for later periods of unfoldment may be wiser than we may first think. Direct aura control has many potential dangers, the most nefarious of which is addiction to the intoxicating astral and etheric high that it can produce.

When, for example within the Middle Pillar exercise, we draw into ourselves large amounts of etheric and astral force, we literally bombard our consciousness, and intense feelings may result. This is due to the sudden expansion of the etheric and astral bodies. As the etheric expands we may feel 'spacy' and larger in size and energetically blissful. As the astral expands we may experience intense emotions, flashes of light, sudden impulses, or visions. Many of us find these experiences are enjoyable over and above the intention of transformation or purification of the aura itself. All such experiences however are to be dealt with and analyzed with the same calm consideration that we should bring into all our magical and spiritual work. We should ask if we are performing practices, such as the Middle Pillar for its intoxicating effects or to genuinely help us transform and serve.

Another basic principle required in the understanding of aura control is that just as we develop, grow and maintain our physical body through the consumption, digestion and excretion of physical substance (food, Water, Air), so too with our non-physical subtle bodies. Our etheric body is connected to and draws in the etheric substance around us to maintain its form, as do the astral and the mental bodies. Whereas we all know the effects of a diminished, polluted or unhealthy food supply, few of us think of the effects similarly tainted etheric, astral or mental substance may have upon us. If we are not 'fed' on any plane, we wither and fade. If we are fed unhealthy substances we become unhealthy and distorted:

> 'We all live in a particular environment, and our subtle body absorbs whatever is within that immediate environment and breathes out its own emanations into it ... we are constantly interchanging each other's magnetism as we share each other's air. We may be largely unconscious of this but it accounts for spontaneous sympathies and antipathies.' Dion Fortune and Gareth Knight, *The Circuit of Force*, p.182

Recognizing these simple facts, though often conceptualized in different ways, most religious and esoteric traditions take steps to ensure a healthy maintenance of all levels of the human being. Hence we find techniques to clear the etheric, astral and mental counterparts of both areas of worship and esoteric work, as well as living areas.

Focusing firstly on the etheric level, many traditions recommend retreats to the country areas, mountains or seaside where etheric energy is purer and in abundance. Other examples will present themselves to you upon reflection, though the essential idea is clear: to try and surround ourselves as much as possible with clear etheric energy. Of course this is not always possible in daily life – our work places and communal areas of entertainment or social interaction are beyond our control. This is where techniques to cleanse the etheric body of any unclear energy come into their own. Again, one of the classic methods in the Golden Dawn is the Lesser Ritual of the Pentagram, though simple techniques such as quickly interspersed hot and cold bathing and Epsom salt baths are also very effective. When it comes to our own private spaces, our room or homes, however we can and should keep them clear. Often this is very simple and requires nothing more than an ordered, emotionally balanced life to be lived within the space.

The astral component of our living and working space is slightly different and I am sure we can all recall houses, rooms or buildings that seem charged with a particular emotional energy or presence. These charges originate from the human interactions of the people living and working within them. That is to say it is we humans who can infect a house or a building with the feelings of depression and discord or bless it with the sense of peace and harmony. If we live in a highly astral-emotionally charged area our own personal emotional-astral body will naturally absorb some of its energies.

Methods to avoid such absorption fall into three main categories, the first two of which are utilised by the Golden Dawn and other Western traditions. Firstly, placing a wall or a filter against the energy; secondly, consciously charging our own astral spheres with the particular astral energies we desire, or thirdly removing our astral-emotional bodies from the area as much as possible. This latter method may partly explain the incidents of dissociation within children and teenagers living in highly tense or emotionally distressing households. By dissociating or daydreaming they are actually moving themselves to a different astral 'area' and absorbing (hopefully) healthier energies. Of course the converse does not necessarily follow – a dissociated child does not necessarily indicate an unclear emotional-astral environment. This movement into another 'area' can also make living in the world problematic, especially when the person does not have the desire or skills to return at will.

While the vast majority of this 'charging' of place occurs without the conscious recognition of the people involved, there are many ways to achieve it consciously. Again the Golden Dawn has numerous methods, most of which will be covered in our chapter on invocation. Other less obvious methods include the traditional religious and esoteric rules of polite and refrained interaction with other members of a community. Correctly followed, such etiquette allows only selected emotional energies to be visibly present and therefore affect the astral-emotional tenure of a house or community building. Such an approach plays an extremely important role in the creation and maintenance of the traditional Western lodge egregore or 'group-mind'. Group-minds often have a reflective property in that they mirror back to the individual group members an amplified rendition of the composite of emotions and aspirations expressed under its auspices. A group that always meets with the emotional ideals of honesty and compassion towards each other will find their group mind displaying such a quality. However, a group that meets with bickering and deceit will find those emotions amplified and infecting the group. Careful guidance of the topics of conversation and forms of etiquette can help keep a group mind clear and focused.

When it comes to living within a household or a spiritual community, sharing the daily round of life together, rather than the few hours a month of a magical lodge, this principle has limitations. Ultimately it is only effective if all individuals are actively transforming or at least owning any negative thoughts and feelings towards others rather than simply repressing them. Otherwise unspoken thoughts and feelings become the raw material for not only individual emotional energy but also, where people share on a spiritual level, the communal astral-emotional state. The modern psychology of open expression has advantages here, though again only if all people involved are assertive enough to be able to hold their own emotional space and not hang onto resentments and harbour destructive thoughts.

When it comes to surrounding ourselves with healthy mental body energy and blessings, the Western esoteric traditions have historically sought to do this through the time-honoured techniques of initiation, meditation, study and contemplation. When we receive a genuine initiation into a wisdom tradition we are linked to the tradition in many ways – physically through lodge attendance, etherically and astrally through shared magic and worship and on the mental body level through direct linkage to the non-physical components of the tradition. This last linkage, which occurs at initiation, is kept intact, nurtured and expanded through meditation and other spiritual practices. It ensures that our personal mental bodies are 'fed' the clearer energies and blessings of the tradition and lodge. This is one of the many reasons that we should always approach initiation and joining an esoteric tradition with care and much thought. We need to be sure that we wish to be connected to and fed by the energies, ideals, divinities and powers that the tradition embodies and draws from. This applies equally to decent, effective 'good' traditions as much as to those corrupted or debased through ego focus or lower motivations. Just because a tradition works on the 'light' side of things does not mean that we may suit it or that it may suit us.

THOUGHT AND WILL IN AURA CONTROL

As shown obliquely in the discussion above, we have control over all of our subtle bodies through the power of thought and will. Similarly most of us reading this and practicing the Golden Dawn have control over our physical bodies – we can move where we want, often eat what we want, and through a bit of hard work achieve an incredible level of material comfort compared to the non-Western populations of the world. In this we are reminded of our blessings, for without the physical freedom and comfort we take for granted every day, we would have far less control over our subtle bodies and those parts of our being historically considered more 'spiritual'. It is important to understand that when we are struggling to find food for our children or escaping war and famine, 'spiritual' thoughts and aura control go out the window.

However, we all can right now choose and direct the quality of our subtle bodies through the application of will and thought. Often this is simply achieved through focus, decision and mental attitude. As we choose to change our subtle bodies and consciousness we automatically attract similar qualities from the astral light around us. It is as if we as individuals are lumps in custard – our consciousness is formed of the same raw material as that around us but at a different level of transformation (lumpiness). When we become even slightly less lumpy, more custard automatically flows into us and out of us. So too within the etheric, astral and to some extent mental worlds, when we focus and develop a particular quality within us, we begin to attract similar qualities to us.

There are numerous books and courses around that illustrate this principle, which is a foundation stone of the New Age movement and the older New Thought ideas. Within the Western traditions and the Golden Dawn this principle is reflected in the understanding that the human being is a microcosm or little universe that reflects and is connected to the greater universe or macrocosm. Unlike the many New Age and New Thought propaganda machines however, the Western traditions posit limits on the ability to change our physical world and our physical selves through the application of thought alone. This is due to the nature of the physical universe, Malkuth, which by its very nature creates human beings who develop a consciousness in separation from 'the One'. In Christian terminology this is one explanation of Original Sin, or that which cuts us off from God and Unity. Following this further we see that the stories and myths of the great masters and Incarnations of divinity, who knowing themselves truly to be one with the All, were able to change the material world by thought and simple action. We ourselves as limited human beings alas cannot, despite the protestations of many New Age teachers.

Knowing that we are limited beings and cannot totally change ourselves or the world by thought alone, the Western traditions teach the study of our selves, our 'little universes' which are connected with and a reflection of the greater universe. What develops or inhibits this connection and the extent to which this connection can 'channel' universal blessings that may transform us and heal the world, forms one of the main areas of study within Western magic. The more we discover, accept and change that which inhibits our connection with the greater universe and God, the more we can allow God to enter into us and thereby fashion us as effective tools for service. This is of course the whole point of Western magic and the Golden Dawn in particular. Aura control is one of the best ways of speeding this process of changing and letting go of the blockages to God. However, it will not help us discover, accept or own our limitations. This requires introspection and honesty.

Within our etheric and astral bodies we will find 'areas' or 'pockets' of stuck energy, emotion and thought. This is perfectly normal and part of being human. These pockets are often containers for difficult emotional states and ideas that we normally do not focus upon. The use of purifying, banishing and balancing practices such as the Lesser Ritual of the Pentagram help break down the walls of these pockets of energy and allow the stuck energy within them to flow freely and the emotions or thoughts to be more conscious. Deeper and more intransigent pockets of astral-emotional energy that lie within our unconscious are transformed later through initiation and Inner Order work.

Before any serious attempt at aura control is attempted these pockets within the etheric and astral bodies need to be cleansed and balanced to some degree. Without such cleansing the energy and emotions, images or thoughts in the pockets may be heightened and exaggerated. This occurs when the extra etheric and astral energy we bring into our subtle bodies enters the pocket but does not flow freely through it. Thus the extra energy, using a very base analogy, like water in a balloon, swells the pocket to beyond its accustomed 'size' and the emotions or energy there becomes distorted. When this occurs the results can be unpleasant and sometimes quite debilitating both emotionally and physically.

Before proceeding with the practices below please ensure that you have practiced the Lesser Ritual of the Pentagram daily for a number of months. While it is impossible to determine the exact number of months for any one individual, we can say at least three months. However, you may need more or less time than this depending on any practices of a similar nature you may have undertaken before the LRP and the 'raw' state of your subtle bodies to begin with. It is best to err on the side of caution and extend the three months if you have any doubts.

The Middle Pillar Exercise

This is the second of the two most utilised pieces of Golden Dawn tradition, the first being the LRP. Originally the Middle Pillar was not taught the way we know it today; it was created by Israel Regardie from several GD principles and techniques. The exercise is fundamentally Golden Dawn in its technique and method of application and since it is simpler than the original versions and still effective, it is reproduced in its popular format here. In some respects the Middle Pillar is a Western equivalent of some Eastern Kundalini yoga practices. It is designed to awaken centres of force within the subtle bodies and allow the generation of tremendous amounts of etheric and astral energy. The awakening of the centres not only allows the full expression of this energy, but also causes specific changes of consciousness and hopefully personal transformation. Further material upon the connection of the Middle Pillar and its adaptations with Kundalini Yoga can be found in Regardie's *The Middle Pillar*, *Modern Magick* by Donald Michael Kraig and *Tantra for Westerners* by Francis King.

The philosophical basis for the Middle Pillar comes from the Qabalah which has been discussed in Chapter One. The middle pillar of the three pillars of the Tree of Life is known as the Pillar of Mildness and Equilibrium. It is the place of reconciliation between the two contending forces of the Universe – love/hate, hot/cold and active/passive, for example. To attain the middle pillar is to equilibrate the two contending forces and as such is the aim of all Western magicians. To live out the middle pillar within one's life is to act in a flexible, just and balanced manner, even throughout those aspects of life that tend to pull us towards one of the pillars of the opposites. A key point here also is the living out of life, rather than escaping from it or withdrawing ourselves into attachments of spiritual bliss, divorced from the world.

The exercise of the middle pillar also provides us with several other benefits. Firstly, it gives the higher aspects of consciousness a psychic mechanism by which they can contact and influence the everyday self. This occurs when the astral body is enlarged and purified with the energy from the mental plane through the use of the divine names. This allows our mental body a way of communication with our astral body, and the mental plane. Secondly, the exercise allows the regular practitioner to tap into enormous amounts of several distinct types of spiritual force, which can then be used in a number of different ways, often to balance consciousness. This occurs through the 'plugging in' of our etheric and astral bodies into the great power sources of the universe. Thirdly, it encourages the expansion and development of inspired intuition (referred to in the chapter on meditation and divination). And fourthly, it has great benefits on the physical health and wellbeing of anyone who uses it regularly. This occurs through the spread of the energy throughout the etheric body and by the increase of breath and lung capacity.

The Middle Pillar exercise is one of these apparently simple exercises within the Golden Dawn tradition that moves far more deeply than is immediately obvious. Of course the more we are conscious of everything it does, the more transformation will occur, the more it has to teach us. So before proceeding with the full exercise I suggest that you start with these simpler versions, paring back the Middle Pillar to see its effect on each level – physical, etheric, astral, mental and spiritual. All five of these exercises may be performed back to back in one session.

MIDDLE PILLAR EXERCISE ONE – THE PHYSICAL

After performing a preliminary LBRP, stand in the centre of your worship and workspace facing East. Stand straight and relaxed, hands loose by your sides. Your neck and shoulders should be relaxed, head level and upright. Feel your feet directly on the floor. Using yoga terminology this posture is called *tadasna* (the mountain pose) and your whole body should be like a mountain solidly existing between the Earth below you and the heavens above. Pay attention to just your physical body, do not breathe any differently or visualise or invoke anything. Just relax and feel what it is like to consciously stand in this position. Notice what effects it has upon your physical sense of wellbeing and also your energy levels and emotional state. You may find that all three levels are affected, but pay closer attention to the effects of the physical body. This is the position, the posture we normally use in the Middle Pillar and every time we effectively perform the exercise our physical bodies will be affected in just this way.

MIDDLE PILLAR EXERCISE TWO – THE ETHERIC

After noticing the changes to your physical body, now focus upon how the energy in your body feels. After at least three months of the LRP and other exercises as previously discussed this should be relatively straightforward. Simply focus on the energy in your body and get a sense of it clearly, how strong it is, areas of weakness or strength and how it flows. Again, do not breathe any differently or visualise anything. Nor should you attempt to analyse any of your findings concerning the state of your energy-etheric body. Now begin to breathe deeply. After a few minutes of this, on the next out breath simply hum or vibrate 'mmm' for the full length of breath. Keep doing this: breathe in and hum out. While doing this do not concentrate on any emotion or spiritual power or blessing, simply feel the power of the hum or vibration. Continue this for about five minutes. Stop and breathe normally. Again focus upon how the energy in your body feels. Notice what changes there are to your etheric body – has the level of energy changed? Does your energy flow better? Whenever we perform the middle pillar exercise, similar changes to the etheric are produced solely by the use of rhythmic deep breathing and vibration of sound. It is the breath itself and the sonics of the names we use that effect the etheric body. In this etheric-body-only version we use a generic sound without esoteric meaning in the GD context to limit our effects on the etheric.

MIDDLE PILLAR EXERCISE THREE – EMOTIONAL-ASTRAL

Now notice the state of your emotions and mind. What feelings are present, what internal chatter and noise is present? What level of calmness is within your mind? Once you have a clear sense of this, proceed with the following visualisation. Here we simply want to focus on the visualisation itself and not imagine any change of emotion, any spiritual quality nor focus on any esoteric or personal responses to the colours used. (Please refer to diagram 11 on page 138 if you are unclear as to the locations of the centres mentioned).

Visualise above the crown of your head a pulsating and glowing ball of radiant white light about six inches in diameter. Concentrate upon this ball of light for a while and its whiteness.

Pause for a while and then visualise a shaft of brilliant white coming down from the ball through the centre of your head and resting in your neck area. Here it changes to a ball of clear lavender light. See both balls of light, white and lavender at once, before concentrating upon the lavender.

Pause for a while and then visualise a shaft of brilliant white coming down from the lavender ball coming to a rest in your heart centre. Here it changes to a ball of yellow-gold pulsating light. See all three balls of light, white, lavender and yellow-gold at once before concentrating upon the yellow-gold.

Pause for a while and then visualise a shaft of brilliant white coming down from the ball of gold light coming to a rest in your genital area. Here it changes to a ball of clear and rich violet light. See all four balls of

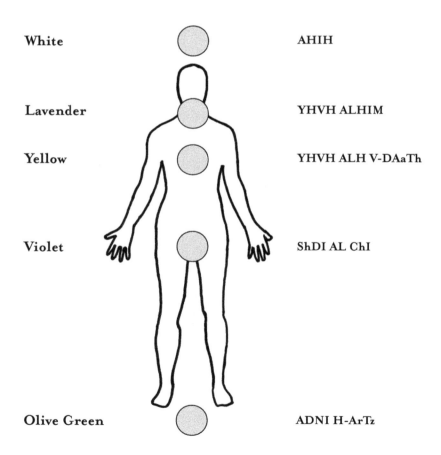

White		AHIH
Lavender		YHVH ALHIM
Yellow		YHVH ALH V-DAaTh
Violet		ShDI AL ChI
Olive Green		ADNI H-ArTz

Diagram 11: the Middle Pillar and Tree of Life on the Human Body

light, white, lavender, yellow-gold and violet at once before concentrating upon the violet.

Pause for a while and then visualise a shaft of brilliant white coming down from the ball of violet light between the centre of your legs until it comes to rest below the soles of your feet. Here it changes to a ball of clear olive green light upon which you stand. See all five balls of light, white, lavender, gold-yellow, violet and olive green at once before concentrating upon the olive green.

Pause and let all the images of the balls of light disappear. Now notice the state of your emotions and mind. How have your emotions and internal chatter changed? Is there any change to your level of calmness and balance? Again, the full middle pillar exercise affects us on the emotional-astral plane and this is largely through the focused use of colour and visualisation. Remember the Golden Dawn understanding that 'colours are not symbols of forces but are the forces themselves.'

MIDDLE PILLAR EXERCISE FOUR – THE MENTAL BODY

Again pause for some time. Next we will move to working with the mental body, which while limitless in time and space can be affected and worked with via certain practices. As mentioned in the first chapter the mental body is affected by the power of divine names. This is not simply the vibration of the names but also opening to the spiritual blessings behind the names. These blessings, in the Qabalistic worldview, are seen as aspects of the unknowable One Being, each name referring to a particular aspect. Ultimately opening to these aspects of the One is a lifelong journey, deepening each time we connect via meditation and work with the name and being in question. For our purposes here we can approach this level of mental functioning through meditation on the meaning of the names as we repeat them to ourselves.

So standing ready we focus upon the awareness of that level of being beyond our emotional thoughts and inward chattering. It is as if we dive through this level like diving into a swimming pool, moving beyond it and deeper through it to arrive at the core mental activity that underlies it. Make note of what you are aware of here. It will probably be very hard to explain, so do not try to conceptualize the awareness in words.

Now we focus upon the crown centre once more, this time not visualising anything nor breathing in any particular way. We now hear and imagine repeating the name AHIH within this space. There is no need to imagine vibrating it, simply repeat the name every so often while inwardly pondering and opening to the mystery of its meaning: 'I will be.'

Repeat this for a few minutes. Next focus upon your throat centre and repeat this same meditative process with the name YHVH ALHIM, 'The Root of Being of the One and the Many.' Continue with the heart centre, YHVH ALH V-DAaTh, 'The Root of Being of the Goddess of Knowledge', then the genital centre, ShDI AL ChI, 'Almighty Ever Living Goddess' and finally the centre below the feet, ADNI H-ArTz, 'The Ruling power of the Principle of Embodiment and Form'.

Now pause once more and focus again inwardly beyond the level of your emotional-astral body. What changes, if any, can you notice?

MIDDLE PILLAR EXERCISE FIVE – THE SPIRITUAL BODY

As we mentioned in Chapter One, none of the few techniques we can utilise to try and stimulate activity within the Spiritual body are guaranteed to work. Mystery is at work here rather than will, even our higher wills, and in many situations all we can do is prepare the temple of our being and hope it will be indwelled by the One. Therefore when we perform the Middle Pillar exercise there is only a possibility that it will directly affect our spiritual body, and to be honest there is no way of quantifying this possibility or even hedging our bets. All we can do is to honestly aspire to the One (and the various aspects of the One represented by the divine names) and try and cultivate a selfless desire for spiritual experience. The mental body, the experience of the Neschamah in GD terms, is beyond the ego and beyond the personal self. When we choose to align our personal selves with its desires in service then we may be able to activate our spiritual body.

Some magicians tend to shy away from the desire for mystical experience and connection with the One Being (however conceived) since they view religion and magic as separate endeavours. I do not share this view and encourage inclusion of the great longing to connect with the One (as expressed through the five divine names) to be included as part of the Middle Pillar exercise. We can practice this for each centre after completing the mental body exercise above. Again focus on the name, but this time without meditation. Simply see it as a doorway to the Highest and consciously choose to allow your full self connection with that aspect of the Highest principle, however you relate to it. Inwardly, using whatever words, thoughts or emotions that are meaningful, ask the One Being to allow you to connect with that aspect so you may become a vehicle for those blessings within your world and everyday life. There is no hard and fast rule as to how long to keep asking and desiring the connection for each centre. Simply move on when you are ready.

When you have concluded these five exercises, finish with a Qabalistic Cross, thanking the One Being. I suggest that you perform these five separated versions of the Middle Pillar several times before moving onto the complete and combined exercise below. Examination of the complete exercise shows why the Middle Pillar is such a potent tool for transformation, as it combines techniques and principles to awaken and align all our subtle bodies within one harmonious technique.

INSTRUCTIONS FOR THE COMPLETE MIDDLE PILLAR EXERCISE

1. LBRP.
2. Either remain standing straight up, feet together, or lie flat on your back on a comfortable but firm surface (a bed is not generally a good idea).
3. Relax awhile with some deep breaths and close your eyes.
4. Visualise a pulsating and glowing ball of radiant white light about six inches in diameter above the crown of your head. Concentrate upon this ball of light for a while and its whiteness.
5. When ready take a deep breath, hold and then slowly vibrate אהיה AHIH (Ehh-Heh-Yah). As you vibrate see and feel the ball of light become stronger and brighter. Try to centre the resonance and vibration within the ball of light. This may at first sound patently silly considering the ball is above your head, but it does occur after a while.
6. Repeat the above step several (at least another three) times. Each time watch the ball grow brighter and more potent. As you become more experienced with the Middle Pillar you should extend the length of time within each centre to around five minutes, vibrating all the time.
7. Pause for a while and then visualise a shaft of brilliant white coming down from the ball through the centre of your head and resting in your neck area. Here it changes to a ball of clear lavender light. See both balls of light, white and lavender at once before concentrating upon the lavender.
8. When ready, take a deep breath, hold and then slowly vibrate יהוה אלהים YOD-HEH-VAU-HEH ELOHIM (Yodh-Heh-Vowh-Heh Elo-Heem). As you vibrate, see and feel the ball of light become stronger and brighter. Try to centre the resonance and vibration within the ball of light.

9. Repeat the above step several (at least another three) times. Each time, watch the ball grow brighter and more potent.

10. Pause for a while and then visualise a shaft of brilliant white coming down from the lavender ball through your lower neck and chest and coming to a rest in your heart centre. Here it changes to a ball of yellow-gold and warm pulsating light. See all three balls of light, white, lavender and yellow-gold at once before concentrating upon the gold.

11. When ready, take a deep breath, hold and then slowly vibrate ודעת יהוה אלוה YOD-HEH-VAU-HEH ELOAH VA-DAATH (Yodh-Heh-Vowh-Heh Elo-Ah Vah-Daa-ath). As you vibrate, see and feel the ball of light become stronger and brighter. Try to centre the resonance and vibration within the ball of light.

12. Repeat the above step several (at least another three) times. Each time watch the ball grow brighter and more potent.

13. Pause for a while and then visualise a shaft of brilliant white coming down from the ball of gold light through your stomach area and coming to a rest in your genital area. Here it changes to a ball of clear and rich violet light. See all four balls of light, white, lavender, gold-yellow and violet at once before concentrating upon the violet.

14. When ready take a deep breath, hold and then slowly vibrate אלהי שדי SHADDAI EL-CHAI (Shaah-Dai El-Chaye. The 'Ch' is pronounced hard as in 'loch'.) As you vibrate, see and feel the ball of light become stronger and brighter. Try to centre the resonance and vibration within the ball of light.

15. Repeat the above step several (at least another three) times. Each time watch the ball grow brighter and more potent.

16. Pause for a while and then visualise a shaft of brilliant white coming down from the ball of violet light through the centre of your legs until it comes to a final rest below the centre of the soles of your feet, so that you are standing on it. Here it changes to a ball of clear olive green light. See all five balls of light, white, lavender, gold-yellow, violet and olive green at once before concentrating upon the olive green.

17. When ready, take a deep breath, hold and then slowly vibrate אדני הארץ ADONAI HA-ARETZ (Ah-Don-Aye Ha-Aar-Retzz). As you vibrate see and feel the ball of light become stronger and brighter. Try to centre the resonance and vibration within the ball of light.

18. Repeat the above step several (at least another three) times. Each time watch the ball grow brighter and more potent.

19. Pause, and again see all five balls of light glowing and pulsating together, linked by the shaft of white light. During the first month or so of practice, you may like to stop here by performing the Qabalistic Cross or continue on with steps 20-26 below. After a month or so you need to continue with the steps below every time.

THE CIRCULATION OF THE LIGHT

20. Concentrate upon the ball of light above your head. Visualise coming from it bright and glowing white light that moves slowly down the left hand side of your body. See and feel the light and energy move down the entire left hand side of your body. Take as long as you need to accomplish this. As you get more experienced you should be able to direct the light down the left hand side of your body during one long out-breath.

21. When the light arrives at the centre below your feet, visualise the light being absorbed into that light, and a current established between the centres above your head and below your feet. When more experienced this should occur as you hold your breath after the out-breath of step 20.

22. Pause a while and then send the light up your body from feet to head in a similar manner but now up the right hand side of your body. As you get more experienced, do this in a single slow in-breath, extending from the holding of the breath in step 21. When the light arrives at the centre above your head, visualise the light being absorbed into that centre and a current established between the centres above your head and in your feet. You have now established a full circular polarity between your Kether and Malkuth centres. Hold your breath here before repeating the entire process again several times. Each time the light passes Kether and Malkuth see it get stronger and more intense.

23. Next, perform an identical process but this time direct the light and energy from your Kether down the front of your body into your Malkuth. Pause the light there and let it grow stronger before drawing it back to Kether up the back of your body. Again, when experienced these actions should be done with the breath: sending down with the out-breath; pausing in Malkuth with the hold breath; drawing up with the in-breath; and pausing in Kether with the hold breath.

24. Now concentrate upon your Malkuth centre. Visualise arising from it a bright and glowing white light that rises up and through your body. Move the light up a step at a time, through your whole body.

25. When the light arrives at your Kether, visualise the light spilling over from your head, over your whole body on all sides, down to the centre below your feet. This is like a fountain of light, falling down to the Malkuth. The light is drawn into Malkuth, below the feet, and then moves up your body again.
26. Continue this process for several minutes, feeling the light and energy grow each time it passes your head and feet.
27. Finish by performing the Qabalistic Cross.

AWAKENING THE FULL TREE OF LIFE WITHIN THE AURA

The original Golden Dawn exercise upon which the Middle Pillar was derived worked with the full Tree of Life. The reason why we, like many contemporary magicians, have focused first on the middle pillar is to establish a strong, balanced foundation before proceeding to develop the full Tree. Once you have become proficient in the Middle Pillar exercise and are confident that its benefits have become activated in your daily life, you may wish to proceed to the full Tree version. There is no need to describe this in detail. The pattern and formula used within the Middle Pillar exercise is maintained using all ten of the Sephiroth, rather than just the five upon the middle pillar. The original Golden Dawn version worked with the Tree as reflected onto the outer surface of the auric egg. This is a complex undertaking and for our purposes the Tree of Life may be awakened within our body as shown in diagram 11.

It is best to awaken the ten Sephiroth in the traditional order, either working down from Kether to Malkuth or up from Malkuth to Kether. At this stage continue to use a simple shaft of white light to connect the Sephiroth, as in the Middle Pillar. Other, more complex versions have the full twenty-two paths visualised in their respective colours. The Sephiroth and the correspondences required for this exercise are given in table three opposite.

INVOCATION OF FORCE WITHIN THE AURA

While the Middle Pillar and full Tree of Life exercises are designed to awaken within our subtle bodies a number of spiritual forces within a balanced harmony, there are occasions where we may wish to work with a single force or spiritual blessing. In most esoteric traditions this would not be done until we were proficient with an exercise, like the Middle

Table 3: Divine Names and Colours of the Sephiroth

Sephiroth	Divine Name	Meaning	Colour	Location
Kether	אהיה AHIH (Ehh-Heh-Yah)	I will be	White	Above the head
Chokmah	יהוה YHVH (Yodh-Heh-Vowh-Heh)	Root of Being	Grey	Left side of brain/head
Binah	יהוה אלהים YHVH ALHIM (Yodh-Heh-Vowh-Heh Elo-Heem)	Root of Being of the One and the Many	Black	Right side of brain/head
Daath	יהוה אלהים YHVH ALHIM (Yodh-Heh-Vowh-Heh Elo-Heem)	Root of Being of the One and the Many	Lavender	Throat
Chesed	אל AL (El)	The One. Unity	Blue	Left shoulder
Geburah	אלהים גבור ALHIM GBUR (Elo-Heem Gee-boor)	Strength and Power of the One and the Many	Red	Right shoulder
Tiphareth	אלוה ודעת יהוה YHVH ALYH VDAaTh (Yodh-Heh-Vowh-Heh Elo-Ah Vah-Daa-ath)	Root of Being of the Goddess of Knowledge	Yellow	Heart centre
Netzach	יהוה צבאות YHVH TzBAOTh (Yodh-Heh-Vowh-Heh Tsab-ae-baoth)	Root of Being of the Manifold Forms of Life	Green	Left hip
Hod	אלהים צבאות ALHIM TzBAOTh (Elo-Heem Tsab-ae-baoth)	The One and the Many within the Manifold Forms of Life	Orange	Right hip
Yesod	שדי אלהי ShDI ALChI (Shaah-Dai El-Chaye)	Almighty Ever Living Goddess	Purple	Gential centre
Malkuth	אדני הארץ ADNI HARTz (Ah-Don-Aye Ha-Aar-Retz)	Lord and Ruling Power of Earth and Principle of Embodiment	Olive Green	Below the feet

Pillar, which works with a harmonious balance of energies. Typically, a specific spiritual blessing of force is only brought into our subtle bodies for a clear and defined purpose such as:

◆ Working through an initiatory or training programme where we focus upon one aspect of ourselves at a time. Within the Golden Dawn the most obvious example is the four 'elemental' or personality grades of Zelator, Theoricus, Practicus and Philosophus. Within these grades we focus upon and transform the four elemental principles within us, one at a time. A Theoricus initiate may then charge and call into her aura the single elemental principle of Air.

◆ A planned and willed remedial action designed to strengthen aspects of ourselves which we find lacking through introspection. For example, if after performing the elemental mirror of self in Chapter One we realise we are lacking in Water qualities and we seriously wish to remedy this situation, we may bring into our aura the spiritual blessings of Water.

◆ A magical action or healing that requires a specific energy or spiritual blessing. For example, if we wish to perform political magic to give a political leader more compassion when making, for example, refugee policy, we could charge our aura with the blessings of Chesed. We could then, via our will, direct this energy from us into the letter we write to them.

In all of these cases, there are direct and practical reasons for the charging of our auras with a single energy. What we need to avoid is the direct charging of our auric sphere with a spiritual blessing only because we 'like' it or it appeals to us at an ego level. To do so would result in an imbalance and stagnation in our unfoldment and service to the One. In the examples above, all actions are dictated by our will. Also, we would not 'hold onto' the single blessing, no matter how wonderful it felt. Even in the elemental grades we are required to move from one grade to the next, from one element to another so we do not stay working with our favourite and thus stagnate. It is for this reason that initiates in most Golden Dawn Orders are seriously advised against proceeding with the four elemental grades unless they are committed to seeing all four through to the end.

Most of the principles involved in charging our auras with a specific energy have already been dealt with in the discussion of the Middle Pillar above. All we are doing here is narrowing our focus onto a specific set of symbols and names that are the gateways for the spiritual blessing we wish to contact. Such a technique enables us to quickly and easily experience the power of the sacred names of the Sephiroth, the Elements, the Planets or other sacred powers of the Universe. There are a few different variations on a theme for this technique. The most important points are the colours associated with the divine blessing chosen, the vibration of the divine names, and the circulation of the names throughout the whole aura.

PREPARATION FOR INVOCATION OF FORCE WITHIN THE AURA

Re-study the correspondences of the blessing and spiritual force to be worked with a day or two beforehand. It doesn't work as well reading up with five minutes to go. Study all you can about the force and the symbols of the force, particularly why those symbols are used, and the meaning of the divine names of the force to be invoked. While this technique can be used for any divine name or power associated with the Sephiroth, it is best to confine your work to the divine names as given above for quite some time. Become familiar with the Hebrew letters of the name to be used as well as the appropriate colour and its opposite or flashing colour. When working with the elemental principles, use the colour of the element and the name from the Supreme Invoking Ritual of the Pentagram in Chapter Five. The colour of the power invoked is the ground colour upon which the divine name is written in Hebrew in its opposite colour.

PRACTICE OF INVOCATION OF FORCE WITHIN THE AURA

This is best done sitting with spine straight.

Perform an LBRP around yourself, rather than any temple space you use.

Relax with the four-fold breath. Breathe in for four, hold for four, breathe out for four, hold for four and then return to breathing in for four. Do this for three to five minutes.

Perform the Exercise of the Middle Pillar without circulating the light.

Inwardly or outwardly ask for the aid of your Sacred Ones and the powers you seek to connect with, stating why you wish to invoke this force into your aura.

Table 4: Colours of Forces for Invocation of Force in the Aura

Force	Ground Colour	Name and Colour
Air	Yellow	יהוה YHVH (Yodh-Heh-Vowh-Heh) in **violet**.
Fire	Red	אלהים ALHIM (Elo-Heem) in **green**.
Water	Blue	אל AL (El) in **orange**.
Earth	Olive Green or Black	אדני ADNI (Ah-Don-Aye) in **red-orange or white**.
Kether	White	אהיה AHIH (Ehh-Heh-Yah) in **black**.
Chokmah	Grey	יהוה YHVH (Yodh-Heh-Vowh-Heh) in **white**.
Binah	Black	יהוה אלהים YHVH ALHIM (Yodh-Heh-Vowh-Heh Elo-Heem) in **white**.
Chesed	Blue	אל AL (El) in **orange**.
Geburah	Red	אלהים גבור ALHIM GBUR (Elo-Heem Gee-boor) **in green**.
Tiphareth	Yellow	יהוה אלוה ודעת YHVH ALYH VDAaTh (Yodh-Heh-Vowh-Heh Elo-Ah Vah-Daa-ath) in **violet**.
Netzach	Green	יהוה צבאות YHVH TzBAOTh (Yodh-Heh-Vowh-Heh Tsab-ae-baoth) in **red**.
Hod	Orange	אלהים צבאות ALHIM TzBAOTh (Elo-Heem Tsab-ae-baoth) in **blue**.
Yesod	Purple	שדי אלחי ShDI ALChI (Shaah-Dai El-Chaye) in **yellow**.
Malkuth	Olive Green	אדני הארץ ADNI HARTz (Ah-Don-Aye Ha-Aar-Retz) in **red-orange**.

With eyes opened or closed, visualise the name chosen before you in Hebrew. The letters should be coloured in the colours already worked out. They should be seen clearly and brightly. Once the vision is clear, see them resting upon a cloud of light which is the colour of the Sephira or the colour of the element.

While building up the vision of the name, inwardly vibrate the name to begin to enliven the image before you.

Once the vision of the coloured cloud of light and the name in the opposite colour resting upon it is clear and bright, breathe the cloud and name into your Tiphareth (heart) centre. This should be done with a full physical inhalation and a strong inner visualisation.

See the cloud of coloured light and the name resting in your Tiphareth centre. Build up the image while inwardly vibrating the name. Feel the blessings of the name pulsating within your heart space.

Now will and see a ray of divine white light from your Kether move down your body and into your Tiphareth centre. There it moves into the cloud and activates and energizes the name further.

On a deep inhalation, by will and vision move the cloud and the name up through your body to your Kether centre. Once the name and cloud is there, begin to circulate the image of the name and cloud through your aura as you inwardly vibrate the name. This circulation should be familiar to you from the Middle Pillar exercise and you should use the same method as described there. It is important, as you circulate the cloud, to see your whole aura change colour into the coloured light of the cloud, with the name moving through your aura. Inwardly vibrate the name so that a full vibration matches one complete circulation of the name. Remember to breathe fully and deeply as if you were outwardly vibrating the name.

Circulate the name slowly and carefully through all three modes of the Middle Pillar circulation. Repeat this for at least ten minutes (20 or 30 minutes is better).

When complete, cease vibrating and allow the name to fade.

When ready give the Sign of Silence astrally and then physically to return. The Sign of Silence is a physical sign given to seal the auric sphere. It is described in Chapter Ten.

Make notes on the experience as soon as possible.

If we analyse the steps of this practice we can see how several fundamental principles of the Golden Dawn tradition are being used, most particularly the use of 'names and images'. The need to make a deeper or 'higher' connection than that symbolised by and found within the astral Yetziratic realms is also highlighted. The study of and meditation upon the names *before* the practice should bring this about. Also of interest in this practice is the resting of the name in the Tiphareth (heart) centre before the circulation. This is because in esoteric and Qabalistic theory the heart governs and is linked to the whole being and body. By first transforming the energy of the heart space to a particular pitch or frequency, the rest of our aura or sphere of sensation is more likely to be transformed.

Aura control works with what the Golden Dawn termed 'the magical mirror of the universe'. As human beings made in the image of the One and the Many (Elohim) we have reflected within our auric spheres all the powers of the universe. When we attune our auras to a single power, or a group of powers, we are forming a powerful link between ourselves and the macrocosmic and universal blessings beyond ourselves. We may then be able to call upon and invoke these blessings far more easily and with more control than otherwise. We may even find ourselves becoming a link or channel between the universal powers and our everyday world. However, this is seldom anything as sensational as discarnate entities whispering in our ears giving us advice. More often it is a very everyday knowing and desire to open ourselves to deepen our service to God and humanity in particular ways. Apart from the pure elemental and Qabalistic powers, the Golden Dawn used aura control techniques with such forces and symbols as the Tattwas, the Enochian Tablets, and the Seven Planets. Later magicians, such as Colonel Seymour from the Society of the Inner Light, used a range of symbols and motifs derived from myths. These were built into the whole aura or a particular chakra.

When we work to control and direct our aura, we are for a short period of time totally transforming our astral body (provided of course we are focused and do not drift off). This is a very powerful undertaking, one that can be extremely beneficial for our unfoldment. Unwisely done however, imbalance can result. To avoid such imbalances the technique should not be edited or abbreviated. To do so may result in one or more of the esoteric principles inherent in the technique being accidentally violated.

For example, let us say a person untrained in the esoteric arts of the West wishes to open themselves to the greater universal powers of compassion. Their motives are to increase their own compassion for the world. They decide to 'meditate' and 'open themselves' to universal compassion. For the sake of argument let us say their motives are clear and unmixed. Let us also say there are no blockages to connecting with the forces of compassion, which we symbolise as Chesed in the Qabalah. By simply 'tuning in and opening' the person's astral body will indeed become infused with the Compassionate qualities of Chesed. However, the astral body, in the presence of such powerful forces can easily become diffuse and its boundaries dissolve. The person will finish her mediation session feeling very compassionate, but could quite easily come away with a distended astral body, half within this world and half within the Chesed realms. This will become all the more likely through repeated practices of the simple 'opening' technique.

By contrast, the invocation of force within the aura technique first strengthens all our bodies through the Middle Pillar. The force invoked is then controlled and is invoked solely into our auric sphere and astral body. This is done via the three modes of circulating the light. We are therefore not only invoking the force we desire but also clarifying and enhancing our own boundaries at the same time. Nor does our consciousness, our astral body, ever leave the habitual space it occupies within the etheric and physical bodies. We stay here and call the force to us, as opposed to accidentally drifting off into Chesed. The focused and willed vibrations, breath and visualisation ensure our continued presence in this realm. The person practicing this technique will therefore have a clear sense of self, be far more grounded and able to enact the powers of compassion within this real flesh and blood world than someone simply 'opening' themselves to compassion.

ASSUMPTION OF GODFORMS

Another aspect of aura control utilized within the Golden Dawn is the assumption of the Godform. While the most crucial instances of this technique occur during the various initiation ceremonies, several solo rituals also make use of this process. Within the GD and other Western mystery traditions, the phrase 'assumption of a Godform' is used to describe taking on the power, energy, divinity and qualities of a specific deity. It is achieved largely through control and manipulation of the aura and the astral body. This differs from the channelling of a God or Goddess as occurs, when successful, in Pagan Drawing Down the Moon rituals. In these ceremonies, the Priestess *becomes* Goddess. She will lose consciousness, and her own sense of will to varying degrees, up to and including full possession and total lack of consciousness. While this full-on uncontrolled channelling is desirable in some Pagan traditions and Wicca, it is not within the Golden Dawn tradition.

Within the GD, the aim is to be able to consciously and at will utilise the powers and qualities of a deity for specific purposes. This is not using the deity in question, but rather the qualities and powers associated with the deity throughout millennia and tradition. There is a distinct difference here. By assuming the Godform of a particular deity, the energy coming from the magician (or a particular officer within a ceremony) will be a *reflection* of the spiritual powers of a deity. However, the will of the magician or officer will still prevail. That is, the officer can still perform the specific actions and say the specific words required for the ceremony to be successful while projecting the power of the Goddess or God in question. This of course is a great advantage over uncontrolled possession by the Gods – at least in Golden Dawn ceremony and ritual. There are various methods and techniques for assuming a Godform, and a few ideas are briefly described in the published Golden Dawn corpus. The method below is probably one of the most complete that can easily be utilised by people with a range of experience in Golden Dawn rituals. The choice of deity depends upon your needs.

ASSUMING A GODFORM – PRACTICE

Perform a LBRP around yourself.

Perform the Middle Pillar Exercise with the circulation of the Light.

Maintain and visualise strongly the central pillar of light. This should run clearly from Kether to Malkuth, from crown to below the feet.

Visualise strongly the image of the deity in question. Build this image up making the colours vibrant and bright.

Either

A: Place this visualisation around your auric egg. This is imagined as if the image was painted in *glowing* colours upon the whole surface of the auric egg. The image should be stretched around the entire sphere or egg. This is hard to do and, if needed, you may concentrate on placing the image on the front part of your auric sphere only. However, please consider this an interim step towards imaging the deity around the full aura.

B: Visualise the image of the deity forming over and around your body. As this is done your arms are within the arms of the deity, your legs within the deity's legs etc. This should be done very slowly and with care. As you do this, always maintain the glowing white central column of your middle pillar.

Hold the Godform as long as possible. It can be strengthened by saying or softly vibrating the name of the deity.

WITHDRAWING A GODFORM – PRACTICE

Cease visualising. Allow the image to fade.

Focus upon your central column again. See it clear and white.

Bring down the white light from Kether around your auric sphere, in the same three motions of the Circulation of Light exercise. However, make sure you visualise and direct the light around the edge of your auric egg, not your body.

When your auric sphere is fully filled with white light, give the Sign of Silence. Thank the deity.

The beauty of this method is that it allows the will of the magician to be fully present while the Godform is still very strong and active. This is achieved via the central column of the Sephirotic centres being maintained as white light. This is where all the astral and etheric energy from a magician comes. Typically in ceremony, energy will enter through the Kether and Malkuth points and emerge from the central column through the Tiphareth (heart) centre. The energy is then modified into the energy of the particular deity as it travels through the image built up on the sphere of sensation. This is akin to white light being modified by passing through a stained glass window. Any energy coming from the magician will be a reflection of the deity unless he is deliberately channelling or directing other energy.

One final point to consider is the nature of the deities, the Goddesses and Gods themselves. The Golden Dawn traditionally viewed the deities as symbols of universal forces, which the magician could use as he or she willed. While respect was counselled and required, the Gods and Goddesses were never worshipped. From wherever we approach the Golden Dawn, from whatever angle we look at it, the use of Godforms calls us to seriously examine our attitude towards the Gods and Goddesses. We all need to make our own mind up here, find our own way to relate to these Beings, however we see them. What I can advise here though is to do exactly what has been said – please make up your own *mind*. Do not enter the practice of working with Gods unless you have previously thought about it deeply. An unconscious approach to these powers or Beings may be more problematic than a conscious utilitarian and disrespectful approach.

INVOCATION – STANDARD GOLDEN DAWN RITUALS

So far in this book we have looked at the Golden Dawn tradition, its underpinning frameworks of the Qabalah and the principles of sacred names and sacred images. In Chapter Two we learnt how to clear our energy fields and consciousness through banishment. Chapter Three introduced us to the techniques of meditation and divination, both of which require the techniques and practices of Chapter Two to be effective. In Chapter Four we began to look at the invitation and invocation of sacred forces, but limited our exploration to the area of life and the world easiest to affect – our own energy systems. In this and the next chapter we take what we have learnt and explored in all these chapters and examine how to affect areas beyond ourselves – our temples, our homes, and the world – through magical invocation.

When studying invocation we have to realise that it is one of the most glamorised and popular areas of Golden Dawn and Pagan magic as it is practiced in the world today. Within the popular culture and much of the New Age and magical community, invocation, along with its complementary technique of evocation, *is* magic itself. The magician is seen as someone who calls forth spiritual powers, Beings and magical currents to work her will in the world. Little thought is given as to why the magician may do this, or the many various disciplines required to enable the magician to invoke effectively – such as those detailed in the preceding chapters. Nor has there been much analysis of the methods and rationale behind invocatory techniques by contemporary magicians or Pagans. The result has led to the production of books, internet sites and even training materials from Lodges and Covens that simply give the words used in the invocation as the invocation itself. As we shall see, the words of invocation, while important, are only a small aspect of the whole process.

We may define invocation as the bringing forth or calling **into** ourselves, a temple, a physical space or an object, some specific and desired force, energy, astral current or deity. Good invocations will work at the etheric, astral and mental levels. Really excellent invocations will also involve the spiritual plane. The physical plane is not affected – at least outside of fantasy novels, myth or delusion. Invocation differs from **evocation,** which from one point of view calls something **out** of us, or from another point of view, calls something **out** of whatever inner realm it normally inhabits.

Since invocation works upon the inner planes, it requires effort and magical work to be enacted upon those planes. This is why the most beautiful invocations in the world, if read by a computer or a BBC newsreader will have absolutely no effect. Nothing would be occurring on the inner planes. The specific spiritual blessings we are seeking to connect with and call into our temple need a connecting point to the temple. This can either be through the subtle bodies of the magicians involved or the subtle components of the temple itself. In the first case, as part of dramatic invocation, the spiritual energy comes first into the magician's subtle bodies. She then directs it from her sphere out into the temple. In the second case, a portal or opening is made in the subtle component of the temple, which is linked directly to the spiritual blessing required. This linking of the inner aspects of a physical room is not easy and is why invocations are normally only attempted in consecrated temples or circles. The act of consecration and the repetition of spiritual work within a room affect its subtle and inner nature, making it more in harmony with the forces and blessings generally desired to be invoked.

The creation of portals within a temple through which specific forces can be invoked is one of the main aims of group ceremonial magic. Such a portal not only affects and transforms the operator who invokes the portal, but potentially everyone in the temple also. By now you would be familiar with this technique as this is exactly what the inscriptions of the pentagrams achieve in the Lesser Invoking Ritual of the Pentagram. One of the main gifts the Golden Dawn has given to the broader magical and Pagan communities is a logical series of standard, potent and transparent techniques designed to invoke specific energies and spiritual blessings through temple portals. This is all done with the minimum of fuss and very little waffle. Unlike other traditions that offer a mish mash of invocatory techniques and practices, the GD with its coherence and rationality, its straightforward and explicable approach to magic, presents a series of techniques to create portals and invoke spiritual blessings from all the realms within the subtle universe. We will examine these portal creation techniques and their inner workings in depth in this chapter before moving onto examine dramatic invocation in the next. The techniques are:

The Lesser Ritual of the Pentagram (discussed in Chapter Two)
The Lesser Ritual of the Hexagram (discussed in Chapter Two)
The Rose-Cross Ceremony
The Analysis of the Keyword
The Supreme Ritual of the Pentagram
The Watchtower Ceremony
The Supreme Ritual of the Hexagram

As with most magical work, the primary effect of these ceremonies is within the Yetziratic or astral realm. The ceremonies work by connecting with Briatic currents and powers and bringing them into the world of Yetzira, thereby promoting balanced and clear change directed by will. Hopefully we are also grounded and clear enough to Earth these blessings into the realm of Assiah, the material realm, changing our world and everyday life. Working within these realms, the ceremonies all make heavy use of the two key principles of the Golden Dawn; names and images, and colours. Specifically, within the world of Yetzira, the Pentagram and Watchtower ceremonies work with the elemental powers, though at differing levels and in different ways. The Hexagram techniques work with the planetary powers and those of the Sephiroth. The Rose-Cross focuses largely upon the Sephira of Tiphareth and the blessings of Christ. The table below summarises the main realm of the effects of each ritual. Please bear in mind this mapping is not hard and fast, and a ceremony can, at times, affect realms not directly related to it. Also bear in mind, once again, that 'the map is not the territory' and the only way to understand all this is to actually work with the ceremonies and spiritual powers themselves.

Table 5: Subtle Planes Affected by Golden Dawn Rituals

Ceremony	Main Realms of Direct Effect
Lesser Ritual of the Pentagram	Sub-elements of Earth in Malkuth of Yetzira.
Lesser Ritual of the Hexagram (generic)	Four elements of the 32nd path between Yesod and Malkuth in Yetzira.
Rose-Cross Ritual	Tiphareth of Yetzira.

Analysis of the Keyword	Tiphareth of Yetzira, drawing on Chesed, Geburah and Kether of Yetzira.
Supreme Ritual of the Pentagram	The full four elements in Yetzira: Earth having its main centre of effect in Malkuth of Yetzira; Air, Tiphareth of Yetzira; Water, Chesed of Yetzira; and Fire, Geburah of Yetzira.
Watchtower Ceremony	The full four elements in Yetzira: Earth having its main centre of effect in Malkuth of Yetzira; Air, Tiphareth of Yetzira; Water, Chesed of Yetzira; and Fire, Geburah of Yetzira.
Lesser Ritual of the Hexagram of the Moon	The four elements as they occur within Yesod of Yetzira.
Lesser Ritual of the Hexagram of Mercury	The four elements as they occur within Hod of Yetzira.
Lesser Ritual of the Hexagram of Venus	The four elements as they occur within Netzach of Yetzira.
Lesser Ritual of the Hexagram of the Sun	The four elements as they occur within Tiphareth of Yetzira.
Lesser Ritual of the Hexagram of Mars	The four elements as they occur within Geburah of Yetzira.
Lesser Ritual of the Hexagram of Jupiter	The four elements as they occur within Chesed of Yetzira.
Lesser Ritual of the Hexagram of Saturn	The four elements as they occur within Binah of Yetzira. May also, on occasions, be used with Chokmah or Kether of Yetzira.
Supreme Ritual of the Hexagram of the Moon	Yesod of Yetzira or the planetary energy of the Moon within Yetzira.
Supreme Ritual of the Hexagram of Mercury	Hod of Yetzira or the planetary energy of Mercury within Yetzira.
Supreme Ritual of the Hexagram of Venus	Netzach of Yetzira or the planetary energy of Venus within Yetzira.
Supreme Ritual of the Hexagram of the Sun	Tiphareth of Yetzira or the planetary energy of the Sun within Yetzira.
Supreme Ritual of the Hexagram of Mars	Geburah of Yetzira or the planetary energy of Mars within Yetzira.
Supreme Ritual of the Hexagram of Jupiter	Chesed of Yetzira or the planetary energy of Jupiter within Yetzira.
Supreme Ritual of the Hexagram of Saturn	Binah of Yetzira or the planetary energy of Saturn within Yetzira. May also, on occasions, be used with Chokmah or Kether of Yetzira.

A couple of points to bear in mind:

◆ The Supreme Hexagram rituals, with enough spiritual integrity and deep inner contacts, may affect the powers of the Briatic world. So for example, the Supreme Hexagram of Mars can potentially have effects upon Geburah in Briah. However, this again is very advanced magic and mystical experience, and most of the people who believe they have achieved such a state are in actuality blinded by their own state of illusion.

◆ When working with the paths that connect the Sephiroth on the Tree there are a few different approaches. One of the most sensible and common is simply to use two sets of rituals, one pertaining to each of the two Sephiroth connected by the Path. For example, if we were working within the inner realm symbolised by the Path of Peh, connecting Hod and Netzach, we would use hexagrams of both Mercury and Venus. Another approach is to determine the appropriate ritual with reference to the correspondences to the Paths listed in Chapter One. Peh corresponds to Mars and we would use the Hexagram of Mars. However we should be clear we are using this hexagram to work with the powers of the Path of Peh not the sphere of Mars, and the ritual would be altered accordingly. The exact changes will be clear when we examine the ritual later in this chapter. Which method we use is largely a matter for personal choice and conviction as both seem to work for different people.

Once we have really understood this analysis, the sheer utility and power of these ceremonies then begins to take shape. We now have a map of a number of techniques through which we can invoke the blessings of the complete inner realm of Yetzira, the realm of magic. With this map and our knowledge of Qabalah we can quickly ascertain what rituals can help us in invocation. Of course these particular techniques from the Golden Dawn are not full invocations and other work may be required to connect fully with the spiritual blessings we desire. They do however link and open our space and our spheres to the realms from which we seek the spiritual blessings that will transform us and serve the One. The 'other work' just mentioned will be detailed in the next chapter. All the rituals that follow rely for their effectiveness upon the method of vibrating or intoning the sacred names called 'the vibratory formula of the Middle Pillar'. So before examining each of these techniques in turn, we will look at this process.

THE VIBRATORY FORMULA OF THE MIDDLE PILLAR

This technique seems to be an original Golden Dawn innovation. I have found no earlier references to anything like it; though a Sufi I met a few years back said that certain schools of Sufism have used a similar process for centuries. It is used to awaken a greater degree of power and energy from the names we vibrate. Please do not feel overwhelmed when you look at this technique. After several months spent vibrating the divine names within the LRP and the Middle Pillar, the process will flow easier than you expect.

The vibratory formula rests upon several magic principles for its effectiveness, many of which we have already covered.

◆ Any force or power exists both within the human being ('microcosm', or small world) and within the universe ('macrocosm' or large world). In this perennial magical tradition, the human being is mirror or reflection of the whole universe.
◆ There is a natural polarity or current of energy that exists between any inner human force and the corresponding outer, universal force. One of the aims of magic is to strengthen this polarity.
◆ The awakening of either force, microcosmic or macrocosmic, may induce the awakening of the corresponding force. When the macrocosmic, or actual in-the-sky moon, is full, our own inner full moon energy is awakened. Similarly, if we awaken our own inner full moon energy we can potentially awaken and call forth macrocosmic full moon energy into our temple that can be felt and experienced by others – regardless of whether the physical moon is full or not.
◆ Inward visualisation of different colours awaken different energies.

THE PRACTICE OF THE VIBRATORY FORMULA

The description here is a simplification and codification of the published Golden Dawn techniques, which vary slightly within a number of published documents. This is the technique to learn and practice for this formula. Once learnt it can be applied to any name you vibrate. In ritual and group ceremony the technique is done at considerably more speed than the practice described here. Also, standing in the form of a cross and the Neophyte Signs are dropped. These are useful aids for mastering the practice, but once mastered they are not required in ritual, though some magicians and Orders retain them.

LBRP.

Relax with some deep breaths for a minute or two. Use the four-fold breath as taught in Chapter One. Keep up the four-fold breath for the rest of the practice. All other actions will be in time with the breath.

Stand in the form of a cross facing East. This cross formula brings about a sense of balance to the etheric energy within the body. Throughout the initial practice sessions, it may take a while to achieve the full visualisations. If this is the case do not suffer unduly and drop the form of the cross until you are ready to vibrate.

Visualise before you, several feet away from your body, a cloud of divine white light.

Once you have achieved this and the image of the cloud can be maintained easily, it is time to visualise the name to be vibrated resting upon the cloud. If the name is Hebrew, they should be seen in Hebrew; if Enochian the English equivalent as indicated in this book will suffice. All names should be visualised in the appropriate colour required. For the minor rituals of the LRP and LRH visualising the names in flashing gold will suffice. Ideally, for the major rituals the names should be visualised with each individual letter coloured to the King Scale of Colour as published in the Golden Dawn and reproduced in table two of Chapter One. However, achieving such a level of visualisation with each individual letter a different colour is not possible for many newcomers to the Golden Dawn. Nor is it required for most purposes. It will suffice here to visualise the name in the corresponding colour of the force to which the name belongs. So if you are vibrating a divine name of Water, use blue; divine name of Hod, use orange. For names of Kether which should be white, see them outlined in flashing gold.

Now empty your lungs. On the next inhalation imagine you are breathing in the name and cloud of white light. As you breathe in, inwardly vibrate the name. See the name and cloud enter through your nose and then rest in the centre of your chest, in the heart and Tiphareth centre.

Pause, feeling and seeing the cloud of light and the coloured name pulsating in your Tiphareth centre.

On the next inhalation imagine a ray of white light comes from above your crown, Kether, originating from your Higher and Divine Genius. It moves through the top of your head and comes to rest in the heart centre and causes the name there to grow larger and brighter. As this happens inwardly vibrate the name.

On the next out-breath, visualise the name moving down the rest of your central column to rest under your feet, in your Malkuth centre.

Feel and see the name under your feet, and as you do so inwardly vibrate the name. Keep the name there until you are ready to vibrate outwardly. Visualise the name strongly as you wait.

When ready, on an inhalation draw the name back up to your heart and then, without a pause, vibrate the name outwardly. Traditionally this is done using Projecting Sign from the Neophyte Grade. Instructions for giving this sign and its magical effects are described in Chapter Ten.

As the name is outwardly vibrated, see it go out of your auric sphere to the ends of the universe in that direction. This will happen quickly. Once there, the name awakens the macrocosmic, universal power of the name.

On the next inhalation draw into your auric sphere the macrocosmic name. See it come from the direction, in much larger letters than the name you sent out. Traditionally this is done using the Sign of Silence. Again, see Chapter Ten for information regarding this sign. Drawing back the reflux of the awakened macrocosmic name and blessings can literally be overwhelming. Israel Regardie recommended having something soft beneath you in case the sudden influx of energy caused you to fall! I have never experienced the reflux of the name to this degree, but it is often very powerful, so be prepared.

Pause and feel the energy in your aura and subtle bodies.

SOME POINTERS ON THE VIBRATORY FORMULA

During a banishing ritual, the name is visualised taking with it to the ends of the universe all the unbalanced energy associated with that name. This is then burnt up or dissolved at the communion point of the microcosmic and macrocosmic names and then recycled by the universe. Some magicians then forgo seeing the large Macrocosmic names being drawn back in. Some retain this procedure. Experiment and see what works for you.

During ritual when you need to inscribe lineal forms, such as the pentagram in the Supreme Ritual of the Pentagram, it is important to time your breath to match your hand movements. There is no one way of doing this. Provided it is clear and consistent and the required effects are produced, it is fine. Brevity is a must in group ceremony, and we need to learn to time our inhalations to be able to *produce powerful, short vibrations* when needed. Practice here is the key. Personal experience and experimentation with this formula is the only way to make it work for you in your vibration of divine names. As you experiment with the breaths etc, it is important to include five key aspects of the ritual.

◆ Seeing the name before you in some fashion.
◆ Drawing the name into your heart and then down to below your feet.
◆ Infusing the name with the power and light of Kether.
◆ Projecting the name out to awaken the Macrocosmic force of the name.
◆ (Except when banishing) Drawing the awakened force into your being or temple.

THE ROSE-CROSS RITUAL

Unlike the other rituals discussed here, the Rose-Cross is designed to focus mostly upon the energies and blessings of a single Sephira, that of Tiphareth. It cannot be adapted for any other Sephira or plane. It also is a method of invoking the blessings of Christ and the mystery of His Incarnation. It has been a favourite of Christian orientated magicians and practitioners since the early days of the Golden Dawn. However, as it rests upon a universal spiritual principle, and its benefits, beauty and transformation can be accessed by a person of any faith who approaches it with care and respect. We will give the ritual first followed by the inner workings and symbolism. For this ritual it may necessary to refer to diagrams 13-15 as you read.

INSTRUCTIONS FOR THE ROSE-CROSS RITUAL

If a Lesser Banishing Ritual of the Pentagram has not been performed, perform the Qabalistic Cross.

1. From your altar, light a stick of incense. The most suitable fragrances are frankincense, sandalwood or myrrh.
2. Go to the South-East corner of the temple or room. Inscribe the lineal Rose-Cross figure with the incense stick as shown diagram 12.

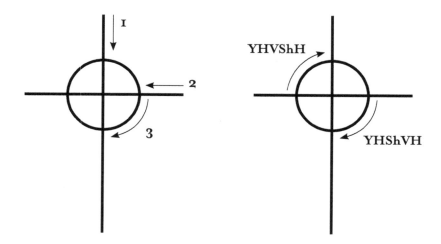

Diagram 12: Lineal Form of   Diagram 13: Tracing of the
the Rose-Cross   Divine Names on the Rose-Cross

3. Touch the centre of the Rose-Cross with the incense stick and vibrate
    YHShVH (Yeh-hesh-u-ah).
4. Holding the incense stick at the level of the centre of the Rose-Cross
    move to the South-West.
5. Trace another Rose-Cross and vibrate **YHShVH**.
6. Holding the incense stick at the level of the centre of the Rose-Cross
    move to the North-West.
7. Trace another Rose-Cross and vibrate **YHShVH**.
8. Holding the incense stick at the level of the centre of the Rose-Cross
    move to the North-East.
9. Trace another Rose-Cross and vibrate **YHShVH**.
10. Holding the incense stick at the level of the centre of the Rose-Cross
    return to the South-East to complete your circle and touch the centre
    of the already existing Rose-Cross with the incense stick.
11. Holding the incense stick at the level of the centre of the Rose-Cross
    move to the South-West.
12. Turn around and proceed across the temple towards the North-East,
    slowly raising the incense stick above you as you move.
13. In the centre of the temple, face above and trace another Rose-Cross
    (above you) and vibrate **YHShVH**.
14. Continue on to the North-East, slowly lowering the incense stick to
    the height of the centre of the Rose-Cross.

15. At the North-East, touch the centre of the already existing Rose-Cross with the incense stick.

16. Turn around and proceed towards the South-West, slowly lowering the incense stick as you do so.

17. In the centre of the temple face below and trace another Rose-Cross (below you) and vibrate **YHShVH**.

18. Continue on to the South-West, slowly raising the incense stick to the previous height as you do so.

19. At the South-West, touch the centre of the already existing Rose-Cross with the incense stick.

20. Proceed on towards the North-West.

21. At the North-West, touch the centre of the already existing Rose-Cross with the incense stick.

22. Turn around and proceed across the temple towards the South-East, slowly raising the incense stick above you as you move.

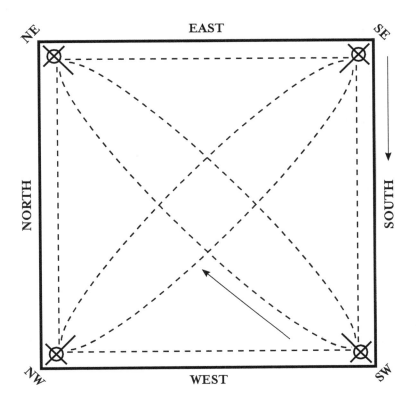

Diagram 14: Movements in the Rose-Cross Ritual

23. In the centre of the temple face above and touch the centre of the Rose-Cross already above you and vibrate **YHShVH**.
24. Continue on to the South-East, slowly lowering the incense stick to the height of the centre of the Rose-Cross.
25. At the South-East, touch the centre of the already existing Rose-Cross with the incense stick.
26. Turn around and proceed towards the North-West, slowly lowering the incense stick as you do so.
27. In the centre of the temple face below and touch the centre of the Rose-Cross already below you and vibrate **YHShVH**.
28. Continue on to the North-West, slowly raising the incense stick to the previous height as you do so.
29. At the North-West, touch the centre of the already existing Rose-Cross with the incense stick.
30. Proceed on towards the North-East.
31. At the North-East, touch the centre of the already existing Rose-Cross with the incense stick.
32. Proceed on towards the South-East.
33. At the South-East, touch the centre of the already existing Rose-Cross with the incense stick.
34. Staying in the South-East, trace another larger Rose-Cross figure. As you trace the bottom half of the circular rose vibrate **YHShVH**, and without a pause, as you trace the top half of the rose vibrate **YHVShH** (Yeh-hoh-vah-shah). Pause and touch the centre of the rose with the incense. See diagram 13.
35. Go to the centre of the room, face East and re-affirm and visualise the six Rose-Crosses around you, above you and below you. There is no need to finish this ritual with a Qabalistic Cross, though some people do.

SYMBOLISM AND ANALYSIS OF THE ROSE-CROSS RITUAL

Unlike the Pentagram and Hexagram techniques the Rose-Cross does not create an astral portal through which the consciousness of the magician can be directed. Nor is it open to as much modification as the Hexagram and Pentagram techniques. It does however use the same basic principles and is one of the 'standard' Golden Dawn rituals that are learnt and mastered by GD magicians worldwide. The ritual should always be preceded by at least the Qabalistic Cross. It does not have to be closed by the Qabalistic Cross, and in fact some GD magicians believe that it should not. The ritual fully encloses the temple or room with a stilling effect on the astral and etheric levels, which is self-enclosed and often womb-like. Some people believe that rituals like the Qabalistic Cross are inharmonious with this feeling. The ritual is often concluded by the Analysis of the Keyword, which is consonant with the nature of the Rose-Cross. Instructions for the Analysis of the Keyword are given next in this chapter.

The Rose-Cross figures should be visualised as flashing golden crosses surmounted by a ruby red rose of five petals in the centre. If this visualisation is not possible, then visualise the lineal form of the Rose-Cross in flashing gold light. Use the vibratory formula of the Middle Pillar when you vibrate the divine names. When moving from one point to another visualise a veil of white light being drawn across as you move. This is also applied when moving from corner to ceiling or floor and back again. The ritual is a very effective preparation for deep meditation or any operation that requires a profound level of peace and serenity. The ritual, unlike the LBRP, should not be used to banish any unwanted forces or vibrations, but merely to quiet and astrally seal the atmosphere of a place. If unwanted vibrations or feelings are felt, use the LBRP, not the Rose-Cross – or an LBRP then a RC. As a general rule the RC should not replace the LBRP and I have seen serious problems occur when this is done on a long term basis.

The two divine names used within the ritual contain much potent symbolism. Yeheshuah (YHShVH) or יהשוה is one symbolic version of the Hebrew name of Jesus. It represents the human being receiving the influx of the Holy Spirit, symbolised by the letter Shin (Sh). With the influx of such a deep level of consciousness and spiritual grace, the elemental nature of humanity is transformed. This is seen in the Tetragrammaton, YHVH, being transformed by the spirit, Shin (Sh) to form YHShVH. Here the Yod (Y) of YHVH represents Fire, the first Heh (H), Water, the Vau (V), Air, and the final Heh (H), Earth. The name YHShVH symbolizes the deep spirit living within humanity, as shown by the role of Jesus in Christian mythology. This links in with the consciousness of Tiphareth, which is the Sephira attributed to the Rose-Cross.

When looking at the attributions of the elements upon the Pentagram and the name YHShVH we see that the name is formed following the letters from Yod in an anti-clockwise motion; diagram 15. The direction is anti-clockwise (to the left), because Hebrew is written to the left. The name also relates to the Tree of Life as shown in diagram 16. The second name Yehovashah (YHVShH), vibrated only once at the end of the ritual, is also a name of Jesus. The single vibration of this name forms the function

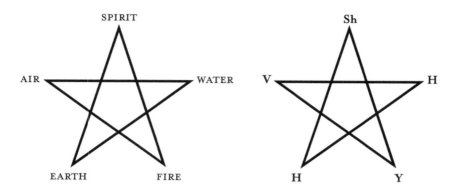

Diagram 15: YHShVH Attributed to the Points of the Pentagram

of Earthing and grounding to the world of Assiah the spiritual blessings brought about by the repeated vibrations of YHShVH. YHVShH shows that the Holy Spirit, the letter Shin (Sh), is placed between Earth (final 'H') and the other three elements (YHV). It is thus the transmitter of the spiritual blessings invoked to the Earth plane or Assiah. The function of YHVShH in helping to ground the spiritual blessings of the name is also shown by the alternate correspondence of Shin on the Tree of Life to Yesod, diagram 16. Here the Holy Spirit, Shin, resides in Yesod, which

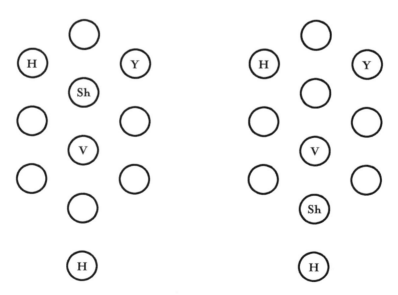

Diagram 16: YHShVH Attributed to the Tree of Life

calls to mind certain links between Yesod and Daath in the Qabalah. The single vibration of this name fully Earths the divine blessings, since by its vibration the full Middle Pillar below Kether has now been called into operation.

EFFECTS OF THE RITUAL

The effects of this ritual are quite unlike that of any other Golden Dawn ceremony. Most important are the spiritual blessings invoked by the divine names. The mystery being enacted and revealed here is that of the Incarnation of Christ – that the One Being is also human, flesh and blood like us. This is a central and core mystery of the Christian esoteric tradition and I suspect this ceremony was derived from one of the Christian esoteric Orders which preceded the Golden Dawn. The mystery of the Incarnation is firstly worked here through the powers of the name (as shown above) and also a number of other factors.

Firstly, the Rose-Cross is inscribed at the six directions of space, enclosing the temple area completely. These six directions refer not only to Tiphareth as the sixth Sephira, but also to the cube, which has six faces. The cube is one of the main symbols of matter and the physical universe. Jesus, as Spirit Embodied, is then called into the temple from all the directions that define this real flesh-and-blood existence. He thus becomes present everywhere, all around us within the temple (Christian Mystics assure us He is present everywhere at once). This is why we vibrate His name to all directions, not to a specific quarter or place in the circle like the Pentagram and Hexagram rituals.

Also of interest is the use of an incense stick as a tool, an innovation which is atypical of the Golden Dawn and points therefore to something important. Firstly, the smoke from the incense helps spread the etheric energy from the intonation of the names around the temple. It helps to create the sphere of etheric energy and blessings that nearly everyone who witnesses the Rose-Cross senses. It also helps to ground and Earth spiritual blessings of Christ from the mental plane (the names) through the astral plane (the images) to the etheric (the incense) and even into the physical. For these reasons performing the Rose-Cross ritual using another tool or simply the hand is not as effective.

The number of vibrations of the divine names is also important. In total YHShVH is repeated nine times. These nine repetitions refer to Yesod, and thus to ungrounded force, as seen by the earlier examination of the letters of the name placed the upon the Tree. The single vibration of the name YHVShH brings the number of vibrations up to ten, the number of Malkuth, thus Earthing the force. It also explains why the two names are vibrated without a pause as the Rose is drawn in the final Rose-Cross. The documents reproduced in *The Golden Dawn* and copied in other works instruct the magician to merely link up with the Rose-Cross below on the second passing and not to vibrate the divine name (our step 27). These instructions do not follow the original Golden Dawn practice, where the name was vibrated at this step. Forgoing this vibration could lead to an imbalance between above and below and a lesser degree of the Earthing of the forces.

THE ANALYSIS OF THE KEYWORD

While this ritual does not function like the others under discussion I am placing it here as it is a classic example of the invocatory formulas used within the Golden Dawn. It is also often used as a follow-on to several of the rituals here and the LVX Signs within it are also used in other rituals. Many people, magicians and otherwise, believe that this ritual is one of the most beautiful and potent rituals within the Golden Dawn tradition. It is used heavily by magicians both within the Golden Dawn and outside. It stems from the opening of the Adeptus Minor initiation ceremony and contains much symbolism pertinent to that grade and Tiphareth.

DESCRIPTION OF THE KEYWORD RITUAL

Some form of ritual that uses the energies and symbolism of Tiphareth needs to be performed as a precursor to this ritual. This means, for most occasions, a LBRH (preceded by a LBRP) or a Rose-Cross ritual needs to be performed. The Rose-Cross does not take the place of a banishing ritual and an LBRP may need to precede it. The LVX signs are shown in diagram 17.

1. Stand facing East. If you are using a central altar, be West of the altar.
2. Relax and centre for a few minutes.
3. Place your arms out in the form of a cross. Breathe deeply for another minute.
4. Vibrate: **I**
5. Vibrate: **N**
6. Vibrate: **R**

7.   Vibrate: **I**
    (Some people vibrate all four letters as one word: **INRI**).
8.   Vibrate: **י YOD**
9.   Vibrate: **נ NUN**
10.   Vibrate: **ר RESH**
11.   Vibrate: **י YOD**
    (Some people vibrate all four letters as one word: **י ר נ י YOD NUN RESH YOD**).
12.   Still in the form of a cross say: 'The Sign of Osiris Slain.'
13.   Move arms to make an L. Say: 'The Sign of the Mourning of Isis.'
14.   Move arms to make a V. Say: 'The Sign of Apophis and Typhon.'
15.   Fold arms on chest and bow head, to make an X. Say: 'The Sign of Osiris Risen.'

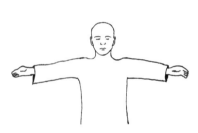

SIGN OF OSIRIS SLAIN

SIGN OF MOURNING ISIS

SIGN OF APOPHIS AND TYPHON

SIGN OF OSIRIS RISEN

Portal Sign 1, Opening the Veil: *Stand normally and extend your hands in front of you with the back of the hands touching, palms turned outward as if to spread open a veil or a curtain. Then, part the imagined curtain by making the motion to spread the imaginary curtain wide enough to walk through.*

Portal Sign 2, Closing the Veil: *Stand normally and extend your hands in front of you, arms and hands extended wide – as wide as the imagined curtain opened in the Opening of the Veil. Now close the imaginary curtain by bringing the hands together in front of you. As the hands meet, turn them so the backs of the hands are touching. Draw the hands back from in front of you to down by your side.*

Diagram 17: LVX Signs and Portal Grade Signs

16. Make the L shape (Mourning of Isis) once more and say: 'L'
17. Make the V shape (Apophis and Typhon) once more and say: 'V'
18. Make the X shape (Osiris Risen) once more and say: 'X'
19. Return arms to the form of a cross and say: 'Lux! The Light of the Cross.'
20. Say: 'Virgo, Isis, Mighty Mother'.
21. Say: 'Scorpio, Apophis, Destroyer'.
22. Say: 'Sol, Osiris, Slain and...'
23. Fold arms on chest in the X shape (Osiris Risen) and say: '...Risen'.
24. Lower arms by your sides. Slowly raise them and your head, to look up, arms towards the sky, palms inward, as you say: 'Isis. Apophis. Osiris.'
25. Looking up, vibrate: **IAO** (eeee-aaayyy-oooo).
26. If not in the vault vibrate: **EXARP. HCOMA. BITOM. NANTA.** (Ex-ar-pay; Hay-coh-mah; Bay-ee-toh-em; En-ah-en-tah) (Some people insist on this step, but some leave it out).
27. Lower hands as you say: 'Let the Divine White Light descend'.
28. Feel the divine light moving over and through you.

SYMBOLISM WITHIN THE ANALYSIS OF THE KEYWORD

This ritual in some ways is the Inner Order equivalent of the Qabalistic Cross. Not that the Qabalistic Cross is unused in the Inner Order. It still is, but the functions of the Qabalistic Cross as an opening point and a finishing point is often replaced by the Keyword within Inner Order work. The Qabalistic Cross's primary function is to link the Outer Order member with the Light and to balance that light within her in the form of a Cross. Just as the Qabalistic Cross symbolizes Malkuth, Yesod, Hod and Netzach (the Outer Order), the Keyword works with the formula of regeneration and redemption and uses the powers of Tiphareth (Osiris), Geburah (Apophis) and Chesed (Isis). It specifically uses the sacrificial principle to redeem the destructive side of the magician to bring about full compassion and the divine light. It thus symbolises the Inner Order work from Adeptus Minor (Tiphareth) to Adeptus Major (Geburah) and finally, Adeptus Exemptus (Chesed).

The form of the ritual reproduced here is not definitive. It changes slightly and is used differently throughout the Inner Order work and from ritual to ritual and Order to Order. However, these notes can be readily applied to any version with a bit of thought. These brief notes are also not meant to be definitive on the inner working of this ritual and only marginally explorative on its symbolism, which is vast and can easily involve many years of study. While the symbolism of the ritual and the symbol itself can be found in a few other books listed in the bibliography, few attempts at exploring the inner work have been published before. The multi-layered symbolism within the ritual should be studied in depth and meditated upon before performing it. In this way you will gain the full transformational benefits of the ceremony and not simply be moved by its power and beauty.

The Keyword is **I.N.R.I.** It is called the Keyword because the formula of magic and transformation contained within its symbolism is the key to the function and workings of the Adeptus Minor grade of the Golden Dawn. As we have seen, the GD uses the Qabalistic technique of embedding formulae within single passages, words or even letters. The multi-layered meaning of INRI is explored well in the works listed in the bibliography and I would benefit no-one in reproducing my own thoughts which are so indebted to those of others. Seek out the works mentioned or surf the Net.

This ritual centres on these four letters, INRI, which tradition says were written upon the cross of Jesus Christ as an abbreviation for 'Jesus of Nazareth, King of the Jews' (in Latin). There are, however, numerous other meanings regarding these four letters. For example, 'Igne Natura Renovatur Integra' which means 'All of nature is renewed by Fire.' The Hebrew letters for INRI are important here also: Yod, Nun, Resh, Yod. Here we are backtracking through history and moving behind the Christian formula to the ancient Hebrew, and ultimately linking with the formula of Osiris (recalling that the wisdom of Moses and the Hebraic Qabalah has its mythical roots in the Egyptian Mysteries).

The Zodiacal and planetary correspondences of these letters also point to a deep mystery embedded within them: Virgo, Scorpio, Sun, Virgo. Using the Tarot correspondences this formula may be rendered like this: the **Hermit** moves through **Death** and is reborn through the **Sun**, to become the **Hermit** once more.

As part of the ritual, three Egyptian Gods who embody these mysteries are invoked and worked with: Isis (I), Apophis (Set) (N) and Osiris (R). Put simply, we see here the mystery of the regeneration of the Higher Self from the death of the lower identity through the illumination of the shadow or demonic self, which is symbolised by Set, Death and Scorpio. The repeated performance of this ritual energizes this formula into our being, thus paving the way for deep and full transformation and service to the One. Of interest also is the use of the Godform of Christ, overlaying a parallel mythology. This was done, as in other advanced

Golden Dawn ceremonies, to help fuse the various mystery systems and symbols of antiquity into a workable whole, which may be approached by people of any faith who are open to the Divine and to service. It also signals the depths of this universal mystery – the mystery of divine transformation within the human being – by holding its passage across at least four mythic traditions.

Another central word throughout the ritual is LVX, Latin 'lux', for Light. The L is attributed to Isis, the V to Apophis and the X to Osiris. The first letter of the names of these three Gods produces the composite divine name, **IAO**. This name was considered by some Gnostic traditions to be the supreme name of God, and relates to Kether upon the Tree of Life.

The ritual also embodies the mystery of the Solar cycle throughout the year. The various arm movements in the ritual invoke the four turning points of the solar cycle. The Sign of Osiris Slain (the form of the Cross) refers to the two Equinoxes. The Equinox is a time of balance (between day and night) thus linking to the balance of the Cross. Also at the Equinox, either the light or the darkness is giving way or being sacrificed to make room for the other, which provides another link to the sacrificial symbolism of the cross. The Sign of the Mourning of Isis (the L) refers to the Summer Solstice. Isis mourns the life force of Osiris who was cut down at His peak, just as the force of the sun is at its peak at the Summer Solstice. The Sign of Apophis (the V) refers to the Winter Solstice; the restriction of space between the hands reflecting the restriction of the light at this time of year. The Sign of Osiris Risen, the crossed arms on the chest, refers to the synthesis of the difference between the light/dark ratio at the Solstices and Equinoxes. This links in with the synthesising nature of the Sign – using the combined energies of the three previous signs to produce redemption or regeneration.

THE INNER WORKINGS OF THE ANALYSIS OF THE KEYWORD

Because of the complex nature of this ritual, I will reproduce segments of the ritual and then a commentary upon them.

1.   Stand facing East. If you are using a central altar, be West of the altar.
2.   Relax and centre for a few minutes.
3.   Place your arms out in the form of a cross. Breathe deeply for another minute.

Commentary: We face East, as in most Golden Dawn rituals, to link to the new light and life of dawn and related spiritual blessings. The Cross here balances us within a four-fold formula. It therefore has links to the four lettered names about to be vibrated. Also, the extended period of holding the arms out as the Cross places physical strain upon our shoulders and back muscles and thus opens our etheric energy centres in the shoulders and the heart. These three centres related to Chesed, Geburah and Tiphareth, the energies worked with in this ritual. It is best to wait to begin vibration until some small strain is first felt but not until it becomes painful.

4. Vibrate: **I**
5. Vibrate: **N**
6. Vibrate: **R**
7. Vibrate: **I**

Commentary: Some people vibrate all four letters as one word: **INRI**. I have found that the difference is not always that great in terms of the blessings of the divine light received. However, in understanding the individual form aspects of the word and thus the whole formula of the Adeptus Minor mysteries, the separate vibration may be more effective. In group ritual the single vibration is used for brevity. These letters (or the word) should be vibrated using the full vibratory formula of the Middle Pillar, while remaining in the cross. The colours of the letters should either be flashing gold or the colours of the corresponding Hebrew letters (see below). What occurs here is that not only are the spiritual powers of the letters invoked, but the actual formula of regeneration embedded within them is also brought into our spheres. This is hard to really articulate or put into words, but it occurs through the formula of energies behind the letters and the historical usage of the letters. It is quite distinct and the more we study the symbolism of the letters outside the ritual the more open our astral body, everyday consciousness will be to the mental plane blessings of the formula.

8. Vibrate: **י YOD**
9. Vibrate: **נ NUN**
10. Vibrate: **ר RESH**
11. Vibrate: **י YOD**

Commentary: This is essentially a repetition of the INRI letters above. They are vibrated according to the vibratory formula and are seen either in flashing gold or the colours given in table two.

12. Still in the form of a cross say: 'The Sign of Osiris Slain'.

Commentary: At this point we take on the Godform of Jesus Christ on the Cross. This is done by imagining yourself as Jesus. (There appears to be no traditional description of this Godform, presumably because the Golden Dawn leaders assumed everyone knew it well anyway.) Facing East, you should imagine yourself upon the Cross, exactly as Jesus. The Sun behind you is setting in the West, the Three Holy Women, without whom Christ would not be, are the foot of the Cross. This Godform is used to help you to open and identify with your approaching death, calmly and clearly, knowing it is a vehicle of ultimate compassion. You should feel it is your last few moments alive as Christ. This Godform activates the already open heart centre and brings forth the first stirring of the first aspect of the Tiphareth energies, that of sacrifice.

13. Move arms to make an L. Say: 'The Sign of the Mourning of Isis'.

Commentary: Here we take on the Isis in mourning Godform. The head, moving to the left shoulder, activates the Chesed centre. This occurs because the top of the head in this ritual is the centre of the Neschamah (the mental body) principle, and as this is moved down into the Chesed centre, Chesed becomes active. The upright right arm limits the power of the Geburah centre from the right shoulder, thus allowing the energy of astral and etheric bodies to be more open to the blessings of Chesed. The Godform here is of the traditional Isis figure, mourning with tears of grief moving down her eyes and cheeks. (Some Orders operating from a mystical Christian perspective use a Godform of a mourning Virgin Mary.) This Godform invokes the first stirring of the Mercy and compassion of the Chesedic energies. The Godform of Isis that can be used here is: 'Isis has the face and body of translucent gold. She is crowned with a Throne over a vulture head-dress of blue and orange. The vulture head is red. Her robe is of blue, bordered with gold. Her ornaments are blue and orange and she carries a blue ankh and a lotus wand with a green flower and a blue stem. She stands on blue and orange.'

14. Move arms to make a V. Say: 'The Sign of Apophis and Typhon'.

Commentary: Here we take on the Godform of Apophis, Typhon or Set. Once more there are no traditional descriptions of these forms for this ritual. The Godform of Omoo Szathan from the Neophyte Initiation ceremony can be used here: 'black bodied and skinned with a lizard-like head with a tail and standing on black. The Nemyss is olive green, collar of russet and citrine. He wears a white apron'. The two arms at the forty five degrees should be positioned so that the palms are facing away from the body. This sends the energy out of our auric sphere and helps invoke and bring forth the dispersing and destructive energy of the Godform and Geburah. The head thrown back, allows for the ascent of our own inner Setian or destructive forces to arise from the base of our spines, empowering the Godform. These forces are used and regenerated later. At this point it is essentially our own 'shadow' sides that are being called forth for control and transformation.

15. Fold arms on chest and bow head, to make an X. Say: 'The Sign of Osiris Risen'.

Commentary: By the quick movement and bowing of the head, all the energy and spiritual forces previously raised are drawn into the Tiphareth (heart) centre. Thus, the combination of the first aspect of Tiphareth (the sacrifice), the compassion of Chesed and the destruction of Geburah are all gathered together and synthesised to help bring about the second aspect of Tiphareth, rebirth. This is achieved also through lowering of the head and the crossing of the arms, the Geburic energy of the right shoulder moving to the left shoulder through the heart centre and vice-versa for Chesed. The arm positions show that Mercy and Severity both sacrifice themselves to their polar opposite; knowing that each alone is not balanced. They do this through the sphere of sacrifice and will, the heart, Tiphareth. The left arm should be placed over the right, indicating that Chesed, Mercy, is above Geburah, Severity, reflecting the order of Sephiroth on the Tree of Life. The lowering of the head brings our Neschamah (mental body) into our Tiphareth centre, awakening it further.

During this whole action we take on the Godform of Osiris Risen or the Resurrected Christ. This is the typical Osiris Godform from the Outer Order: 'He wears the tall white crown of the South (of Egypt), flanked by feathers striped white and blue. His face and skin are green, the eyes blue, and from his chin hangs the royal beard of authority and judgement, blue in colour and gold tipped. He wears a collar in bands of red, blue, yellow and black, and on his back is a bundle strapped across his chest by scarlet bands. He is in mummy wrappings to the feet, but his hands are free to hold a gold Phoenix wand, a blue crook and a red Scourge. The hands are green. His feet rest on a pavement of black and white'. This brings forth the second aspect of Tiphareth, rebirth, into our sphere. At this stage we have completed one enactment of the formula of the letters INRI, which we invoked at the beginning of the ritual.

16. Make the L shape once more and say: 'L'

Commentary: Here we visualise our two arms forming a brilliant white 'L', the joining point of which is in the heart, Tiphareth centre. When our arms move out of the sign, we should see the 'L' of light staying there, formed in our astral body. This and the subsequent letters will help attract the light of the LVX current from the inner Golden Dawn tradition into our astral body. On an etheric level the same energetic movements with the arms occur as in point 13.

17. Make the V shape once more and say: 'V'
18. Make the X shape once more and say: 'X'

Commentary: Once more we visualise our two arms forming brilliant white letters and allow them to remain in our sphere when our physical arms move out of the sign. The heart centre is once more the meeting point for the two arms of light.

19. Return arms to the form of a cross and say: 'Lux! The Light of the Cross.'

Commentary: Here we visualise our whole body as a brilliant cross of dazzling white light. We have now performed the second repetition of the INRI formula. The first focused upon the mythological transformation of the Gods with our own energies empowering the Godforms. This second repetition focused upon the hidden formula of the Light, LVX within INRI and within the forms of the Gods.

20. Say: 'Virgo, Isis, Mighty Mother'.

Commentary: We stay now in the form of the Cross of Light, energised fully from point 19, to attract into our spheres the deeper macrocosmic blessings associated with the Keyword. We begin these with the fusion of the energies of Virgo, Isis as the Great Mother. As we say these words we visualise above and before us, at the reaches of our auric sphere, the sign of Virgo (♍) in blue light, and then the image of Isis as Mother, as described previously, or any figure of Isis we are familiar with. This invokes these energies into our spheres, ready to be synthesised later. The image of Isis here should not be mourning and should be seen in intense glowing colours.

21. Say: 'Scorpio, Apophis, Destroyer'.

Commentary: The same as point 20 occurs here, but with a Scorpio sign (♏) in red light and the image of Apophis or Typhon as described earlier in glowing colours or any image of Set we are familiar with, also in glowing colours.

22. Say: 'Sol, Osiris, Slain and…'

Commentary: Again, the same, but we see the vivid image of sinking Sun rather than the symbol for the Sun. Then we see the image of Christ Crucified upon the Cross in vivid, glowing colours.

23. Fold arms on chest and say: '…Risen'.

Commentary: Etherically and astrally this is equivalent to point 15, with the drawing in of the various blessings into the Tiphareth centre. Here we see the image of Osiris Risen, as described earlier, in glowing colours at the edges of our auric sphere. This completes the third repetition of the INRI formula. In the first we used Godforms to awaken our own energies and shadow; in the second we invoked the Light of the Gods, and in the third the Gods themselves are imaged, as being before us. This is a systematic approach towards the culmination below.

24. Lower arms by your sides. Slowly raise them and your head, to look up, arms towards the sky, palms inward, as you say: 'Isis. Apophis. Osiris.'

Commentary: With our arms at our sides, we draw up our full energy towards Kether, opening as we do so our link to the Earth through our Malkuth. This will help Earth and ground the spiritual force and blessings we are about to invoke. As we raise our hands and eyes upwards we call the names of the Gods. Here we invoke the full power of Chesed, Geburah and Tiphareth. As we do so we visualise the streams of spiritual blessings as large coloured rays of light, coming into the edge of our auric spheres above us. The light does not move through the auric sphere into our physical body at this stage. As we say 'Isis' we see the Chesedic blue ray coming in. Then as we say 'Apophis', the Geburic red ray. Then finally as we say 'Osiris', the Tipharetic yellow ray. As all three of these rays of light come in, they combine to produce dazzling white light. This is a synthesis of these forces, above us now in our Microcosmic auric sphere.

25. Looking up, vibrate: **IAO** (eeee-aaayyy-oooo).

Commentary: This is the final climatic point of the ritual. With the Vibration of IAO, the divine white light just synthesised above us opens up and draws forth vast amounts of macrocosmic light and spiritual blessings. As we vibrate the name the light will expand and pour forth and we then open ourselves to receive it. The divine name here is the synthesis of the three Gods just invoked, and thus functions as the final 'I' of the INRI formula. We have thus completed four repetitions of the formula, bringing in the power ever more deeply as we go and also linking to the Qabalistic formula of YHVH. In terms of the progression outlined in the commentary to point 23, we have moved now from our own energies, to the Light, to the Gods and now to the sources of power that we clothe as the Gods, the Sephiroth.

26. If not in the vault vibrate: **EXARP. HCOMA. BITOM. NANTA.**

Commentary: Some people insist on this step, but some leave it out. I believe that it is a useful step when conducting the ritual as part of a group ceremony but may be omitted in our own practice. The vibration of these names literally moves the divine Light above us to the four quarters of the temple. It enlivens the whole temple with the Light. As we vibrate these names we visualise the light moving towards the East (Exarp), then West (Hcoma), then South (Bitom) and finally North (Nanta). These four Enochian names are the names of the spirit of the four elements and their vibration will help attract the light towards the elemental quarters.

27. Lower hands as you say: 'Let the Divine White Light descend'.

Commentary: With the slow movement of the hands downward, the divine light is brought into the temple or auric sphere and body. There is no actual visualisation or work here. At this point, if you have performed the ritual well, all you need to do is open yourself to the blessings of the light as it moves through you. The hands should be moved down to the sides, palms facing the Earth. This will allow the light to move easily through your auric sphere and to be Earthed and grounded through your Malkuth centre. When performed well you will find that the divine white light moves through the various subtle bodies, from mental body down to the physical. It thus re-vitalizes and re-energizes our whole being.

THE SUPREME RITUAL OF THE PENTAGRAM

These rituals use the full formula of the pentagram to invoke and banish the complete range of elemental energies. These rituals are contained in the Pentagram Lecture, an original GD document reproduced in part in Regardie's works, and it is recommended that you read that lecture in conjunction with these notes. These rituals should not be worked until mastery of the LRP, LRH, the Middle Pillar exercise and extensive work with the four elemental principles. As well as being a powerful method of invoking the elements, these rituals can, in advanced Golden Dawn magic, be used to invoke the Zodiacal forces also. The twelve Zodiacal powers are considered to embody the full powers of the Briatic world. The Sphere of the Zodiac corresponds to the Sephira of Chokmah, the highest Sephira within Briah. The God names that are associated with the Zodiacal powers are the twelve permutations of the four letters YHVH, the divine name of Chokmah. This is advanced Golden Dawn magic and traditionally was not approached until after extensive work within the Inner Order and will not be discussed here. We will first give the instructions for the ritual followed by a discussion on the symbolism and inner workings.

THE SUPREME INVOKING RITUAL OF THE PENTAGRAM INSTRUCTION

The methods of inscribing the various pentagrams and making the signs referred to below can be found in diagrams 17-19. The Hebrew spelling of the divine names has already been given in the description of the LRP in Chapter Two and table four in Chapter Four. The other names here are angelic or Enochian and when vibrated should be seen spelt as they are given here. The Supreme Banishing Ritual is performed in the same manner as the invoking but using the banishing forms of the Pentagram.

1. Stand in the centre of your temple space and perform the Qabalistic Cross.
2. Go to the Eastern quarter. Inscribe an invoking spirit active pentagram while vibrating **EXARP** (ex-ar-pay). (See diagram 18 for the inscriptions of the various pentagrams).
3. Inside this pentagram inscribe the spirit wheel sign while vibrating **AHIH** (eh-hey-yah).
4. Give the LVX signs towards the East.

5. Inscribe an invoking Air pentagram while vibrating **ORO IBAH AZOPI** (eh-roh ee-bah-hay ah-oh-zohd-pee).

6. Inside this pentagram inscribe the symbol of Aquarius while vibrating **YHVH** (Yod-Heh-Vow-Heh).

7. Give the Theoricus sign to the East. This sign and the other elemental signs are shown in diagram 19.

8. Touch again the centre of the pentagram, and keeping your arm at the same level, circle round the perimeter of the temple sun-wise until you face the Southern quarter.

9. Inscribe an invoking spirit active pentagram while vibrating **BITOM** (bay-ee-toh-em).

10. Inside this pentagram inscribe the spirit wheel while vibrating **AHIH** (eh-hey-yah).

11. Give the LVX Signs towards the South.

12. Inscribe an invoking Fire pentagram while vibrating **OIP TEAA PDOCE** (oh-ee-pay tay-ah-ah pay-doh-kay).

13. Inside this pentagram inscribe the sign of Leo while vibrating **ELOHIM** (Ell-oh-heem).

14. Give the Philosophus sign to the South.

15. Touch again the centre of the pentagram, and keeping your arm at the same level, circle round the perimeter of the temple sun-wise until you face the Western quarter.

16. Inscribe an invoking spirit passive pentagram while vibrating **HCOMA** (hay-coh-mah).

17. Inside this pentagram inscribe a spirit wheel while vibrating **AGLA** (ah-glah).

18. Give the LVX signs towards the West.

19. Inscribe an invoking Water pentagram while vibrating **MPH ARSL GAIOL** (em-pay-hay ar-sel gah-ee-ohl).

20. Inside this pentagram inscribe the sign of Scorpio while vibrating **EL** (Al).

21. Give the Practicus sign to the West.

22. Touch again the centre of the pentagram, and keeping your arm at the same level, circle round the perimeter of the temple sun-wise until you face the Northern quarter.

23. Inscribe an invoking spirit passive pentagram while vibrating **NANTA** (en-ah-en-tah).

24. Inside this pentagram inscribe a spirit wheel while vibrating **AGLA** (ah-glah).

25. Give the LVX signs towards the North.

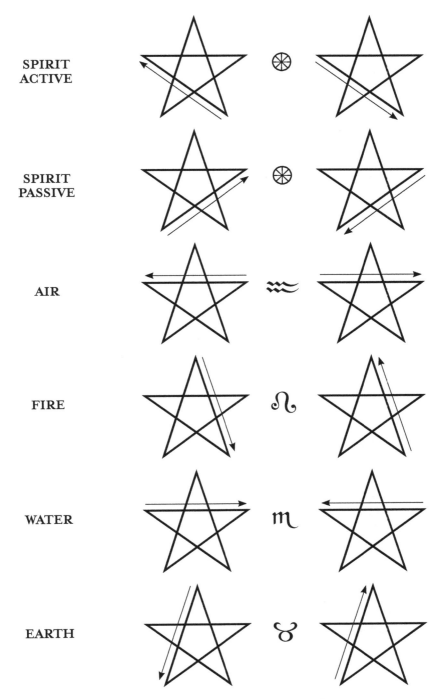

Diagram 18: Spirit and Elemental Pentagram Inscriptions

26. Inscribe an invoking Earth pentagram while vibrating **MOR DIAL HCTGA** (em-mor dee-ahl hec-tay-gah).
27. Inside this pentagram inscribe the sign of Taurus while vibrating **ADNI** (Ah-don-aye).
28. Give the Zelator sign to the North.
29. Touch again the centre of the pentagram and keeping your arm at the same level, circle round the perimeter of the temple sun-wise until you face the Eastern quarter once more, completing the circle of place.
30. Go to the centre of the temple, facing East. Hold your arms out in the form of a cross and say/vibrate:

"Before me **RAPHAEL** (Rah-Feyh-El)
Behind me **GABRIEL** (Gahb-Bree-El)
On my left hand, **MICHAEL** (Mee-Cai-El)
On my right hand, **AURIEL** (Ohr-Ree-El)

For about me flame the pentagrams.
And above me shines the six-rayed star."

31. Finish with the Qabalistic Cross.

BRIEF INNER WORKINGS OF THE SUPREME PENTAGRAM RITUALS

1. Qabalistic Cross. Normal inner workings.

2-3. Inscription of Spirit Pentagram. Traditionally the magician at this point would be advised to take on the form of their Higher and Divine Genius or higher self. This presupposed connection with the Higher Genius through work following the Adeptus Minor initiation. By taking on this form, like a Godform, the magician was connecting his Yetziratic self and astral body with his Neschamah, as symbolised by the form of the Higher Genius. However, without a deep connection and specific image given to you via prolonged contact with the Higher Genius, such advice is worthless. It is far better at this point to simply imagine your whole aura filled with dazzling white light. The visualisation of light within your aura needs to be practiced for an extended period before using it during the SIRP or similar rituals. The intense visualisation of white light, when merged with genuine desire to go beyond the ego self, should result in a movement of consciousness from the astral to the mental realms, from

Yetzira to Briah. Practice your visualisation until this transformation occurs. Only then can it be used quickly and easily in ritual. Here the light is seen to fill your astral body and aura, helping you to bring the effects of the mental body into your etheric and physical bodies.

Once this light is established, the pentagrams are formed in a similar manner to those in the LRP – energy is drawn from crown and feet centres and merged in the heart and then sent into the hand and/or tool (the mode of pentagram inscription for each element is given in diagram 18). This energy is now projected out to form the pentagram in the air. Both the pentagram and spirit wheels are visualised as being made of flashing white light, hanging in the air before you. The spirit wheel, like all symbols in invoking Pentagrams, is drawn as much as possible from left to right, clockwise. The names are vibrated using the vibratory formula of the Middle Pillar. The energy and force invoked is drawn back through the magician, her hand going back over the left shoulder (for right handed folk) as the force comes into the temple. It should be willed and seen to fill the entire temple.

4. The LVX Signs. The Golden Dawn used a number of body and arm movements to indicate a certain grade of initiation and therefore a certain aspect of consciousness. The LVX signs here key the magician into the Adeptus Minor grade and thus to the higher consciousness of the spirit. The physical formation of the signs also causes energetic changes in the etheric body of the magician that open and consolidate the heart centre, thus allowing greater connection to the spiritual blessings just invoked. For someone not initiated into the Adeptus Minor grade by an authentic Order, meditation upon the signs and use of the Analysis of the Keyword, described earlier in this chapter, can provide a solid link between the formation of the signs and the consciousness required. However you can use the signs as part of this pentagram ritual without such preparation to begin with. The visualisation used here follows that of the second repetition of the keyword in the Analysis of the Keyword ritual – the arms are seen to be glowing white bars of light (see page 171). This affects the astral body of the magician. This is in contrast to the elemental grade signs, described below, which have no visualisation attached and effect only the physical and etheric bodies of the magician. This difference is resonant with the nature of spirit and the elements.

The magician now, through the LVX signs, has opened her etheric and astral bodies to the force of the spirit pentagram. She now uses the blessings and presence of spirit in the inscription of the elemental pentagram that follows. This helps in the balancing and ordering of

Air – Theoricus Grade Sign.

'Stand with feet together and raise both arms, upwards and back, palms up as if supporting a weight.' The hands and fingers should be facing in towards each other, above the head.

Fire – Philosophus Grade Sign.

'Raising the hands to the fore-head, and with the thumbs and index fingers forming a triangle and apex.' The hands should actually rest upon the forehead, the triangle enclosing the 'third eye' centre. The elbows should be out from the body, so that the arms themselves also form a triangle.

Water – Practicus Grade Sign.

'With the hands together, raise the arms until the elbows are level with the shoulders. With the thumbs and fore-fingers make triangle on your breast'. The triangle points apex down and covers the heart centre.

Earth – Zelator Grade Sign.

'The sign is given by raising the right hand to an angle of forty-five degrees'. The arm starts by the side and is slowly raised up. The palm is facing down. At the same time the left foot is advanced six or so inches.

Diagram 19: Elemental Grade Signs

the raw elemental force, as spirit rules and balances the elemental principles.

5-6. Inscription of the Air Pentagram. The magician now takes on the Godform of the Kerub of Air – Ha-Hathor, or visualizes their aura being filled with yellow light for Air. The Kerubim are the Gods and Goddesses of the elemental powers in Yetzira. Their function is to provide a more stable and controlled expression of the elemental powers. Visualising the aura filled with the coloured light of the element provides a more diffuse, though equally as strong, invocation. The four Kerubim are shown and described in diagram 20.

The pentagram is formed in the same manner as the spirit pentagram, but with changes to the colour of the light visualised, in this case yellow for Air. The magician, clothed with the Godform or filled with yellow light, visualizes the astral realm of Air before her. This should be easy, following your work with the elemental principles. She then sends a ray of her Ruach or will to connect with it, often done by directing the will out on a long out-breath. She then inscribes the pentagram as she vibrates the name, the name going out to awaken the elemental power, the pentagram to draw and invoke that power into the temple and also to provide the portal by which it may enter and be modified and filtered. The energy and blessings are, again, drawn through and over the magician into the temple. The Sign of Aquarius is inscribed in the centre of the pentagram, again from left to right. It should be seen in glowing violet light, the opposite to the yellow light of the pentagram. This sets up a polarity between the inner and outer regions of the pentagram which strengthens it upon the etheric level and increases its capacity as a portal.

7. The sign of the Theoricus grade is given here, this grade relating to the element of Air. The various grade signs are used within the Supreme Pentagram Ritual to connect the magician's subtle bodies with the elemental powers and forces invoked by the pentagram. The signs are linked to the etheric level microcosmic elemental powers of the magician by their traditional use in the Golden Dawn and instruction during the various initiation ceremonies. When we as Golden Dawn magicians perform these signs, their effects upon our etheric body, together with their traditional usage, helps to awaken the elemental energy from within us. In context of the SIRP this establishes a rapport between the magician and the elemental powers just invoked, which allows the elemental energy to flow more clearly from the astral portal into the magician and temple. The signs help to open our etheric bodies to the elemental blessings just invoked, in this case, Air. In other contexts the signs also function as a form of salute and acknowledgment to any elemental Beings invoked or banished. However, in the SIRP we are not invoking or inviting elemental Beings, simply the power and blessings of the element itself.

8. Here, like in the LRP, the energy continues to be directed out from the tool or hand and a wall of white light is visualised as we walk around the circle or temple.

9-29. The same inner workings as above, only varying the element, colour, Godform and sign as required for the pentagrams of Fire, Water and Earth. The Zodiacal sign is always seen in the opposite colour of the element: violet for Air (yellow), green for Fire (red), orange for Water (blue) and red-orange for Earth (olive green).

30-31. These steps use exactly the same inner workings as the Lesser Ritual of the Pentagram. However, we should note that since our pentagrams in the SIRP have worked with the full elements, rather than the sub-elements (as in the LRP), the invocation of the Archangels will be a lot stronger and a lot clearer.

We can see how the Supreme Pentagram uses the same pattern as the Lesser Pentagram. Once you have learnt the various names, signs, and godforms, it is a very easy ceremony. It is quick and effective and has many uses, which can be found by exploration and thought. When it comes to the Supreme *Banishing* Ritual of the Pentagram, the Pentagrams are traced in their banishing mode, the glyphs still drawn but from right to left. As both are traced their energy is drawn back in on the etheric level through the tool and hand of the magician. They are erased on the astral level via the visualisation of the symbol formed of light being wiped away as you trace over it. The vibration of the name sends all energy and blessings back into the mental realm. The pentagrams are not, unless for a particular purpose, left hanging in the air as in the Lesser Pentagram ritual where they remain to balance and protect the temple or magician.

Finally, the ritual is easily adapted to consecrate a temple with a single elemental blessing. If you were required to invoke solely the element of Earth you could use the Supreme Pentagram as follows.

Perform the Qabalistic Cross in the centre, as normal.

Invoke the spirit passive and Earth Pentagrams with appropriate names, signs etc (steps 23-28) at the East. Use the inner work described above.

East, Air: Ha-Hathor.
'Her face and limbs are of translucent gold. Upon her head she wears a scarlet sun disk resting between black horns. She has a black Nemyss, her robes are orange. She has a young girl's countenance and behind her are spread large and shadowing wings.'

South, Fire: Tharpesht.
'She has the form of a Lion with large and clashing wings. The colouring is very lively and flashing green with ruby and flame-blue and emerald green.'

West, Water: Thomoo.
'She has the face and form of a great eagle with large and glistening wings. The colours are mostly blue and orange with some green.'

North, Earth: Ahapshi.
'He has the face and form of a Bull with heavy, darkening wings, and the colours are black, green, red with some white.'

Diagram 20: Four Kerubim Images and Descriptions

Touching again the centre of the pentagram and keeping your arm at the same level, circle the temple sun-wise until you face the Southern quarter.

At South, West and South repeat the invoking spirit passive and Earth Pentagrams as above.

Complete the circle in the East.

At the centre ask for and invoke the great Archangel Auriel to be present before, behind, to our right and to your left:

'Before me **AURIEL**
Behind me **AURIEL**
On my left hand, **AURIEL**
On my right hand, **AURIEL**

For about me flame the pentagrams.
And above me shines the six-rayed star.'

Finish with the Qabalistic Cross.

Our temple now would be completely charged with and linked solely to the elemental powers of Earth and any Earth work or connection would be greatly magnified, resulting in deeper transformation.

Opening By Watchtower

This ritual has become one of the most popular 'Golden Dawn' rituals utilised by the modern magical and Pagan communities. It works with the four elemental principles like the Supreme Pentagram, but in a deeper manner and drawing on other formulas to create a potent and balanced opening ceremony for many magical operations. It was culled from the Inner Order ceremony for the Consecration of the Vault of the Adepti in the 1930s by Israel Regardie. There are a large number of versions of this ceremony in print. Almost every new magical book has a slightly different version. Regardie himself has several versions to his credit, reflecting his long magical career, and no version should be taken as definitive. I do not give detailed instructions here as to exactly when to intone the divine names – during the inscription of the pentagrams or after. I have found, for this ritual at least, it makes little difference and personal experiment and preference is important. This ritual should not be worked until mastering the Supreme Pentagram rituals as it utilises the pentagram techniques heavily. Once again, we will present the instructions for the ceremony followed by an analysis of its symbolism and inner work. The various tablets and tools mentioned in the instructions are also explained in the analysis.

OPENING BY WATCHTOWER INSTRUCTIONS

1. Stand West of the central altar, facing East. Announce: Hekas Hekas Este Bebeloi (Hay-kas hay-kas ess-tay- beeb-ee-loy).
2. LBRP
3. LBRH
4. Go to the South. Pick up the Fire symbol. Shake the symbol three times to the centre of the tablet. Move sunwise once around the temple, holding the symbol on high while reciting:

And when after all the phantoms have vanished thou shalt see that holy and formless Fire, that Fire which darts and flashes through the hidden depths of the universe. Hear thou the voice of Fire.

5. At South shake the symbol three times at the top of the tablet. With the tool inscribe a large circle in the air. Within the circle inscribe an invoking Fire pentagram and Leo sign in centre as you vibrate/say:

    OIP TEAA PDOCE. (oh-ee-pay tay-ah pay-doh-kay). *In the names and letters of the great Southern quadrangle, I do invoke ye, ye angels of the watchtower of the South.*

6. Turn and move to the centre, placing Fire symbol on the South of the altar.
7. Go to the West. Pick up the Water symbol. Shake symbol three times to the centre of the tablet. Move sunwise once around the temple, holding the symbol on high while reciting:

So therefore first the priest who governs the works of Fire must sprinkle with the lustral Waters of the loud resounding sea.

8. At the West shake the symbol three times at the top of the tablet. With the tool inscribe a large circle in the air. Within the circle inscribe an invoking Water pentagram and Scorpio sign as you say/vibrate:

    MPH ARSL GAIOL. (em-pay-hay ar-sel gah-ee-ohl). *In the names and letters of the great Western quadrangle, I do invoke ye, ye angels of the watchtower of the West.*

9. Turn and move to the centre, placing Water symbol on the West of the altar.

10. Go to the East. Pick up the Air symbol. Shake symbol three times to the centre of the tablet. Move sunwise once around the temple, holding the symbol on high while reciting

    Such a Fire existeth extending through the rushings of Air, or even a Fire formless whence comes an image of a voice. Or even a flashing light, abounding, revolving, whirling forth, crying aloud.

11. At the East shake the symbol three times at the top of the tablet. With the tool inscribe a large circle in the air. Within the circle inscribe an invoking Air pentagram and Aquarius sign as you say/vibrate:

    ORO IBAH AZOPI. (eh-roh ee-bah-hay ah-oh-zohd-pee). *In the names and letters of the great Eastern quadrangle, I do invoke ye, ye angels of the watchtower of the East.*

12. Turn and move to the centre, placing Air symbol on the East of the altar.

13. Go to the North. Pick up the Earth symbol. Shake symbol three times to the centre of the tablet. Move sunwise once around the temple, holding the symbol on high while reciting

    Stoop not down into that darkly splendid world wherein continually lieth a faithless depth and Hades wrapped in gloom, delighting in unintelligible images, precipitous, winding, a black ever-rolling abyss, ever espousing a body unluminous, formless and void.

14. At the North shake the symbol three times at the top of the tablet. With the tool inscribe a large circle in the air. Within the circle inscribe an invoking Earth pentagram and Taurus sign as you say/vibrate:

    MOR DIAL HCTGA. (em-mor dee-ahl hec-tay-gah). *In the names and letters of the great Northern quadrangle, I do invoke ye, ye angels of the watchtower of the North.*

15. Turn and move to the centre, placing Earth symbol on the North of the altar.

16. Go West of altar facing East. With spirit symbol describe invoking active and passive spirit pentagrams and spirit sigils as you say/vibrate:

    EXARP BITOM (ex-ar-pay. bay-ee-toh-em) (Active) **NANTA HCOMA** (en-ah-en-tah. hay-coh-mah) (Passive) *In the names and* *letters of the mystical tablet of Union, I invoke ye, ye divine forces of the spirit of life.*

17. Place spirit symbol down. Give the Portal sign of Opening of the Veil. Then recite:

I invoke ye, ye angels of the celestial spheres, whose dwelling is in the invisible. You are the guardians of the gates of the universe, be ye also the guardians of this mystic sphere. Keep far from us the evil and the unbalanced. Strengthen and inspire us so that we may preserve unsullied in this abode of the mysteries of the eternal gods. Let our spheres be pure and holy, so that we may enter in and partake of the mysteries of the Light divine.

18. Either remain here or move to South East edge of the circle and say:

The visible sun is the dispenser of light to the Earth. Let us therefore form a vortex in this chamber so that the invisible Sun of the spirit may shine herein.

19. Circumambulate, meaning walk in a circle, sun-wise, three times around the temple. Give the Sign of the Enterer each time you pass the East. After completing three full circles, return back to West of the altar and face East.

20. Recite the adoration to the Lord of the Universe below. At the end of each line give the sign indicated as follows:

Holy art though Lord of the Universe (Sign of the enterer)
Holy art thou whom nature hath not formed (Sign of the enterer)
Holy art thou the vast and the mighty one (Sign of the enterer)
Lord of the light and of the darkness (Sign of silence)

CLOSING BY WATCHTOWER INSTRUCTIONS

Please note, even though some others omit this section, if the place of working is not a room permanently set aside as a temple etc, it is best to banish, and not to simply use the YHShVH YHVShH formula alone, step 23. This is done by reversing the pentagrams as in the instructions below.

21. Go to the West of the altar, facing East. Then go to the North East. Perform the reverse circumambulation, circling anti-sunwise, three times around the temple, giving the Sign of Silence each time you pass the East.

22. Return back to West of altar and face East. Then inscribe the banishing
    pentagrams. This is done with the same words except replacing
    the word 'banish' for 'invoke' and using the appropriate banishing
    pentagrams. The order in which the pentagrams are banished can
    vary from magician to magician and Order to Order. For initial
    explorations with this ritual I suggest the same order as used in the
    invoking: Fire, Water, Air, Earth, spirit active, and spirit passive. The
    banishing is done with same tool that was used to invoke.

23. Return back to the West of altar, facing East. Say:

    *I now release any spirits and powers that may have been attracted to
    or imprisoned by this ceremony, by the power of* יהושה יהושה
    YHShVH YHVShH (Yeh-hesh-u-ah Yeh-hov-ash-ah) *I now declare
    this temple duly closed.* (Clap your hands together once, very smartly).

VARIANTS WITHIN THE WATCHTOWER CEREMONY

Before going into the inner workings of the ritual, we will discuss some
of the published variants within this ceremony and the reasons for them.
In this way it will be easier to decide which version you may wish to use,
not simply following this version blindly.

TABLETS

Almost every version of the ceremony requires a tablet of some sort at the
quarters, and sometimes at the centre. This follows traditional practice,
which holds that when properly consecrated these tablets become
talismans and gateways for the elemental forces. The most powerful
tablets are the full Enochian Tablets which are shown in black and white
in diagram 21. Israel Regardie in his book *Ceremonial Magic* advises the
use of sigils as a substitute, though such an act may cause a traditional
GD magician to shake their heads a little. This is because the sigils are
said to regulate the power of the tablets, and without any tablets the sigils
cannot do anything.

Donald Michael Kraig recommends using the Hermetic triangular
symbols of the elements, but then goes on to recommend a (incorrectly
coloured) Tablet of Union at the centre, thus confusing symbol systems. If
the Hermetic triangular symbols of the elements are used at the quarters,
an eight-spoke spirit wheel is probably the best symbol to have at the
centre. I have used both miniature Enochian Tablets and the Kerubic

FIRE

d	o	n	p	a	T	d	a	n	V	a	a
o	l	o	a	G	e	o	o	b	a	u	a
O	P	a	m	n	o	V	G	m	d	n	m
a	p	l	s	T	e	d	e	c	a	o	p
s	c	m	i	o	o	n	Ay	m	l	o	x
V	a	r	s	G	d	L	b	r	i	a	p
o	i	P	t	e	a	a	p	D	o	c	e
p	s	u	a	c	n	r	Z	i	r	Z	a
S	i	o	d	a	o	i	n	r	z	f	m
d	a	l	t	T	d	n	a	d	i	r	e
d	i	x	o	m	o	n	s	i	o	s	p
O	o	D	p	z	i	A	p	a	n	l	i
r	g	o	a	n	n	P	A	C	r	a	r

WATER

T	a	O	A	d	v	p	t	D	n	i	m
a	a	b	c	o	o	r	o	m	e	b	b
T	o	g	c	o	n	x	m	a	l	G	m
n	h	o	d	D	i	a	l	e	a	o	c
p	a	t	A	x	i	o	V	s	P	s	N
S	a	a	i	x	a	a	r	V	r	o	i
m	p	h	a	r	s	l	g	a	i	o	l
M	a	m	g	l	o	i	n	L	i	r	x
o	l	a	a	D	n	g	a	T	a	p	a
p	a	L	c	o	i	d	x	P	a	c	n
n	d	a	z	N	z	i	V	a	a	s	a
i	i	d	P	o	n	s	d	A	s	p	i
x	r	i	n	h	t	a	r	n	d	i	L

E	X	A	R	P
H	C	O	M	A
N	A	N	T	A
B	I	T	O	M

AIR

r	Z	i	l	a	f	A	y	t	l	p	a
a	r	d	Z	a	i	d	p	a	L	a	m
c	z	o	n	s	a	r	o	Y	a	v	b
T	o	i	T	t	z	o	P	a	c	o	C
S	i	g	a	s	o	m	r	b	z	n	h
f	m	o	n	d	a	T	d	i	a	r	i
o	r	o	i	b	A	h	a	o	z	p	i
t	N	a	b	r	V	i	x	g	a	s	d
O	i	i	i	t	T	p	a	l	O	a	i
A	b	a	m	o	o	o	a	C	u	c	a
N	a	o	c	O	T	t	n	p	r	n	T
o	c	a	n	m	a	g	o	t	r	o	i
S	h	i	a	l	r	a	p	m	z	o	x

EARTH

b	O	a	Z	a	R	o	p	h	a	R	a
u	N	n	a	x	o	P	S	o	n	d	n
a	i	g	r	a	n	o	o	m	a	g	g
o	r	p	m	n	i	n	g	b	e	a	l
r	s	O	n	i	z	i	r	l	e	m	v
i	z	i	n	r	C	z	i	a	M	h	l
M	O	r	d	i	a	l	h	C	t	G	a
O	C	a	n	c	h	i	a	s	o	m	t
A	r	b	i	z	m	i	i	l	p	i	z
O	p	a	n	a	L	a	m	S	m	a	P
d	O	l	o	P	i	n	i	a	n	b	a
r	x	p	a	o	c	s	i	z	i	x	p
a	x	t	i	r	V	a	s	t	r	i	m

Diagram 21: The Enochian Tablets

Diagram 22: Four Kerubic Heads for Air, Fire, Water and Earth

symbols of Angel, Lion, Eagle and Bull to great effect – diagram 22. If the Spirit Pentagrams are to be invoked over the altar, it is best to have some form of spirit symbol, even a rose at the centre of the altar. Instructions on making and consecrating these tablets, including the Enochian Tablets can be found in the Ciceros' book *Making and Consecrating Magical Tools* and it would be redundant of me to reproduce my own versions here. There are probably similar instructions on several internet sites also. As with all ceremonies though, look for and work out the inner workings as they probably will not be clear or explicit.

SPIRIT PENTAGRAMS

In some versions, like the one above, the active and passive spirit pentagrams are invoked at the centre after the four elemental pentagrams. In other versions the appropriate spirit pentagram (active for Air and Fire and passive for Water and Earth) is invoked *before* the elemental Pentagram in the same quarter, following the Supreme Pentagram ritual. Some authors, in what seems an act of blind faith, leave them out entirely. In the Western magical tradition the elemental forces are seen to be 'blind forces' – that is the forces are not controlled or directed by any force that is coherent and intelligent beyond its own nature. Without the spirit pentagrams somewhere the elemental forces invoked would at best cancel each other out, and at worst be harmful to the magic being worked. We can understand this better if we look at the elemental make-up within ourselves. Without the controlling principle of our sense of self, within Tiphareth, our differing elemental natures may not act in concert or harmony. Our thinking self of Air may not act in the same way as our passionate, erotic self of Fire. It is our choices, derived from the higher spirit, which enables harmony to occur.

While the spirit pentagrams are needed, we need not go the way of Regardie in *The Complete Golden Dawn System of Magic* and have them at the quarters *and* the centre. The key to choosing whether to have the Spirit

Pentagrams at the quarters or at the centre is dependent on the magic to be performed in the temple opened by Watchtower. If the magic is to focus on or take place upon the central altar, then the pentagrams above the altar are required. If the magic is to take place in various quarters or upon the astral level through travel in the Spirit Vision, pathworking or whatever, then the spirit pentagrams at the quarters are to be preferred. Finally, the inscription of the circle, in which the pentagram is inscribed, is designed to help confine the elemental power to that particular area of the temple. This assists in containing the elemental force and helps to avoid adverse interaction with the other elements.

SHAKING THE TOOLS

In some versions the tools are shaken three times before the circling of the temple with the element and three times afterwards. In others, only three times before the circling. In a few versions, they are not shaken at all. The shaking of the tools a total of six times was part of the consecration of the Vault of the Adepti ceremony, six being the number of Tiphareth, the Sephira corresponding to the Vault. Three shakes before and three after shows the union of the triangles of aspiration and inspiration; God and man, heaven and Earth, and therefore all that occurs between the two sets of three, being placed 'under' the presidency of this union. The circumambulation of the elements is, in this symbolism, under the control or direction of the union of Goddess and humanity, heaven and Earth.

The shaking three times reflects a part of the formula from the opening of the grade initiation ceremonies of Zelator through Philosophus. This is the Invoking Whorl or Whirl (for a partial description of this see *Z-5 Secret Teachings of the Golden Dawn, Book Two: The Zelator Ritual 1=10* by Pat Zalewski). This formula is only workable with a full Enochian Tablet at each quarter as shown in diagram 23. However, three shakes can be done, one to the left, one to the right and one in the centre, to invoke energy of balance. Personally I have found that for general workings, the series of two sets of three seems the best for the symbolic energies it invokes even without a vault as described above.

CLOSING

Most versions of the ritual do not use banishing pentagrams in the closing. This is for two reasons. Firstly, the ritual is derived from the consecration of the Vault of the Adepti, where no banishing was performed. Secondly, the use of the formula of YHShVH and YHVShH should (hopefully) remove any 'imprisoned' spirits or energy left after the reverse circumambulation, the LBRH and the LBRP. This formula is based on the understanding that the magician is of the Adeptus Minor grade and can therefore, by her own power, control the elemental forces. This is shown in the name YHShVH – the Shin (Sh) being the spirit that rules over the elements of Y (Fire), H (Water), V (Air) and H (Earth). Therefore any elemental spirits and powers are banished by this formula, but the subtle openings to the elemental forces remain within the subtle sphere of the temple – the portal created by the invoking pentagram is not closed. This is why this method of closing should only be done within a dedicated temple space. In which case, like the ante-chamber to the vault of the Adepti, the open portals remain and add to the sacred sphere of the temple. However, within a lounge room used as a temple on a Sunday night, having open elemental portals may prove to be disruptive, and it is wise to do a full closing.

WHICH ONE TO USE – THE WATCHTOWER OR THE SUPREME PENTAGRAM?

Both the Watchtower and Supreme Pentagram rituals focus upon the invocation, in balance, of the four elemental principles. They both work with the blessings embodied in the same divine names drawn from the Enochian tablets, and they both have their primary effects in the world of Yetzira. However, there are important differences between the two ceremonies and understanding these will allow you to choose which ritual suits your purposes and needs for transformation.

One of the main differences is that while the Supreme Pentagram is solely an elemental ritual, the Watchtower has other symbolic and energetic connections. These are most clearly seen in the four invocations that are read as the magician circumambulates with the four elements. Drawn from the Chaldean Oracles, these four verses refer to the creation of the universe from the Original Fire, the Fire that existed before the creation of the material universe, the Fire that pervades and maintains each and every thing within the universe. This is why in both the Water and Air verses, the central theme is Fire, not those elements – which it would be if the ceremony was solely concerned with the four elements. Some authors and groups seem not to have understood this and substituted their own words in place of these verses from the Chaldean Oracles. While essentially there is nothing wrong with this, we should not be replacing words in traditional ceremonies unless we are clear of the function of those words. In this context if we were going to replace these 'Fire' verses, we would need to replace them with words that not merely refer to the elements, but also the creation of the universe through the expression, enfoldment and solidification of the original Fire to produce the material universe and the Earth.

Of course we are not talking about the type of Fire by which we can toast our marshmallows, or even that Fire by which we can perform delicate laser surgery. The word 'Fire' here is an ancient Middle Eastern attempt to convey a hidden interior reality by means of common, everyday experience. Other mystical descriptions refer to 'lucid Fire' or 'interior light' or the Rosicrucian lamp that burnt but was never consumed. When Moses encountered the burning bush, it may have been a description of his awakening to this Fire – the interior divine energy that is alive and burning always – within the natural world. In any case, however we look at this, the Watchtower ceremony in some measure re-enacts the creation of material form from the ever-present and non-material Fire that persisted throughout the universe from the very instant of creation. Apart from the beautiful speeches from the Chaldean Oracles, this is also shown through the invocation of the four elements in their order of Creation, following the YHVH formula; Fire (Y), Water (H), Air (H), Earth (H). This is different from the order of the elements experienced from around the wheel of life as utilised by the Supreme Pentagram: Air (East), Fire (North), Water (West) and Earth (South).

The Watchtower builds up within the entire temple, through the circumambulations which literally spread the energy and blessings of the elements throughout the temple, a reflection of the process of creation. This makes it a powerful temple consecration ritual, ideal for any magic that involves adoration of the material and spiritual universe through communion or contemplation. The circumambulations allow the powers of the four elemental principles to be called upon anywhere in the temple, not simply at the four quarter portals, as in the Supreme Pentagram. However, unlike the Pentagram ritual it cannot readily be adapted for banishment of large scale unwanted and imitable forces.

The Pentagram ritual also combines, in one ceremony, the blessings and currents of both the Enochian and Hebrew magical traditions. No Hebrew angels are invoked in the Watchtower ceremony – it draws entirely from the Enochian representation and pathway to the four elemental realms. There are distinct differences in the blessings and energy received and encountered through the traditional Hebrew Qabalistic and the Enochian elemental approaches. One of the most easy to identify is the warmth and more human nature of the Hebrew tradition, which is hardly surprising considering that the four Archangels of the elements in this tradition are said to be under a mandate to form relationships with human beings.

INNER WORK OF THE OPENING BY WATCHTOWER CEREMONY

Announcement of Hekas Hekas Este Bebeloi. This is the traditional cry from the Bacchanalia, an aspect of the ancient Greek mysteries. It was declaimed to let all know that a sacred act was about to be performed and all profane people and energies should leave. The same symbolism is found in its use within the Golden Dawn and other modern Western traditions. From an inner point of view, what is also occurring is that as the notice given for these energies to be removed, *without a banishing action*, they actually manifest more upon the lower astral and etheric realms. When this occurs they are more easily dispersed with the LBRP than would be the case if this step were omitted.

LBRP – normal inner work.

LBRH – normal inner work.

Shaking the Tool Toward the Tablet. The Tablet should be approached by circling in the temple sunwise towards it. The magician now stands before the tablet. She grounds herself and connects to the Earth through their Malkuth centre, so that all energies and spiritual blessings they receive will be Earthed and affect the material world and their everyday life. The magician picks up the Fire tool. She focuses upon the tablet and then shakes the wand three times towards the tablet, slowly and deliberately. If a tablet other than the Enochian tablet is used, the following occurs: on the first shake a ray of the magician's will or Ruach is directed from her into the tool she is using. This is simply a case of willing your consciousness to move into the tool. This will happen without fuss or hindrance and is easier than it sounds. The magician's astral and etheric bodies are already enveloping the tool she holds, and this action is really just a matter of focus.

With a ray of the magician's will now focused inside the astral body of the tool, the will is directed by the second shake to move into the Fire tablet. Again this is a matter of will and focus. With the third shake, the magician directs the ray of her will to move to the elemental realm beyond the tablet, the realm of astral Fire itself. This will only occur quickly and easily if the magician has a deep connection with the astral realm of Fire by mediation and work with that elemental principle. Like so many ritual

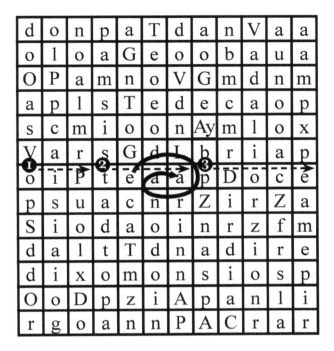

d	o	n	p	a	T	d	a	n	V	a	a
o	l	o	a	G	e	o	o	b	a	u	a
O	P	a	m	n	o	V	G	m	d	n	m
a	p	l	s	T	e	d	e	c	a	o	p
s	c	m	i	o	o	n	Ay	m	l	o	x
V	a	r	s	G	d	L	b	r	i	a	p
o	i	P	t	e	a	a	p	D	o	c	e
p	s	u	a	c	n	r	Z	i	r	Z	a
S	i	o	d	a	o	i	n	r	z	f	m
d	a	l	t	T	d	n	a	d	i	r	e
d	i	x	o	m	o	n	s	i	o	s	p
O	o	D	p	z	i	A	p	a	n	l	i
r	g	o	a	n	n	P	A	C	r	a	r

Diagram 23: Invoking Great Central Whorl on Enochian Fire Tablet

The spiral inward covers eight squares spelling out the name of the King of the Fire Tablet: EDLPRNAA. The names of the Kings of the other Elemental tablets are formed in the same manner.

OIP TEAA PDOCE – The Three Great Holy Secret Names of the One Being from the Fire Tablet formed along the central line. The first name has three letters, the second name four letters and the third name five letters. The Three Great Names of the other Elemental tablets are formed in the same manner.

actions in the Golden Dawn, what appears to be an outer theatrical form has deep inner workings attached to it. These inner workings rely upon previous personal work by the magician to be performed effectively.

If an Enochian Fire tablet is used the three initial movements provide a linkage between the will of the magician and the Elemental King of the Tablet, the most directive and active power of the element. This is done via the Invoking Great Central Whorl or Whirl as shown in diagram 23. The movement of the whorl is traced over the name of the King in three sharp but connected and successive motions. As the letters are traced over in the three actions the same basic inner workings as with the non-Enochian tablet occurs except for two differences. Firstly, the magician inwardly intones the name of the elemental King slowly and clearly, in this case, the King of Fire EDLPRNAA. Secondly, on the final shake the magician links herself to the Enochian Tablet of Fire through the King rather than the general astral realm of elemental Fire. This ensures that all elemental Fire blessings and spiritual energies that are called into the temple are filtered through the Enochian currents and traditions.

The Circumambulation with the Element. Having linked her will and astral body to the elemental realm of Fire or the Enochian tablet of Fire, the circumambulation can now proceed. The magician should visualise herself either as being clothed in the appropriate Godform of the Kerub of Fire described diagram 20 or their aura filled bright red light.

The elemental power of Fire is attracted to the tool and through the inner work of the magician is spread throughout the astral and etheric counterparts of the temple (along with the power of the elemental King if an Enochian tablet is used). The magician should now visualise the astral elemental energy and blessings coming from the tablet into the tool and being spread out, through the temple, as they move around and speak. The tablet itself here is a reservoir, a source of the elemental power that is pulled from it and moved around the temple. The voice actually directs this energy from the tool out into the sphere of the temple, as the voice is a symbol of the Ruach, the will. The visualisations required here are not totally fixed in stone. What is required is that as the magician walks she needs to see the temple being filled with the element in question; in this case Fire filling the whole temple as she slowly walks around saying the verse. Again this will occur easily if deep and effective work with the element of Fire has been conducted beforehand. During the circumambulation it is also important to keep in mind the Original Fire as mentioned earlier.

Shaking the Tool at the Top of the Tablet. On completing the circle the visualisation is briefly affirmed, that is, the magician inwardly sees the whole temple filled with the blessings of Fire. She then performs three more shakes of the Fire tool, this time at the top of the tablet or at the point where the circle that will enclose the pentagram is to be inscribed. These three shakes invoke and draw the power of the element to above the tablet. In the case of the Enochian tablets, this is over the sigil that governs the tablet. This awakens this sigil, which as mentioned previously is one of the regulating principles of the Enochian tablets.

In both Enochian and non-Enochian tablets, the energy just delivered by three shakes of the tool is now used to draw an enclosing circle, which starts and finishes at this point above the tablet. Some writers disagree with this and start the enclosing circle at various points depending on the element. The enclosing circle is visualised as being made of bright red light, the colour of Fire. Etheric energy from the magician is also directed out of her hand and through the tool to create the circle on the etheric level. This etheric energy will be modified by the nature of the tool in question and be transformed slightly, altering it to be in rapport with Fire upon the etheric level. Generic etheric energy leaves the magician's hands and is filtered through the Fire nature of the tool, emerging as Fire-attuned etheric energy.

Inscribing the Pentagram. The magician now inscribes an invoking Fire pentagram, in bright red light. Apart from the change of divine names, the inner workings used here are basically the same as that described in the Supreme Pentagram Ritual, and will not be repeated here. The enclosing circle naturally limits the power of the portal of the Fire pentagram to the Southern quarter of the temple. However, since the will of the adept connected with the element of Fire is spread throughout the temple via the circumambulation, she can call upon the element *at will* to enter the whole temple whenever she chooses to do so. Otherwise the element of Fire is confined to that quarter.

The names used here are Enochian and are derived from the Enochian tablet of Fire as shown in diagram 23. If an Enochian tablet is used, during the vibratory formula of the Middle Pillar the three names, written upon the central line of the tablet, are often used in replacement of the names on the white cloud. That is, the magician on her in-breath draws the names *out of* the tablet, changing their colour from black to red via visualisation as she does so. By breathing the names out of the Fire tablet, the magician increases her own link to the tablet. This is useful in that it allows the adept to control the pentagram as a portal by which to enter the astral realm of the element.

Moving the Fire Tool to the Central Altar. When the pentagram is complete, the tool is returned to the central altar. This is done by moving *directly* to the altar, from the South of the temple to the Southern side of the central altar. This is a simple though powerful action. It enlivens the central altar and directly links it to the Fire tablet, more than if the tool was moved with the magician in a sun-wise circle to the altar. As she walks from the South of the temple to the South of the altar the magician should visualise a direct band of Fire connecting the Fire tablet with the central altar.

The Elements of Water, Air and Earth. The same procedure is followed with the three other elements as described for Fire, with appropriate changes in the inner work.

Inscription of the Spirit Pentagrams. Once the temple is filled and enlivened with the four elemental principles, and the formula of creation as expressed through the enfoldment of the Original Fire, the spirit that 'rules' the elements is now invoked. This follows the formula embedded within the original version of this ceremony, where the temple was prepared as an entry point to the Vault of the Adepti, which is a paramount symbol of the higher consciousness of Tiphareth. In the Western esoteric traditions the four elemental principles are both simultaneously united and bound together as separate but interrelated forces by a fifth power – the spirit. It is the 'active' component of this power of spirit that holds the four powers together, while the 'passive' component of spirit unites them. This can be expressed also as the movement towards manifestation and diversity through the active spirit and the tendency towards dissolution and unity through the passive spirit. Another way of looking at the function of the spirit is to say that spirit active moves around the circumference of the circle connecting the four quarters, and spirit passive resolves all powers into the centre of the circle.

Within the human being this spirit can be referred to the Higher and Divine Genius. The Genius is our 'angelic self' – that unborn and eternal principle that our personality or lower selves revolve around. And if we believe in reincarnation, it is the genius that expresses itself through differing personalities incarnation after incarnation. In terms of the four seasons of the year, the fifth power of the spirit is said to be the Sun. With respect to the cycles of the Sun itself, the fifth spirit power is traditionally known as 'the Sun behind the Sun', identified in both Egyptian and Western traditions as the star Sirius.

The method and inner workings for invoking the spirit pentagram are almost the same as those described in the Supreme Pentagram notes. The key differences are the absence of the Hebrew names and the intention for the pentagrams to be a portal through which the divine forces of life and the angelic powers are to be drawn into the temple. Also, if the Enochian Tablet of Union is upon the altar, the names are drawn from the Tablet upon the in-breath as described previously. Whatever spirit symbol is used to inscribe the pentagrams, once it is enlivened and placed back on the altar it keeps in balance the four tablets and elements – which were previously linked to the altar by the replacement of the tools. At this point the altar is now fully activated. I have noticed that some versions of the Watchtower do not use the spirit wheel sigils, which, like the Kerubic emblems in the elemental pentagrams, fix and regulate the powers of the pentagrams. I cannot see any clear advantage in omitting this step and would recommend inscribing the wheels.

Invocation of the Angelic Powers. With the full activation of the altar, the temple is now enlivened and balanced with the four elements and spirit. Qabalistically this relates to the four Sephiroth of Malkuth through Netzach, all of which are balanced by the active and passive spirit. The next phase of the Watchtower Ceremony focuses upon Tiphareth within Yetzira. Firstly, the magician, standing at the altar facing East, extends her consciousness into to the veil of Paroketh in the world of Yetzira. This veil is the barrier or portal between the regular everyday consciousness of our astral-personality self and the deeper aspects. Extending our consciousness this way is not easy to describe on paper, and was originally one of the oral traditions of the Golden Dawn – one of the many magical skills and techniques that must be experienced rather than taught. In order to extend our consciousness in this fashion we need to have a number of skills and concepts under our belt. Firstly, we need to be deeply familiar with the Tree of Life, particularly the Sephiroth and the Paths of the Middle Pillar. Secondly, we need to be able to remain grounded and Earthed within the temple, as we extend our consciousness. This is a very important point – we **extend** our consciousness to Paroketh and Tiphareth of Yetzira rather than move our consciousness there. This means we remain in Malkuth of Assiah and all the other realms between Malkuth and Tiphareth.

The magician now extends her consciousness in the manner described in Chapter Three when working with the angel HRU of the Tarot. Following this method she extends her consciousness up the path of Samech until she begins to notice a change, at which point she consciously visualizes the power and blessings of the Sun thinly veiled behind clouds. This is the entrance point into Tiphareth – the veil of Paroketh. The magician maintains this image while inwardly intoning the name Paroketh. As difficult and as complex as this sounds, once practiced and experienced this procedure is able to be achieved quickly and efficiently as part of the Watchtower opening. It does however show once more how rituals within the Golden Dawn tradition rely on inner work and prior meditative practices.

At this point the magician is standing before the altar physically and her consciousness is also before the Veil of Paroketh in Yetzira. She now gives the sign of the Opening of the Portal. As she performs the physical sign she intones the name strongly inwardly and extends her consciousness through the veil of clouds to see the light and blessings of the Sun of Tiphareth unimpeded. This opens the veil and allows the Sun and light of Tiphareth to be open to invocation. This opening is achieved simultaneously by the astral form of the magician before the Veil of Paroketh, and by the physical body movements of the sign. The first opens the magician's astral body and consciousness to the influx of the Tiphareth energies, and the second action reflects this upon the etheric and physical levels.

The guardians and angelic powers of Tiphareth are now invoked, and asked to perform clear and definite tasks as described in the words of invocation. This is a hallmark of a good invocation – there is a clarity about which spiritual powers we are addressing and what we are asking them to do. Often we would state why also. During this invocation of the angelic powers, the magician's astral body is surrounded by the angels' power, and this energy and light is brought forth into the astral sphere of the temple. A detailed description of the formula for this process is given in the next chapter.

The Mystic Circumambulation. The magician now withdraws her consciousness down through the various paths and Sephiroth. As she does so she consciously brings with her the light and spiritual blessings of Tiphareth, visualised as intense and dazzling white light, to rest just above the astral and etheric spheres of the temple. The magician now prepares to create the astral and etheric vortex to attract the light. The invocation has brought forth the light into the astral form of the temple, and the circumambulation will move it into the etheric form. This is one the most beautiful and potent parts of the ceremony.

The magician moves to the North-East, the mystical place of conception, ready for the birth of the light into the etheric temple at the East. She attracts the light, through once more opening her consciousness to it and visualising the light moving to rest just above her Kether centre. The words spoken at this point reinforce this action. The magician now moves to East and begins to circumambulate. When she gives the Sign of the Enterer or Projecting Sign, the magician wills and visualizes the light entering her etheric body through her Kether. She then wills the light to move down her middle pillar to her Tiphareth (heart centre) and projects the light out with the projecting sign. As she walks, she continues to draw the light from her Kether and project it out through her Tiphareth. She sees and feels a circle of divine etheric energy being formed as she walks slowly around the temple. This method of energised circumambulation is found in several Golden Dawn ceremonies and has a number of variants. In this particular form the magician herself is the entry point or portal for the light to enter the temple. In other ceremonies, such as the Neophyte initiation, a temple officer at the East is the portal for the light.

One of the difficulties sometimes encountered with this form of circumambulation is a weak creation of the divine etheric circle of light. It exists and is formed strongly on the astral level through the visualisation, but the etheric counterpart is lacking vitality. If this occurs, try visualising and willing the light to come out of your Tiphareth centre *and* your Paroketh (solar plexus) centre. If after a ritual where you perform this action you feel weak or the Paroketh (solar plexus) still feels tingly or active, you should very consciously close and seal the solar plexus centre afterwards. This can be done via your will and clapping the hands together smartly over the centre. Tracing a Qabalistic cross over the centre with your fingers and softly intoning the names will also close and seal the centre. Do not direct the light *solely* out of the solar plexus centre. This can and is done in other Golden Dawn ceremonies, but only for particular purposes.

Adoration to the Lord of the Universe. Here we ask for the blessings, aid and power of the One Being, pure and simple. This adoration follows the four-fold formula of YHVH. Just as the elemental principle of Earth, which relates to the final H, is of a different nature than the first three elements, so too is the last line different from the other three. The first three adore the One while the last is just descriptive of the nature of the One. At the conclusion of the first three lines the Sign of the Enterer, the Projecting Sign, is given. This projects the adoration of the magician towards the macrocosmic East, the place of birth and resurrection. Once the final line is spoken the Sign of Silence is given. This withdraws the current and adoration projected by the first three lines and hopefully brings with it the power and blessings of the One. The Sign of Silence will draw these blessings into the auric sphere of the magician or when a group performs this adoration, as in the Neophyte temple, into the sphere of the temple. This short and simple adoration should be approached with extreme reverence as it is through this adoration and worship that the spiritual plane, the World of Atziluth, may be stirred into action.

After all this is done the temple is now fully opened by the Watchtower Ceremony. Whatever magical work, adoration or worship is required can now be performed. For beginners learning the ceremony, a short silent meditation before closing may be sufficient. The act of opening in and by itself can be transformational as it involves contact with and opening to a number of spiritual powers and blessings.

INNER WORK OF THE CLOSING BY WATCHTOWER CEREMONY

Reverse Circumambulation. The magician now moves to the South-East and stands ready to circumambulate anti-sun-wise, facing towards the North. The visualisation and inner work here begins with the Sign of Silence, which withdraws the current and energy already put out via the Sign of the Enterer during the opening circumambulation. The energy and light enters the sphere of the magician through the heart centre (or heart and solar plexus). The magician here visualizes and wills the white light to move from heart to crown and then back up through the various realms into the sphere of Tiphareth. As she walks she is constantly withdrawing the light and energy into her sphere of sensation and out through her Kether via will and visualisation. As she walks around the temple the second time, a distinct thinning of the etheric form will be noticed. As she walks around the final time all remaining divine etheric energy has to be visualised as being withdrawn until none remains.

Inscription of the Banishing Pentagrams. The banishing of the Pentagrams in this ritual uses essentially the same formula and inner work as the Supreme Banishing Ritual of the Pentagram, described earlier. The Pentagram within the circle is first visualised in the appropriate colour. Then the circle is banished by tracing it over again, starting from the same point, but circling anti-sunwise. As the circle is traced the magician visualises the light that creates the circle being withdrawn into the tool, so that once the circle is complete nothing remains. This is followed by the banishing Pentagram, seeing the light withdrawn in similar fashion. The banishing pentagram here closes the Elemental tablet and returns the power of the Elemental King to his own realm. The energy and power of the quarter is directed into and through the tablet and to the elemental realm in question. The tablet is often sealed at the end by a quick turn of the hand and tool that reverses the central whorl.

Closing with the Blessings of YHShVH YHVShH. The key to this closing is the name, which is a symbolic way of spelling the name Jesus in Hebrew. Just as Christ was a master of the world, so too does this name rule over the four elemental principles. There are many discussions and explorations on the beauty and power of this name, which I recommend you seek out and read. From an energetic and symbolic viewpoint what occurs here is that the magician quickly re-connects to her own Higher and Divine Genius through assuming the Godform, or filling her aura with divine and dazzling white light. This connects the magician to the

Tipharetic energies and blessings and awakens this consciousness to some degree. From this standpoint, when ready, she commands the elemental powers to depart and leave the temple space, Tiphareth ruling over the elements. This form of closing, without the banishing pentagrams, should not be used on its own by anyone unsure of their own connection to their Higher and Divine Genius or the blessings of Tiphareth. Finally, the clap of the hands is a symbolic action to show the completion of the ceremony. At this point a moment of silent prayer and thanks to the One and your Sacred Ones may be performed.

LESSER RITUALS OF THE HEXAGRAM OF THE PLANETS

Much of what is required to be understood concerning the invoking aspect of the Lesser Ritual of the Hexagram of the Planets has already been discussed in our section on the generic LRH and banishment in Chapter Two. Please refer to that section and the diagrams within it while reading this section. It is also recommended that you read the 'Ritual of the Hexagram' notes in the Regardie *Golden Dawn* compilation. The LRH affects the four elemental principles as they occur throughout the various Sephiroth and planes of Yetzira. The LRH of a particular planet or Sephira is normally only performed as a prelude to working with the full energy of that planet or Sephira, which is normally invoked via the Supreme Hexagram ritual. The exact order of rituals will be discussed when we look at the Supreme Hexagram ritual.

There are eight versions of the LRH – the generic one included in Chapter Two and seven others, one for each of the ancient planets. The main difference between the various Lesser Hexagram rituals is the mode of tracing the triangles of the hexagram. This is determined by the following rules:

◆ Start the first triangle from the point attributed to the planet you are working with.
◆ Start the second triangle from the planet opposite the planet you are working with. The opposite planets are shown on the full interlaced Hexagram attributed to the South: Saturn/Luna; Jupiter/Mercury and Mars/Venus.
◆ Inscribe the triangles clockwise to invoke or anti-clockwise to banish.

When it comes to the LRH of the Sun, six hexagrams are required to be traced, one each for the other six planets. This is because esoterically, the sun contains the powers of all the other planets, just as Tiphareth is the mediating and central aspect of the Tree of Life. This means that in the LRH of the Sun, a total of 24 hexagrams are required to be traced – six at each quarter. Also in the centre of each hexagram a solar symbol, the point within the circle, is to be traced. This should be seen in flashing gold.

The rest of the ritual would be exactly the same as the generic LRH described in Chapter Two. The hexagrams are still seen in flashing gold and a wall of white light still formed around the temple. The same divine name, **ARARITA,** is used and is intoned at the conclusion of the hexagram with the tool or hand in the centre. The elemental attributions for the four quarters remain the same regardless of planet. It is the mode of tracing that causes one ritual to be different to the other. For this to be effective, the four forms of the hexagram need to be studied and meditated upon. You should be able to recall them and the various planetary attribution points at will. For this reason I will not show the tracing patterns for the various hexagrams. Also, working out the forms is essential, as authors, publishers and printers make mistakes and more than one Golden Dawn book has reproduced inaccurate hexagram forms and other diagrams. Learn the attributions and the rules and do your own work.

Following the principle that it is by names and images that a ritual invokes or banishes its intended energies, there is a slight problem in the Hexagram schema bequeathed to us via the published Golden Dawn papers. The generic LRH and the LRH of Saturn have the same form, inner work, divine name, visualisation and mode of tracing the triangles. But one is to affect the 32nd Path of Tau and the other Binah in Yetzira. This is a contradiction to GD principles and magic which relies on more than intention to cause magical change. The problem is easily solved by adopting the suggestion given in the LRH of the Sun above: trace a Saturn glyph in the centre of the lesser hexagrams of Saturn, but not in those of the generic hexagram. This glyph should be seen in gold light, as befits the lesser nature of the ritual, and traced after the completion of the hexagram but before the intonation of ARARITA. In this way the divine unifying power of Ararita, as it is drawn through the hexagram, is modified by the glyph to be resonant with Saturn. I suggest doing this with all the planetary lesser hexagram rituals. While not included in the Hexagram notes that are published, I am confident that many sensible and practical Golden Dawn magicians follow this practice. It is a logical addition to the schema and solves a slight inconsistency problem.

SUMMARY OF THE LESSER PLANETARY HEXAGRAMS

Qabalistic Cross. Normal inner workings.

Go to the East of the temple and inscribe the East form of the Hexagram starting from the point attributed to the planet in question. Hexagrams are to be seen in flashing gold light.

Trace the appropriate planetary glyph in the centre of the hexagram. See it in gold flashing light. Now vibrate **ARARITA** using the vibratory formula of the middle pillar.

Move around to the South of the temple, keeping your hand outstretched at the same level and form a wall of white light as you move.

Inscribe the South form of the hexagram starting from the correct position for the planet and repeat the tracing of the glyph and intonation of **ARARITA**. Same inner work as above.

Repeat at West and North, forming a wall of white light as you move between quarters.

Move around, back to the East of the temple, keeping your hand outstretched at the same level, completing the circle of place.

Return to the centre of the temple and finish with a Qabalistic Cross, or continue with the rest of your ritual work.

SUPREME INVOKING RITUAL OF THE HEXAGRAM

Unlike the lesser hexagrams, the Supreme Hexagram rituals work with the complete energy of a Sephira or planet rather than the four elemental principles as they exist in that realm. While they strongly invoke the blessings of a planet or Sephira, they are also often performed to create an astral portal to that planet or Sephira. Once this is created then a deeper, longer and fuller invocation of energies associated with that planet or Sephira is often recited. A Supreme Banishing Hexagram is seldom performed other than to close the portal created by an invoking hexagram previously.

The Supreme Hexagram rituals are advanced Golden Dawn techniques and rest upon skills developed in the other rituals we have been looking at here. They are also only ever performed in a temple or space previously purified and consecrated. The sequence of rituals given shortly shows how the various rituals within the GD fit together and complement each other. The notes on the hexagram reproduced in *The Golden Dawn* are sometimes a little unclear as to the exact requirements and sequence of rituals. However, we can summarise these notes with the following sequence.

USING THE SRH TO INVOKE A SEPHIRA OR PLANETARY ENERGY OR CREATE A PORTAL

Determine where in the sky the planet will be at the time of invocation.
This can be readily determined from any number of astronomy computer programs, or ring up your local observatory. You may find the planet is below the horizon. In this case you need to determine as best you can which direction it is, below the Earth beneath you. An easy example here will illustrate this point. We have decided to invoke the Moon via a Luna Hexagram at 9pm. We check our program or observatory, or our own observations of the moon, and know that she will be towards her Zenith and slightly to the South at this time. We would therefore, when standing at our central altar, face South.

Perform the Lesser Banishing Ritual of the Pentagram
This cleanses the temple in the world of Assiah and the lower realms of Yetzira.

Perform the Generic Lesser Banishing Ritual of the Hexagram
This cleanses the 32nd Path of Tau that connects the world of Assiah and Yetzira, ensuring that all higher energies brought through this path will not be hindered or distorted.

Perform the Lesser Invoking Ritual of the Hexagram of the Moon
This brings into the astral sphere of the temple the balanced elemental principles as they exist within the realm symbolised by the moon and the Sephira of Yesod. The presence of the elemental principles means that they are equally affected, in balance, when the Luna-related force is invoked. The transformation of the elemental principles helps the complete working to affect this Earthy realm, since Malkuth is symbolically a synthesis of the elemental powers.

Face the Direction of the Moon and Inscribe a Supreme Invoking Hexagram of the Moon
Full instructions for this will be given shortly. The magician should face

the direction in question so that the central altar is between her and the planet. In our example the magician needs to face the South, so she stands North of the central altar, facing South. In this way the hexagram is inscribed over the central altar and the altar helps to Earth the energy towards the etheric and physical worlds.

If Required, Perform a Full Invocation of the Moon or Luna Associated Powers
This should be done still facing the direction of the Moon with the Luna portal of the Hexagram before you. If you are to perform transference of consciousness to the Luna realms, you would sit close to the altar still facing the direction and use the hexagram as a portal by which your consciousness travels. Instructions for this are given in chapter seven.

Once Complete, Give Thanks and Inscribe a Supreme Banishing Hexagram of the Moon
Again, this would be done facing South. This closes the portal to the lunar realms.

Perform a Lesser Banishing Ritual of the Hexagram of the Moon
This removes all Lunar energy from the temple space.

Perform the Generic Lesser Banishing Ritual of the Hexagram
This re-cleanses the temple in the 32nd Path and removes any Lunar or other energy from this path that has not previously been grounded to the world of Assiah.

Perform a Lesser Banishing Ritual of the Pentagram
This brings the temple and magician back to normal consciousness and balances their energy. It also closes the ceremony.

INSTRUCTIONS FOR THE SUPREME HEXAGRAMS

The Supreme Hexagrams, you will be pleased to note, use but one form – that of the regular or interlaced Hexagram attributed to the South in the LRH. The attribution of the points and centre to the seven planets follow that already shown in diagram 9. The rules for invoking and banishing also follow what we have previously discussed. We will now look at the rest of the ritual together with the inner workings.

1. Perform the Qabalistic Cross. Normal inner workings, except that you may wish to stay extended in size, as in the LRH.
2. Draw the light down from your Kether centre into your Tiphareth centre and from there into your hand and any tool you are using. Do not draw light up from your Malkuth centre as we are working with non-material worlds, energies and blessings.
3. Start the process for the vibratory formula of the Middle Pillar with the divine name **ARARITA** visualised in the flashing gold light ready for the outer vibration in the next step.
4. When ready, trace the Hexagram starting from the correct point. The hexagram should be formed of flashing gold light on the astral level and from etheric energy directed via your hand or tool. As you trace the hexagram, vibrate outwardly **ARARITA**.
5. Place your hand in the centre of the Hexagram and perform the final part of the vibratory formula, drawing back the blessings to enliven the hexagram further.
6. Start the process for the vibratory formula of the Middle Pillar with the divine name of the planet of the Hexagram visualised in the colour of the planet. In our example the name used for the Luna hexagram is that of the Sephira of Yesod, **ShDI AL ChI**. The divine names of the planets used in the SRH are taken from the Sephira they are attributed to, as shown in column three of table two (p.34). The Hebrew spelling of these names is given in table three (p.145). The colours used are normally those of the first colour given in table two.
7. Trace in the centre of the hexagram the appropriate planetary symbol, starting at the left and moving to the right. The symbol should be visualised in the bright coloured light attributed to the planet. This forms the symbol astrally and it is formed etherically via the etheric energy directed from your hand or tool. In our example, the colour would be bright purple light. As you trace the hexagram, vibrate outwardly the name already vibrated inwardly.
8. Place your hand in the centre of the Hexagram and perform the final part of the vibratory formula, drawing back the blessings of the planet into the temple.
9. Start the process for the vibratory formula of the Middle Pillar with the Hebrew letter of the Path on the Tree of Life attributed to the planet of the Hexagram. These attributions are given in table two along with the colours required. In our example, the reflection of the Moon is attributed to the path of Gimel, running between Tiphareth and Kether. The colour is blue, so we would visualise a blue letter Gimel.

10. Trace in the centre of the hexagram the letter, starting at the left and moving to the right. The letter should be formed of bright coloured light and the etheric energy directed from your hand. As you trace the letter, vibrate outwardly the name of the letter.

11. Place your hand in the centre of the Hexagram and perform the final part of the vibratory formula, drawing back the blessings of the reflection of the sphere of the planet into the temple. This step, the vibration of the letter, is important as it brings into the astral sphere of the temple and the Hexagram portal what the Golden Dawn calls 'the Reflection of the Sphere of the Planet'. This is the aspect of the Path of the Tree of Life attributed to that planet. It is called a reflection as it is not the full power of the planet. Traditionally it is said that the experience of the Sephiroth is objective and the Paths subjective. By invoking the power of the appropriate planetary path, the Supreme Hexagram allows fuller transformation and effects upon the personal, individual and subjective level of the magician.

12. Give the LVX signs. See the notes on the Supreme Pentagram for the inner work required here.

Please note: if you are using the Saturn hexagram for invocation of Chokmah or Kether, use the appropriate divine names and colours for those Sephiroth as given in tables two and three. These Sephiroth do not have planets attached to them and therefore do not have letters or symbols attached to them. The effectiveness of the hexagram will rely entirely on your connection to the blessings of the Sephira and the name. When using the Hexagram of the Moon, the symbol of the Moon varies depending on the phase of Moon at the time of the invocation: Dark, ●; Waxing, ☽; Full, O or Waning, ☾

In the SRH a single hexagram is invoked, not four at the quarters like in the other rituals under discussion. This is because the Supreme Hexagram is mainly designed to open a portal to the appropriate realm, not fill the temple with the energy from that realm. There are few occasions when the entire temple would need to be completely filled with the energy of a planet. On most occasions the portal created towards the centre suffices for the magician's needs. The magician can draw through hexagram-portal planetary energy for consecration of any object, which would be placed on the altar directly beneath the inscribed hexagram. It can also serve as a gateway to the astral realm of the planet in question. There are few other needs for planetary energy.

On those occasions where the entire temple needs to be filled with the planetary energy, the Supreme Invoking Hexagram of the planet may be traced at each quarter in the manner already described. As the magician moves from quarter to quarter she should visualise a wall of bright light, the colour of the planet in question rather than a wall of white light. This is removed at the end of the working when the Supreme Banishing ritual is performed. If any planetary work is to be conducted at the central altar, another Supreme Hexagram would need to be performed as described above. Similarly for transference of consciousness to the astral realm of the planet – this would need to be done through a hexagram-portal inscribed over the central altar and facing the position of the planet in the sky. It should not be done through one of the quarter hexagrams.

DRAMATIC INVOCATION

WE come now to what most people think of as invocation: someone stands in front of the group addressing a spiritual power or Being and imploring them to be present within the temple, group, or object to be consecrated. Within most magical traditions in the West today, including the Neo-Pagan traditions, invocation is practiced in one of two ways. Firstly, through pre-composed invocations, which are learnt prior to the performance of the ceremony and then recited with intent and emotion at the appropriate stage of the ceremony. Or secondly, through spontaneous invocations, which are created on the spot, allowing the words to flow which express the energy or deity to be invoked. Often there is a mix of the two – the general shape and pattern of the pre-composed invocation is learnt, whether consciously or unconsciously, and it then becomes the framework for the spontaneous words to form upon.

Reflecting its ceremonial bias and roots, the Golden Dawn has many pre-composed invocations included within its various ceremonies but no examples of spontaneous invocation. There is also no really clear instructional paper on the subject. The Golden Dawn however, does teach particular and specific techniques for the practice of invocation and keys to ensure its effectiveness. These can be found scattered through a number of papers and ceremonies. Naturally enough they involve more preparation, training and work than the general method previously described. As might be expected, the practitioners of the Golden Dawn and other ceremonial methods of invocation claim that these methods are far more effective than spontaneous invocation. In my experience however, knowing all the keys and techniques of invocation does not guarantee an effective response. In the end, what makes invocation work rests within the magician herself.

How Dramatic Invocation Works

The rationale behind dramatic invocation is that through concentrated effort, a magical current, a deity or the blessing of that deity can be brought into the mental, astral and etheric atmosphere of a temple. As we have seen, the Golden Dawn provides a number of rituals that allow a portal to be created whereby spiritual energy or blessings may enter the atmosphere of the temple. Dramatic invocation, however, works by first bringing the blessings into the astral and etheric bodies of the magician and then throughout the temple. Occasionally invocations of this type are used in conjunction with the various Golden Dawn rituals described in the last chapter; the rituals such as the Supreme Hexagram provide a portal through which the magician may draw the energy and blessings into her body and from there to the temple. However, invocation is more often used when we cannot create a portal through which those powers and energies may come. For example, if we wish to invite the Gnomes of elemental Earth to be present, the Supreme Pentagram can be used to create a portal and provide a further invitation to draw them into the sphere of the temple. However, when it comes to invoking the Great God Pan, there is no ritual that links to His realm as He is beyond elements, planets and Zodiacal signs. It is the same with all the Gods and major spiritual forces throughout the world's cultures.

Of course, some Golden Dawn rituals invoke the blessings of various deities through symbols and portals, such as Christ within the Rose-Cross ceremony. However, it is clear that we are drawing upon only the blessings or energy of Christ in a particular aspect. It is as if we know we are working with the aura of light that surrounds the candle flame, not the flame itself. In most invocations we are trying to draw upon the deepest spiritual blessings we can – the actual flame, or as close as we can get without burning. This mention of burning may seem like following a metaphor too far, but when we work with the Goddesses and Gods we are working with mysterious and powerful Beings (or forces depending on your point of view). They can be as deeply disturbing to our ordered little lives as they are transformational, a view well expressed in the saying:

God is not comfortable –
He is not a kind uncle.
He is an Earthquake.

In most books on magic, when an invocation is given they simply repeat the words of the invocation and do not mention the inner workings of the invocation. This is unfortunate as it gives the impression that by simply reciting the words in an emotive manner the invocation will be effective, which is not the case. That said, both the words and emotion of the invocator are important factors, as it is through them the blessings previously brought into the sphere of the invocator are spread throughout the temple. The words of the invocation are not only about describing the deity or blessings to be invoked, they are also the key to imparting those blessings to the temple and members of the temple. This is because the words and the breath are related to the Ruach or the Will. By linking his words of invocation to his will, the invocator can direct any blessings he is channelling throughout the temple. They will then affect everyone present and the astral and etheric atmosphere within the temple. A good invocation will have this Ruach quality directing it and it can be distinguished quite readily. It is not dramatic emphasis and emotional phrasing or loud directed speech. It is the quality imparted by a magician who has developed their will and has linked it to their speech via a consciousness that can access the blessings of Tiphareth.

It is often mentioned in magical textbooks that the words of an invocation are relatively unimportant, and it is the energy and intent of the magician that is the deciding factor. For solo ritual any words can, *in theory* be used. However, in group ritual, the words and the emphasis upon them are of key importance, as the connotations contained within the words will affect the group. Theoretically one could invoke the Moon Goddess by chanting 'Coke is Life', but the members of the group and the group mind would have so many reactions to this chant that it would not work. This is why the words used are of crucial importance and relevance. They need to stir within everyone present, including the invocator, the emotions, thoughts, images and qualities associated with the deity or blessing being invoked. If they fail to do this, then they should be modified for the next invocation.

Another factor also to consider here is the depth of connection the invocator has with the deity or blessing to be invoked. What relationship have they developed with the deity or force previously? For successful invocations a deep and non-ego based connection between invocator and the power to be invoked is essential. This is something that takes not only time and effort, but also a willingness to go beyond our first reactions and emotional needs for our Goddesses and spiritual blessings. If our connection with our Sacred Ones is largely emotionally based it will not reach further than the Yetziratic (astral) world and consequently the blessings of the deity that are drawn forth will be limited in their effect and transformational qualities.

A good example of this is of would be a New Age 'Priestess' of the Great Mother who has rejected the Christianity of her childhood and has adopted 'the Goddess religion' to compensate for lack of a deeper contact as a child. This woman's contact with the ancient and potent 'Great Mother' Goddess will be limited. Since her primary (unconscious) motivation is to address needs within her emotional life, there will be little Briatic (mental realm) contact, and thus the transformational qualities of the Great Mother in the realm of Briah could not be mediated to others. Also, since the primary contact is within the astral/emotional realm, the contacts with the Great Mother would be *felt* as great emotional or visionary events and be 'real' to the Priestess and others working out similar emotional issues. However, the lack of deep connection will be evident by the lack of real transformation and spiritual unfoldment. Most magical practitioners are prone to some variation of this kind of misunderstanding, particularly when starting out. To avoid this, constant vigilance, self-observation and deep openness to change is required.

THE FRAMEWORK FOR INVOCATION

Invocation pre-supposes that there exists within the non-physical inner realms either the deity or an energy that may be 'tapped into'. For example, some Pagan and Green activists groups regularly invoke 'the spirit of the forests'. If we believe such invocations can be effective, we are working with a theology that assumes that the energy, spirit or blessings of the forests exists in the inner realms and may be tapped into and drawn upon. The question of exactly what inner realms a non-physical force or Being exists within is often not examined. From the perspective of the Golden Dawn's Qabalistic framework certain broad assumptions can be stated. Note well the word assumption – this is a working model open to modification. It also deliberately avoids listing many classes of spiritual Beings. Think of Beings it does not list, and work out for yourself on which realms they exist.

◆ The One exists as all and everywhere at once.
◆ Goddesses and Gods and aspects of the One Being (such as those symbolised by the sacred names) exist with all the worlds from Atziluth through Assiah.
◆ Archangels, Elemental Kings, the Source and 'over-souls' of all aspects of the natural world and nature spirits and the greater or Collective Ancestors exist in the worlds of Briah, Yetzira and Assiah.

◆ Angels, elementals, nature spirits, ancestors, spirits of place, power animals, familiars, and any aspect of the physical world as created by humanity exist in Yetzira and Assiah.
◆ Anything at all envisioned or dreamt, but not physically created, by humanity exists in Yetzira.

For those people who have noticed the inclusion of Assiah in this list and assume I have finally flipped my lid and imagine I have angels round for tea and Goddesses out for lunch, I wish to point out an older and more traditional way of viewing the world. From this perspective, still shared by some traditional cultures, a mountain named after and sacred to a Goddess *is* the Goddess. Certain rivers and trees *are* the ancestors or the various spirits of place, the Genii Loci. Even within a revealed, as opposed to a Pagan, religion such as Christianity we find echoes of this view. St Gregory of Nyssa viewed angels as unlooked-for inspirations and motivations towards good work in the world. From this point of view, a young doctor forgoing material success in the West and working in a leprosy hospital as a result of inspiration is the Assiatic form of the Chasmalim, the Angels of Compassion of Chesed.

The separation between divinity and matter is something we take for granted in the West, but is not the only way of looking at the world. Of course, it has so informed our reality and world that we need to acknowledge that we do hold these points of view and start from where we really are. This is exactly what the Golden Dawn does, knowing that most of us, while inspired and in awe of the natural world, do not find the One, a Goddess, an Archangel or even an angel in our regular everyday life. With this in mind the Golden Dawn teaches us how to transfer the blessings and energy of the deeper realms into our world through invocation and other techniques. It is said that a fully awake human being, such as Christ, would see the inner divinity in all and by simply beholding the world it becomes sacred. This is one of the origins of the custom of pilgrimages to places visited by holy ones. Through their presence and their enlightened beholding, particularly at significant phases of life, the places are sacralised. Pilgrims seek not only to capture the essence of their holy one's journey and become like them, but also to share in the awakened divinity of place.

Many of the various spiritual powers and blessings we seek to invoke and Earth into this world through our Golden Dawn practice do not have forms within Yetzira, the astral realm. When they engage with humanity they assume astral forms. These forms can be created from the macrocosmic astral light around us, our own personal unconscious, or if we are magicians, from our conscious and willed creative powers. When we act in this way, we co-create with the spiritual powers. They use our forms and therefore we are more open to them. When they have ceased engaging with us, we re-absorb the astral forms they used into our personal astral light along with their spiritual blessings. In this way we are transformed more than if we allowed the powers to use forms created either by our culture or unconscious.

Another important point is that most of those powers that traditionally exist in the higher or deeper worlds of Atziluth and Briah also have representations or presence in the lower realms. The Goddess Isis for instance exists within all the realms from Atziluth to Assiah; as her pure being in Atziluth; as her deeper spiritual presence in Briah; as a myriad of images and forms in Yetzira and as the Nile in Assiah. Connecting with Isis in the world of Briah can be a very different experience than connecting with Her forms and images in Yetzira. Ideally of course our connection with Her would involve us invoking Her while camped by the Nile using a Yetziratic form which is enlivened by Her Briatic Power and connecting with Her true essence through our aspiration unto Atziluth.

An underlying assumption of this theology is that the spiritual blessings we are seeking to connect with are infinite, or at least very vast. On full moons a Coven does not worry that by the time they Draw Down the Moon Goddess into their Priestess, She will have already been invoked by another Coven. Similarly, Golden Dawn lodges do not time their ceremonies to avoid clashing with other groups also seeking to invoke the same spiritual blessings. Christ, as one Sunday liturgy says, 'is present on a thousand altars, yet is One and Indivisible'. We may say therefore that there is an infinite pool of inner plane blessings for each force or deity we can connect with. This pool will exist within all the worlds where the powers we wish to invoke exist, and will contain differing aspects of the same force, as shown in our discussion on the Goddess Isis above. Carrying this metaphor further, we can now look at how we may connect to these pools.

Firstly, we will need to know how to find the pool, and how to distinguish from other pools that may look similar. This requires some form of spiritual framework – a language and a map to the inner realms of the universe. This is exactly what the Golden Dawn and the Qabalah provides us with. Having such a map helps avoid the confusion that besets many well intentioned new age groups and courses. Secondly, we will need somehow to draw water from the pool. To ensure that the water drawn from the pool is pure when we receive it, we need to make sure the vessel we use is clean. We will also need to travel, employing will and energy to bring the water into our spaces and our subtle bodies. We will then need tools and methods to spread the water throughout the temple.

Within the eclectic Pagan traditions all of these requirements are met through the use of emotion. That is, it is largely the emotion of the invocator, and in part the group, that ensures the functionality of the relay to the pool. However, sometimes this does not work well. There are two main reasons for this. Firstly, emotion alone is a fickle thing, and is rarely pure. More often than not, our emotion is tinged with other sub-conscious emotions and thoughts. Qabalistically, our emotions of Netzach are often tinged with our unconscious needs and patterns from Yesod. This, in our metaphor, can result in slightly murky water.

More important though is the fact that many of the pools of water we are seeking to connect with exist on a plane deeper than the emotional plane; that is, within the Briatic not the Yetziratic realms. What exists within the Yetziratic realm is more often than not a lot of powerful emotional and astral energy and a series of strong images and ideas. In terms of transformation and connection however, these are not as potent as the full Briatic blessings. This means that when we use emotion alone, we will connect with something that looks and 'feels' like what we are after, but may not be transformational to any degree. This is because **to transform any part of our being, we need to utilize a higher power than the part to be transformed**. That is, to transform emotions, we need to utilize a power higher than emotions. In terms of Qabalah, we need a Briatic contact not a Yetziratic connection.

With reference to the New Age Priestess of the Goddess mentioned earlier, since her connection with the Goddess is largely emotional in nature her invocations are unlikely to go beyond the emotional, astral plane and connect with any force that may transform her. She may see and experience a great deal of Goddess energy and emotions, but transformation will elude her. To avoid this problematic reliance on emotion as the force behind invocations, the Golden Dawn has developed a series of keys to invocation which we will now look at.

KEYS TO INVOCATION

"Invoke Often and Inflame Thyself With Prayer"

Put simply in modern terms this phrase could read: 'Do it a lot and do it with feeling!' Repetition and emotion are the two keys to successful invocation outlined here. I would add four more keys, making a total of six:

1. **Conscious Repetition**
2. **Preparation**
3. **Emotion**
4. **Will (Ruach)**
5. **Imagination**
6. **Trance or altered state of consciousness**

Conscious Repetition. This is the learning and recitation of the invocation over and over until it is learnt thoroughly. This ensures that when it is recited in ritual, no part of the mind is searching for the words. This allows trance or an altered state of consciousness, where we can shift our consciousness to the various realms, to occur. If you are worrying about or searching for the words, it is very likely that some emotional reactions will be occurring somewhere in your psyche. This may keep the whole invocation bogged down at the emotional level. Also if one part of you is searching for words, it makes it much harder for multi-layered consciousness to occur, which as we will see, is important. Remembering words consciously also activates left-brain activity and Beta waves, which is exactly the sort of state we wish to avoid in ritual. **Conscious** repetition (not rote learning) will also allow us to gain a deeper understanding of the *meaning* of the invocation and is in many ways a meditative practice by itself. It helps us engage at a mental body level, and great insights can be gained from what initially may seem like a bunch of words on paper.

Preparation. This consists of three equally important aspects. Firstly, attuning our consciousness and various subtle bodies to the forces and blessings we wish to invoke. This is done via meditation, spiritual connection, worship or other exercises prior to the day of the invocation. In effect it is building a relationship with the blessings and deities whose presence we seek. It is being open to them and their effects in this world at the deepest level we can be. Also, invoking a deity we have not bothered to learn about or open ourselves to is quite simply disrespectful. It would be akin to expecting a member of another culture to come to dinner at our beck and call, for our own personal advantage, while we make one cultural faux pas after another.

The second aspect of preparation is the writing and rehearsal of the whole ritual (if only in imagination) prior to the evening. By knowing exactly what is to occur, and seeing it vividly in our imagination and/or walking it through, our astral body and consciousness becomes attuned to the ceremony and its purpose. In group ceremonies, everyone should do this, regardless of the size of their role. Inner and outer rehearsals such as these are also extremely useful in spotting any unforeseen problems, particularly practical difficulties. Finally, preparation is also the cleansing of the temple and ourselves on the evening of the invocation. We have examined this in depth in Chapter Two and also when looking at the role of the various hexagram rituals in the last chapter. Applying our metaphor, effective preparation will help ensure our vessel is clean and the water that from it is drinkable. The *form* of the ritual is the path from the pool.

Emotion and Will (the Ruach) are considered together, since during invocation it is the emotion **directed by the will** that enables us to go through the various layers of the inner realms to reach the particular pool of blessings we desire. Emotion is like a candle – its light disperses softly in a three hundred and sixty degree arc. When someone expresses deep sadness or anger, we can generally feel it enveloping them, their entire astral and etheric bodies. The Ruach, or our will, shapes the emotion into a narrow beam; much like a slit-lantern does to a candle – so that it is focused and useful for penetrating the layers of consciousness and subtle realms. Emotion is also the raw energy that will draw down the blessings of the spiritual force or deity into the temple. This is another reason why good invocations contain appropriate words, images, sounds and motifs that will stir deep and powerful emotion within all present. This is then directed and contained by the will.

We can look at this Qabalistically. A group of people are fully present physically in Malkuth invoking the Goddess Isis. By their magical skills and cleansings they have controlled and contained any possible disruptive unconscious and subconscious forces emerging from Yesod. If they are really good, they have will have utilised and channelled the immense creative and generative powers of Yesod for the magical work in question. As the invocation progresses, certain words, expressions and images are received by their Hodic spheres, which generate emotions and feelings from Netzach. These Netzachian energies in turn spark off similar Netzachian energies in others, producing a group amalgam of emotions, thoughts and images that are clear and in harmony with the aspect of Isis to be invoked. The Will or Ruach centred in Tiphareth, having control over the four basal Sephiroth, now directs and focuses this group amalgam of emotion towards the Goddess on the inner planes. This will be described in more detail shortly.

We see five points of importance, one for each Sephira. Firstly, everyone needs to be fully present as their body-selves in Malkuth and aware of each other. Without this presence the group harmony is diminished considerably and the spiritual blessings of Isis will not be effectively earthed. Secondly, the Yesodic energies need containing and/or directing. Often when deep emotions are felt our subconscious Yesodic patterns awaken. This will cloud the pure emotion of Netzach with lower and possibly unhealthy images and thoughts. Again, we can use the example of the New Age Priestess of the Great Mother. Because her emotional neediness when Isis is called upon by Her mother names, this person's Yesod, not Netzach, is aroused. Her subconscious desires and fantasies of the Goddess are then energetically present within her sphere and the temple, even if not consciously admitted to or seen for what they are. This will certainly cloud and distort her Netzachian purity of her deeper emotions, and possibly those of others in the group. Incidentally the unconscious of Yesod can also rise up and distort the thoughts and logic of Hod. This is why people are able to convince themselves they are acting sensibly and logically when outsiders can easily see their actions are based on personal needs and fears.

Thirdly, the words, phrases and described images of the invocation must resonate with and open the Hodic spheres of those present. This is one of the reasons why in Golden Dawn group ceremonies the words of invocation are kept standard and largely unchanging. It also explains why many of them were drawn from inspirational works that existed within the culture of the day – that is largely from the Old and New Testaments of the Bible. In this way the founders of the Golden Dawn knew the words would elicit the appropriate responses. Fourthly, everyone present needs to be comfortable with opening and expressing their deeper Netzachian emotions. Again, cleansing helps here as does habitual prayer, worship and thankfulness expressed towards the divine. Fifthly and finally, the Ruach centred in Tiphareth needs to be well-developed. This is achieved only by introspection and spiritual work.

In solo ceremonies the invocator has to be able to do all of these things themselves effectively. In group ceremonies it is possible to have people present who are still learning the magical arts or even attending an invocation for the first time. Provided the cleansings are done effectively and they are open to the ceremony, in general they will not be disruptive. If they are not regular members of the group, the act of including their emotional responses into the group amalgam becomes a little more tricky. Some people will empathize easily and well with the group and its aims and there is no problem. For others more direction is required. This can best be achieved by a simple trick of placing the newcomer next to the invocator or an experienced member of the group who knows what is occurring. The sharing of etheric and astral bodies will help produce the appropriate openness quite easily. If you are working in a circle, try and position the newcomer between the invocator and another experienced member of the group. As the invocator and group member link, they will do so by moving through the etheric and astral bodies of the newcomer and thus bring her into the weave.

Imagination and Trance. Not only does imagination and visualisation create forms within the astral world, they also help to change our consciousness, placing us in a self-directed and controlled trance. By careful use of imagination and visualisation we can fine tune and alter our consciousness and the energetic pitch of our astral bodies to match the blessings or deity we are seeking to invoke. This will greatly aid our chances of a successful higher contact at the Briatic or possibly the Atziluthic levels. Again our imagination is directed by our will. In terms of our metaphor, we internally recreate the 'pool' we wish to link to. This is done mostly through intense and controlled visualisation, but also through the inner reproduction of other senses. For example, when creating the image of the Great God Pan, we would also recreate the smell of His goat body and the intense and haunting music from His pipes. Holding a clear and intense scene of the deity or the blessings before us, we use the emotion and will to take our consciousness to the deity, moving through the inner realms of the universe, which are symbolised in the Qabalah by the Sephiroth and planes. We can then ask and respectfully link ourselves to His blessings.

Continuing our metaphor: in invocation, part of our consciousness needs to be at the level of the pool, taking the vessel we carry to the water. Another part needs to remain grounded in Malkuth, reciting the words and directing the water through the various inner levels into the our aura, the actions and words of the ritual, and thus out to the temple.

PUTTING IT ALL TOGETHER FOR A SUCCESSFUL INVOCATION

Please bear in mind this format is not definitive, and some magicians use different methods. The notes here refer to the inner work of the invocator. Others should support this and not stand by idly waiting for the flashing lights and intense feelings to happen *to* them. After we have given the general format, we will give a full invocation based upon it. Please read both with care.

1. Prepare the temple space and people. This would include prior meditation on the deity or force to be invoked. The temple would be

cleansed by at least an LBRP and LBRH. Depending on the nature of the deity or force to be invoked, other preparation may be required. This should by now be easily determined with reference to the Qabalah and the notes in this book.

2. When ready, go silent and still. If you need to, perform a Qabalistic Cross to connect to the higher. Ground and link to the Earth by opening your Malkuth centre.

3. Either outwardly or inwardly pray for assistance from your Higher and Divine Genius and your Sacred Ones. Outwardly state the intention of the ceremony and why it is being performed. These two actions may be linked.

4. Expand your astral and, if possible, etheric auras to fill the temple, or if consecrating an item (including a Eucharist) to cover the item. This can be done via will and visualisation, seeing your auric sphere growing larger and larger until it covers what is required. There is no need to take a long time with this, it will happen quite readily.

5. Build up clearly the image of the deity or blessings you wish to connect with. It is best here to use traditional images, smells, sounds. Also keep the scene active not static – see the wind blow through the trees and the deity moving, for example. Use all the senses, not just sight. At this stage there should be no engagement with or yearning towards the image or deity. Simply build it up as strongly as possible. This is where your will and training comes in and where an emotionally unbalanced magician or Priestess would fall down a little.

6. Consciously and willingly build up an intense yearning to connect with this deity. At this stage all the emotion, desire and yearning you can muster and experience should be created or released. The yearning here must be controlled so that it does not interfere with your creation and continued visualisation of the deity. One of the difficulties some of us have is feeling deep and intense yearning and desire without it interfering with our will. The key to successful energised yearning is the will, and if not already practiced, I suggest starting now on the will development exercises in Chapter Three. During group ceremony this process and that of the previous step can and should be aided by group work. As the emotion is built up it is often a good idea to have the group softly chanting the deity's name over and over. However, much depends on the invocator and the purpose of the ceremony. If this little technique is used, the chant should be controlled and directed and not descend into a frenzied adoration, getting louder and louder. It should be a soft,

almost whispered chant while everyone focuses upon the inner work previously described. It is designed to build up group emotion and to link the group in a collective endeavour using the name of the deity as the link.

7. When the emotion and yearning is really strong, use your will to channel the emotion towards the image and scene of the deity etc. For most invocations the sense of this will be either going 'up' through the personal Kether centre, or 'down' through the Malkuth centre. In no circumstances should the personal lower centres (Daath through Yesod) be used to transfer consciousness through. Direct your consciousness to be carried by the intense yearning which travels automatically towards the image of the deity you have formed.

8. Connect your consciousness with the image of the deity by focusing your will and emotional yearning *into* the image. This is connecting your consciousness with the astral and Yetziratic representation and blessings of the deity. Typically at this point the image may be more intense or take on a life of its own. Emotions and bliss may be felt, even strong sexual feelings. All of this needs to be experienced but not focused upon. Keep your Ruach intact and focused.

9. Move your consciousness **through** the image of the deity to **the blessings behind** the image. This is transferring your consciousness from the astral, Yetziratic world to the mental, Briatic world and is a crucial part of the invocation. Typically at this point there will be no image, only a deep awareness of the ultimate qualities and intense spiritual presence of the deity in question.

10. Once within the Briatic blessings of the deity, inwardly ask to be filled with the blessings. Open your mental body, your consciousness at this level, completely to the deity. This involves a level of willed surrender that will only occur if you are familiar and have a pre-established relationship with the deity. Remember Goddesses, Gods and other spiritual Beings are awe-ful in the original sense of the word – they fill us with awe. At times this awe, wonder and delight can be as painful as it is blissful.

11. At this point inwardly seek to move behind and through even the Briatic blessings of the deity to the complete Atziluthic **presence** of the deity. To be honest this is unlikely to occur, but there is no greater mystery and service, so there is no harm in asking and trying. What we are trying to do at this level is to engage and merge our spiritual body with that of the deity. If this happens you will know about it and no words, apart from those of great mystics and poets, can convey the experience.

12. Commence reciting the invocation. We see two important points. Firstly, only after all this inner work does the main outer work begin – the words of invocation. Secondly, there is here the need for the ability to be able to split consciousness, part of us at the Briatic realm filled with and open to the blessings of the deity and part of us in Assiah, reciting and controlling our actions. The words of invocation themselves should move through a number of stages reflecting the inner work being performed. At this initial stage of contact, any outer words of invocation are normally **describing** the deity or spiritual force in question. Often many invocations do not focus upon this description of the deity and will simply recite or intone the name of the deity several times. This achieves the same purpose, which is to prepare for the transfer of the Briatic blessings into the lower bodies and temple. A classic example of describing the deity is contained in Dion Fortune's 'Rite of Pan':

Half a man and half a beast
Pan is greatest, Pan is least.
Pan is All and all is Pan,
Look for Him in every man.
Goat-hoof swift and shaggy thigh
Follow Him to Arcady.

13. Begin to transfer the spiritual Briatic blessings of the deity into your astral and etheric bodies. This is done by your will, firstly bringing the blessings into the astral level and the image of the deity. Then direct the blessings into your physical body, which will ensure they are present in your etheric body.

14. Build up the spiritual blessings in your astral and etheric bodies. This in effect is super-charging the auric sphere on these two levels. More and more spiritual blessings are drawn into the auric sphere. Of course, since you have expanded your astral and etheric bodies previously, some of these are automatically transferred throughout the temple. More direction however is given in the next stage described below. At this point, when invoking the spiritual blessings into the auric sphere, the invocatory words are often changed to be **addressed to** the deity. As the invocation builds to a climax, the words may invite or entreat the deity to be fully present. Once more *the* Priestess of the twentieth century, Dion Fortune, provides a good example of this aspect of invocation in her 'Rite of Isis':

O Isis, veiled on Earth, but shining clear
In the high heaven now the full moon draws near,
Hear the invoking words, hear and appear
Shaddai el Chai, and Ea, Binah, Ge

15. Direct the spiritual blessings of the deity energy out of your auric sphere to the whole Temple. Again, this is done via will, visualisation and the expansion of the aura previously achieved. Exactly what is visualised here depends on the invocator and the spiritual force being invoked. Personally at this point I seldom have any visualisation and rely on the spiritual forces being spread via my will and expanded auric sphere. Other people visualise white light or a colour associated with the deity. At this point a pause in the words of the invocation often occurs, and direction of the blessings start when the words of the invocation change so the magician **speaks as the deity**. Some invocations do not utilize this speaking as deity, and simply direct the spiritual blessings throughout the temple. For Eucharists and similar consecrations of holy items, the blessings are directed into the material substance. Here the words of the invocation often reflect the **deity's identification with the material substance**. In this instance the Golden Dawn provides a good example of this aspect of invocation: the invocation of Osiris and consecration of the elemental Eucharist that occurs during the preparation for the Neophyte initiation ceremony. During this invocation the Hierophant takes on the Godform of Osiris and channels His blessing into each of the four symbols of the elements as they are named.

For Osiris on-Nophris who is found perfect before the Gods, hath said:
'These are the Elements of my Body,
Perfected through Suffering, Glorified through Trial.
For the scent of the Dying Rose is as the repressed Sign of my suffering:
And the flame-red Fire as the Energy of mine Undaunted Will:
And the Cup of Wine is the pouring out of the Blood of my Heart:
Sacrificed unto Regeneration, unto the Newer Life:
And the Bread and Salt are as the Foundations of my Body,
Which I destroy in order that they may be renewed.
For I am Osiris Triumphant, even Osiris on-Nophris, the Justified:
I am He who is clothed with the Body of Flesh,
Yet in whom is the Spirit of the Great Gods:

I am The Lord of Life, triumphant over Death.
He who partaketh with me shall arise with me:
I am the Manifestor in Matter of Those Whose Abode is the Invisible:
I am purified: I stand upon the Universe:
I am the Reconciler with the Eternal Gods:
I am the Perfector of Matter:
And without me, the Universe is not.'

16. This completes the actual invocation aspect of the ceremony. Unless she is moving onto similar deep work, it is important that once the invocation is complete the invocator returns her consciousness to normal and grounds. As part of the closing of the ceremony the deity invoked should be thanked. Remember also the closing of the temple should reflect the preparation and, in general, reverse hexagrams or pentagrams should be inscribed.

This simple formula for invocation can be used and modified as needed. Other formulas exist, most notably those that utilise the assumption of a Godform. It is pretty much universally agreed however, that most God-form assumption invocations are not as potent as the full ceremonial forms. However, I would argue that where a practitioner has a deep personal connection with a deity and assumes Her or His form, these invocations could in fact be even more potent and transformational. An obvious example of this is the Christian Eucharist where the Priest says 'This is my Body...' and the bread is consecrated as (or depending on your viewpoint, becomes) the Body of Christ.

In these full and potent Godform invocations steps one through fourteen above are modified and are achieved inwardly through the Godform itself. Again, using ceremonial Christianity as an example, the Godform becomes the vehicle for the Atziluthic, Briatic and Yetziratic blessings to enter the sphere of the Priest, who then **acts as Christ** as he states the Words of Institution that transforms the bread and wine on all levels. For a Godform to work to this depth with potency and clarity it needs to be created and infused with the power of a complete spiritual tradition rather than the work of a single magician. We are, however, moving into a different mystery than that of Western ceremonial magic, one that I cannot say I understand fully. Suffice to say, that for full and shared invocations within the Golden Dawn tradition, the assumption of a Godform should be seen as adding to the invocation, not replacing it. The obvious place it fits in is step 15 where, as the invocation comes to a climax, the magician speaks as the deity.

A Brief Note on Ritual Formation in the Golden Dawn Tradition

Ritual composition and design is a skill and an art by itself, the exploration of which could fill a book. While some authors have done just this, some essential magical principles are often overlooked. Firstly, within the Golden Dawn tradition rituals are never simply 'written'; they are always based upon one or more magical formula. The formula will give the bare bones of the ceremony, and the composer of the ritual then fleshes out the ceremony. In this way we know the ceremony is actually going to have a very clear magical effect. The use of Golden Dawn formulae as the basis for your rituals will also lend them a power and a history that will increase their effectiveness. The formula for a ceremonial invocation given above is based on GD principles and contains within itself other formulas. As far as the GD goes it is actually quite an expanded formula, as most of the formulas are normally given in point form and are a bit opaque to the newcomer. Normally the formulas that underlie advanced Golden Dawn ceremonies are based on those of the various group ceremonies, such as initiation and the Equinox ceremonies. However, even the rituals we examined previously, like the Supreme Pentagram, are based on a formula, which can be modified to produce variants if required.

The second, and in some ways most important aspect of ritual formation, is the general overall principle of being grounded and connected to the Earth. I have mentioned this at length several times already in this book, because it is by staying within Assiah while *also* transferring consciousness to the other realms that full transformation occurs. The only time this principle is altered is when we consciously choose to transfer our consciousness fully to another realm through what the GD calls 'Travelling in the Spirit Vision'. Otherwise any realms we visit or connect with during ceremony or ritual are visited by extension and expansion of consciousness while remaining grounded in the temple space. We can summarise this principle by borrowing a Wiccan phrase:

'Start grounded, stay grounded and finish grounded'.

Or for Travelling in the Spirit Vision: 'Start grounded and finish grounded'.

Practically this means performing something like the Qabalistic Cross or LBRP at the start and end of the ritual and consciously maintaining Earth-plane presence during the ritual. For spirit travel, another, deeper practice of grounding may be required at the end of the ritual. We will give specific grounding exercises in the next chapter when we discuss spirit travel.

A third point to remember when it comes to ritual composition is the use of standard Golden Dawn processes and rituals within the main body of the ritual itself. Cleansings, groundings, transfer and extension of consciousness, invocation in the aura and a host of the other nuts and bolts of magical practice can be quickly and easily achieved through GD techniques. Use these rather than creating your own or borrowing from other traditions. The more the various processes within a complete ritual share a common lineage or underpinning framework (such as Golden Dawn Qabalah) the more harmoniously they will work together.

The next aspect of ritual formation, often discussed in books, is the use of correspondences. We covered this topic briefly in Chapter One. While the use of the various correspondences to Gods and other spiritual powers are useful, such use needs to be intelligent and willed. That is, do not simply reach for the jasmine perfume when working to open yourself to Yesod within Yetzira. Find out why jasmine is corresponded to Kether, meditate on the reason and decide if it works for you. Then try it out **before** the night of the invocation – does it seem to add strength and power to your connection? What I am saying here is that while the correspondences have a traditional power of their own, for their full effect they need to be activated within your own personal sphere before use in ritual.

AN EXAMPLE OF A FULL DRAMATIC INVOCATION

With these basic principles in mind we can now look at a full invocation of the Goddess Isis within the broader Golden Dawn tradition. To give context and to set the scene, we assume that the invocation is taking place as part of an ongoing Mystery group's work with Isis. The purpose of the mystery group is to train and help develop its members so that they may become channels and tools for the neglected spiritual forces of the Western tradition to enter this realm and change society. One of these neglected spiritual forces is Goddess. Rather than seeking to work and form a relationship with the unified and amorphous 'Great Goddess', the group's leaders decide to focus on the Goddess Isis. Isis is chosen because in many ways She is the Goddess of the Western mysteries and the Golden Dawn; the tradition that the group draws its techniques, inspiration and framework from.

Over the last three months all members have been learning and reading the various myths and attributes of Isis and Her worship, from ancient times through to modern. All have received or drawn coloured images of Her. One particular image is relevant for the invocation, showing the Luna Isis, one of the most potent and worked with aspects of Isis in the modern Western traditions. In order to link in with the ancient Egyptian Mysteries, which did not focus too much on the lunar aspect of Isis, it is decided to use Her Egyptian name **Ast-Ah** – Isis of the Full Moon.

The invocation is set for the night of the Full Moon. The Priestess who will be performing the invocation has been an Isian Priestess for the last year and is deepening her established relationship through a series of tasks given to her by the leader. One of these is this full ceremonial invocation, which will be the first that the Priestess will have done with someone who is not part of the group in attendance. A newcomer, who is half-way through a basic course in the Western traditions organized by the group, has been invited to attend. She has been given full information on the group and the invocation.

Prepare the temple space and people. All members, and the guest, have been asked to meditate over the last week upon this Luna image and an associated description of Isis given to them by the Priestess. One particular aspect of the meditation involves the members using introspection to own and name aspects of their personality which may impede the Goddess Isis using them to bring change in the world. Once aware of these, through introspection, members are asked to assign elemental attributions to each aspect before closing with an LBRP. In this way, members will come to the invocation prepared and open for the blessings of Isis and the change She may require.

On the evening, the Priestess who will be invoking meets everyone and briefly asks if anyone has had any problems with the meditations. The group members know that this is not a time for a big discussion but a brief check-in to make sure no one will be entering into the ritual space who is emotionally upset.

The temple is laid out with a central altar and four side altars. The four side altars represent the four elemental principles, and the central altar, that of spirit. The central altar has been draped in a purple and silver altar cloth – colours of the moon. It has small candles of purple, a silver chalice of red wine and jasmine incense. The side altars have lamps in the elemental colours and a symbol to represent the element. Incense is not used for air as it would interfere with the jasmine incense, chosen for the moon.

The members and guest assemble and sit around the walls of the temple on chairs facing inward. The leader of the group makes sure she sits next to the guest. After two minutes of silence, the Priestess stands and asks for the lights to be turned off and the candles and jasmine incense lit. Some Golden Dawn groups have specific candle lighting ceremonies; groups I have worked with never have and do not seem to have suffered from the lack. Experiment and work out your own needs.

Once the candles are lit a member comes forward and performs the LBRP.

Next, another member comes forward and performs the generic LBRH. She then pauses and proceeds with an LBRH of the Moon.

The Priestess comes forward and performs the Supreme Invoking Ritual of the Hexagram of the Moon at the four quarters, around the temple. While she realizes this is not really required, she wishes to invoke all the assistance and help she can for this invocation. She finishes the SIRH with an Analysis of the Keyword at the centre of the temple, omitting the four Enochian spirit names so that the divine Light affects her own sphere the most. She does this to help awaken and stabilise her Tipharethic and higher consciousness.

Connection to the Higher and Grounding. The Priestess asks everyone to stand and face East. They perform a Qabalistic Cross in unison. As they stand at the end of the Cross, the Priestess asks them to ensure they are grounded and linked to the Earth. They do this by opening their Malkuth centre through four inward intonations of **ADNI-H-ARTz**. These done, everyone but her returns to their place and remain standing, getting ready to inwardly support the Priestess.

Prayer and Stating the Intention of the Ritual. The Priestess moves to the central altar and faces the direction of the moon at present. She inwardly prays for assistance from the One, her Higher and Divine Genius and Isis. She now focuses briefly upon each of the elemental altars and the realms they symbolise, and states the intention of the ceremony with these words.

'Spirits of Air, Fire, Water and Earth.
Spirits Active, Passive – those of the reaches above and depths below.
All spirits, in all the realms, hear our intention tonight:

We are the Perth Temple of the Western Mysteries.

We honour and acknowledge the spirits of this living land that sustains and supports us in our lives, together with the original Aboriginal peoples who cared for and continue to care for the land, generation upon generation.

Tonight we seek to invoke the complete and full presence of the Great Goddess Isis in Her Luna aspect, so that we may come to know Her, be touched by Her, be changed by Her and that through that change may be inspired to change our world. And to this end we seek the aid of the One Being, our Higher and Divine Genii, the inner guardians of the Golden Dawn who guide our Temple and the Great Isis Herself. Amen.'

Everyone else responds with Amen.

This form of statement of intent is good as it speaks to the four elemental realms and the realms of mystery. If we remember the Qabalistic correspondence of the four worlds to the letters of YHVH and the four elements, we are speaking to all the realms from Pure Deity in Atziluth to the flesh and blood Beings in Assiah. It is also good practice to name yourself or the group. If you are working within a group that is informal, comes together rarely and does not have a name or strong group-mind, then it is better for each individual present to take it in turns to name themselves. While this is good psychology in that it helps to focus people and 'bring' them to the ritual, it is also a sound magical principle. Remember names have power, and by declaring ourselves we are opening ourselves to the power of the invocation to come. The naming of a group or a temple also does the same for the group mind.

The phase of honouring the Land and the original peoples of the Land is an innovation to the Western magical tradition. Without going into the politics and compassion behind such an act, it is a sound principle in magic to honour and seek alliance with all the spiritual forces that sustain us. The Land is one of these forces and I invite you to add this innovation into your own personal and group practice.

The general purpose of the ritual is now announced. Here there is a little bit of poetry, which helps to focus the first stirrings of awe and worship to Isis. However, any poetry or lyrical phrases should be short and devoid of waffle and complex imagery and motifs. Simply state what you and/or the group intend to do and why. Finally, we ask for aid. Following traditional practice we name the highest and deepest power we can conceive of first – the One Being. It is standard Golden Dawn practice to honour and name our Sacred Ones in descending order of importance or 'power'. This procedure is a core part of Golden Dawn magic and should be followed well, as it ensures a correct movement of blessings and spiritual potency down the planes in the order of Creation. Be aware that some authors, including Israel Regardie, do not follow this procedure, but it is traditional and useful. My personal preference is then also to name the key power of the evening again for dramatic effect, as in this example.

One of the key points in announcing yourself and stating your intention is honesty. If you are doing your first invocation, largely for practice (as you should), simply say something like: 'Tonight I wish to invoke the God Pan to practice my skills in invocation'. If you just want to experience the bliss of the Moon, say 'Tonight we wish to be enlivened and experience the bliss of the Full Moon'. Never put on airs and graces as to what you are doing and more importantly why. Of course, if you find yourself constantly just wishing to experience nice sensations from your magic rather than unfold and develop in your service, some introspection on your motives for practicing magic may be called for. Or be honest with yourself and others – state clearly you practice magic for the experience and the buzz.

Expansion of the Aura. At the culmination of the invocation the wine on the altar will be consecrated and later shared as a Eucharist. However, for the purpose to be enacted in the world, the blessings of Isis should flow through all present and the four elements at the quarters, which represent the totality of the material creation and the world. The Priestess therefore has decided (while composing the ceremony) to expand her aura to the four elements. She takes several slow, deep breaths. As she breathes out, she wills and sees her aura growing larger and larger in all directions. The rest of the temple aids her by visualising this also. It only takes four breaths before she sees her aura large enough to fill the entire temple. She focuses particularly on her aura covering and going around the four elemental altars and symbols. So as to give outer actions to inner experience, and aid the temple in assisting her, the Priestess slowly raises her arms as she expands her aura and drops them softly once complete. The rest of the temple now know to move to the next state of the inner work.

Building up the Image. Half closing her eyes so that she continues to be aware of the temple and the world of Assiah, the Priestess builds up the image previously meditated upon and connected with. The rest of the temple assists inwardly, seeing the image also. The image builds quickly and easily as it has already been created in the Yetziratic and astral realm by the work of the temple over the weeks previously. Staying focused, she allows the image to become alive, adding all the other interior senses – she hears the sound of the sea behind Isis, the soft wind and the flutter of swallows (a bird sacred to Isis). She smells and tastes the sea, feels the wind and the light of the moon.

Building Up the Yearning. From this point on until the words of invocation are said, the inner work of the invocator (in this case the Priestess) often have no outer correspondence. The group supporting them simply do their best to move from stage to stage at the same time as the invocator. It does not matter much if this is not congruent, the aid is simply that, aid – and the real work is still being done by the invocator. In this example, after a short period of building up the image one of the group, who was previously assigned this role, now starts very softly and slowly chanting 'Isis' over and over. The rest of the temple picks up the chant. At this point the Priestess is letting out and generating her desire to connect with Isis at the deepest and most transformational level possible. Her previous relationship and daily worship enables this to happen clearly and consciously. She maintains her Ruach and will – strengthened previously by the blessings from the Keyword – and controls and directs her yearning and emotion. The rest of the temple build up their yearning, consciously keeping themselves and the chant controlled but impassioned, and direct their yearning to the Priestess.

Extension of Consciousness Towards the Image. With the emotion and the yearning getting stronger and stronger, the Priestess now uses the emotion and energy. She consciously collects it and expands, like in the Qabalistic Cross, until she is standing at the ends of the Universe with her feet upon the Earth. She still has eyes half open, maintaining her Assiatic presence. Once as large as the universe, the Priestess pauses and sees vividly once more the image of Isis. She then directs and channels her consciousness out of her Kether centre, which inwardly is at the very ends of the Universe, and through the dazzling white light towards the image of Isis. She feels herself extending, getting closer and closer to the image, which becomes more radiant as she proceeds.

Connection with the Image. The Priestess now in imagination and on the inner levels arrives directly before the image she has been yearning for. She directs her consciousness and looks into the eyes of Isis, perhaps holds her hands, it does matter too much as long as touch and connection occurs. As soon as she does this, there is a notable shift in the astral atmosphere of the temple. The Priestess finds herself in a swirl of intense and alive images and forms of Isis. She also experiences a rush of deep emotions. Momentarily overcome by the astral-Yetziratic blessings of Isis, she focuses her Ruach and moves to the next stage.

Connection with the Blessings Behind the Image. The Priestess has re-focused on the original image, putting aside the rush of other images and sensations. She stands touching Isis and looking into Her eyes. Next the Priestess consciously directs and extends her consciousness *through* the image, moving into and through the body of Isis. Once within the Briatic realm, the Priestess experiences a sense of deep awe and spiritual presence and a profound peace. Again, this is likely to be felt within the astral and mental atmosphere of the temple. This is a state of being that the Priestess has touched upon a few times previously – her consciousness is within the blessings of Isis, the deep presence of Her in the world of Briah. She is only aware of presence, consciousness and mystery at this level. The Priestess inwardly surrenders herself to Isis and asks to be filled with Her blessings and mystery. Typically, most people working at the Briatic Realm will experience this as thought and will, without any interior words being spoken.

Seeking the Real Presence of the Deity. The Priestess now attempts to move even deeper than the spiritual blessings of Isis, seeking Her real and direct presence. The movement towards Atziluth here is very hard to describe, and really I do not see the point in trying. When you have worked deeply in the Briatic presence of a deity, you will probably understand this process, but not likely before. However, mystery is mystery and there is no harm in trying – even on your very first practice invocation – for the pure presence of deity. Mysteries do happen and may occur to us all, regardless of experience. In fact sometimes, the less experience the better. In any case, the Priestess, like most of us, is not graced with the real Presence of Isis. She stands in Assiah at the central altar, and in Briah filled and channelling the blessings of Isis.

Commencement of the Words of Invocation. The Priestess now opens her eyes fully, which should help ensure she is still well grounded, and recites clearly and confidently.

AST-AH, AST-AH, AST-AH

Great ISIS, Queen of the Heavens and all the Stars.
Moonlight in the sky
Goddess revealed,
Pour forth upon the Land and
Come to us, Come to us!

You who are the light sought for in the pathless dark,
You who inspire lovers and poets to madness and death
You who are the source of the ecstatic trance
Pour forth upon the Land and
Come to us, Come to us!

Ripened One
Pregnant Belly of the Sky
Child bringer
Love maker

ISIS of the realms above
We call to you, descend into this temple
Of your eternal mysteries.
Bring to us the blessings of Ah and Nuit.

Bright Queen, be here now.

(Pause)

I am She, Ast-Ah – Isis of the Moon.
I am in all things that live under my sky
Or bathe in my wombic light.
I am the ruler of sea and of tide.

Your tears are mine,
Your juices are mine,
Your milk and your passion entwined are mine.
All passion and draughts belong to me –
Spring Water and wine,
Elixir, nectar and sweet honey from the bee;
All these belong to me.

As the Priestess recites the words of invocation there are several distinct
phases of inner work occurring. The initial vibration of Ast-Ah utilises

the divine names of the lunar aspect of Isis, and helps prepare the transfer of the spiritual blessings from Briah to Assiah. As mentioned in the description of the formula above, it is an abbreviated description of the deity. As the name is intoned, the Priestess channels the Briatic blessings of the Luna Isis into her Astral and Etheric bodies. This is done via her will and also by her imagining the image used to connect with Isis once more. This will very quickly ensure the direction of the blessings into the astral body of the Priestess. She then directs these blessings into her physical body, which will ensure they are moved into her etheric body. When the names are vibrated, the rest of the temple members cease chanting 'Isis' and focus inwardly in assisting the Priestess.

The Priestess continues with the invocation, addressing Ast-Ah directly. As she does so she is drawing more and more of the Briatic blessings into her sphere and thus the temple. The rest of the group assist with this through inner work and yearning to the highest aspect of the Luna Isis they can conceive of. The invocation reaches a peak at the words 'be here now'. By this stage the Priestess is fully channelling the blessings of Isis. She now pauses the invocation before moving onto the next stage. As she pauses she quickly takes on the Godform of the Luna Isis, the exact image she used to yearn towards previously. Through personal work the Godform is activated and becomes real within a few seconds.

The Priestess now opens her arms wide and above her head, making the sign of the crescent moon, a symbol of Luna Isis. She now speaks the final section of the invocation *as* Isis herself. As she does so, she has become a clear and effective channel for the Briatic, spiritual blessings of Isis. Her words and her Will direct the blessings as she speaks to the whole temple, announcing herself as Isis. The blessings flow through easily and quickly upon all the inner planes. Just before she speaks the line 'your tears are mine' she picks up the chalice of wine from the altar and places it near her heart centre. Maintaining her Godform and the channelling of the blessings of Isis, she now looks directly into the chalice and focuses all the blessings into the wine. She concentrates all the remaining blessings into the wine, charging it and consecrating it. The rest of the temple aid this through visualising the blessings, however they see them, entering the wine. The mental plane aspect of the wine is transformed via the blessings channelled. The visualisation and the will consecrate it on the astral level and the extended etheric aura, words and breath – the final words being spoken into the chalice – consecrate and charge it on the etheric level.

Once the invocation is complete, the Priestess replaces the chalice upon the altar. She then pauses while she thanks Isis and returns her consciousness from her extended state to normal. She performs a quick grounding by inwardly intoning **ADNI H-ARTz** four times, strengthening her Malkuth centre. Once this is done, she proceeds to invite everyone to stand around the central altar to receive the Eucharist, the wine of Isis of the Moon. She picks up the chalice once more and addresses the temple and the universe.

'All who wish to partake of the moon-wine of Ast-Ah, Isis of the Full Moon, draw close and receive Her blessings, given freely to all.'

The temple move to stand in a circle around the central altar. Once everyone is settled, the Priestess says:

'Let us give our names and affirm our openness to the touch of Isis as we drink her consecrated wine tonight'.

She pauses and then she names herself before drinking carefully from the Chalice. She turns to the person to her left (sunwise) and looks him in the eye before passing the chalice on. This person then names himself, communes and passes the chalice on in a like manner. When all have drunk, the chalice ends up back with the Priestess. She holds the chalice on high and says:

Ast-Ah, Isis of the Full Moon
Thanks and blessings for your presence and gifts tonight.
May we all remain open to your ways and your touch, now and forever!
Amen.

All respond with 'Amen'.

She then places the chalice back down. The remaining wine will later be poured forth upon the Land as libation and thanks for its blessings and sustenance.

There is only minimal inner work occurring here. The mystery of the consecrated Eucharist, the embodying of Isis within the wine is transformational in its own right. The naming of each person and the affirmation of being open to the touch and change of Isis is important. These actions and affirmations, though small, can over time affect us all deeply and powerfully. Never underestimate the power of willed openness to the Goddesses and Gods.

Everyone but the Priestess now returns to their place. The Priestess now covers the chalice with a thick cloth and places it inside the altar.

This is to prevent the wine being accidentally deconsecrated, even to a small degree, through the banishing that is to follow.

The Priestess now performs a Supreme Banishing Hexagram Ritual of the Moon around the temple, reversing the circle that was formed in the opening.

Another member comes forward and performs a generic Lesser Banishing Ritual of the Hexagram. She pauses and then continues onto the Lesser Banishing Ritual of the Pentagram, effectively returning the temple space to 'normal.' Everyone now gathers once more around the altar.

The Priestess closes the temple with the following words:

"To those who have aided our spiritual endeavours tonight we give you thanks and blessings: the One Being of All, the Land that sustains and supports us all, our Higher and Divine Genii, the inner guardians of our temple, and, above all Ast-Ah –Isis of the Full moon. Thanks and blessings. Amen."

All respond Amen and the temple is closed.

If you take your time and compare this full version of an invocation, the notes on the formula it is based on and the other notes in the previous chapter, you will find a wealth of Golden Dawn keys and pointers to successful dramatic invocation. This example was purposely chosen to show how the Golden Dawn can provide direct methods of communion with spiritual powers many think are outside its scope, in this case, the Goddess. This invocation of the Luna Isis is pure Golden Dawn in essence. A few Golden Dawn purists will be horrified, as will some Neo-Pagans who think the Goddess is their domain. Regardless of our religious background and the Sacred Ones we worship, the Golden Dawn can help us deepen our relationship and service to them.

CONNECTING WITH AND VISITING THE INNER PLANES

AN INTRODUCTORY TALE

ONE day when I was still a young boy growing up in England my father gave me a piece of advice: 'believe nothing of what you hear and only half of what you see'. I never really appreciated this advice, or my dad, until I was much older. The occasion that prompted my long overdue appreciation occurred when I was studying at university. Along with some friends, I had formed a student club to discuss aspects of the New Age and the esoteric. Our first treasurer was a talkative guy named James. He was about twenty, tall, thin and fair with a mass of red hair and active in student politics. After a few months fulfilling his duties very well James stopped attending to his responsibilities, and the club's finances were getting in a bit of a mess. He didn't return my calls and it was hard to contact him. I had number of quite important bills to pay and required his signature on the cheque alongside mine. All in all I was getting quite annoyed.

One day I happened to be walking through the Student Guild area, where the student politicians liked to hang out and feel important, when I saw James walking towards me. I went right up to him and he greeted me, something I did not return but leapt straight into listing the problems he had caused. I was asking him why he wasn't returning my calls and why he had, in effect, stopped being treasurer without notice – hardly letting him speak. His responses were basically that he had no idea what I was talking about – 'what calls?', 'what club?' 'what esoteric thingy?' James kept repeating that he had no idea what the hell I was on about – none at all – while I kept repeating my list of problems. I was simply not listening to him, believing he was trying to evade the issue. Then after at least thirty seconds of this, I started to actually *think* – evading responsibility is one thing, but denying knowledge that the club even existed carried it a bit far.

With my first real thought of the day (as opposed to patterned behaviour) something dreadful and very embarrassing happened: James changed into Michael, an old school friend. I was literally seeing and speaking to James one moment and the next his face, his body, changed into Michael. I even saw James' face transmute, like in a Hollywood special effects movie – it dissolved and reformed as Michael. Of course, I had been talking to Michael all along and had 'mistaken' him for James. Michael too was about twenty, tall, thin and with red hair. He was simply visiting the university for the day; I had never seen him there before and was walking in the area I could expect to find James. My automatic pilot turned on and, for that very brief but crucial minute or so I was speaking to James, not Michael. If I had been stopped half way through that minute I would have sworn black and blue and bet my life it was James before me.

After the incredible embarrassment and humiliation, I was shaken enough by my automatic behaviour to try and learn from this experience. Depth psychologists and mystics have for centuries told us we see only what we create and not what is actually 'there'. In fact some traditions, Buddhism for example, insist we can never truly know what is 'there', only our perceptions of it, which are always clouded by some distorting factor or other. Buddhism calls this 'maya' or illusion. In my case this distorting factor was my tendency not to observe, not to think, and to expect things to be how they always have been. My unthinking desire to sort it out with James, a chance meeting with someone who looked vaguely like him (and who greeted me by name) in an area where I knew James could be, placed me in an illusion as powerful as one the most brilliant stage hypnotist could weave. Once in this illusion it took a conscious thought, rather than unconscious talking and chatter, to break free.

One of the most amusing and interesting aspects of this experience was the method of change from James to Michael. In my illusion my mind used the only form it knew to show change from one human being to another – the way it was shown in the movies I watched as a kid and a teenager. I expect that if the Hollywood convention of changing one person to another was through a small pop and an explosion of pink smoke, I would have seen that rather than the melting and reforming.

When I reflect on this experience I wonder how many other times in my life have I acted in this way. Also, what illusion am I experiencing right now? More importantly I wonder how we may break free from the illusions. Spiritual traditions state quite clearly it is only through regular spiritual practice we can become illusion-free. When interacting with the universe beyond Malkuth, I use, and earnestly recommend, the advice given to me years ago by my dear old dad:

'Believe nothing of what you hear and only half of what you see'.

THE INNER REALMS

One of the fundamental differences between the esoteric and exoteric viewpoints in the Western world is the acknowledgment of the inner, non-physical realms of the universe and the belief that we can interact with them and the Beings that inhabit them. This viewpoint is found in just about every traditional culture in the world. Our own modern Western culture is unique in denying the existence of the inner realms and the denizens thereof. The Golden Dawn, as with most magical traditions, not only asserts the reality of the inner realms and its people, but insists that we can and should interact with them, that humanity benefits and grows through such interaction. Again, traditional cultures the world over posit that the harmony of the world in some way depends upon regular human interaction, in the correct manner, with the otherworld or the inner realm. Such a belief is taken to an interesting conclusion in the modern interpretation of the Faery tradition by Scottish writer and musician R.J. Stewart. The human being, Stewart asserts, is actually an incomplete being; a mere third of the complete Being which consists of human, spirit animal and Faery all working in alliance as one.

Drawing from the Middle Eastern traditions, which recognise the One within the Many, the Golden Dawn does not see such a lack in the human being, but does require its initiates to form an alliance and good relationship with a variety of inner plane Beings. In addition the Golden Dawn initiate is required to be in balance with the inner realms, being able to exist within them and explore them at will. The Golden Dawn insists on these qualities, as it is through conscious human interaction with the inner world that a number of important transformations occur.

Firstly, a visit by a human being potentially links the inner planes to the physical realm of Malkuth. This is because we humans are incarnated beings existing in Assiah and Malkuth. The more connections and links between an inner realm and Malkuth, the more its qualities and mysteries are embodied in the physical world. Secondly, every inner realm we visit, explore and harmonise with has a corresponding energy and blessing within us, as explained in chapter one – 'as above, so below'. By harmonising with the inner realms of the greater universe, we harmonise and balance our own inner nature, increasing our unfoldment and potential for effective service. Thirdly, while visiting the inner realms we interact with real, though non-incarnate Beings. While these Beings have a life and purpose of their own they can be a source of great wisdom for us human beings, and we for them. This wisdom is not generally the sort that can be taught or written into a book: rather it pervades our consciousness and beings. Occasionally however, the wisdom can be direct and practical. A good example of this is the farming wisdom given by the contacts of the founders of the Findhorn community in Scotland.

Finally, an interesting result of conscious interaction between humanity and the elemental inner plane Beings is the transference of the spirit to them and their plane. This stems from the traditional Hermetic understanding of the nature of the relationship between humanity and the elemental kingdoms. In this view, shared by the Golden Dawn, human beings are considered to be made up of the four elements and also the fifth – the Quintessence, the spirit. The four elemental kingdoms do not have spirit and are very desirous to come into contact with it, as it is through contact with, and the presence of spirit, that evolution occurs. This is why, traditionally, the elemental Beings are amongst the easiest of non-corporeal spirits to engage with.

Another way of expressing this point of view stems from the understanding that humanity is made in the image of the One. That is, we have been created to be the self-reflective and self-cognizant aspect of the world (at least at this stage of the world's unfoldment). We are to be the facilitators of a current of blessing stemming from the Unmanifest One and directed to the Manifest All. By being conscious and allowing God to move through us, God is transferred to all we behold and touch and engage with. The vehicle by which this occurs is the spirit within us. This is what the great poet Rainer Maria Rilke means when he writes 'all that I see has become, by my beholding it'.

When we move into the elemental realms and engage with elemental Beings we help form a circuit between the Unmanifest One and the elemental Beings and kingdoms. While we are the bridge that allows this to occur, we cannot consider ourselves as better or more important than either of the two other aspects of this circuit; the Unmanifest or the elemental Beings. A wire is no more important than the two ends of the electric circuit it connects, as all three points are needed for electricity to flow. This is what true alliance is about – the realization that we are required to work in partnership and harmony with other Beings for the mutual unfoldment of all. This requires a shift in consciousness from seeing ourselves as important in our own right, the view of the 'Natural Man' as the GD would put it, to seeing ourselves as but one interconnected aspect of the great unfolding of the manifest universe, the view of the initiate. In terms of our electrical metaphor above, we need to see that the electricity is the important thing, not ourselves as the wire.

Within the ceremonies to open and close the 'elemental' grades in the Golden Dawn some of the spirit that is invoked is given to the elemental Beings as a gift at the closure of the temple. When we work in alliance with the elemental Beings our conscious presence also provides them with spirit. However, this spirit comes directly from our own beings and thus we form a personal bond, a sacred pact with the Beings. Such a bond and deep link is wonderful, but it is also a responsibility. Before we form these bonds and alliances with the elemental Beings, or other inner plane Beings, we need to be consciously aware of what we are doing. Not because they are in any way dangerous, but because like any relationship it needs time and effort to make it work.

This approach flies in the face of the common Western magical approach to the elemental Beings and the approach used by most Golden Dawn magicians historically and probably today. The traditional approach is one of control tempered with respect. That is, the magician was taught they must respect the elemental Beings but ever within a framework where they are to learn to control and invoke the Beings at will. From this perspective the magician must always ensure they are in complete control of any transaction with any elemental being or power. The magician must learn the appropriate 'words of power' (that is the state of consciousness behind the words) that will enable her to control and order the elemental Beings at will, though with a mind for their wellbeing at all times. This is possible since humanity partakes of the essence of God and the realm of pure spirit.

The rationale behind this view (without examining the ideology that supports it) is that by correct and proper control over the outer elemental Beings, the magician will develop similar control over her inner elemental powers, and thus her personality. Certainly, it is possible to use this approach and be able to control the outer elemental Beings. Correct use of the appropriate names and symbols (and our own inner understanding of them) can give us control over the elementals. And there are times when such a degree of power is useful. However, from my own view and that of the Order I belong to, a more respectful, harmonious and less human-centred approach is that of alliance, not control. This follows our general philosophy of wishing to be in harmony with the universe as it occurs around us. It draws from the understanding discussed earlier that the electricity, not the wire, not the generator and not the light bulb, is the most important thing.

With respect to the transformation of consciousness, working in alliance with the elemental powers is equally as effective as controlling them. With respect to using the elemental Beings to assist us in traditional practical magic for our own ends (finding buried treasure and the like), working in alliance is less effective. With respect to nature and the planet, I believe it is far more effective and places a stick in the spokes of the great wheel of anthropomorphic patriarchy that has dominated the world for the last 1500 years. Of course, the use of methods to subjugate the elemental Beings to our wills, even if we are able, may also exact a heavy personal price. Beings that are under control may, when that control slips or is ineffective due to illness and so on, rebel against their masters. The Rev. W.Y. Ayton, one of the early and most accomplished Golden Dawn magicians, warned against converse with spirits saying, 'even the elemental spirits turn against one at the end'. Rev. Ayton would have been using traditional control methods of conversing with the elemental Beings, rather than an alliance approach.

CONNECTING WITH THE INNER REALMS

From the esoteric point of view we are always in contact with the inner planes. When we meet someone we interact with them on the etheric, astral and mental planes as well as the physical. When we ponder and day-dream we create briefly lived forms that exist in the astral plane. When we pay a visit to a friend's new home, part of us 'feels' the astral and etheric atmosphere. At a football match our astral-emotional body merges with the group astral body and mind of our team's supporters. Some authorities and teachers also insist that at every moment non-incarnate Beings, guides, angels and others are vying for our attention. What we are seeking as magicians is not only contact with the inner planes but also conscious and directed connection and interaction. Essentially there are two ways to do this:

1. We can 'move' our consciousness into a specific inner plane or connection with a specific inner plane being. This may be a partial transference of consciousness focused on the use of a symbol, or the classic 'astral' travel scenario, where we perceive ourselves to be in a different world and can move about at will. The Golden Dawn calls this experience of the astral, Yetziratic, plane 'Spirit Vision' as it is so

often heavily focused on the visual aspect of inner awareness. Partial transference of consciousness through the use of a symbol is called 'Skrying in the Spirit Vision' and full transference is called 'Travelling in the Spirit Vision'.

2. We can 'open' our consciousness as it exists in this realm of Malkuth to the influx of a specific inner plane being. In the broad sense of the word this is 'channelling' – the reception of inner plane wisdom or blessings.

Traditionally the Golden Dawn insisted that the first approach was the only safe and reliable one. Consequently it developed and taught only techniques designed for this form of interaction and communication. The second method was, and often still is, eschewed by GD Orders because of the methods employed by spiritualists and mediums which result in passivity and a lack of will within the medium. This is counter to the whole magical approach which is centred on the use of the will and conscious choice. Also from the GD perspective, many mediums do not use enough protective and consciousness-raising techniques to ensure adequate filtering of problematic Beings and energies. Two old GD techniques using tools called 'the Ring and the Disc' or 'the Tripod' appear outwardly to be forms of opening the consciousness in Malkuth to the inner realms. However, upon examination of the inner work involved it is clear that there is an extension of consciousness, identical to the method used in invocation, and the magician's will is never affected or placed in any form of passivity.

Since the days of the original Order some groups have developed techniques that allow an influx of communication into Malkuthian consciousness without the loss of will or any form or passivity. Most notable in this direction are the Society of the Inner Light and the Servants of the Light. While having no essential difficulty with this form of inner plane connection, where the will is intact, I believe the techniques that allow it to occur can only be effectively taught in person. I will therefore not be discussing them here.

TRANSFERRING OUR CONSCIOUSNESS TO THE INNER PLANES

Before any attempts are made to transfer our consciousness into the inner planes we need a very good internalized understanding of exactly what we are trying to achieve. We need to know exactly what realm we are travelling to and why. Our studies in the Qabalah and the framework outlined in the previous chapters provide this for us. As part of Golden Dawn magic the initiate is required to visit, explore and harmonise with many different inner planes. The exact sequence of inner planes varies depending on the particular Order, but most start with visiting the astral or Yetziratic realm of the four elemental principles. Many contemporary Orders require their initiates to visit the inner elemental realms as part of their work through the 'elemental' grades of Zelator through Philosophus. Traditionally, the vast majority of inner plane travel was reserved solely for initiates of the Inner Order, the theory being that they would be able to remain balanced and sane and resist the lure of ego inflation and distortion that is part and parcel of inner plane work. Sadly many people were not able to resist the pull and glamour of the astral realm, and the whole 'astral travel' business has suffered a bad reputation ever since.

When conducted with care and following the traditional safeguards, visiting the inner realms can be a highly productive part of a Golden Dawn magical curriculum. The benefits of such visits have been given previously and we need now to focus on the potential downside of inner plane connection. The biggest and most serious danger comes from our own egos and unconscious. It is important to remember that our inner plane exploration will be almost completely within the world of Yetzira, the realm of astral light. The astral light is completely malleable and can be formed into literally anything. We can thus encounter any 'thing' in our travels. Many inner plane Beings have no astral form and assume forms when they communicate with us. The forms they assume may bear little relation to their inner essence and we need to find other methods of judgment than those based on what something looks like. A simple method is what I call the 'Four F's': **Form, Function, Feeling and Fruition.**

♦ Our world, the world of matter, flesh and blood (Assiah) is concerned with **Form**. We recognise what is what, who is whom, by what it or they look like, taste like etc. When we are ungrounded however, as in the personal story at the start of this chapter, our consciousness does not function as fully within Assiah as it needs to. We may then try and discern what is 'real' in the material world through our consciousness in Yetzira, the astral realm, a realm open to the distortion of our subconscious. This is what occurred when I 'saw' James instead of Michael in the world of Assiah. My consciousness, resting mostly within the astral plane, was distorted by my preconceptions and superimposed my astral reality over my physical reality. This is why delusion is often best avoided by being grounded and a dose of plain common sense. It also explains why the Western traditions, including the Golden Dawn, insist that initiates live a solid and practical life in the real world of families and work as well as the magical realms.

◆ The astral world (Yetzira) is concerned with **Function** – a being there can vary in what it looks like to a large degree, but it will function and act in the same manner regardless of the form it assumes. For example, five magicians may encounter a Salamander (one of the elemental Beings of fire) and may each see a Being that looks completely different from each other. However, it will still be a Salamander. We can discern if it is a Salamander from how it acts and functions, not what it looks like. If it expands from and is delighted to be on the receiving end of an invoking fire pentagram, chances are it is a salamander. If we assume that all Salamanders look like lizards made of fire, we are judging from a standpoint of form and have mistaken the planes. If we call a salamander to us and then refuse to interact with it because it has the form of a bird not a lizard, we may have given up a good opportunity to grow and learn. It will also offend the Salamander, making contact more difficult next time. All Beings we see on the astral plane should be tested through function not form. This method of discernment is crucial in Golden Dawn inner plane work and we will return to it shortly.

◆ The mental world (more or less Briah), is concerned with **Feeling**. This is not the emotional type of feelings we all experience every day, but rather the direct intuitive apprehension of knowledge. It is the experience of a self to another self without the span of time or thought. It is the feeling of clear presence. If we are functioning within Briah fully we do not judge or make opinions, we simply know. Again, please do not confuse this with the regular 'knowing' we can all have from time to time, the 'lower intuition'. This form of testing should not be applied to any astral experience. If we have a vision, if we have emotions, imagery, sounds etc, we are functioning within Yetzira and the test of function not feeling applies. Testing by feeling in the astral world of Yetzira can be very problematic as our feelings on this level are open to distortion from within and without our selves.

◆ The Spiritual World (Atziluth) is concerned with **Fruition** – the experience of unity with a spiritual presence or being and the transformation of self after it recedes from the experience. When this occurs it is a touch of divinity and is very recognisable. Again there will be no vision or inner experience of a world at this level of interaction, a level most of us, most of the time, do not engage in.

It is very important to understand these concepts before attempting to explore the inner planes, either by skrying or travelling within them. Put simply, just because you encounter a being dressed as an Egyptian adept with gold light all around them, it does not mean they are an adept. Forget about what you see, what you hear and what you feel. Examine how the supposed adept functions. Do they shun or embrace the vibration of divine names? Do they wish to follow you when you ask them not to? Do they give advice and wisdom that will help your unfoldment? Or does it simply make you feel important and useful? In short, what they do is far more important than what they look like.

The Golden Dawn developed many techniques to help us discern what exactly it is we encounter on the inner realms, but none of them are guaranteed to work for everyone. If we have a strong inner desire for illusion, we will come across delusion at some point. There is nothing essentially wrong with this, and it is certainly not a good reason for forgoing the exploration of the inner realms. We are all deluded at some time in our lives. How we handle that delusion is the crucial issue here. Do we let it take over our lives, or do we contain it and not make rash decisions until we have sat and thought a while? As we have said before, it is unwise to make decisions that affect our outer lives based on inner plane information alone.

The Golden Dawn approach is to test every inner plane experience and every inner plane being, every step of the way. We will explore these methods of testing extensively shortly. For now I wish to add that in addition to the spiritual and ceremonial methods of testing, one of the keys to ensure we do not succumb to temptations of our own unconscious is to make some solid, practical rules and stick by them. Such rules may include not visiting the inner realms more than once a week; not accepting any information that presents you as important or superior to others; not changing any outer relationship or outer aspect of your life based solely on information from an inner source. These all seem very sensible and obvious, but it is surprising how easily common sense can go out the window once we engage with the inner realms in this fashion. Of course, having a stable and full outer life with family commitments means that there is less chance of us dropping everything and rushing off to find the Holy Grail based on a map given to us by an inner guide. This is one of the many reasons some Orders encourage or only accept initiates over the age of thirty.

How to Test the Inner Experience and Inner Beings

Testing any inner plane Beings we contact is an essential part of the Golden Dawn. I have heard some teachers advise against this process on the grounds that it is rude to test the Beings we contact. No genuine inner plane Being will object to being tested or be affronted by your initial 'mistrust'. In fact most of the methods of testing actually assist the Being in question (in a small way). Testing can be done through a number of processes.

Correspondences to the Realm in Question

If we enter the astral realm of elemental Earth and find ourselves surrounded by the ocean and face to face with a mermaid, we know that something has gone wrong. At best we have wound up in the Water sub-element of Earth, and at worst we are lost within our own mind. In either case, we should withdraw and start again. There is no reason to be rigid in our assessment here, as some of our own preconceptions may bar our experience, as in the case of the salamander mentioned previously. However, we do need to be sensible, and if your vision or the Beings you encounter do not match the obvious and broad qualities of the realm in question, then be prepared to close down and start again.

Vibration of Divine Names

This is the paramount way of testing. Once we have entered an inner realm we should at once vibrate the corresponding divine names on our entry to the realm. This should strengthen our image and perception of the realm. If the image and perception fade or disappear when we vibrate the sacred names, we can assume they were not fully in resonance with the realm. The intonation of the names calls forth the mental plane blessings into the astral realm. This will enliven and empower any astral images and forms in harmony with the mental plane blessings and disperse those forms which are not in harmony. When we encounter any being within the inner realm we should ask them if they are there to aid us in the name of the Divine name in question (vibrating the name towards the being). Any authentic inner plane being from the realm will be happy to be asked this, as the vibration of the name towards them will direct mental plane blessings towards them and increase their own power and energy. If they are not happy with the vibration of the names, shrink from them or begin to disperse after the name has been vibrated, they are not to be trusted and are to be banished at once (see below).

THE PENTAGRAMS AND HEXAGRAMS

These are not ordinarily used to test, but to banish. If there is a problem or a being does not test well, banish using the corresponding pentagram or hexagram in question in conjunction with the divine name. This should be made inwardly in the appropriate colour towards and over any being and the vision before you. Once you have performed the banishing it is time to close the vision or journey. You may then also like to perform a banishing Lesser Ritual of the Pentagram to complete the breakage between your sphere and the realm or being in question. Occasionally, where the vibration of divine names does not yield a strengthening of the vision, you may wish to use the appropriate invoking pentagram or hexagram of the element in conjunction with the divine names. This is rarely required however. Under no circumstance are we to inscribe an invoking pentagram or hexagram of a different nature towards an inner plane being. For example, we would never inscribe an invoking fire pentagram towards a being of elemental Water. This would be a cruel act and would cause the being harm and distress.

THE USE OF ELEMENTAL TOOLS OR SYMBOLS

If you have been using elemental tools or symbols within the Watchtower and other ceremonies you may wish to have the appropriate one by you when you undertake the journey into the inner realm. In this case, you take the astral form of the tool or symbol with you, visualising yourself holding it as you move into the realm. Provided your consecrations and work in the Watchtower has been correct, your elemental tool will give off and generate an elemental energy field of its own. This can be used to test the Beings you encounter, and these tools are often remarked upon by the Beings themselves.

THE SEVEN WANDERERS

This is one of the most innovative and wonderful adaptations of traditional Qabalistic wisdom within the Golden Dawn. The traditional correspondence of the seven ancient planets (the 'wandering stars') to the seven double Hebrew letters (those with two sounds) was used by the GD in a very practical manner. Since each of these letters, when correctly approached, helps invoke a particular stream of blessings from the Briatic plane, they can be used to bring those blessings into any experience or vision on the astral, Yetziratic plane. This affects and transforms the astral experience in a particular and very distinct manner, depending on the letter in question. By observing the effects of the introduction of one of these seven streams of blessing into an astral experience, the astute Golden Dawn magician can then determine several things regarding the source of the vision.

There is of course no point in using these seven Hebrew letters without having established a good relationship with the inner powers they represent. Within the traditional Golden Dawn the establishment of this relationship was a slow and methodical process. Firstly, the letters themselves were intellectually learnt within the Neophyte Grade. Then at the Zelator grade initiation the astral forms of the letters and their connections to the mental plane blessings were carefully placed within the astral aura of the candidate. These astral forms were then developed throughout the rest of the Outer Order and strengthened considerably within the Adeptus Minor initiation. Therefore, by the time the Inner Order magician was required to use them in astral work, the relationship was well established. Since most of us cannot rely on expert initiations such as these, we need to really work with the letters via meditation prior to using them to test our astral visions and experiences.

During the vision the Hebrew letters can be drawn in the air and vibrated over the image (or card in the case of skrying) and towards any Beings in question. They are best seen very large and in glowing white light. Unlike the divine names of the realm in question, the Seven Wanderers are used to test for specific distortions in the perception of the inner realm. The divine names ensure the connection to the inner realm; the Seven Wanderers test how we interact with that realm. They should therefore only be used after the experience or vision has been thoroughly tested by the divine names and the other suggestions above. Specifically the Seven Wanderers or seven double letters test for the following distortions.

Tau, brings forth spiritual blessings related to **Saturn**. This letter is used to test if our vision or experience is being derived from our memories. While in one respect there is nothing wrong with this, as often a form has to be given to the formless, we need to know where the form is being derived from. Also memories are seldom neutral and have many emotions and thoughts attached to them which may cloud or distort our inner experience.

Kaph, brings forth spiritual blessings related to **Jupiter**. This letter is used to test if we are constructing or creating the inner experience ourselves. This refers mainly to the construction of the astral forms and the astral realm we are in. I have had experiences where the entire vision and experience has vanished or altered considerably after testing in this fashion. Within the Golden Dawn many of the Beings we may encounter in the inner plane use forms consciously created by the magicians themselves. These consciously created forms, called Telesmatic Images, together with the less consciously created forms that draw from our own astral light, should still be tested. The vibration of the letter Kaph will ensure that the formless spiritual Beings we are in contact with are in control of the forms, not our own unconscious minds. Another, very simple test is to try and control the actions of the Beings you are interacting with. If you are able to influence a group of gnomes to dance the hokey-pokey, it is a fair bet that *you* are controlling those forms not any spiritual being.

Peh, brings forth spiritual blessings related to **Mars**. We would trace and vibrate this letter to ensure that our inner impatience or anger does not affect our vision or experience. While our banishing rituals and preparation should have quieted our emotions, as soon as we engage on the inner levels through astral travel there is a chance that our subconscious or unconscious feelings will be aroused. Often distortion due to inner, unconscious anger or impatience is experienced as a fast, roller-coaster or cavalcade of imagery, one action moving into the next without resolution. If you have this type of inner experience, try testing with the letter Peh. The letter is also useful whenever you sense any impatience or anger within the environment you are in, or from the inner Beings. In this case it is often our own anger that is distorting the vision, and vibration of the letter Peh will calm these energies considerably.

Resh, brings forth spiritual blessings related to the **Sun**. This is one of the most crucial tests and should be applied for every inner experience or vision. Resh tests if the experience and vision is simply appealing to our vanity and ego. This is mainly due to our own construction or distortion of the experience. Occasionally however, the inner plane Beings, especially elementals, will help us along a bit in our delusion. They do this more out of giving us what they think we wish for than out of malice or spite. If they encounter someone whose unconscious wish for power is lit up within the astral light, they may help spin a yarn that fulfils this fantasy. The vibration and work with the letter Resh will help expose and reduce visions produced or distorted by our own vanity and those aided by inner plane Beings. Again, I have had whole worlds full of life and colour disappear when I have tested this way. Because we human beings have so many unmet unconscious needs, desires and fantasies hanging over from our childhood and youth, it is essential we ensure they do not distort our inner experiences. The use of Resh will go part way towards this.

Daleth, brings forth spiritual blessings related to **Venus**. Related to the Resh above, Daleth is used to test if the vision or experience is simply fulfilling our pleasures. Whenever we experience any sense of pleasure, eroticism or blissing out within our visions, we should immediately test with this letter. Our desires and hedonistic tendencies can distort the astral light as much as any other inner aspect of ourselves. The transference of consciousness to the inner realms can release these aspects of our selves and because they are so highly energised, whole astral experiences and worlds can form around them. These are completely subjective to us and will not aid in our unfoldment or experience of the actual inner realms. So despite how wonderful they seem, and how much pleasure we are experiencing, they should be dissipated, and the letter Daleth will help us to do so.

Beth, brings forth spiritual blessings related to **Mercury**. The letter Beth tests if we are imagining and creating the whole experience. It differs from the letter Kaph which tests if we are constructing the images and forms and the control of those forms. Beth is used when we wish to know if the whole damn experience is being created and conjured up from our subconscious or unconscious. It will remove those areas of the vision created or distorted by our imaginations. Sometimes certain aspects of the vision or experience may disappear only to be replaced by something else, also created by our imagination. For example we may be standing watching a great cloud of purple light above a tree-scape. After vibrating and tracing Beth the cloud changes into a silver dragon. We should not assume that the silver dragon is 'real', and test again with Beth. Occasionally we will find that vision after vision is removed by the letter Beth only to be replaced by another imaginative product. This indicates there is no actual connection with the inner realm you are seeking, that your consciousness is elsewhere, that something was not right in your connecting method. When this occurs it is best to banish the vision, close down and examine what went wrong.

Gimel, brings forth spiritual blessings related to the **Moon**. The final letter of the Seven Wanderers, Gimel is used to remove and still any wandering thoughts. If the vision is indistinct and wandering, often the vibration and inscription of Gimel will solidify it and make it more real. Also if we find ourselves quite strongly in the realm but our thoughts appear to be wandering by their own volition, the letter Gimel can help still our thoughts and help us to focus where we are. One of the effects of the intonation of this letter is to bring forth completely balanced, undifferentiated astral light into the experience and vision we are having. It thus provides more 'raw material' by which the vision and forms are created. It should therefore only ever be used after the vision has been tested well via the divine names of the realm.

KEYS FOR SUCCESSFUL EXPLORATION OF THE INNER REALMS

Before looking at the specific forms of techniques used with the Golden Dawn to explore and connect with the inner realms, let us examine a few of the qualities and keys to successful exploration regardless of the method used.

Charging the Astral Body. As we discussed in chapters one and four, the etheric and astral bodies of the magician can be consciously charged with the qualities and blessings of a particular spiritual force or inner realm. If our astral bodies are charged in this way when they are directed, by will, out of their habitual abodes of the etheric body they will tend to travel to the inner realm corresponding to the spiritual charge. Like attracts like in the astral realm and if we fill our astral spheres with the elemental principle of Water, we will have much more chance of connecting with and entering the astral realm of Water than if we did not. It is for this reason that Invocation of Force within the Aura, meditation and preparation of the temple through invoking rituals are often undertaken prior to transfer of consciousness to the inner realms.

One of the most interesting aspects of the Western initiatory traditions is the insistence that their ceremonial initiations provide the initiate with 'authority' to visit the inner realms and without which non-initiates simply cannot. In reality this 'authority' is simply the placement of certain symbols within the etheric and astral bodies of the magician. These symbols represent the inner realm in question and are linked to the mental plane blessings of that realm. The symbols can be activated and brought into action via vibration of specific names, the formation of certain signs or the performance of rituals and other processes. When activated they draw particular energy and blessings into the astral body of the initiate. This in turn will allow easy access to the inner realm when they seek to travel there. Non-initiates can certainly visit the same inner realms. We will however be required to charge our astral bodies with the appropriate energies by our own devices and effort, not with the aid of tradition or a lodge. This is one of the downsides of working on our own. The upside is that it forces us to really understand and make use of the magical principles of the Golden Dawn and to do our own work.

Use of Symbols. Within the Golden Dawn, transference of consciousness to the inner realm is always performed through the use of a symbol which represents and connects the inner realm to this plane. In other traditions and schools, symbols may or may not be used. The use of symbol in this way helps the magician to transfer her consciousness to the desired inner realm and not get 'lost' within their own consciousness. The symbols are used as a gateway to the inner realm and also provide a link for the Briatic blessings behind the symbol to be present and assist the magician. The symbols used need to be deeply understood by the magician. It is extremely unwise to transfer consciousness through a symbol you do not know or only have a superficial intellectual understanding of. Travel within the inner realms is much like travel in foreign cities: as novices we stick to the well known and well lit areas. Failure to do so, wandering off to somewhere we have only vaguely heard of, may result in an unpleasant and possibly dangerous experience.

Being Grounded. While being grounded and earthed within our regular lives does not aid or hinder our transference of consciousness to the inner realms, it greatly improves our chances of successful and meaningful interaction. Success here is measured in how useful the interaction and inner plane experience is in our transformation and service. Being grounded with plenty of common sense, not seeking some inner plane joy ride, means that our inner exploration can have a real use and a real effect in our lives and the world. Without this quality we are more likely to engage in delusion and fantasy fulfilment as discussed previously. Being grounded will also help earth and activate fully any blessings we receive when we explore the inner realms.

Strong Visualisation Skills. The more we can visualise, the more astral light is at our command and disposal. With good visualisation skills we can provide well developed forms for a range of inner plane Beings to inhabit and use within the world of Yetzira. At the end of the encounter the astral light returns to our own sphere as the being departs into the mental, Briatic realm. The more astral light we provide and re-absorb, the greater the Briatic blessings which will be absorbed into our astral bodies. Visualisation and the creation of astral forms within the inner realms is one of the key vehicles for Briatic blessings to enter our astral-Yetziratic selves. While a few people have naturally existing and well established links to Briah, the majority of us require a bridge, and visualisation provides that bridge. As mentioned in Chapter One, when the Golden Dawn talks about visualisation it means real, perceived images, not the 'sense' of an image.

A Willingness to Leave Assiah and Enter the Inner Realms. To enter the inner realms we need to will ourselves to do so. Experiencing the inner realms is very different from a day-dream or fantasy, which flows along nicely and where we stay within our own spheres. It is also different to New Age guided visualisations, which are actually not designed to enter the macrocosmic inner worlds, but solely to explore our own inner realms (and for which they are very useful). Full transference of consciousness into the inner realms can be quite off-putting for some people, for a variety of reasons. If a magician does not fully wish to enter the inner realms and does not address her disquiet, her experiences will be limited. Any reluctance you have to engage in this form of Golden Dawn activity needs to be addressed and looked at clearly. Inner plane exploration is a key part of the Golden Dawn, but for some people may require the kind of commitment and dedication others find is called for when learning ceremony or invocation. Each of us will at some point in our magical and spiritual unfoldment be called to persevere and commit to aspects of the tradition that do not automatically fit with us.

Respect for Inner Realm Beings. Like being grounded, respect will not aid or hinder our transference of consciousness but will greatly determine our successful navigation of the inner world. We need to approach the inner realm with the awareness that we are visitors and novices. We are there to learn and explore. We should not assume we have more rights or even power than the Beings we encounter. Remember also that communication between humans of different cultures is difficult enough and here we are attempting communication between humans and non-humans. Be patient, kind and maintain an open mind.

An important piece of advice is to approach the inner plane Beings with the knowledge and thought that they really exist independent of you, that they are not an aspect of your unconscious. Outside of the experience, as a belief and a world-view you may see the inner plane Beings as simply part of yourself. But when you connect with them, do so with a 'suspension of disbelief' and know them to be real. Taking a similar situation in modern life, if we wish to be entertained by the latest action movie, we do not enter the theatre consciously knowing and reinforcing to ourselves that 'it is not real'. We allow the drama to unfold and our adrenalin levels to rise, to grip the seat and be affected emotionally and physically. Later we may discuss the acting and special effects over coffee, but not during the movie. We can apply the same principle with the inner planes and the Beings that live there.

GOLDEN DAWN TECHNIQUES FOR EXPLORATION OF THE INNER REALMS

The two Golden Dawn methods of inner plane exploration, Skrying and Travelling in the Spirit Vision, have been so well associated with the elemental Tattwa symbols that it is probably best to briefly discuss the Tattwas before progressing any further. For most modern magicians and groups the Tattwas are normally the first, and often only, symbols used to connect and explore the inner realms. Many people believe that Travelling in the Spirit vision refers exclusively to the use of the Tattwas. This is not the case, though it is wise to confine our Skrying or Travelling to the Tattwas exclusively for some time. Once we are familiar with the Tattwas and elemental realms, we can then move onto the other realms and symbols of the Golden Dawn tradition.

The inclusion of the Tattwas in the Golden Dawn magical system is something of an anomaly as they are not historically part of the Western esoteric tradition. They originate as part of certain aspects of the Hindu Tantric systems. Their adoption and modification by the Golden Dawn seems to have been something of a cross between expediency and esoteric politics. Their efficacy and ease of use (as adapted by the GD) would have greatly appealed to the founders of the GD as would have their inclusion in the Theosophical literature of the day. While promoting and exalting the Western traditions, the Golden Dawn did not exist in a vacuum. Many of its members were also important members of the Eastern influenced Theosophical Society, which produced a book, *Nature's Finer Forces*, dealing with the Tattwas. Much of this book was later summarised into a GD document, and a practical system of working with the symbols developed. It is this practical system that has come down to us as part of the exploration of the inner realms. The rest of the Tattwa system, as presented by the Theosophical Society and adapted by the GD, has not passed the test of time and has largely been jettisoned by the contemporary magical community.

Some contemporary magicians, in an attempt to hark back to the pure roots of the Western Mysteries, suggest replacing the Tattwa symbols with the by now familiar Hermetic triangles of the elements. Personally, I feel that the inclusion of the Tattwas within the GD shows how living traditions are continually changing and growing. I do not see the system as alien and unworkable and it has, over the last hundred years, become a distinct part of the Golden Dawn tradition.

There are twenty five Tattwas in all, five for each of the elements and spirit and twenty for each of the sub-elements. The main five Tattwas are:

Element	Tattwa	Symbol
Earth	Prithivi	Yellow Square
Air	Vayu	Sky Blue Circle
Water	Apas	Silver Crescent
Fire	Tejas	Red Triangle
Spirit	Akasha	Black Oval

All the symbols should face upwards towards the top of the card or page. There are variants in colours from book to book and group to group; Vayu is sometimes green; Tejas is sometimes orange; Apas is sometimes white and Akasha is sometimes deep purple or indigo. The sub-tattwas, representing the sub-elemental realms, are formed by placing the inferior Tattwa symbol within the centre of the larger, superior symbol. For example, Fire of Water (Tejas of Apas) would be seen as a red triangle within a silver crescent, as shown in diagram 24. Air of Water (Vayu of Apas) would be a blue circle within a silver crescent. The sub-elements such as Earth of Earth or Fire of Fire are depicted by a smaller symbol formed of the opposite colour within the larger symbol. For example, Prithivi of Prithivi, Earth of Earth will be depicted as a violet or mauve square within the yellow square. Tejas of Tejas would be depicted as a green triangle inside a red triangle.

PRITHIVI
EARTH

VAYU
AIR

APAS
WATER

TEJAS
FIRE

AKASHA
SPIRIT

TEJAS OF APAS
FIRE OF WATER

Diagram 24: The Elemental Tattwa Symbols

SKRYING AND TRAVELLING IN THE SPIRIT VISION

The only real difference between Skrying and Travelling within the Spirit Vision is the degree of the transference of consciousness into the chosen inner realm. When we skry we consciously and purposely maintain our consciousness within the realm of Assiah to a large degree. If we travel in the Spirit Vision we attempt to move our consciousness into the inner realm as much as possible. In Golden Dawn practice, skrying can be used to establish a connection with the inner plane first before deciding to travel within it. However, there is always a conscious decision to change the mode of operation, and skrying should never simply slip into travelling. Also, once the decision is made to move from skrying to travelling, the full preparation and rules for travelling must still be followed.

When we skry we use a physical symbol, often made of coloured card, which becomes the portal through which we transfer our consciousness. The symbol represents a particular inner plane and is derived from one of the many symbol systems used within the GD tradition: the elemental Tattwa symbols, the symbols of the seven planets, the Hebrew letters etc. Once we have transferred a 'beam' or a projection of our consciousness through the symbol, we stare into the symbol with our eyes open and allow images to form. This is a more directed and focused form of the generic skrying done with the classic crystal ball or the bowl of inky water beloved of witches the world over. The use of the symbol, together with our preparation, directs our consciousness into the specific inner realm we wish to explore, rather than simply 'tuning in to whatever comes'.

Skrying in the Spirit Vision is one of the more underrated and overlooked aspects of the Golden Dawn magical corpus. Most people prefer to launch straight into travelling to the inner realms and ignore skrying altogether. The technique however has a number of useful aspects, all of them due to the strong maintenance of the consciousness within Malkuth. Firstly, it allows the magician to explore an inner realm by remote, as it were, with the astral body largely remaining within the etheric body. While this does not diminish the possibilities of delusion it does limit its effects to that area of consciousness projected into the inner realm in question. This means that we are less likely to experience the intoxicating astral buzz and false bliss that is often a result of astral travel. Our Ruach is less affected, simply because there is less of it within the inner realm to be affected. We can however explore the inner realm as fully as if we were travelling within it. Of course, the absorption of inner plane blessings and spiritual energies is also lessened by having less of our Ruach within the inner realm. But for beginners it is often a good way of exploration while lessening the effects of our own delusions.

In addition, the maintenance of the connection with the physical body and the physical realm is a great way of developing the skill of directed splitting of consciousness, where we are aware of the inner world and the outer world at once. As we saw in the last chapter, this skill is a crucial part of dramatic invocation. It also is required in just about every form of advanced Golden Dawn magic. Skrying also helps develop links to the chosen inner realm and the subtle bodies of the magician. Whereas travel within the inner realms also develops these links it does so only at the mental and astral levels. Skrying, because Malkuthian consciousness is maintained, helps to Earth these links into the etheric body of the magician also. The links are built up slowly over time as the magician uses the symbol as a skrying portal for a prolonged period. After a while these links may be discernible by clairvoyant astral and etheric vision and are normally seen as the symbols themselves. Skrying in this fashion can help build into the etheric body those links and symbols traditionally placed within the magician at the time of her initiation. It is therefore a useful skill to acquire as part of our exploration through the traditional Golden Dawn grade structure, discussed later in Chapter Nine.

THE PROCESS OF SKRYING IN THE SPIRIT VISION

Choosing the Symbol. This is determined by the inner plane you wish to explore. We should not simply flit around and explore only those realms that take our fancy. Within the Golden Dawn there is a clear sequence of realms to be followed which changes for each grade. This sequence will be outlined in the curriculum within Chapter Nine. The inner realms appropriate to the beginner, together with their symbols, colours and divine names, are listed in table six at the end of this chapter.

Making the Symbol Card. These days some of the symbols can be purchased, occasionally even with the correct colours. Despite this it is always preferable to make the symbol card yourself (this does not mean simply printing it out from the Internet either). Making the card connects it with your subtle bodies. The cards are normally made from paste-board or thick card and are coloured by either brilliant acrylic paint or pasting the appropriate colour paper to the card. Generally they should be around 7-12cm in size.

The colours of the symbols are very important and should be as bright and as clear as possible. Most of the cards, apart from the elemental Tattwa cards, will have two colours. The first is the ground colour or the background colour of the card. This is the colour attributed to the realm to be explored. The second colour is known as the 'charge' colour and is the colour of the symbol itself. This is always the opposite of the ground colour. For example, the symbol card of Mars will have a ground colour of red with the symbol ♂ in green superimposed upon it. The card for Hebrew letter Aleph will have a ground of pale yellow and the letter itself in the charge colour of violet. Because of this juxtaposition, coloured paper, where the glyphs are cut out and stuck on the ground colour, often produces a brighter, more brilliant result than painting one colour over another. Green painted on red dulls the green considerably. If the symbols are to be painted, it is best to paint them first in white and then apply the colour after the white paint has dried. This reduces the dulling effect of one colour upon the other. The symbol cards for the Tattwas should be formed of black card about 15cm or so square. The symbol of the Tattwa itself should be cut from bright paper about 7cm in length should be stuck in the centre of the black square.

The divine names associated with the inner realm in question should be written on the back of the card. The back of the card does not need to be comprised of two colours. If it is, use the same colour scheme for the front of the card. Otherwise write the names in black or gold. Throughout the making of the card your mind and concentration needs to remain focused on what you are doing and why. It is a good idea to continually and softly intone the divine names as you make the symbol card as this will help link your subtle energies to the card. When you have finished making the card, you should seal it with a sealant or some PVA glue. Once dry, wrap it well in cloth or a bag, either white or the colour of the force in question.

Choosing the Time for the Exploration of the Inner Realm. Many magicians set a great deal of importance to the timing of their magic, believing they should only work at the most auspicious time according to the ebb and flow of inner forces. While it is true that the inner cycles, particularly those of the moon, can affect the quality and availability of certain inner forces, the inner realms are always there to explore. With the correct training and approach the Golden Dawn magician is capable of connecting with any inner realm at any time, with the possible exception of the two Equinoxes in March and September. If, however, you do wish to match the time of your inner exploration with the times when the subtle forces of the inner realm are strongest, you can consult the various Tattwa (elemental) tides and planetary hours tables as published in *The Golden Dawn* and available on the Internet.

The Temple or Place of Working. This should be arranged as follows. There should be a central altar with a black altar cloth. The symbols of the four elements placed on the altar at its East, South, West and North. At the centre should be a symbol of the spirit or the Golden Dawn cross and triangle. This reproduces the material universe, comprising the four elements and the indwelling spirit. This will help ground and solidify your astral experience and produce a greater degree of transformation. You should place a chair near the altar so that you are facing the direction appropriate to the inner realm in question. The planets move so you will need to locate the appropriate position as described in the last chapter on invocation.

Preparation – Cleansing. Perform an LBRP. If exploring any other realm besides the elements, follow this with a generic LBRH.

Preparation – Consecration. For the elemental realms perform a Supreme Invoking Ritual of the Pentagram of the element at the four quarters around the temple. If you are wishing to explore a sub-elemental realm, say Fire of Water, then the Supreme Pentagrams of both elements are invoked. The pentagram for the larger or superior element, in this case Water, is always invoked first. Also the smaller or inferior elemental pentagrams are normally made with the symbol of the superior element. In this case the pentagrams of Fire would be inscribed with the Water tool.

For Sephiroth and Planetary forces, perform the appropriate Lesser Invoking Hexagram around the temple space. Follow this by the appropriate Supreme Invoking Hexagram inscribed over the altar, facing the direction where the planet is at the time of working.

For the Paths on the Tree of Life perform the Lesser Invoking Hexagrams of the two Sephiroth the path connects. The hexagram of the superior or 'higher' Sephira is invoked first. For example, if we wish to explore the realm symbolised by the letter Teth which connects Chesed and Geburah, we would invoke first the lesser hexagram of Jupiter (Chesed) followed by the lesser hexagram of Mars (Geburah). Follow the lesser hexagrams by invoking the two Supreme Hexagrams of the Sephiroth over the altar, superior Sephira first. This is probably best done facing East for all occasions, but you can face the direction of the planet of the superior Sephira if you wish. For those paths that connect with Malkuth use the Saturn hexagrams for Malkuth, replacing the Saturn glyph with the crossed circle ⊗ and YHVH ALHIM with the divine name **ADNI H ARTz**.

To be perfectly honest many magicians and Orders simply omit or simplify this step of consecration as it does extend the process somewhat. I do not recommend omitting this, especially for beginners as this preparation does enhance the chance of a successful contact with the desired realm. However, I am aware that many people do report success without such elaborate preparation. If you do wish to simplify, but not shorten the process, this step can be replaced by an Invocation of Force within the Aura of the symbol as described in Chapter Four. In both cases the subtle bodies of the magician are infused with the required energies.

Grounding and Centring. Sit in your chair with the symbol card in front of you on the altar. It is best to lean it against something or use a book or photo stand so you can see it at eye level. If it is face up on the altar you will find your neck soon becomes strained. Relax and centre using the four-fold breath for several minutes. Now ground by opening your Malkuth centre and intoning **ADNI H ARTz** several times. If you have a tool or a symbol that you work with that connects with the inner realm in question, pick it up. For example, if you were exploring the realm of Fire, you would pick up either your red lamp or Fire wand. If you are exploring a sub-element pick up the tools for both elements, with that of the superior element in your dominant hand. For Fire of Water for example, you would hold the cup in your right hand and lamp in your left (if you were right handed).

Awakening the Symbol. Stare passively at the symbol for thirty seconds to a few minutes while maintaining the four-fold breath. Continue this until you see a flash of colour around the edge of the symbol. This is a natural optical effect caused by the eyes staring at the coloured symbol and the slight movement of our eyes. It is important to relax during this process and blink normally. This staring and breathing will link you to the symbol card on the etheric and astral levels.

Opening the Portal to the Inner Realm. Once you have seen the flash of colour, inscribe over the card the appropriate supreme pentagrams or hexagrams, vibrating the divine names into the card, imagining they are travelling through the card and into the realm in question. The pentagrams and hexagrams should be made quite small in front of the card. Use the same supreme pentagrams and hexagrams you used in the consecration of the temple. If you are working with a path on the Tree of Life, at the completion of both hexagrams, vibrate the letter, imagining the vibration moving through the card and entering the realm. Repeat this complete set of pentagrams, hexagrams (and if required, vibration of the Hebrew letter) several times.

Making Contact. Describing how to skry is quite difficult. Essentially what you are required to do is to imagine and direct your perception into and through the symbol. This should not be too difficult as your astral body and consciousness will, by now, be vibrating at the energetic pitch of the inner realm. Once you feel you have achieved this, you should simply stare passively at the symbol and open yourself to the perception of images or visions. By focusing outwardly on the symbol and portal to the inner realm, your inner perception and consciousness will be only of that realm. The repeated staring at the same outer scene without changes allows the outer visual aspect of the mind to become relaxed and in some sense bored. This in turn allows your inner vision to superimpose itself upon the outer vision. In this way you will perceive what is occurring in the inner realm, not the outer realm of the card on the altar. Most people see these images and visions with their inner sight while staring at the symbol. A few people have the perception of the inner realm literally occurring within the 7cm symbol, like a miniature TV screen. Neither mode of perception is better or more accurate.

Once any sort of vision or image appears to you, vibrate the divine names of the realm in question into the symbol once more. It is best to do this outwardly, not just inwardly, as this helps maintain the Malkuthian consciousness essential for successful skrying. At this point the vision should clarify and strengthen. Keep vibrating the name until the image grows strong and clear. Of the few writers and teachers who mention Skrying in the Spirit Vision at all, most will let you believe that skrying can only ever deliver images and scenes of the inner realm and not contact with inner Beings. I have not experienced such limitation, and pretty much all that can be experienced via travel in the Spirit can be achieved by skrying. The only difference is intensity of experience and the level of consciousness that is transferred.

In any case it is best for the first few attempts at skrying and travelling to confine your exploration to simply getting there. Once you have a strong and clear image of the inner plane which is strengthened through the vibration of the divine names, it is time to close the vision and return, as described below. This may seem a bit of a damp sponge, but it is a good discipline to follow and trains you in the all important movement into and out of inner realms before you explore them. In this way, when you do explore, you will be able to confidently and quickly move out of and cut the connection to the inner realm should you need to.

Exploring the Realm. Upon your fourth and subsequent skrying practices you may explore the realm. The traditional approach here is to keep vibrating the divine names of the realm into and through the card until a guide appears. This guide will be one of the inner plane Beings and will likely have been attracted to the vibration of the name and the Briatic blessings you are calling into the realm. Once you have a vision of the guide you should calmly and respectfully test him by the use of the divine names and if appropriate, the grade signs.

Once the guide has 'passed the test' you may journey or converse with them. Do not explore the realm without a guide of some form. From now on you should remain clear and calm and test the vision and any information you receive through the use of the Seven Wanderers and the other methods outlined earlier in the chapter. The Hebrew letters of the Wanderers should be traced before and over the symbol card and the vibration directed into the card and realm.

It is best to confine your exploration to no more than 10-15 minutes, especially for the first dozen or so attempts. Later, when you are more experienced, you can increase the length of exploration, but always no more than half an hour at the outside. Each exploration will be different and each will have the potential of helping you to harmonize with the realm and Beings that dwell there. You must use your own judgment and discernment in these explorations, utilizing your testing procedures well and judiciously. Remember to keep your consciousness within this realm also. The inscription of the symbols over the card will help this, but you may also like to outwardly describe what you see and what is occurring. This is an excellent way of maintaining a connection with this realm. If you wish, you can set up a voice recorder and make a record of your journey, which should be listened to after you have closed the temple and fully returned.

Closing the Vision. When ready to return, you should thank your guide. As part of your thanks vibrate once more the divine name of the realm towards them. If you were travelling in the Spirit Vision it would be essential to return down the same road or paths you have travelled since entering the realm and returning to the portal by which you entered. With skrying, since there is only a partial transference of consciousness, you can withdraw through the symbol card at any point. To do this, take a deep breath, and as you do so, consciously withdraw yourself and your Ruach from the realm. At the completion of the breath perform a Sign of Silence, withdrawing your gaze and focus from the card. This simple method, when performed well, should suffice for skrying. Now ground by opening your Malkuth centre and intoning **ADNI H ARTz** several times.

Closing the Portal to the Inner Realm. Inscribe over the card the appropriate supreme *banishing* pentagrams or hexagrams, consciously seeing and imagining that portal is sealed. Use the banishing versions of the same supreme pentagrams and hexagrams you used to open the portal. If you have been working with a path of the Tree of Life, do not, as in the opening, vibrate the letter of the path. The hexagrams or pentagrams should only need to be inscribed once. Once closed, wrap the symbol card up and place it within or by the altar. This will avoid its etheric and astral charge being banished and cleared when the temple is closed.

Closing the Temple. The banishing forms of any supreme hexagram or pentagrams invoked at the opening now need to be inscribed over the altar and/or around the temple. If you have been working with realms other than the elements, the banishing versions of any lesser hexagrams invoked at the opening should now be performed. Follow this by a generic LBRH. Finally, for all realms, finish with an LBRP.

THE PROCESS OF TRAVELLING IN THE SPIRIT VISION

Much of the procedure for Skrying applies to Travelling in the Spirit Vision and to avoid repetition I will refer to the skrying instructions where appropriate.

All of the steps from **Choosing the Symbol** through to **Grounding and Centring** are identical to skrying.

Internalizing the Symbol. Unlike skrying, where the symbol card itself becomes a portal through which we can direct part of our consciousness, in Travelling we re-create the symbol internally as part of our inner vision. The symbol is then imagined and expanded so that it becomes a doorway through which we direct and transfer our consciousness into the inner realm. With the Tattwa symbols this is done by staring passively at the symbol for thirty seconds to a few minutes while maintaining the four-fold breath. Continue this until you see a flash of colour around the edge of the Tattwa symbol. The flash of colour will be very bright, almost fluorescent, and the opposite of the colour of the Tattwa itself. The black background of the card will assist this process. Now either close your eyes directly, or move your gaze onto another piece of black card or paper, and see the symbol in the glowing complementary colour. Once you can see the symbol formed of glowing light in the complimentary, or opposite colour, close your eyes.

What is occurring here is a natural optical effect which most of us have experienced accidentally at some point in our lives. By staring at the coloured symbol for a period of time the image has been temporarily impressed onto the retinas of our eyes, but formed of the opposite colour. Thus, we will see a bright fluorescent violet-mauve square of light when working with the yellow square Prithivi Tattwa. Esoterically this colour is considered the astral colour of the element and can help us connect with the astral inner realm. Having a clear inner image of the Tattwa symbol formed from its opposite colour, begin to imagine it growing larger and larger, until it fills your inner vision and is as large as a doorway. Hold the image of the Tattwa-doorway clearly for a few deep breaths, seeing it strongly.

In all but the Tattwa symbols most magicians simply reproduce the symbol inwardly as it is seen outwardly. For example, the symbol of Mars would be seen and expanded until it is seen as a large green doorway with the red glyph of Mars upon it.

Passing Through the Portal. Once you have doorway-symbol in front of you, pause and consciously connect with your intention and desire to pass into this particular inner realm. Once you are clear of this, it is time to project your consciousness through the portal and into the realm. An early Golden Dawn document suggests that the magician 'pass, spring or fly' through the portal. This is really a matter of the direction of the Ruach and is greatly increased by the use of the Sign of the Enterer or the Projecting Sign. The sign can be given outwardly as well as inwardly via visualisation. As you make the sign and thrust out your arms, send your consciousness out and through the portal. This method of projection of the Ruach will take very little time if you have built up your will as suggested in Chapter Three and performed the various spiritual practices within this book.

Making Contact. As soon as you get a sense you have passed through the portal or see any form of vision, inwardly vibrate the divine names of the realm in question. These should be vibrated as if you are within the realm with the portal behind you, directing the vibration into the realm. As with skrying, at this point the vision and your sense of presence in the realm should clarify and strengthen. Keep vibrating the name until the vision grows strong and clear. Also, like skrying, it is best for the first few attempts at travelling to confine your exploration to simply getting there. Once you have a strong and clear image of the inner plane which is strengthened through the vibration of the divine names, it is time to close the vision and return as described below.

Exploring the Realm. This is essentially the same as skrying, including contacting a guide, but with more of your consciousness being present within the realm. It is important therefore to use the traditional methods of testing and strengthening the vision, especially the use of the Seven Wanderers. The main difference at this stage between skrying and travelling is the need to keep track of where you travel within the inner realm and the paths you took. Later when you close the vision and seek to return through the same portal, you will need to back track and travel back along the same paths. It is therefore important to keep a clear head and your wits about you. The same limits concerning duration of the exploration applies to travelling as it does to skrying.

Closing the Vision. When ready to return, you should thank your guide. As part of your thanks, vibrate once more the divine name of the realm towards them. It is now essential to return down the same road or paths you have travelled since entering the realm and returning to the portal by which you entered. You should arrive back at the portal and clearly see it there as a doorway once more. If the image is vague, spend a bit of time consciously creating and building it. Once ready and standing before the portal, give the Sign of the Enterer and project your Ruach back through the portal. This is the reverse of the process that took you into the realm. Once you are through the portal, turn back to face it. Then inwardly inscribe the appropriate supreme banishing pentagrams or hexagrams over the portal. You may vibrate the names outwardly also if you wish. Once the portal has been closed by the banishing pentagrams or hexagrams, see the symbol itself grow smaller and smaller until it disappears.

Grounding. Give the Sign of Silence and then open your eyes. Now stand up and repeat the Sign of Silence outwardly. This first sign will have closed and sealed your astral body, the second has more of focus on your etheric. It is very important now to ground. This can be done in a number of ways, the simplest being by opening your Malkuth centre and intoning **ADNI H ARTz** a dozen or more times. Because grounding is such a crucial aspect in Travelling in the Spirit Vision you should not skimp this part of the process. If after a dozen or so vibrations you still feel spacey or ungrounded, sit down and consciously connect and focus just on your feet for five minutes. Then stand once more and repeat the vibrations of **ADNI H ARTz**.

Closing the Temple. This uses the same procedure as outlined in skrying.

PATHWORKING

Pathworking has become very popular and fashionable within the esoteric communities over the last thirty or so years. The term however is not used consistently and can be a little confusing. It originally stemmed from the structured inner exploration of the paths of the Tree of Life by methods identical or similar to those just described. These days it may refer to any guided inner journey to connect with a particular spiritual force or power (as opposed to guided visualisations which seek to connect with aspects of our own selves). Historically, such guided journeys, where a facilitator reads out what is to be inwardly visualised, had no place within the original Golden Dawn, though towards the end of the classical GD era some temples were developing rudimentary forms of pathworking scripts.

The usefulness of pathworking scripts lies not in the events and images of the journeys described and re-created interiorly, but the effects on the astral body such visualisations produce. An effective pathworking will involve the systematic reproduction of a series of visual forms and symbols that will change the energetic pitch of the astral body so that it is resonant with the desired inner realm. They will not ordinarily automatically transfer consciousness to the inner plane, nor will the Beings they instruct you to visualise necessarily be actual, macrocosmic inner plane Beings. This is why the majority of good pathworking scripts lead the path-worker to a certain place or event and then allows them to explore individually. The path-worker at this point has the spiritual energy of the inner plane within their astral body and from there they may make contact with the inner realm. They will have also, through following the visualisations, created forms resonant with the inner plane Beings and these forms may come to be inhabited by those Beings.

The historical and traditional Golden Dawn approach to exploration of the inner planes, including the paths of the Tree of Life, does not involve pathworking. If you do engage in this practice however, which can be beneficial, please continue to use the traditional Golden Dawn methods of testing the visions and Beings.

INNER REALMS TO EXPLORE WITHIN THE GOLDEN DAWN TRADITION

While the Golden Dawn offers many inner realms to explore, it is best for the beginner to confine themselves to those of the elements, planets, Sephiroth and paths on the Tree of Life. All of these can be explored using the techniques of Skrying and Travelling in the Spirit Vision. The tables below give the symbols, colours and divine names of these realms.

Table 6a: The Elements – The Tattwas

Element	Tattwa	Symbol	Main Divine Name	Other Divine Names
Earth	Prithivi	Yellow Square	אדני	Mor Dial Hctga
Air	Vayu	Sky Blue Circle	יהוה	Oro Ibah Azopi
Water	Apas	Silver Crescent	אל	Mph Arsl Gaiol
Fire	Tejas	Red Triangle	אלהים	Oip Teaa Pdoce
Spirit	Akasha	Black Oval	אהיה	יהשוה

Table 6b: The Planets

Planet	Symbol	Ground Colour	Symbol Colour	Divine Name
Saturn	♄	Black	White	יהוה אלהים
Jupiter	♃	Blue	Orange	אל
Mars	♂	Red	Green	אלהים גבור
Sun	☉	Yellow	Violet	יהוה אלוה ודעת
Venus	♀	Green	Red	יהוה צבאות
Mercury	☿	Orange	Blue	אלהים צבאות
Moon	☽	Purple	Violet	שדי אלחי

Table 6c: The Ten Sephiroth

There are many symbols that may be used for the Sephiroth. I have chosen to use the various polygons as they are simple to make and visualise. The various shapes should be made solid, that is, not with lineal outline like a pentagram but simply as a shape cut out of coloured paper. Please see diagram 25. Alternate symbols can be found by consulting any good book on the Qabalah, or on the Internet.

Sephira	Symbol	Ground Colour	Symbol Colour	Divine Name
Kether	Point within the circle	White	Black	אדני
Chokmah	Cross within the circle	Grey	White	יהוה
Binah	Triangle within the circle	Black	White	יהוה אלהים
Chesed	Square within the circle	Blue	Orange	אל
Geburah	Pentagon within the circle	Red	Green	אלהים גבור
Tiphareth	Hexagon within the circle	Yellow	Violet	אלוה ודעת יהוה
Netzach	Heptagon within the circle	Green	Red	יהוה צבאות
Hod	Octagon within the circle	Orange	Blue	אלהים צבאות
Yesod	Nonagon within the circle	Purple	Yellow	שדי אלחי
Malkuth	Decangle within the circle	Black	White	אדני הארץ

Table 6d: The Twenty-Two Paths of the Tree of Life

Once again there are a few traditional symbol systems within the Golden Dawn that can be used to explore the inner realms of the Paths of the Tree of Life. I have chosen the most traditional and simplest, the letters of the Hebrew Alphabet. They are coloured according to the most active and most suitable colour system, the King Scale. Other symbols can be found

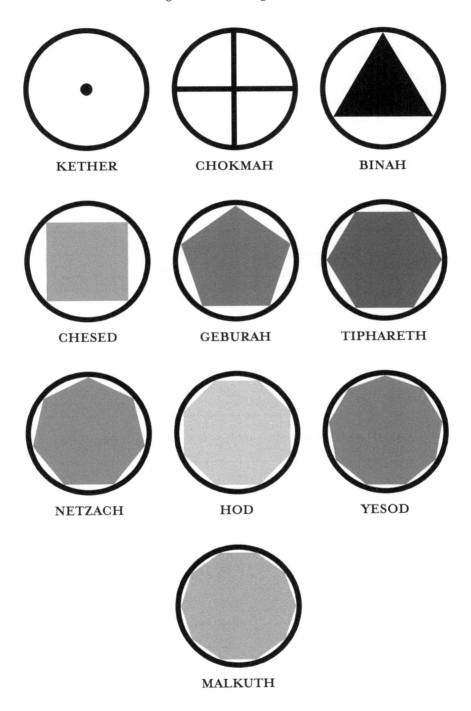

Diagram 25: Polygons of the Sephiroth

in other books and on the Internet. While the Tarot trumps are attributed to the Paths of the Tree and can be used as portals, they are best left until after complete exploration using the letters alone. The Tarot cards, at least in the Golden Dawn, are designed to be a compendium of the spiritual blessings of the Paths within each of the four worlds, Atziluth through Assiah. It is best to experience and become familiar with the unmixed Yetziratic experience before moving on to more advanced work.

Letter	Hebrew	Ground Colour	Letter Colour
Aleph	א	Pale yellow	Strong violet
Beth	ב	Yellow	Violet
Gimel	ג	Blue	Orange
Daleth	ד	Green	Red
Heh	ה	Red	Green
Vau	ו	Red-Orange	Green-Blue
Zayin	ז	Amber	Indigo
Cheth	ח	Orange	Blue
Teth	ט	Yellow	Violet
Yod	י	Yellow-Green	Crimson
Kaph	כ	Violet	Yellow
Lamed	ל	Green	Red
Mem	מ	Deep Blue	Orange
Nun	נ	Green-Blue	Red-Orange
Samech	ס	Blue	Orange
Ayin	ע	Indigo	Amber
Peh	פ	Red	Green
Tzaddi	צ	Violet	Yellow
Qoph	ק	Crimson	Yellow-Green
Resh	ר	Orange	Blue
Shin	ש	Red	Green
Tau	ת	Indigo	Amber

EVOCATION

We briefly defined evocation in Chapter Five when examining invocation; a magical process which from one point of view calls something (normally a 'spirit') **out** of us, or from another point of view, calls something **out** of whatever inner realm it normally inhabits. This spirit or energy is then coerced and forced into a Triangle of Art (a physically drawn triangle on the floor of the temple) so that it can manifest to some degree. Within the Golden Dawn and most magical traditions there is no class of magic that is more difficult and requires a greater degree of spiritual wisdom than evocation. As a form of solo magic nothing is more complex and difficult to achieve. Apart from some ceremonial initiations there are few group rituals that require the same level of technical expertise and confidence. And, while unwise exploration of the inner realms can be as dangerous as evocation, it requires prolonged abuse of the process. With evocation, a single stupid and unlucky act can have disastrous consequences, most of which result from unplanned connection with a negative or 'demonic' power:

> 'Depending on the nature of the [unwanted, negative] spirit, and the degree of its manifestation, it is likely that the spiritual progress of the magician is at an end – at least as far as his current incarnation is concerned.' (*Complete Golden Dawn System of Magic*, vol. six, p.28)

Because of its reputation and glamorised image of the mage conjuring up spirits for his command in an incense laden temple, while scantily clad female 'assistants' watch on, evocation can appeal to people who would do best to avoid magic entirely. These people would be best served by compassionate psychotherapy or counselling rather than magic. Fortunately, due to the sheer complexity of the method and the lack of many decent, fully descriptive works on the subject, few people have the energy and intelligence to attempt evocation at its fullest. Due to the complexity and level of magical expertise and spiritual wisdom required for safe evocation I will not be describing the process in detail. We include it here simply to show how it fits into the complete Golden Dawn system.

Now that we have dispensed with the warnings and literary head shaking, we need to explain why evocation is a part of the Golden Dawn tradition. While it is clear that most of the extant methods for evocation focus on the control of spiritual powers, some demonic, some angelic, for personal gain, the Golden Dawn approach is far different. Somewhat like Witchcraft and Magic itself, evocation has been redefined and re-invented for the modern world. While there is no doubt the word 'Witch' historically had only negative connotations, it has been retrospectively applied as a positive label to some historical practitioners of magical art and spiritual wisdom. Specifically, it has been given to those people who drew the inspiration for their healing and spiritual arts from sources and blessings not sanctioned by the various Churches. By labelling in this way, modern Witches form a spiritual and mythic link with the past, which greatly enhances their Craft and spiritual practice. This link however does not extend to the realms of practice or theology – the actual craft and beliefs of the modern Witch are very different to her historical predecessor. Similarly, the theology of modern evocation, focusing as it does upon spiritual unfoldment and personal responsibility, is far different to that which underpinned historical evocation. The link between the past and present however is maintained, as the Golden Dawn, in its unique way of spiritual re-interpretation, has kept the core structure and processes that comprise evocation, but entirely changed its focus.

The purpose of evocation is to manifest a spiritual force within the etheric plane so that our interaction with it will affect our material bodies and lives to a degree generally not available by other processes. It is this etheric manifestation that is meant by the often quoted words 'manifest to visible appearance'. The evoked spirit, if all goes well, will have an etheric body that will be visible to anyone within even the mildest form of altered state. The raw material for this etheric body is not produced by the spirit themselves, but rather it is formed largely from excess etheric material derived from the magician. Having a spiritual power at this level of manifestation, standing right in front of us, will enhance and actualize whatever contact we have with them. This can be immensely beneficial, but can also be catastrophic if things go wrong. This is why botched or unwise evocations can prove so damaging – the negative force has direct access and connection to our etheric, and in some cases, physical bodies.

Of course any astral (and even possibly mental) plane damage we receive is also greatly enhanced.

We may understand this principle a little better by looking at daily life. We all know that doing something 'for real' is always different than when we learn about it intellectually or practice it in a class or a school. No matter how good a training course is or how elaborate the role playing exercises are, when we actually get out there and 'do it for real' we learn far more. In fact, as anyone skilled in any job will tell you, by doing the job we in some way embody the skills required of us. The same process occurs in evocation.

If we face our fears of a particular demonic or negative force, stare it in the eye and command its obedience to our Higher will, then its power and influence over us will diminish. This will occur far more in evocation than in any inner plane exploration, since we face it solidly and completely within our plane, with our full conscious Malkuthian awareness. Perhaps it is stating the obvious, but facing any form of negative power in this manner requires a great deal more courage and will than any inward guided visualisation. It also requires the magician to be completely and utterly confident that they can connect, hold and embody a Briatic level of consciousness at will, even when facing a demon. It is for this reason that evocation within the Golden Dawn is reserved for the Inner Order and is the special task of the Adeptus Major, a grade connected to the higher consciousness, will and strength of Geburah.

For evocation to be successful, at least within the Golden Dawn framework, the etheric body that the spirit uses to manifest has to be formed largely from etheric energy and substance derived from the magician herself. As part of the ceremony, the magician consciously and purposefully extrudes and projects a great deal of etheric substance, which is then used by the spirit as an etheric vehicle. Of course this creates a vital and potent link between the spirit and the magician and when done correctly, any interaction with the spirit will affect the magician on virtually all the planes, etheric to mental. The Triangle of Art the spirit is forced to manifest within allows the magician to control and limit the effects the spirit may have upon her. This is why correct and accurate formation of the triangle, on all the planes, is of crucial importance. Without such a safeguard, the spirit, who is using our etheric substance for their body, is potentially able to link themselves to our etheric body or damage it considerably.

The use of the magician's etheric substance as a vehicle for manifestation, even when done correctly, may exact a heavy price. This is why 19th century French magician Eliphas Levi collapsed after witnessing a successful evocation of a spirit: his etheric body was so weakened by the experience that it directly affected his physical body and wellbeing. Unless we are in excellent health and are fit, we simply cannot spare large quantities of etheric substance without ill effects. This is one of the reasons why MacGregor Mathers, co-founder of the Golden Dawn, insisted magicians be in top physical condition.

In some traditions, historical and contemporary, the etheric substance by which the spirit manifests is derived from sources other than the magician, most notably sacrifices of small animals. Without examining the ethical considerations and magical complications associated with animal sacrifice, from the Golden Dawn's perspective such an act would be magically and spiritually pointless. The crucial characteristic of spiritual evocation is that the spirit *does* form its body from the etheric substance of the magician. If it was formed by etheric substance drawn from the death of a pigeon, there would be far less etheric and daily life effects on the magician. Indeed there would be no point in the evocation at all. For evocations aimed at affecting the material world rather than spiritual unfoldment, the use of etheric substance obtained from sacrifice would, in theory, work. However, putting ethics aside once again, there are so many magical difficulties associated with sacrifice, especially in our culture, it is a field left well alone. On a related note, some books urge the use of incense and herbs as a source of etheric energy for spirits to manifest within. Even if incense and herbs alone could provide the quantities and type of etheric substance required (which they cannot), the same situation would apply: the required etheric link between spirit and magician would be absent or weak. Within the Golden Dawn, all evocations use etheric material acquired from the magician herself.

THE NATURE OF NON-PHYSICAL BEINGS AND SPIRITS

One of the features of medieval magic is its vast catalogue of demons and arch-demons, each being allocated a particular sphere of activity over which it ruled and could therefore effect changes. For example, following the instructions of the magical textbook *The Lesser Key of Solomon the King*, an evocation and command of the demon Gomory would help the magician 'procure the love of women'. If the magician required money rather than love or sex, he could evoke and command Andromalius, who would help him uncover 'hidden treasures'. And so it goes on: for nearly every conceivable human desire, there is a demonic or angelic power able to make our wishes come true. Occult historian Christopher McIntosh refers to this as a 'Kafkaesque civil service with a labyrinth of departments and strange rules and formalities' (*The Devil's Bookshelf*, p.33). While it is easy to smirk at such conceptions, the basis for this demonological classification stems from the same sources as the Qabalah. Just as the Tree of Life can be used to map out and examine every facet of life, the vast catalogue of demons and their activities can provide a map for the demonic, evil and destructive aspects of our selves. At least this is the view of certain modern demonologists, who view demons as personifications of hidden, destructive unconscious impulses. Others, subscribing to the older beliefs, care little for the hidden, evil side of humanity and view the demons as real Beings that can provide material results.

Some magical writers and teachers make a sharp distinction between these two beliefs, viewing them to be somewhat in contrast to each other. Of course the Golden Dawn tradition has room for any point of view, its spiritual practices and techniques working either way. However, from the modern Western magical viewpoint distinctions between what is 'within us' (aspects of ourselves) and what is 'outside us' (another 'real' being), break down. The modern psychological and secular view, which has influenced modern magic more than could be wished for, is that each of us is a real individual with an unconscious which is the source and storehouse of any demons we may perceive. The demons, the angels, the astral worlds are all within us, within the individual, within her mind and unconscious. This is shown graphically in diagram 26.

Any similarities between the demon or angel or inner plane as experienced by Jane and Toby exist because, as human Beings, our inner psyches are similar and will therefore produce similar fantasies. In some ways the pre-modern, magical worldview is directly opposite this: the astral realms, the demons and angels are outside the individual not within. It is our individual consciousness that exists inside the greater world and myriad of planes, with Beings and spiritual energies all around us, as shown in diagram 27. The similarities between Jane and Toby's experience of a demon are simply because they are experiencing the same demon or same class of demon.

The modern magical viewpoint, as exemplified by the Golden Dawn, encompasses both these views. Its basis is fundamentally that of the pre-modern view of the world; the individual human being exists within a world comprised of a range of other non-physical Beings. However, drawing upon the Hermetic axiom 'as above so below' the Golden Dawn recognises that each human is a magical mirror of the universe and has within themselves a reflection of all the powers of the greater universe around them. Within each of us, at some level of our psyche is a reflection of the astral elemental kingdoms, the angel Haniel and the demon Belial. Many of these powers are dormant and exist only in potential within us, waiting to be activated by spiritual work or life circumstances. Some we use and are aware of every day; just as right now you are using the Sephira of Hod within you to read this book. Some inner powers may only emerge into conscious awareness years after they have affected our 'conscious' decisions; such as a man marrying a woman who unconsciously reminds him of his mother. Any good depth psychologist will assert vigorously that our everyday lives and decisions are affected by our unconscious needs and desires far more than we think.

Both the hidden and conscious aspects of our psyches are linked to the greater non-physical world around us. Whatever energy or state of emotion is activated within us at any given moment is potentially forging a link between ourselves and the greater, macrocosmic equivalent. So when we are filled and deeply moved by compassion we are in some way opening ourselves to the greater compassionate energy of the Sephira of Chesed. The extent to which this opening occurs is dependent on a number of factors, including how strong our sense of self is; how strong are the barriers around our Ruach and astral selves. People with a poor sense of self often feel a deep emotion or engage in an exciting concept and find themselves 'lost within' the feeling or thoughts that seem to run around inside them. What occurs is that the original deeply felt emotion connects the individual to the corresponding universal energy which floods into them and overpowers their consciousness and Ruach. They are then unable to feel anything else, or find themselves in the grip of obsessive thoughts and ideas.

Through the processes of socialization, growing up in a less than perfect environment and simply the nature of being human, our psyche develops in such a way as to occlude or hide many aspects of ourselves, negative and positive, from our conscious awareness. Using traditional psychological language, these unexpressed and unacknowledged aspects of our self form part of what is called the unconscious. From the modern secular psychological perspective, the unconscious is contained entirely *within* the individual human being. From the modern magical perspective the unconscious is not only within the individual, but is also potentially connected to the greater macrocosmic realms; in fact the 'out there' non-physical world posited by the pre-modern magical world view. This is partly understood in those psychologies that recognise the collective unconscious. We can see this by looking at diagram 28.

From the modern magical perspective it is sometimes hard to define an encounter with an inner plane entity as being definitively an aspect

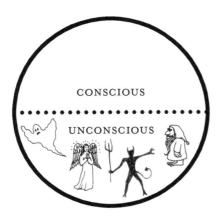

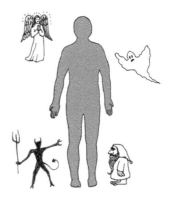

Diagram 26: Modern Secular/
Psychological Worldview

Everything is inside the individual.
The circle marks the barrier of the
self, the dotted line the barrier
between the unconscious and
conscious.

Diagram 27: Historical and
Pre-Modern Magical Worldview

Non-physical beings exist as real
entities outside the human being.
They populate the real universe.

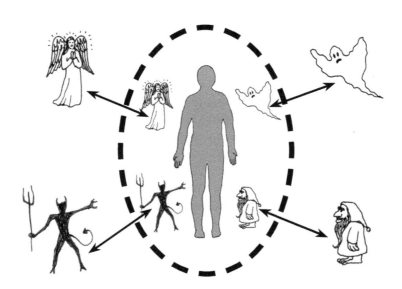

Diagram 28: Modern Magical Worldview

The inner and the outer connect and interact. Within each human there
is a mirror of the universe outside, including reflections of non-physical
beings. The dotted line represents the barrier of the individual – depending
on its permeability, outside beings can connect with the person.

of the unconscious or a real, macrocosmic being. The reflections of the demonic and angelic powers we each have within our unconscious can easily become linked to and empowered by the greater universal powers. In this context, what is 'ours' and what is 'not ours' in one sense becomes meaningless. The unconscious by definition is not under conscious control or scrutiny and may be empowered by powers and Beings that certainly existed before we as individuals were born and will continue to exist after we have died. This vast 'power' of the unconscious is understood by the best depth psychologists who approach working at this level with almost as much care as a magician preparing for evocation.

When the more destructive or creative aspects of the unconscious are activated and impinge upon our sense of self they may open us to the greater macrocosmic powers, of which they are a reflection and to which they are linked. Unless the unconscious is activated consciously with care and guidance we can find ourselves in trouble. Fortunately it is rare that such activation occurs without either conscious volition or stupidity. Unfortunately, within the modern world a lot of stupidity is accepted as normal or harmless. This includes unwise psychedelic drug use and consciousness changing sexual practices, both of which can activate unconscious aspects of ourselves or open us to unwelcome astral Beings. The traditional magical injunctions regarding the use of drugs and healthy sexual relationships stem from this awareness.

Within the Golden Dawn tradition evocation is practiced within the Inner Order, mostly at the Adeptus Major grade. By this stage the magician has realised and internalized the modern magical worldview outlined above. She is therefore keenly aware that the demons and spirits she evokes are both from her self and the collective macrocosmic human and non-human worlds. The results of the evocations, since the demons are controlled and placed under the *divine* will, affect her sphere as well as the greater world. The work therefore is seen quite rightly as a service to the world. Also at this level of consciousness the magician is fully aware that her ordinary everyday consciousness is a lens and a focus for her higher self that is united with the One. She therefore has little concern about personal development as such and begins to focus more and more on transpersonal service. This comes to fruition during the following grade of Adeptus Exemptus, as we shall see in the next chapter on initiation.

AN EVOCATORY TECHNIQUE BASED ON THE RITUAL OF THE PENTAGRAM

The discussion above gives a simple rundown on the purpose and rationale of evocation within the Golden Dawn tradition. While it is not possible to give the actual techniques for evocation here, some of the same principles used in evocation are found in a technique based on the Pentagram Ritual. The technique is designed to help break down and remove a particular habit of thought, emotion or action. It is especially useful for those habits and patterns we are conscious of but seem to have little control over. However it is not designed as replacement for psychotherapy or counselling. Nor is it designed to affect and transform those deeper aspects of ourselves stemming from unconscious desires and needs. For example, I once used the technique with good results when I found myself habitually annoyed, for no logical reason, with one of my university tutors. A single performance of the technique and I found myself free of my petty but distracting habit. It would not however have worked, and would have caused a few problems, if I attempted to use it to rid myself of a persistent habit based upon unresolved unconscious forces. For example, a habit of being attracted to women who looked like my mother could be based on unresolved unconscious mothering issues. Trying to change this habit would stir up the unconscious issues.

It is important to understand this distinction, as use of the technique to try and remove or alter a deep seated aspect of the self which is driven by unconscious needs can be harmful. Use it only to remove minor habits and patterns which are annoying and which you are sure are not driven by strong unconscious forces. Introspection and honesty is required here and this technique should not be practised until you are experienced in magic and self-honesty. I would not recommend its use by anyone with less than a year of serious daily work with the LRP and inner exploration. While there are other practices within the Golden Dawn tradition that seek the same ends, this technique can be used by people of any grade and utilises the skills used in the LRP and SRP. Also, while the technique utilises a triangle as a prop, just like evocation, it is clear here that the 'spirit' evoked or called forth is nothing more than a personification of a conscious personality trait. Again note the difference: in evocation the spirit may be seen as a personification of an *unconscious* force; in this procedure the spirit personifies an aspect of ourselves we know and are very familiar with.

Outline of the LRP Evocatory Technique and Inner Work Required

Several of the steps within this process require certain magical and energetic actions to be performed quite quickly, without pausing to build up the required visualisations. Please ensure that your visualisation and energy direction skills are developed before attempting the ritual. Read through the ritual carefully at least twice to get a sense of what is required. If necessary, you should practice the skills required before the night of the ritual.

Props Required: White card or paper; pens or ink in the four elemental colours; white or black cloth; gold cord, card or chalk; wand, sword or piece of dowel.

1. Decide on the area of the personality you wish to be removed or changed. For example, I may be very unhappy at the way I interrupt people when they are speaking, but my simple will does not seem to change this personality trait of mine. Through introspection and clearly examining myself I am clear that the habit does not mask deep unconscious force and needs. It is not, for example, an expression of long-held inner rage at being ignored by my alcoholic father while a child. In short, it does not carry much of an emotional 'charge'.

2. Write down in your magical journal exactly what you wish to do. In our example: 'Change my habit of interrupting people when speaking with them'. It is best to keep the statement clear and simple.

3. Using the procedure outlined in the Elemental Mirror of Self exercise in Chapter Two, decide on the elemental attribution of the quality in question. In our example here, I decide that interrupting is an excessive negative Air self quality. The trait is obviously talking too much and communication relates to Air. The trait is also a way of using my intellect to avoid hearing what people are saying, and the intellect again relates to elemental Air.

4. Name the quality in question. Here you create a new and unique name that has never been used before in any context. Do not name it 'Fred' or 'Helen' for example. Make up a nonsensical name that is not in use in any language or symbol system or jargon that you know of. There are lots of ways of performing this naming process. You can create a name whose sound matches the quality. Or just allow some gibberish to form in your mind. Another way is to take the first letter of the words of the sentence describing your intention, using them as

an acronym. Add vowel sounds if you think you need to. So in our example, we would have: 'Change **My H**abit **O**f **I**nterrupting **P**eople **W**hen **S**peaking **W**ith **T**hem', which gives 'CMHOIPWSWT'. If I was really doing this, I would probably decide this name is too long and simply shorten it to 'Cmhoip'. There is no right or more correct way of naming the trait and you should decide the method each time you perform the ritual. It is important not to write the name or the working out of the name in your journal; do it on a spare piece of paper.

5. On a fairly large piece of white paper or card write the name of the quality in the colour of the element you assign it to. So I write Cmhoip in yellow for Air.

6. Wrap the paper in a piece of cloth so it cannot be seen. White or black cloth is fine.

7. Arrange your temple or work space so that you can turn around, like in the ordinary LRP, but have space beyond the reach of your arms at the quarter of the element in question. So for example, I would make sure I can do my LRP circle with plenty of space East (for Air) outside the reach of my arms: see diagram 29. If I was working with a quality or trait relating to Water I would ensure that there was plenty of space West of my LRP circle.

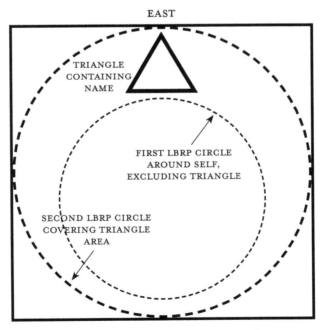

EAST

TRIANGLE CONTAINING NAME

FIRST LBRP CIRCLE AROUND SELF, EXCLUDING TRIANGLE

SECOND LBRP CIRCLE COVERING TRIANGLE AREA

Diagram 29: Temple Set-up for LRP Adaptation

8. On the floor outside of the LRP circle, draw or place an equilateral Triangle large enough to contain the piece of paper or card you have written the name upon. This triangle can be formed from cord, drawn on the floor or made out of paper or card (with a hollow inside) etc. The colour of the triangle should be gold, so use gold cord or card etc. The Triangle should be made and positioned so that when you face that quarter you are looking at its base, not a point.

9. Place the paper, still covered by the cloth, within the triangle. The cloth should now be placed over the paper but not wrapping it, so that it can easily be flicked off with a wand or other tool at the appropriate moment.

10. Perform an ordinary Lesser Banishing Ritual of the Pentagram around yourself. Make sure you are focused and clear in this ritual and do not let your mind wander.

11. State out loud your intention for your ritual and ask your Higher and Divine Genius and your Sacred One(s) to help you. Here it is a good idea to use the form of statement of intention described in chapter six where the elemental powers are addressed as witnesses to the rite. So in our example here, I would use words like:

'Spirits of Air, Fire, Water and Earth.
Spirits Active, Passive – those of the reaches above and depths below.
All spirits, in all the realms hear my intention tonight:

I am Peregrin Wildoak / Frater XYZ of the Golden Dawn tradition of Western Magic.

I honour and acknowledge the spirits of this living land that sustains and supports me in my life, together with the original Aboriginal peoples who cared for the land, generation upon generation.

Tonight I seek to personify, banish and remove my habit of interrupting people when speaking with them, so that I may become a more balanced and harmonious person. And to this end I seek the aid of the One Being, and my Higher and Divine Genius. Amen.'

12. Cleanse some incense. There are a number of ways of doing this and many good techniques can be found on the internet and in other books. When choosing your method always pay attention to the inner work required. In the ritual there is no need to burn copious quantities of incense as it is not used to add etheric energy to any manifestation. Also simple stick incense should be used as it makes the sealing actions with the incense later on a lot easier. A simple method of cleansing

incense would be to use the formula based on the LRP described in the Personal Empowerment Ritual in Chapter Three.

13. Perform a full Middle Pillar exercise, circulating the light. This will open your Kether and Malkuth centres and provide you with the various spiritual energies required to make the process effective.

14. Perform another Qabalistic Cross and then, as in the inner work for the LRP, draw energy from your crown centre and from the Earth into your heart centre. Allow the energies to mix in your heart, and then direct the energy out through your active hand.

15. Move to the quarter where the triangle is located, in our example the East. Focusing on the energy being directed from your hand, point your fingers to the top of the triangle and visualise a stream of gold light being directed into the edge of the triangle. Start with the point facing away from you and move sun-wise. Trace around the perimeter of the triangle from point to point and back to the first point, all the time directing and seeing the gold light enter the edge of the triangle. As you do this, see a wall of gold light form from the triangle upwards so that a three sided pyramid is formed of translucent gold light. Do this tracing of the perimeter three times, sending gold light into the perimeter of the triangle, all the time forming the walls of the golden pyramid of light. This whole procedure needs to be done with care and thought. The energy you are directing from your hand will form the pyramid on the etheric level; the image you are forming with your mind of the golden pyramid of light will form it on the astral level. Your directed Ruach will keep the astral form intact and solid. Since the 'spirit' to be contained within the triangle is but a personified aspect of your conscious astral self, there is no need for mental plane energy to contain and limit it. In deeper and more powerful evocations concerned with unconscious forces, divine names are inscribed and awakened around the triangle that provide mental plane energy and blessings.

16. Pause and cease mixing the two energies of Kether and Malkuth in your heart.

17. If you have one, use your ritual wand, staff, sword, or dagger to flick off the cloth covering the paper. Flick it so it is moved well away from the triangle. If you do not have ritual pointed tool of some sort, just use a twig or a branch or a piece of dowel. For this level of work the lack of a consecrated item is not a problem.

18. Put down your ritual tool. Pause and once more see and build up the image of the pyramid of translucent golden light formed over and around the physical golden triangle on the floor.

19. Stand facing the triangle. Look at the name on the paper. Reconnect your mind and emotions with the quality the name represents. Remember the times when this quality has been active and has impinged upon your life. Recall the memories clearly and really feel this. Take as long as you need, but do not go into the memories; just experience the energy from them.

20. Now take a deep breath, and imagine all the memories and feelings you have just reconnected with are drawn into your solar plexus. You may like to move your hands to help this happen as you breathe deeply. Take as many deep breaths as you require to really get a sense of the memories, thoughts and emotions connected with the quality residing in your solar plexus centre. What is occurring here is that your Ruach and will are literally altering your astral and etheric bodies. The astral substance connected with the traits is being forced into a particular 'area' of your subtle body, the solar plexus centre. This centre is connected with the lower will as well as the veil between the higher and lower consciousness. It is the place from which we may easily direct etheric and astral substance out of our subtle bodies.

21. Project out of you this combined energy of emotions and memories. This is directed out from your solar plexus using the Sign of the Enterer (see next chapter). The energy should be directed out with your Ruach and follow the direction of your hands and eyes, which should be pointing to and focused on the name in the triangle. See, direct and feel the energy go out of you and into the paper, feel the quality leave your being and enter the triangle. Do the Sign another two times, making three times in total, emptying your self completely of the quality in question. These should be done with direction, strong will and quite quickly.

22. Quickly draw energy from your Kether and Malkuth centres into your heart centre and then into your hand and ritual tool, if you have one. See your hand or ritual tool glowing in gold light. With your hand or ritual tool make a sharp cutting motion over your solar plexus region, cutting off any links between you and the quality in the triangle. Do this three times also. The combined Malkuthian and Ketheric energy directed into your the etheric hand or the ritual tool will, together with the Ruach, remove and cut away any etheric links you have with the etheric energy projected out of you into the triangle. The strong image of the gold light formed from Malkuth and Kether combined, and your will achieves the same on the astral level.

23. Follow the cutting with the Sign of Silence, which seals your auric sphere. See yourself in a sealed auric egg of softly glowing golden light. This will seal you on both the etheric and astral levels. At this stage we have removed and projected the astral and etheric energy associated with the trait from our spheres. It has been directed into and naturally forms around the name which expresses it. The amalgam of etheric substance and astral light has been sealed from us and is contained and trapped within the golden pyramid formed from the combination of Ketheric and Malkuthian blessings and our own will. What remains now is to banish or remove the energy completely, transforming it so that it will never affect us in the same way again. At this stage some teachers and authors suggest seeing or visualising a form to express the energy, a little being trapped inside the triangle, an imp or a demonic form. There is absolutely no need to do this. While it may solidify the astral form of the projected energy a little, such a visualisation will not help with its removal or transformation. The astral and etheric energy should already have been completely removed from your sphere and the banishing to follow next is the important step, not seeing a personified being that expresses your habit. Do not spend any time trying to see anything in the pyramid. If any images or visions present themselves to you, simply ignore them and carry on to the next step.

24. Banishing. Now using the regular inner workings, trace over the pyramid a Supreme Banishing Pentagram of the element to which the name and quality is attributed. So in our example I would trace a banishing Air pentagram with the complete inner workings as found in Chapter Five on invocation. The pentagram should be traced squarely over the pyramid and the names intoned directly towards the paper or card. The pentagram should be inscribed and the names intoned powerfully a total of four times. With all of these pentagrams, direct and imagine both the names and the pentagram moving into the pyramid and transforming the astral and etheric energy of the quality in question. Some teachers suggest seeing the pentagrams spin like windmills and chop the energy in the triangle to pieces, which adds an element of drama to the ritual. The main transformation however will occur through the power of the Divine names of Briah, not the visualisation of Yetzira. Directing and seeing the names entering the paper or card is far more important that the visualisations of the pentagrams moving into the card. The Briatic power of the divine names and the banishing pentagram form will effectively banish and transform the etheric and astral form of the

personality trait residing in the pyramid. The pentagram is repeated four times to ensure this is done completely and also to link to the principle of embodiment and the material plane.

25. Pause a little. Next trace all four banishing Pentagrams of the LBRP over the pyramid in the correct order, intoning the divine names into the paper. This is similar to the cleansing of the incense at the start of the ceremony. These inscriptions are done to remove any etheric substance or astral energy associated with the personality trait that is not comprised of the element to which it is attributed. In our example, I attributed the personality trait to the element of Air but it is unlikely that the complete trait operates through and is contained within my elemental Air self. A small percentage of it may operate through and be comprised of my Fire or Water selves. The inscription of the four Lesser pentagrams remove any remaining traces of the personality trait within the pyramid.

26. Pause and perform another Qabalistic Cross. Now pick up your cleansed incense stick and, with the full inner workings, trace over your solar plexus area a small Rose-Cross as described in the Rose-Cross ritual in Chapter Five. The form of the Rose-Cross should be the final form, where both **Yehusha** and **Yehovashah** are intoned as the rose is inscribed. This is done to seal and close your solar plexus centre. The incense, your will and the action itself will seal the centre within your etheric body. The visualisation and the divine name will seal the centre within your astral body.

27. Banish the pyramid. Now that the etheric and astral components of the personality trait have been banished and you are sealed, the astral and etheric structure of the pyramid can be dismantled. Firstly, pause and see once more the pyramid of gold light. Now begin to trace over the triangle with your hand or ritual tool as you did when you created the pyramid in point 15, this time however moving anti-sun-wise. Start, as in point 15, with the point facing away from you and trace around the perimeter of the triangle, from point to point and back to the first point. As you do so see the golden walls of the pyramid dissipating. Do this reverse tracing of the perimeter three times, willing and seeing the pyramid dissolve and disappear as you go, so that by the end of the third circuit it is entirely gone. This procedure effectively removes and disperses the etheric and astral forms of the pyramid.

28. Pick up the paper and without examination or thought or emotion either burn it or rip it into very small pieces. At this point also burn or destroy any other pieces of paper with the name on. What you are

doing here is removing what the Golden Dawn calls 'the material basis' of the personified personality trait, the link to the material world of Assiah.

29. Remove or rub out the triangle. This removes the triangle-pyramid upon the physical plane, just as it has previously been removed on the etheric and astral levels.

30. Perform a normal LBRP but this time around the whole room, making sure you include the area the triangle was located – the second circle shown in diagram 29. By ensuring that the LRP circle includes this area the dispersed etheric and astral form of the triangle is removed from your temple space. The LBRP also closes and re-cleanses the temple once more.

31. Thank your Higher and Divine Genius and your Sacred One(s). As in the calling for aid, use a form similar to that described in Chapter Six, for example:

'To those who have aided my spiritual endeavours tonight I give you thanks and blessings: the One Being of All, the Land that sustains and supports me and my Higher and Divine Genius. Thanks and blessings. Amen.'

32. Dispose of the ash or paper thoughtfully. Never use or say the name you created again; forget about it completely.

INITIATION AND LINKING TO THE GOLDEN DAWN MAGICAL CURRENTS

'A true initiation never ends' ~ Western magical saying.

THERE has been so much mystification and hype concerning ceremonial initiation within the Western traditions that it is almost an impossible task to write about it from a down to earth perspective. Despite the publication of most of the Golden Dawn papers and access to some of the most transformational spiritual techniques ever developed, people will still wait years for initiation rather than deepening their spiritual unfoldment and service now. And despite many sensible and accurate descriptions of the initiation and its purpose, it is still seen as an event that somehow makes one different from other people – more advanced, one of the elite – an attitude that is in complete contrast to the actual purpose of initiation. These and other misconceptions hinder our understanding of this core aspect of the Golden Dawn tradition and must be let go of if we are to go deeper than the occult stereotypes so prevalent in Western esoteric circles.

THE PURPOSE OF CEREMONIAL INITIATION IN THE WESTERN TRADITIONS

Initiation means simply 'to begin'. The late W.E. Butler, an adept in a Western Magical tradition stemming from the Golden Dawn, believed we should not say we are 'initiates' (noun), but rather 'initiate' (verb), to indicate that we are all, no matter our experience, *continually beginning* our spiritual unfoldment. In the Golden Dawn this is the beginning of a new mode of awareness, where we no longer walk in the sleep of everyday life but are alive to our own inner divinity and the call of God. Much has been written on the magical and general theories of initiation which cannot be described here due to space, and which can be found within many books available from the public library system. Here we will focus solely on the process of initiation within the Golden Dawn with reference to the broader Western lodge tradition. For further information on the Western traditions of magical initiation please read the excellent *Inside a Magical Lodge* by John Michael Greer.

Like all fraternal and magical lodge traditions in the West, the Golden Dawn initiations are ceremonial in nature. The person being initiated is normally referred to as the candidate. Those members of the lodge performing the initiation are normally referred to as officers. During the initiation the candidate, who is often blindfolded, is directed and moved around the temple space, often as part of a symbolic journey. Each initiation takes place in a specially prepared temple space that contains both physical props and subtle forces and Beings resonant to the purpose of the initiation. During the initiation the candidate may be shown symbolic images or diagrams, addressed by various officers and have specific spiritual blessings placed within their subtle bodies. This may be achieved via contact with consecrated items such as holy water and incense, the use of Godforms around the officers, invocation or other magical means. The whole sequence of magical actions within the ceremony is well orchestrated and works in concert to produce the required changes in the subtle bodies and consciousness of the candidate.

There are various opinions within the Western magical traditions concerning initiation and the spiritual and psychological effects it may or may not have. We may summarise these opinions in several broad statements, each of which looks at initiation from a differing perspective.

1. Ceremonial initiations, when correctly performed, will without a doubt promote a change of consciousness within the initiate. That is, a new state of consciousness, a new level of spiritual awakening will be delivered to the initiate. With each new or subsequent initiation they will become more spiritually advanced than those who do not have those initiations.
2. Initiation is a process, not a series of ceremonies, and the actual initiation is through our own personal work and life circumstances. Life itself is the initiator. The ceremonies are simply a recognition of the state of consciousness already achieved as well as a booster or 'leg-up' towards further unfoldment within the process.
3. Ceremonial initiations, when correctly performed, offer a series of energetic keys to the initiate. If these are taken up and used by the initiate within their own personal work, they will then promote a

distinct change in consciousness and spiritual advancement. Often this may involve unexpected or dramatic changes in life circumstances. When these new life circumstances are entered into fully they may provide a vehicle through which the new state of consciousness may be developed.

4. Ceremonial initiations are mostly designed to recognise work within a particular occult or magical discipline or Order. They have little or nothing to do with spiritual or moral development and are simply markers of who is an 'elder' within a tradition and who is not.

5. Ceremonial initiations within the magical traditions are predominantly designed to promote greater magical powers or mastery of the various forces of the universe, both internally and externally. They have little to do with spiritual advancement or the mystical awareness of God and the transformation of consciousness.

The way the members of the original Golden Dawn viewed its initiatory schema appears to have elements of all five perspectives. The ceremonies were designed to change the initiate's consciousness (1). It is also clear from the commentaries upon the initiations that the initiate had to work his own process (2) and activate the keys of the ceremony within his daily life through will and surrender (3). However, it is also clear that the initiations themselves, *regardless* of the spiritual unfoldment or magical attainment of the individual, were used as prerequisites to hold certain offices within an Order (4). And there is certainly plenty of evidence that while the initiations increase an individual's capacity for magic, they may not promote an expansion of consciousness towards a mystical awareness of God (5).

THE GOLDEN DAWN INITIATORY SCHEMA

The Golden Dawn initiatory system is one of the most comprehensive and complete esoteric formulas to be found within the Western traditions. Its beauty and power is seldom appreciated even today – simply because many people and many Orders do not work the initiations fully. The complete system is predicated upon several fundamental magical theories:

◆ By a series of invocations and other magical work, something dead or inert can be brought to life. In initiation, this 'something' is the candidate who is 'dead' to the Light or other spiritual forces and blessings.

◆ The psyche and the subtle bodies when under stress are receptive to an influx of both symbols and forces. Once implanted these symbols and forces, when activated by magical work, will grow and cause changes within the psyche and subtle bodies. These will affect our consciousness and help us transfer our consciousness to various inner realms at will.

◆ A person can be charged with particular forces and spiritual blessings by placing her in close proximity with those forces or blessings. This can be explained by using the analogy of a piece of metal becoming magnetised when placed next to a strong electromagnet.

The original Golden Dawn comprised seven ceremonial initiations. These seven ceremonies form part of a theoretical approach to spiritual unfoldment that includes becoming one with the Divine and encompassing the entire Universe. This nonsensical and grandiose vision has prompted much delusion and madness over the years, and really should be let go of today. In this full schema there are twelve initiations, though until the break up of the Golden Dawn few people claimed any of the higher degrees at all. These, together with their elemental and Sephirotic attributions are:

Grade	Number	Element	Sephira
Neophyte	$0°=0^\square$	—	—
Zelator	$1°=10^\square$	Earth	Malkuth
Theoricus	$2°=9^\square$	Air	Yesod
Practicus	$3°=8^\square$	Water	Hod
Philosophus	$4°=7^\square$	Fire	Netzach
Portal	—	Spirit	(Paroketh)
Adeptus Minor	$5°=6^\square$	—	Tiphareth
Adeptus Major	$6°=5^\square$	—	Geburah
Adeptus Exemptus	$7°=4^\square$	—	Chesed
Magister Templi	$8°=3^\square$		Binah
Magus	$9°=2^\square$		Chokmah
Ipsissimus	$10°=1^\square$		Kether

Despite the number associations and attributions to the Sephiroth, we must bear in mind that the aim of initiation is really to live life as fully as possible, mediating the divine as we participate in the world, and not to escape to the top of the ladder. The seemingly natural tendency to focus on 'climbing the ladder of initiation' is one of the more damaging internalized aspects of our culture. Our desires to become a more advanced magician or obtain a higher grade, no matter how deeply hidden or cleverly disguised by our egos, must be looked at, owned, recognised and then surrendered. This is often far harder and requires more sustained effort than we initially think. While it is certainly true that we do develop and deepen and in some ways are more advanced that we were previously, we are still here, still human and still required to be of service to our world and God.

THE THREEFOLD FRAMEWORK OF THE WEST

Despite the apparent complexity of the Golden Dawn initiatory system, it stems from a very simple framework indeed. The same straightforward framework underlies nearly all Western initiatory grade systems. This structure had its origins in the various Craft guilds of the middle ages which recognised three levels of skill and mastery within a particular trade: the beginner, those more advanced and the few who had more or less mastered the trade completely. With the influx of esoteric ideas and thought into the Craft guilds and the development of Speculative Masonry (that is, Masonry practiced by men who worked with the mind and not with physical stone), these three levels were used as a general framework to map out spiritual unfoldment. These Freemasonic terms for these levels, together with the general magic titles corresponding to them, are:

1. **Entered Apprentice**   **Novice**
2. **Fellow Craft**   **Adept**
3. **Master Mason**   **Master**

The magical Rosicrucian traditions from the seventeenth century onwards also used this basic model and divided their traditions into three Orders corresponding to the three stages just outlined. This approach was developed further into the grade system adopted by the Golden Dawn:

NOVICES: FIRST ORDER – 'THE GOLDEN DAWN'
Neophyte 0=0 (as link)
Zelator 1=10
Theoricus 2=9
Practicus 3=8
Philosophus 4=7

ADEPTI: SECOND ORDER – ROSAE RUBEAE ET AUREAE CRUCIS
Portal (as link)
Adeptus Minor 5=6
Adeptus Major 6=5
Adeptus Exemptus 7=4

MASTERS: INVISIBLE THIRD ORDER
Crossing the Abyss (as link)
Magister Templi 8=3
Magus 9=2
Ipsissimus 10=1

We can now look at each stage in turn, bearing in mind that the map is not the territory and there are plenty of other ways to understand all of this.

THE NOVICE: NEOPHYTE AND THE SO-CALLED 'ELEMENTAL' GRADES

The Neophyte Ceremony, despite it being the first initiation, is in some ways the most important of the whole ceremonial structure of the Golden Dawn tradition. It brings the candidate from the darkness to the Light, a metaphor for their own higher consciousness. She is purified, consecrated and put in touch with the Light. The ceremony also links the initiate to the spiritual energy and tradition of the Golden Dawn and its inner currents of magic. This is a non-physical linkage between the Neophyte's auric sphere and the standing pattern of Golden Dawn magic on the astral and mental realms. It is achieved via the *etheric and astral link*, placed within the etheric and astral bodies of the candidate during the ritual. The ceremony also welcomes and links the Neophyte into the particular Order, temple or group. The full text of this ceremony together with a description of the magical formula that underpins it may be found in *The Golden Dawn*. There are now a number of redactions of the various GD initiation ceremonies available online and in some newer books, and it is worth looking them up for deep study.

The keywords for this initiation are **light** and **connection** and the essence of the Ceremony is beautifully symbolised by the speech of the three chief officers at the climax of the ritual:

Inheritor of a dying world, we call thee to the living beauty.
Wanderer in the wild Darkness, we call thee to the gentle Light.
Child of Earth, long hast thou dwelt in Darkness,
Quit the Night and seek the Day.

The next four initiations are concerned with balancing the psychological and astral make-up of the magician. These grades (**Zelator, Theoricus, Practicus** and **Philosophus**) are assigned to the four elements and during them the initiate is charged with the power of the appropriate element. All four of these ceremonies do the following:

◆ Place within the subtle bodies and psyche of the initiate certain symbols and symbol structures (relationships between symbols) that will be utilised in further magical work or that will cause changes in the consciousness and thought patterns of the initiate.
◆ Raise to the conscious awareness of the initiate possible changes in her personality, life and exterior surroundings that if acted upon will produce greater balance and harmony. For example, following the Zelator initiation where the elemental principle of Earth is 'injected' into the initiate's subtle bodies, she may become aware of the right diet and exercise regime for her body-self. This may occur for all of the subtle forces placed within the candidate, not just the elemental powers.
◆ Raise the shadow side of the personality into consciousness awareness (so it is no longer shadow). So, in our example, the new Zelator may become consciously aware for the first time of just how much they dislike or ignore their body-Earth-self. Here the term 'shadow' means all we have suppressed or ignored, not only the 'negative' aspects.
◆ Cause changes in the personality and life of the initiate that will promote greater balance and harmony. The spiritual reality here, shared by most magicians, is that the energy and spiritual blessings directed into the initiate during these initiations can, on occasion, actually cause physical changes to the 'outside' world of the initiate.

The keywords for all of these initiations are: **Change** and **Balance**. The text for these initiations can be found in *The Golden Dawn*. These four initiations should never be considered separately, just as the four elemental principles in Malkuth are never found unmixed or alone. All four initiations form in effect a four-fold sequence, and can be considered one initiation having four phases at four distinct times and ceremonies. Nor should we consider them to be elemental grades alone, since they contain much more then elemental energies, for example Sephirotic and planetary energies. Later in this chapter we will examine the multi-layered nature of these four initiations in depth.

Looking at these four initiations with reference to changes in consciousness, the work of the Novice magician within the Outer Order is to consciously control and place in balance all the various components of the personality self. These are symbolised by the elements; Body-Self (Earth), Thinking-Self (Air), Feeling-Self (Water), Passionate-Self (Fire). With this in mind, the state of consciousness of the Philosophus initiate waiting for their Portal initiation should be one where they can, at will, exercise control over and promote balance within their whole personality. This would include their physical body-self, fitness, health and material life; their thought process and rational and concrete minds; their emotional patterns, nature and expression; and their sexuality, passion, will and intuition.

Such a person would necessarily be positive towards life and would know how to solve, accept or work towards solving, any problems they would come up against. They would be able to draw extra elemental energy from the Macrocosmic realms of the elements and other planes when required to keep them functioning well and healthily. For example they would be able to draw upon the powers of Air if they found themselves muddy in thinking or upon the powers of Earth if their physical health was low in vitality and spark. With the balance of the mind, will, emotions and body such a completed Novice magician is well placed to traverse the link to the Adept Order through the Portal Grade. This balance would also have produced a great sense of blessing and gratitude towards the universe and the One Being, and we could expect a magician at this stage to have deepened her relationship to her Sacred One(s) and mystical awareness of the One.

However, the magician at this stage is still a Novice, an Apprentice. Looking at the transformation of consciousness, we see that regardless of the balance of the elemental selves, the Outer Order magician is still vulnerable to the uprising of the un-regenerated aspects of the Self. They are exactly those stubborn aspects of the unconscious that we discussed in the last chapter on evocation. When these unconscious aspects and desires rise or merge into consciousness, which will occur from time to time, the long created balance of the personality is disrupted and may even fall apart for a time. We have all experienced this: just when we think we've got our act together and everything is going well, something comes along and knocks us for a six and we find ourselves acting how we never expected to. This is simply a part of being human; but for someone who has spent a considerable period of time balancing their personality, it can be a bit disheartening. A more balanced personality, however, means that it is less likely the entire balance will be knocked around, or that it will take long to recover our poise and balance.

From an esoteric point of view, such a spontaneous arising of unconscious aspects into the consciousness occurs because the magician is simply re-arranging the various component parts of the elemental personality self, rather than transforming it. They are essentially balancing and perfecting within the world of Yetzira, the world of the conscious personality and sense of self. As discussed previously in this book, sometimes to effect deep transformation we need to utilise a level of consciousness above or higher than the area of self we wish to transform. With respect to the elemental self, we need to access the realm of spirit, the Quintessence, which is found in Tiphareth. This is the work and consciousness of the Adept grade, foreshadowed by its linking grade of the Portal.

THE ADEPT – THE INNER ORDER GRADES

The grades within the Inner or Second Order need to be examined individually if we are to be clear about the states of consciousness they may produce when worked fully. Please be aware that there are many people within the magical community claiming and acting from all sorts of high grades but whose actions do not reflect the consciousness of those grades. This does not undermine the essential nature of the grades in question, but does point out the inherent dangers in magic discussed throughout this book.

The Portal grade is a link between the Outer Order (Neophyte through Philosophus) and the Inner Order (Adeptus Minor onward). To it is assigned the element of Spirit, and it thus 'caps' or finishes off the elemental and other changes undergone in the Outer Order. It is a highly complex ritual and one which will produce a large degree of transformation. It aims to:

◆ Place within the subtle bodies and psyche of the initiate certain symbols and symbol structures (relationships between symbols) that will be utilised in further magical work or that will cause changes in the consciousness and thought patterns of the initiate.
◆ Cause changes in the life and personality of the initiate that will bind together the energies and new ways of being, associated with the four elemental initiations, into a cohesive and unified whole.
◆ Prompt (and keep on prompting) to the conscious awareness any possible changes within the personality of the initiate associated with the elemental grades that were missed, ignored, deliberately shunned and denied previously.

◆ Prepare the initiate's mind, unconscious and subtle bodies for the forthcoming Adeptus Minor initiation.

The keywords for this initiation are **Unification** and **Preparation.** The Portal grade, as link, is commonly by necessity an uncomfortable place to be and the state of consciousness in some ways may be likened to adolescence. The magician is neither a Novice, nor yet really an Adept, just as a teenager is neither a child nor an adult. The Portal magician exists in a liminal state, a place between the end of one path and the start of another. During this period one often feels displaced, unsure of the Path and of spirituality itself. Also during this time, further changes in consciousness arise from the depths of the various elemental selves. All of this is by way of preparation for full entry into the Inner Order through the Adeptus Minor initiation. A fully functioning Portal magician, on the threshold of Adeptus Minor has, in the words of the grade, 'passed through the hour of cloud and of night'. She has had the lights go out one by one and has stuck fast to her Path, continued to balance her elemental personality self and now awaits to move into a deeper realm of consciousness.

Typically, it is said, living with a person undergoing the Portal grade, like any 'dark night of the soul' experience, is not easy. The magician may feel he is 'dying' or 'ebbing away'. From one point of view this is true, as the Portal is a period where the magician passes through the veil between the lower four Sephiroth of everyday life and the higher Sephiroth. During this period any elemental imbalance of the personality is shed and falls away, just as a dying person slowly sheds their life and energy.

The Adeptus Minor ceremony is powerful and beautiful. It has no peer in any other extant Western system that I, and every writer and magician I've come across, are aware of. Symbolically this ceremony causes the death of the lower self to achieve the birth of the Higher Self. Specifically it aims to:

◆ Place within the subtle bodies and psyche of the initiate certain symbols and symbol structures (relationships between symbols) that will be utilised in further magical work or that will cause changes in the consciousness and thought patterns of the initiate.
◆ Cause changes in the initiate that will permanently allow her to consciously, at will, move her consciousness from the persona self of the lower four Sephiroth to her Higher and Divine Genius centred in the Sephira of Tiphareth.

♦ Connect the initiate with the spiritual blessings and magical currents of the inner order of the Golden Dawn, the Rosae Rubeae et Aureae Crucis (and through them, the Rosicrucian magical and spiritual currents).

♦ Produce a state of acceptance within the initiate's lower (personality) self towards the will of the Higher and Divine Genius.

♦ Produce within the initiate an expansion of love and compassion, as symbolised by the figure of Christian Rosencreutz.

The keywords for this initiation are: **Higher Consciousness** and **Love**.

Due to all her magical work and the ceremonial impetus of the initiation, the consciousness of the Adeptus Minor is in stark contrast to that of the Portal magician. She has arisen anew like the dawn from the long dark. Specifically there is an influx of tremendous Briatic blessings and spiritual light and this shines through all her life and work. The main characteristic shift is the falling away of the personality concerns of life and the lack of lower, personal will in life choices. This is due to what is known as the 'Knowledge and Conversation of the Holy Guardian Angel'. This refers to a process whereby the consciousness transmutes and the control of our personality self is handed more and more to the greater consciousness that is behind our lives. This process is something we all experience every so often – the difference is that traversing the full Adeptus Minor grade makes it a permanent state of affairs, a hard wiring of consciousness. As part of this, the complete elemental personality self is re-made. This is the Adept nature of the grade – the magician is able to alter and transform her elemental make-up and outer personality at will through alliance with her Higher and Divine Genius. This can involve radical transformation and change that from the outside perspective can seem very harsh and painful, but from the magician's perspective is perfect.

Again, we all have moments of this all the time in our spiritual work and we can easily delude ourselves into thinking that these constitute an Adept level consciousness. However, the full Adeptus Minor magician never even thinks about this consciousness, she simply knows that she is a projection of the angelic power of her Higher and Divine Genius. She can, at will, surrender to and become that power and blessing. This is not dissociation of the personality, but rather the perfecting of it. This form of consciousness is typified by the ideals of the Rosicrucian fraternity, the mythic mystery Order behind nearly all Western magical traditions. These ideals are symbolically expressed in the foundational Rosicrucian document as:

- To heal the sick, and for free.
- To adopt the garb and customs of wherever one finds oneself.
- To find and train a worthy successor for the Order upon his death.
- To meet together at least once every year.
- The name Christian Rosencreutz would symbolise their ideals.

Bearing in mind these were written during the early 1600s, we may translate these principles in clearer, modern language as:

- Providing healing and spiritual service to humanity, both on the outer and inner planes, with nothing expected or taken in return. This is counter to the practice of charging for medicine, house clearings, healings and spiritual support common in today's secular and spiritual communities.
- Keeping silent and anonymous in our unfoldment and spiritual service, so that our egos are less likely to become involved. Again this runs counter to the tendency to exalt one's self with titles and claims to be a 'Rosicrucian', an 'adept' or to advertise how much we have helped those less fortunate than ourselves.
- Helping to train and induct others so that the service to humanity will continue. This motivation for teaching and passing on the tradition is counter to the modern practice of commercial teaching and expensive weekend courses offering 'mastership' in spiritual healing techniques. It also runs counter to the often found inner motivation of teachers to collect as many students as possible as a way of shoring up their fragile egos; 'he who dies with the most initiates wins!'
- Joining together to share spiritual aspirations, be recharged and essentially be peer-reviewed, helping to ensure we do not wander off on our own ego led tracks.
- Continual aspiration towards that state of consciousness symbolised by Christian Rosencreutz, the mythic founder of the Rosicrucians. Christian Rosencreutz is the epitome of 'a just man made perfect', an adept who upon his illumination used all his spiritual gifts and efforts in the service of humanity, without focus on his self.

With reference to the magical work that promotes this state of consciousness, the Adept's sphere of activity is the full Yetziratic realm and the astral plane, just as the Apprentice's sphere was the personality. The Adept connects with the deeper objective forces of Yetzira, symbolised by the full elemental powers, the planets, the Sephiroth and the Zodiac. She learns to navigate and move into the various realms of Yetzira at will. By doing so she is able to connect with and draw down all the powers and blessings she needs in order to re-make her personality self and to promote healing and spiritual growth in others. She also has the ongoing expanded awareness of the Higher and Divine Genius and is more and more able to obtain whatever magical or spiritual instruction she requires without reference to an outside human agency. However, she may often choose to maintain a connection with the physical Order so as to work in harmony with other Adepts in their service to humanity. All of this however takes a considerable amount of work, unfoldment and inner initiation and will not be suddenly 'there' the day after the physical initiation ceremony.

With the true alliance of the Higher and Divine Genius, the Adeptus Minor now navigates her way towards a deeper journey. Once she has re-made the elemental personality self, and formed alliance with some of the deeper Yetziratic forces, she is ready to begin the work symbolised by the Adeptus Major and Adeptus Exemptus grades. These two grades can never really be considered separately, as they are working on the same plane and towards the same ends. Originally the Golden Dawn's Inner Order never worked grades higher than that of Adeptus Minor. Later these ceremonial degrees were added, though each Order seems to have created their own particular form of the ceremony. There is still debate as to whether these ceremonial degrees can have any direct transformational powers at this level of consciousness. Certainly, if they are to do so, the majority of the work would need to be performed at the deeper levels of Yetzira, with an Adept team drawing down the full power of Briah. In any case, ceremonially initiated or not, the next phase of unfolding involves moving into the realm of the Higher and Divine Genius itself.

Previously the area of self that has been worked on has been the lower personality self; the incarnated self that will die when the body dies. This has been made possible through alliance with the Higher and Divine Genius. Now, at the major Adept levels, the 'soul level' becomes the sphere of operation. Quoting a phrase from the Zelator ceremony, 'this is a mystery, very admirable and recondite'. The essential mystery here is that the soul cannot grow and expand except through incarnation. Without the experience of Malkuth, wherein Kether is concealed, the soul exists but does not evolve. The soul needs the mystery of the full incarnation of Malkuth, and through the experience of life itself, it can then begin to evolve. It does this when the soul's consciousness, which is symbolised as the Higher and Divine Genius, engages deeply with the now balanced and harmonized personality self.

The Higher and Divine Genius cannot work this transformation on its own, but needs the incarnated self to work with it. The incarnated self brings to the soul (through the Higher and Divine Genius) the mystery of Kether within Malkuth. And just as the lower self requires the higher blessings of Tiphareth for full transformation, so too does the soul require a 'higher' force for its evolution. This higher force is Unity within Diversity, or Kether incarnated in Malkuth. This is part of the mystery of the incarnation of humanity, the Fall in Christian terms, or to express it in the (paraphrased) words of the Goddess channelled through Aleister Crowley:

> 'I am divided for love's sake, for the chance of re-union; for
> the joy of re-union is all and the pain of dissolution as nothing'.

The One Being divides itself so that it may know itself through re-union which produces greater bliss and purpose in the Universe. We, as divided parts of the One, need to consciously choose to Unite once more and return to the One. In acting and living this choice we will necessarily come across those forces that seek to hinder this unification. We are then required to face and transform those forces and finally to express this unified state in the real, flesh and blood world. This then, is the work of the Adeptus Major and Adeptus Exemptus.

The Adeptus Major, working fully with the Sphere of Severity, Geburah, has the active task of facing and overcoming the negative aspects of her soul. These negative qualities or facets of the soul can be viewed as coming from a number or sources. As we discussed in the last chapter on evocation, we have within each of us reflections of all the powers of the universe. This includes the evil or negative powers, often referred to by the Qabalistic term, Qlippoth. Some magicians also believe that negative aspects of the soul are the result of negative Karma attached to the soul from previous incarnations. Then there are the macrocosmic or human collective negativities that are part and parcel of being human. The main outer work of the Adeptus Major is a prolonged series of Evocations where she will manifest, face, and transform all the negative aspects surrounding her soul, whether they are 'hers' or not.

The Adeptus Exemptus, working within the Sphere of Mercy, Chesed, accepts passively and completely any remaining imbalances of the soul or Karma. Rather than outwardly and actively confronting the imbalance, her acceptance, equilibrium and love 'works out' and transforms the imbalance inwardly. The Adept at this level will also be connected to and mediating the full streams of blessing her spiritual tradition has to offer. She will be an inspiration and a teacher. The main outer, visible work of the Adeptus Exemptus is typified by the phrase 'good works' – healing, teaching, and taking on the pain and Karma of other people through love and sacrifice. The Adept at this level will exemplify the saying: 'in the Western traditions the Adept does not teach the path; he does not show the path; he is the path'.

This Soul level adjustment is understandably very rare. I think that most of the people claiming to be initiates at these levels are either claiming temple grades (markers of their status within a particular Order) not states of consciousness, or they are seriously deluded. Israel Regardie once said that by claiming a grade above Adeptus Minor, one automatically casts doubt on the validity of that grade. This is because Adepts at this level are not only few and far between, but would also not claim any grade outwardly at all and would work in silence for the betterment of humankind.

THE MASTER

Trying to talk about the next phase of unfoldment is almost impossible. It is rather akin to someone trying to describe an orgasm who has never experienced one, but more so. Consequently I will not say much. Tradition teaches us that through the resolution of Karma, imbalance and impurities, the tension in the Soul is lessened and one no longer needs to incarnate. Thus the Adept Exempt now moves inevitably towards that much famed and much misunderstood phase called 'Crossing the Abyss'. The Crossing is said to be the phase of unfoldment where the Adept becomes a fully illuminated and divine being. One of the biggest misunderstandings concerning this process is the fact that the Adept, that is John Smith or Jane Doe, does not actually cross the Abyss at all. At this advanced stage the Higher and Divine Genius behind John has become so prominent that John hardly exists at all in any real sense. It is therefore the Higher and Divine Genius that undergoes this process, which is a deeper reflection of the surrender of the lower self to the Higher Self during the Adeptus Minor grade. Here the Higher and Divine Genius surrenders itself to God.

Another misunderstanding about Crossing the Abyss is the belief that a person can choose to do it, that it is the result of willed action. ('What are you doing over the weekend?' 'Oh, I thought I'd cross the Abyss on Saturday – how about you?') This shows a complete misunderstanding. The Adept Exempt is in such harmony with the Universe and her own Higher Soul that the process of the Crossing simply occurs without any conscious decision at all. One day, one finds oneself walking across the Abyss and the Crossing is accomplished easily, since it happens at the ripe moment. All the talk about the perils of Crossing is due to that fact that people *choose* to cross. If you ever hear anyone talking about planning to Cross the Abyss, it is a fair bet they are suffering some delusion or have misunderstood the entire process. That said, if one does consciously choose to attempt a Crossing, then yes, they will face many grave perils, death being the least of their worries.

It is taught that those who cross the Abyss are beyond the need for incarnation and form the Invisible Third Order, the perfected Guardians of the Western traditions existing in the realm of Briah. However, if they choose to stay embodied, they become Masters of the Temple, showing they have mastered the material Universe. At this level of Mastery one has access to all human knowledge without learning it, can control every aspect of their body and mental functions. They would, as they progress to the stage of Magus, even be able to have perfect control over all matter and could perform miracles and transmute matter, like Christ. Beyond this, there is only complete Union and becoming God, in the Sphere of Kether. Again, these are mere words to reflect a pale understanding of a spiritual state deeper and beyond most of humanity at present. The Third Order, when contacted spiritually, do not even seem human at all, having gone beyond the familiar traits we recognise as human characteristics, and yet they are the sources of the deepest compassion and spiritual blessings of our tradition. We can gain a partial understanding of this mystery by reflecting on the fact that is Binah that emanates Chesed – the dark restriction of Saturn that gives birth to the expansion and magnificence of Jupiter.

Initiatory Progress within the Golden Dawn

If initiation into the various Golden Dawn grades is effective we will not only acquire magical skills and knowledge. We will also learn more about ourselves, the One Being and the world. As a result we should find ourselves more connected to humanity, more compassionate and more consciously involved in the round of daily life. Any notions of us as initiates (the 'twice born') being in any way better or more advanced than regular humanity (the 'once born') should, as we unfold, lessen and eventually give way to the awareness of the deep connection throughout whole of humanity. Similarly, as we move through the grades, our genuine desire for service to the world and humanity should increase and grow. If these changes do not take place we can say that the initiations have not 'taken', their full transformational potential has not yet been realised.

With reference to Western magical initiations in general and Golden Dawn initiations in particular, remembering four key points will help us gain the most from our initiations and also help place their purpose and importance into perspective.

♦ Firstly, progress through any particular path of initiation does not translate as progress in 'spiritual advancement' within other spiritual paths, or even becoming a better human being. A high degree initiate in one system of initiation is only high in that system – their advancement is not transferable to other systems. Also, despite their higher initiatory status they may still be fundamentally flawed as human beings, as the evidence furnished by the history of modern and contemporary magic aptly points out. In Golden Dawn terms, an Adeptus Minor initiate cannot readily assume the same status in other ceremonial or spiritual paths as she does in a Golden Dawn temple. She may also be as mad, vicious or deluded as some of the original public Golden Dawn magicians.

♦ Secondly, the Golden Dawn grade system of 'advancement' through ceremonial initiation does not imply that a fourth degree Philosophus is 'better' or more 'advanced' than a first degree Zelator. It simply shows that a Philosophus is working in a different magical area than a Zelator; with the element of Fire rather than the element of Earth. While it is true that the deeper initiations require successful completion of earlier initiations, they are not better or more powerful. All parts and aspects of our being are equally holy.

♦ Thirdly, initiation is a gift from an Order to an initiate, one that should inspire the initiate to give equally in turn. Sadly however, it is a gift most of us involved in the Western esoteric traditions may never receive and will have to learn to live without. This is simply because of the lack of sensible, accessible and properly functioning magical Orders within the West today. However, it is quite possible to create your own Order rather than waiting for one to appear or bemoaning the lack. To this end I sincerely recommend John Michael Greer's *Inside a Magical Lodge*. Seriously, forming a magical Order is not out of the question and may not only be spiritually fulfilling, but may also provide a much needed service.

♦ Finally, the whole aim of any authentic Western tradition's initiatory process, including the Golden Dawn, is to help prepare the initiate for service through love. This is expressly stated in the Golden Dawn through words repeated by thousands of magicians the world over at each Equinox:

'the Soul by true direction must be brought to the study of Divine things, that it may offer only clean oblation and acceptable sacrifice, which is love expressed towards God, humanity and the Universe'.

SELF INITIATION AND INITIATORY WORK WITHIN THE GOLDEN DAWN TRADITION

At this point we need to explore the concept of self initiation, if only because it is an idea very common within the magical community at present. While I believe that it is possible for a magician to undergo a magical process that will result in similar effects as a full Golden Dawn initiation, I do not believe it is possible to do this via a single self-initiation ceremony. There are two main reasons for this. Firstly, within the Golden Dawn the initiations are extremely complex magical actions. They rest upon and require clear and empowered connections to particular magical currents and a level of technical skill far in advance of a newcomer to the grade. Put simply, if someone had the skill to initiate themselves into the Neophyte grade with its complex formula and impact of twenty two godforms etc, all within a single self-initiation ceremony, they would not need to be initiated.

Secondly and most importantly, ceremonial initiations always require passivity on behalf of the initiate. While this becomes a little less in the deeper grades of some traditions, it is still a requirement. The initiate is literally acted upon by the officers and spiritual forces invoked. The same effects simply cannot occur if we were to call the forces and seek to act on ourselves. The very act of invocation would alter our subtle bodies and we could not receive the various complexly created structures and energies the initiation is designed to instil.

If we as solo magicians wish to engage with the initiatory method of the Golden Dawn, and there are very good reasons for doing so, we need to find ways of affecting our subtle bodies in the same manner as the initiation ceremonies themselves. During initiation we receive a gift of many hundreds of hours of inner and spiritual work on behalf of the initiating team. It is these hours of effort and spiritual work, combined with the blessings of inner plane Beings, that all come together into a coherent whole that will (hopefully) change the initiate. We simply cannot hope to achieve this by ourselves in a single ceremony, no matter how good we are at visualising various officers or Godforms around us.

The way forward is to analyse exactly what each initiation does and what changes it produces. Once we are clear of these, we can then design a curriculum of magical practice designed to produce these changes within us. We may need to use different magical processes than those found in the initiation ceremonies, but provided the end result is the same there will be no difficulty. In short we can design an initiatory process that will, over a period of time, change our various subtle bodies and our psyche and result in us effectively being initiated whatever grade we are working with. We will now apply the first stage of this process; analysis of the initiations.

THE NEOPHYTE CEREMONY

The Neophyte ceremony is one of the most powerful and beautiful ceremonies I have ever had the privilege to be a part of. When enacted correctly the transformation it can achieve in open and sincere initiates can be staggering. This transformation comes about through the complex magical formula within the ceremony which known as the Z Formula. Essentially the Z formula is designed to bring something to life, in this case bringing the candidate to a new spiritual life. This transformation is one of the two main aims of the Neophyte initiation, the second being to link the initiate to the Golden Dawn tradition on the inner planes. Sadly, there is no easy way to duplicate the full Z formula within a simple ceremony or daily practice that a beginner may perform. Happily however, similar effects can be achieved through prolonged daily practice of the rituals within this book, particularly the LRP and the full Middle Pillar. An approach to this daily practice and work is given in the curriculum at the end of this chapter. The other aspect of the initiation, connecting to the Golden Dawn, may be accomplished by the Connection Ceremony in the next chapter. The link formed needs to be subsequently enhanced through a simple daily process and regular solo Equinox ceremonies, both of which are also detailed in the next chapter.

THE FOUR ELEMENTAL OR PERSONALITY GRADES

These four grades are sometimes cursorily practiced or even omitted in modern Golden Dawn Orders. This is due to the belief that they are solely concerned with the elemental principles and anything else within the ceremony is obsolete or redundant occult lore. Aleister Crowley, who was normally dead on the mark magically, once wrote that these grades were of 'little magical interest, value or importance'. Other magicians, including Israel Regardie, have suggested regular performance of the Watchtower Ceremony or other elemental practices will effectively replace the effects these ceremonies have upon the initiate. Such a view shows an elemental bias and a lack of understanding concerning the other spiritual forces these ceremonies awaken and direct into the candidate. The table below summarises some of the major spiritual blessings invoked and placed into the candidate as part of these grades. A few other forces are not discussed here as it is impossible to describe how to bring them about without revealing certain esoteric formulae best left unpublished. These formulae act directly upon the more delicate aspects of the subtle bodies and can be quite dangerous if approached unwisely.

Table 7: Major Components of the Elemental Grades

	Zelator	Theoricus	Practicus	Philosophus
Element	Earth	Air	Water	Fire
Sephiroth	Malkuth	Yesod	Hod	Netzach
Planet		Moon	Mercury	Venus
Paths		32nd Path of Tau, Reflection of the Sphere of Saturn	31st Path of Shin, Reflection of the Sphere of Fire; 30th Path of Resh, Reflection of the Sphere of the Sun	29th Path of Qoph, Reflection of the Sphere of Pisces; 28th Path of Tzaddi, Reflection of the Sphere of Aquarius; 27th Path of Peh, Reflection of the Sphere of Mars
Tarot		Universe	Judgement; Sun	Moon; Star; Blasted Tower
Main Symbols Placed in the Subtle Bodies	22 Hebrew Letters as Mother, Double and Single	The Abode of Shells; The Serpent on the Tree	Eden Before the Fall	Eden After the Fall

By simply looking at this table, without even reading or undergoing them, we begin to get a sense of the richness of these ceremonies. The multi-layered nature of these ceremonies means that an open and humble initiate can expect a great deal of change to occur in the months following each grade. Since the ceremonies work with universal forces the types of change may be roughly predicted, though each initiate is different. While it would take a whole book to examine the full initiations, we need to be aware of the main spiritual forces within each ceremony and how they connect from ceremony to ceremony. The meditations and rituals for the solo magician to practice that will awaken these forces within her are detailed in the curriculum at the end of this chapter.

THE SECOND ORDER GRADES

All of the second Order grades, including the link grade of Portal, will not be discussed here. They are far too potent and complex to examine in anything short of a book by itself. They also involve connection with and use of the Rosicrucian Rosae Rubeae et Aureae Crucis spiritual blessings. One of the more enigmatic aspects of the Rosicrucian mysteries, as shown in the *Chemical Wedding of Christian Rosencreutz,* is that many of those who actively seek connection at this level or believe they are worthy of it, do not find it. Esoterically, this points to the need for silence and gestation following the balancing of the outer personality through the grades previously discussed. Within the original Golden Dawn there was a minimum waiting period between the Philosophus and Portal initiations and between the Portal and Adeptus Minor initiations. These minimum periods, as scanty as they were, were there for good and practical magical reasons. It is very unwise to progress too far and too fast.

In any case, anyone diligently working through the curriculum within this book, will, after they have completed the Philosophus work, be well and truly able to apply the same analysis to the Portal grade if they wish. They may then develop their own personal Portal curriculum, and since one of the aims of the Portal grade is to revisit and re-activate the previous four grades, this is no bad thing. The ceremonial Portal initiation activates the various 'elemental' grades within the candidate once again. However this is done under the guidance of a number of deep spiritual forces, including the Higher and Divine Genius of the candidate himself. In this way a subtle but important emphasis is placed upon certain aspects of the initiation, to match the still existing weaknesses of the candidate. No generic magical curriculum can cater for this need for individual attention. Any Portal initiatory sequence needs first and foremost a prolonged period of deep reflection and self-observation. In this way we may see what powers and spiritual blessings we require to continue our unfoldment and service.

THE INITIATIONS AND THEIR USE TODAY

In the original Order it was only after the Adeptus Minor initiation that the real hard core magical work began. The essence of this work is simple – the total transformation of the lower self of the initiate to allow the Higher and Divine Genius to shine through in an ever deepening manner. This is a life long work, as we all need a lower self, a personality, to interact with the world – all we can do is to perfect it more and more as a vehicle for our Higher and Divine Genius. In the original schema, the Outer Order prepared the ground of the personality so that it would not be overwhelmed by the power of the Higher and Divine Genius contacted and embedded into the personality at the Adeptus Minor grade. Then, after this initiation, the Higher and Divine Genius rebuilt and modified the persona self so that it could shine through clearly more and more, transforming the magician into a greater servant of the One Being.

This original initiatory system was designed in a particular way and with some assumptions which today, for many people, do not exist. In the Victorian era most people seeking esoteric knowledge and spiritual transformation had done little direct and practical self-change or transformational work. Today people who approach the Golden Dawn may have done much work in other traditions, or a little or none at all. The Outer Order initiations or equivalent processes, *when performed correctly*, will produce more change and transformation in people who have already begun their own transformation than those who have not. The effects can be far more dramatic and powerful than they would have been in the original Order. This is because, if we have done some other self-change work, not only are we open to changing but our subtle bodies are more open and free.

The dramatic effects that may be produced by these initiations or initiatory processes require some equally potent balancing daily practice techniques. It is for this reason that the majority of modern Orders now teach Outer Order members rituals and exercises other than the Lesser Ritual of the Pentagram, which originally was the only piece of magic taught at this stage. It is for this reason that various Inner Order rituals and processes are within this book and are suggested as part of the magical curriculum outlined later.

THE NEVER ENDING INITIATIONS OF THE GOLDEN DAWN

In the Golden Dawn tradition it is very clear that once we have undergone an initiation it will continue to effect us forever. For example, looking simply at the elemental powers, just because we have moved through and been initiated in Theoricus (Air), this does not mean that our Zelator (Earth) and Neophyte (connection) initiations now cease to be active. Certain parts of their transformational powers are indeed 'capped' by the subsequent initiations, but not all. So, for example the Zelator (Earth) initiation keeps working, but in the background of our lives, *except when further Earth balancing is required to allow Air balancing to occur.* When this is required the Zelator initiation may again 'kick in' to provide the required Earth-balance for the Air-balance to 'sit upon'.

To illustrate this, imagine our psyche is composed of 100 boxes, as shown in diagram 30, existing in each of the four realms, Earth, Air, Fire and Water. Imagine these are laid on top, or over one another, like in the 3-D chess of Star Trek. As we live and breathe and move in the everyday world, we exist on all four dimensions at once, being a coherent and whole personality. It is, however, theoretically possible to become just one of the elements; all aspects of life exist in each elemental realm within us. Even though thinking is assigned to the element of Air, there is still a place within us that thinks totally from the Earth perspective, and another that thinks totally from the Fire perspective. This is why, for example, an Earth elemental can still undertake 'non-Earth' actions such as thinking, writing, feeling and so forth.

Let us suppose, for example, that the squares B2 and E9, relate to interacting with women and our attitude towards studying respectively. This is the same for each of the four grids. The Earth B2 shows our Earthly way of interacting with women; the Air B2 shows our Airy manner and so on. Now, when we are initiated into the Zelator grade which balances the elemental Earth energy within us, the changes that come about may cause us to become quite balanced in the Earth element. This may occur, lets say within 54 of the squares out of the 100 total Earth squares, meaning that we are about half way balanced in Earth, as shown in diagram 31. Then we are initiated into the Air element and our Air 'grid' of 100 boxes gets injected with balancing Air energy. Again, for the sake of clarity, let's say another 54 squares will get balanced, again shown in diagram 32. This process moves along fine so long as the 54 Air boxes affected are in the 'same position' (aspect of our personality), affecting the same aspect of life, as the previous 54 Earth boxes affected. If they are not, then the Earth energy within this area of life will become reactivated

	0	1	2	3	4	5	6	7	8	9
A		■	■	■	■	■				
B		■	■	■						
C		■	■	■						
D		■	■	■						
E		■	■	■						
F										
G	■	■	■	■	■	■	■	■		
H	■	■	■	■	■	■	■	■		
I	■	■	■	■	■	■				
J										

Areas of Personality Balanced in Earth

	0	1	2	3	4	5	6	7	8	9
A	■	■	■	■	■	■	■	■	■	■
B	■	■	■	■	■	■	■	■	■	■
C	■	■	■	■	■	■	■	■	■	■
D	■	■	■	■	■	■	■	■	■	■
E	■	■	■	■	■	■	■	■	■	■
F	■									
G	■									
H	■									
I	■									
J										

Areas of Personality Balanced in Air

	0	1	2	3	4	5	6	7	8	9
A	■						■	■	■	■
B	■						■	■	■	■
C	■						■	■	■	■
D	■						■	■	■	■
E	■						■	■	■	■
F										
G										
H										
I										
J										

Areas of Personality Requiring Earth Balance Before Air Balance Can Occur

Diagrams 30-32: Grid of Elemental Personality Qualities

and cause or suggest changes in our lives that will produce the Earth balance required to allow the Air to balance, to 'sit on top' of it.

Looking at again at our squares B2 and E9, relating to interacting with women and our attitude towards studying. Via the Zelator initiation the square B2 is balanced in Earth but the square E9 is not. When the Theoricus initiation is taken, both squares are activated, both aspects of life – relating to women and studying. The first, B2 becomes balanced in the Air element. The second, E9 cannot because there is no balance in the Earth element behind it. The energy from the Theoricus initiation (and subsequent work) will, through the etheric-astral link which connects all initiations, activate the Zelator energy once again. The Zelator energy will then move to balance our attitude towards studying, E9, within the element of Earth. Once this is done, the Air within E9, our attitude towards studying, can be balanced.

Even with this coarse example we can see that by the time we've got all four elemental energies within us it means that we are constantly 'moving' back and forth between elements, balancing all the while. And what applies to the elemental powers also applies to the Sephiroth and other aspects of these initiations. Of course, this is presented here as being a perfect situation. Reality is never as clear cut. What this does show is how the process of initiation becomes more and more intense and solid as we progress. Understanding why and how this occurs is important. It is all too easy during the later grades of initiation to get despondent at the intensity of it all, especially when you suddenly find you are confronted with something your thought you had finished with two initiations ago.

A GOLDEN DAWN MAGICAL CURRICULUM

This curriculum outlines a course of magical study and practice for spiritual unfoldment based upon the Golden Dawn grades Neophyte to Philosophus. It takes into account the need to replicate, as far as possible, all the spiritual blessings and symbols the initiate would be exposed to as part of the traditional initiatory schema. It therefore has additional meditations not found in the historical curriculums. It also attempts to provide for the deep spiritual and personal changes that magic brings about by utilizing techniques and rituals historically practiced only within the Inner Order. It does *not* include those items of occult pedantry found within the traditional curriculums that served no other purpose than to exalt the dry, intellectual knowledge of the Order's founders.

Even today many magical curriculums glory in the memorization of medieval magical and alchemical terms and symbols without reference to any practical, spiritual process. This curriculum focuses upon practical, spiritual magic and the intellectual framework required to understand and engage in this magic fully. It is a basic approach and gives the minimum work required.

Rather than repeat a great deal of already published information, reference is continually made to the historical curriculum of the Golden Dawn. This is contained within the knowledge lectures published in *The Golden Dawn* and you will need access to this book to fully engage with this curriculum and the Golden Dawn. The practices and meditations given should be practiced in the order suggested. Please do not rush through this curriculum. I suggest spending between one and two years per grade.

APPROACHING THE GD TO CONNECTION WITH GOLDEN DAWN CEREMONY

At some point during this period you will need to make your own black robe and obtain the props listed in Chapter One. You will also need to make your lamen ready for the Connection Ceremony as described in Chapter Ten. All of these can be done at any time.

PRACTICAL

Visualisation exercises. These should be practiced until you can pass the tests suggested in chapter one. From then on repeat the test at regular intervals and if required, continue practice.

Elemental Mirror of Self. Do this at least twice during this phase.

Four Fold Breath. Practice this method of conscious breathing until you are able to incorporate it easily into all your other practices as required.

Lesser Banishing Ritual of the Pentagram. Perform this daily. After at least a month's practice you can perform the Lesser Invoking Ritual of the Pentagram in the morning and the banishing in the evening.

Will Development. Begin the practices in Chapter Three. Perform the Personal Empowerment Ritual if required. The most important exercise here is the self-observation exercise. Continue these exercises throughout the *entire* curriculum.

Meditation. Begin meditating as soon as you can. Pay attention and perform the relaxation technique as often as required. During this phase use only the Neophyte meditation.

Middle Pillar Exercise. After at least three months' daily work with the LRP you can move onto the Middle Pillar exercise. Practice the five preliminary exercises described in Chapter Four at least once. Then you may practice the full exercise, daily if possible.

SUPPORTING THEORY AND PONDERING

Golden Dawn. Read as much as you can about the Golden Dawn tradition. Use discrimination.

Reflection and Writing. Consciously work out and write down your own personal spiritual and magical aspirations and motivations, and how the Golden Dawn tradition can help you unfold into these.

Once you are sure that the GD tradition is right for you and you right for it, perform the **Connection Ceremony** from Chapter Ten. After this you will symbolically be in the Neophyte grade.

NEOPHYTE TO ZELATOR

Continue practicing the LRP and the Middle Pillar.

Magical Use of the Password. Practice this process as often as possible; daily would be good.

Meditation. Continue to focus upon the Neophyte meditation, but now add the four elemental powers. Meditate also upon:

'the symbol of the Sun – the point within the circle – in flashing gold light. Picturing the symbol strongly, endeavour to feel the spiritual qualities and powers that are *behind* the symbol and which the symbol represents in our world.'

SUPPORTING THEORY AND PONDERING

First Knowledge Lecture in *The Golden Dawn:* learn, memorise and think about the qualities and symbols of the four elements; the names and symbols of the Zodiac; the triplicities of the Zodiac; the names and symbols of the seven planets; the Hebrew alphabet and correspondences as described in Chapter One; the English names and basic structure of the Tree of Life.

Qabalah. Read as much as you can with discrimination. There is a lot of good material, as well as much that is unhelpful, on the Internet these days. As you read, ponder and think. Work out the meaning of the Tree for you, in your life.

Magical Theory. Again, as you read, ponder and engage actively with the texts. At this stage, focus on those works that help you to really understand the magical worldview. Then critique them and see if they are logical and sensible.

Reflection and Writing. (1) Reflect upon and write about how your connection with the tradition has changed, or not, since performing the connection ceremony and using the password. (2) Write about your experience and understanding of the four elemental powers. (3) Write about your experience with the Neophyte meditation and what it means.

Once you have achieved all this you may move into the Zelator grade work.

ZELATOR TO THEORICUS

Continue practicing the LRP, the Middle Pillar and the Magical Use of the Password.

Elemental Mirror of Self. Do this at least once during this phase. Notice any changes from your previous mirror and reflect upon them deeply.

Meditation. Throughout this period focus upon the symbols of the Zelator grade as described in the Second Knowledge lecture in *The Golden Dawn*: square; cube; salt; Earth triplicity. Also meditate upon:

Earth Triangle: Visualise the Hermetic symbol for Earth in either black or olive green light. Picturing the symbol strongly, endeavour to feel the spiritual qualities and powers that are *behind* the symbol and which the symbol represents in our world.
Saturn Symbol: Visualise the symbol for Saturn in black or deep indigo light. Picturing the symbol strongly, endeavour to feel the spiritual qualities and powers that are *behind* the symbol and which the symbol represents in our world.

The Seven Double Letters of the Hebrew Alphabet. As described in Chapter Seven.

FROM THE ZELATOR GRADE CEREMONY

Carefully read the ceremony at least twice. Meditations should now be performed with the following symbols and blessings:

MALKUTH. Meditate upon each of the following: the divine name **ADNI H ARTz**; the Archangels **Metatron, Samael** and **Sandalphon** and the phrase:

'Form is invisible alike in darkness and in blinding light'

The Red Cross inside the White Triangle. This is the symbol of the grade.

The Sword and the Serpent This diagram can be found in the second Knowledge Lecture in *The Golden Dawn*. It shows the *descent* of the power of the One Being via the Lightning Flash sword though the ten Sephiroth in order, from Kether to Malkuth. It also shows the *ascent* of consciousness from Malkuth back to Kether connecting all the Sephiroth and Paths of Tree of Life in reverse order.

Invocation of force within the Aura of Malkuth. Following the instructions in Chapter Four, invoke the blessings of Malkuth into your aura. Do this at least ten times.

Lesser Ritual of the Hexagram. Practice this regularly in banishing mode for three months before engaging in Skrying or Travelling in the Spirit Vision as described below. Practice the invoking only after a month's practice with the banishing.

Invocation of Force Within the Aura of Elemental Earth. Do this several times a week for three months before engaging in Skrying or Travelling in the Spirit Vision.

Spirit Vision. This should not be performed until all other meditations and practices are accomplished. Perform at least five Skrying in the Spirit visions with the Prithivi Tattwa. After these are successfully accomplished perform at least five Travels in the Spirit Vision within Prithivi.

SUPPORTING THEORY AND PONDERING

Second Knowledge Lecture in *The Golden Dawn:* learn, memorise and think about the Tree of Life with the Serpent of Wisdom upon it; the Hebrew names and spellings and English translations of the Sephiroth; the Hebrew names and spellings and English translations of the divine names of the Sephiroth; the Hebrew name and brief description of the essence of the four Qabalistic worlds; the Hebrew names and English translation of the Ten Houses of Assiah attributed to the Sephiroth.

Qabalah. Learn, memorise and think about: the attributions of the 22 Hebrew letters to the paths of the Tree of Life. Continue reading widely with discrimination, focusing upon Malkuth and Assiah.

Reflection and Writing. (1) Reflect upon and write about the element of Earth within and without you. (2) Write about your experience with all of the meditations above. (3) Write about your understanding of Malkuth. (4) Write about your experience within the Spirit Vision.

Once you have achieved all this you may move into the Theoricus grade work.

THEORICUS TO PRACTICUS

Continue practicing the LRP, the Middle Pillar, LRH and the Magical Use of the Password.

Elemental Mirror of Self. Do this at least once during this phase. Notice any changes from your previous mirror and reflect upon them deeply.

Meditation. Throughout this period focus upon the symbols of the Theoricus grade as described in the Third Knowledge lecture in *The Golden Dawn:* waxing, waning and full moon symbols; Air triplicity; the numbers nine and five and the Qabalistic connection between them. Also meditate upon:

Air Triangle: Visualise the Hermetic symbol for Air in yellow upon violet light. Picturing the symbol strongly, endeavour to feel the spiritual qualities and powers that are *behind* the symbol and which the symbol represents in our world.

From the Theoricus Grade Ceremony

Carefully read the ceremony at least twice. Meditations should now be performed with the following symbols and blessings:

YESOD. Meditate upon each of the following: the divine name **ShDI AL ChI**; the Archangel **Gabriel** of Yesod, the letter **Tau**. The phrase:

'Quit the Material and Seek the Spiritual'

The Red Cross inside the Inverted White Triangle. This is the symbol of the grade.

The Banners of East and West. Pictures of these banners may be found in colour within Regardie's *The Golden Dawn*. Meditate first upon the Banner of the East. Do this several times. Repeat with the Banner of the West. Now perform another meditation with the Banner of the East following a Middle Pillar exercise. Again this should be repeated several times. This sequence of meditations will help, in part, to give the solo magician the same benefits as are found within the 32nd Path of Tau component of the Theoricus ceremony.

The Phrase:
'Be thou therefore prompt and active as the sylphs, but avoid frivolity and caprice; be energetic and strong like the salamanders but avoid irritability and ferocity; be flexible and attentive to images like the undines, but avoid idleness and undue changeability; be laborious and patient like the gnomes but avoid grossness and avarice. So shalt thou gradually develop the powers of thy soul, and fit thyself to work in deep and true alliance with the Spirits of the elements.'

Invocation of Force Within the Aura of Yesod. Do this at least nine times.

Lesser Ritual of the Hexagram of the Moon. Practice this regularly in banishing mode for three months before engaging in Skrying or Travelling in the Spirit Vision as described below. Practice the invoking only after a month's practice with the banishing.

Invocation of Force Within the Aura of Air. Do this several times a week for three months before engaging in Skrying or Travelling in the Spirit Vision.

Spirit Vision – Air. This should not be performed until all other meditations and practices are accomplished. Perform at least five Skrying in the Spirit visions with the Vayu Tattwa. After these are successfully accomplished perform at least five Travels in the Spirit Vision within Vayu.

Spirit Vision – Yesod. Perform at least five Skrying in the Spirit visions with a symbol of Yesod. After these are successfully accomplished perform at least five Travels in the Spirit Vision.

Spirit Vision – the Path of Tau. Perform at least five Skrying in the Spirit visions with letter Tau. After these are successfully accomplished perform at least five Travels in the Spirit Vision.

SUPPORTING THEORY AND PONDERING

Third Knowledge Lecture in *The Golden Dawn:* learn, memorise and think about the Qabalistic division of the soul and a brief description of the essence of these divisions; the three mothers, seven doubles and twelve single letters of the Hebrew alphabet; the symbol of the moon when placed on the Tree of Life.

Qabalah. Continue reading widely with discrimination, focusing upon Yesod and Yetzira

Esoteric Knowledge. Read widely with thought concerning the astral world and the inner planes. Apply your knowledge of the Qabalistic Division of the Soul to any other paradigm you read about.

Reflection and Writing. (1) Reflect upon and write about the element of Air within and without you. (2) Write about your experience with all of the meditations above. (3) Write about your understanding of Yesod. (4) Write about your experiences within the Spirit Vision.

Once you have achieved all this you may move into the Practicus grade work.

PRACTICUS TO PHILOSOPHUS

Continue practicing the LRP, the Middle Pillar, LRH and the Magical Use of the Password.

Elemental Mirror of Self. Do this at least once during this phase. Notice any changes from your previous mirror and reflect upon them deeply.

Meditation. Throughout this period, focus upon the symbols of the Practicus grade as described in the Fourth Knowledge lecture in *The Golden Dawn:* the symbols of the rhomboid and Vesica; the number eight; control of emotions. Also meditate upon:

Water Triangle: Visualise the Hermetic symbol for Water in blue upon orange light. Picturing the symbol strongly, endeavour to feel the spiritual qualities and powers that are *behind* the symbol and which the symbol represents in our world.

Mercury Symbol: Visualise the symbol for Mercury in orange upon blue light. Picturing the symbol strongly, endeavour to feel the spiritual qualities and powers that are *behind* the symbol and which the symbol represents in our world.

Jupiter Symbol: Visualise the symbol for Jupiter in blue upon orange light. Picturing the symbol strongly, endeavour to feel the spiritual qualities and powers that are *behind* the symbol and which the symbol represents in our world.

FROM THE PRACTICUS GRADE CEREMONY

Carefully read the ceremony at least twice. Meditations should now be performed with the following symbols and blessings:

HOD. Meditate upon each of the following: the divine name **ALHIM TzBAOTh**; the Archangel **Michael** of Hod; the letters **Shin** and **Resh.**

The Red Cross above the Inverted White Triangle. This is the symbol of the grade.

The Garden of Eden Before the Fall. This diagram can be found in colour in Regardie's *The Golden Dawn*. It is best if you make your own. You should meditate and ponder upon this diagram constantly throughout this grade. After a month or two of meditating upon it, re-read the description of the diagram within the Practicus ceremony. With your knowledge and experience, re-write this description in today's English so that anyone can understand it.

Invocation of Force Within the Aura of Hod. Do this at least eight times.

Lesser Ritual of the Hexagram of Mercury. Practice this regularly in banishing mode for three months before engaging in Skrying or

Travelling in the Spirit Vision as described below. Practice the invoking only after a month's practice with the banishing.

Invocation of Force Within the Aura of Water. Do this several times a week for three months before engaging in Skrying or Travelling in the Spirit Vision.

Spirit Vision – Water. This should not be performed until all other meditations and practices are accomplished. Perform at least five Skrying in the Spirit visions with the Apas Tattwa. After these are successfully accomplished perform at least five Travels in the Spirit Vision within Apas.

Spirit Vision – Hod. Perform at least five Skrying in the Spirit visions a symbol of Hod. After these are successfully accomplished perform at least five Travels in the Spirit Vision.

Spirit Vision – the Path of Shin. Perform at least five Skrying in the Spirit visions with the letter Shin. After these are successfully accomplished perform at least five Travels in the Spirit Vision.

Spirit Vision – the Path of Resh. Perform at least five Skrying in the Spirit visions with letter Resh. After these are successfully accomplished perform at least five Travels in the Spirit Vision.

SUPPORTING THEORY AND PONDERING

Fourth Knowledge Lecture in *The Golden Dawn:* learn, memorise and think about the correspondences of the Tarot to the Tree of Life; the colours of the paths of the Tree of Life; the attribution of the elements, Zodiacal signs and planets to the paths of the Tree of Life; Mercury upon the Tree of Life.

Qabalah. Continue reading widely with discrimination, focusing upon Hod and Briah.

Esoteric Knowledge. Read widely with thought concerning esoteric psychology and the inner make up of the human being.

Reflection and Writing. (1) Reflect upon and write about the element of Water within and without you. (2) Write about your experience with all of the meditations above. (3) Write about your understanding of Hod. (4) Write about your experiences within the Spirit Vision.

Once you have achieved all this you may move into the Philosophus grade work.

PHILOSOPHUS

Continue practicing the LRP, the Middle Pillar, LRH and the Magical Use of the Password.

Elemental Mirror of Self. Do this at least once during this phase. Notice any changes from your previous mirror and reflect upon them deeply.

Meditation. Throughout this period, focus upon the symbols of the Philosophus grade as described in the Fifth Knowledge lecture in *The Golden Dawn:* the Fire triplicity; Universal love and service expressed through the symbol of Venus (see below for a more amplified description than that within *The Golden Dawn*); Fire as the agent of sacrifice; Sulphur upon the Tree of Life.

Fire Triangle: Visualise the Hermetic symbol for Fire in red upon green light. Picturing the symbol strongly, endeavour to feel the spiritual qualities and powers that are *behind* the symbol and which the symbol represents in our world.

Venus Symbol: Visualise the symbol for Venus in green upon red light. Picturing the symbol strongly, endeavour to feel the spiritual qualities and powers that are *behind* the symbol and which the symbol represents in our world. Also meditate upon the image of Venus superimposed upon the Tree of Life, and open your mind to the symbolism and power of this juxtaposition.

Universal Love (to be performed only after meditation on Venus upon the Tree of Life has produced definite results). Visualise within your heart centre the symbol of Venus in green light. With this image in mind endeavour to feel love radiating from your heart towards all humanity, the Earth and God. Keep doing this, practice after practice, until you can feel yourself alive with pure compassion. Close each meditation with the image of Venus, like a badge of love towards humanity, within your heart.

Mars Symbol: Visualise the symbol for Mars in red upon green light. Picturing the symbol strongly, endeavour to feel the spiritual qualities and powers that are *behind* the symbol and which the symbol represents in our world.

FROM THE PHILOSOPHUS GRADE CEREMONY

Carefully read the ceremony at least twice. Meditations should now be performed with the following symbols and blessings:

NETZACH. Meditate upon each of the following: the divine name **YHVH TzBAOTh**; the Archangel **Haniel** (or **Uriel**) of Netzach; the letters **Qoph** and **Tzaddi** and **Peh.**

The Red Cross below the White Triangle. This is the symbol of the grade.

The Garden of Eden After the Fall. This diagram can be found in colour in Regardie's *The Golden Dawn*. It is best if you make your own. You should meditate and ponder upon this diagram constantly throughout this grade. After a month or two of meditating upon it, re-read the description of the diagram within the Philosophus ceremony. With your knowledge and experience, re-write this description in today's English so that anyone can understand it.

Invocation of Force Within the Aura of Netzach. Do this at least seven times.

Lesser Ritual of the Hexagram of Venus. Practice this regularly in banishing mode for three months before engaging in Skrying or Travelling in the Spirit Vision as described below. Practice the invoking only after a month's practice with the banishing.

Invocation of Force Within the Aura of Fire. Do this several times a week for three months before engaging in Skrying or Travelling in the Spirit Vision.

Spirit Vision – Fire. This should not be performed until all other meditations and practices are accomplished. Perform at least five Skrying in the Spirit visions with the Tejas Tattwa. After these are successfully accomplished perform at least five Travels in the Spirit Vision within Tejas.

Spirit Vision – Netzach. Perform at least five Skrying in the Spirit visions with a symbol of Netzach. After these are successfully accomplished perform at least five Travels in the Spirit Vision.

Spirit Vision – the Path of Qoph. Perform at least five Skrying in the Spirit visions with the letter Qoph. After these are successfully accomplished perform at least five Travels in the Spirit Vision.

Spirit Vision – the Path of Tzaddi. Perform at least five Skrying in the Spirit visions with the letter Tzaddi. After these are successfully accomplished perform at least five Travels in the Spirit Vision.

Spirit Vision – the Path of Peh. Perform at least five Skrying in the Spirit visions with the letter Tzaddi. After these are successfully accomplished perform at least five Travels in the Spirit Vision.

SUPPORTING THEORY AND PONDERING

Fifth Knowledge Lecture in *The Golden Dawn:* learn, memorise and think about the Hebrew spelling, English translations and essence of the Three Veils of Negative Existence; divine names and Beings of the Elements both in Hebrew and English; the names in English only of the Qlippoth upon the Tree of Life.

Qabalah. Continue reading widely with discrimination, focusing upon Netzach and Atziluth. Read and ponder upon the Qlippoth and evil.

Esoteric Knowledge. Continue to read widely with thought concerning esoteric psychology and the inner make up of the human being.

Reflection and Writing. (1) Reflect upon and write about the element of Fire within and without you. (2) Write about your experience with all of the meditations above. (3) Write about your understanding of Netzach. (4) Write about your experiences within the Spirit Vision.

LINKING TO THE GOLDEN DAWN

GOLDEN DAWN CONNECTION CEREMONY

THE purpose of this ceremony is simply to link to the Golden Dawn currents and magical blessings. Do not expect spiritual insight, bliss or an expansion of consciousness. While these experiences can occur during the full Neophyte Ceremony, the Z formula that allows them to take place is necessarily absent from this ceremony. Some magicians would maintain it is impossible to connect with the Golden Dawn tradition without temple initiation through a 'legitimate' Order. However, magical experience the world over has shown this is not the case. The best explanation of how and why 'non-authorised' connection to the Golden Dawn and other magical traditions may occur is given in John Michael Greer's *Inside a Magical Lodge*. Basically, the inner plane currents of any tradition that are not guarded and contained by unbroken group work can be 'picked up' by anyone of sincerity using the symbols of that tradition. The break up of the original Golden Dawn Orders (which did not fully occur until the 1970s) and the revelation of the Golden Dawn symbols and passwords means that the inner plane blessings of the tradition are now open to anyone who desires to and can connect with them.

PREPARATION

One of the most important acts of preparation prior to performing this ceremony is the choice of a password. Within the Golden Dawn, the password is changed every Equinox (around March 21 and September 21). It reflects and embodies the purpose and direction of the particular temple or Order for the following six months. In this ceremony you should choose a password that will reflect your projected magical and spiritual path between the date of the ceremony and the next Equinox. At the Equinox you will stop using this password, choose another and link it to yourself as an embodiment of your spiritual unfoldment for the six months following. We will discuss the password a little later when we are exploring the Equinox Ceremony.

At this stage you will need to perform some active meditation with your spiritual unfoldment over the next period as your meditation object. Please do not expect to encounter an inner plane Adept who will whisper the password you with a nod and a wink. All you are doing is conditioning your consciousness to focus on your spiritual unfoldment itself. After the meditation, which may need to be repeated, you may simply know what password to use, or you can simply *think* what would be appropriate. Your thought processes, if you performed the meditation correctly, will be influenced by your inward work and you will choose correctly. Often passwords are taken from the Qabalah. Some Orders consciously use the names of the ten Sephiroth in sequence; so in effect they have a five year plan (two passwords per year) and see themselves as working through a spiritual current over that period, only to start again with a new current at the end of the five year sequence.

Another important preparation is the creation of a Neophyte Lamen. This is a circular 'badge' about 10 or 11cm in diameter and is suspended from your neck by a white ribbon falling over your heart centre. Instructions for lovely lamens can be found in *Making and Using Magical Tools* by Chic and Sandra Tabatha Cicero. However, an easy way to make a lamen is to use a plain wooden drink coaster you can buy from

Diagram 33: Golden Dawn Neophyte Lamen

craft shops. One side is painted with clear white acrylic; the other has the symbol of the Neophyte upon it as shown in diagram 33. This is best created by painting the whole side white and sticking on a circle cut out of black paper. After that, cut out the triangle from white paper and stick that on. Or design and print the whole thing off from your computer. Create a couple of holes in the top white area with a compass. Thread through some fuse wire or other thin wire to make a loop. Now thread through the loop a length of white ribbon the correct length and tie the two ends in a knot. Finish by sealing the lamen with some clear lacquer.

TEMPLE SET UP FOR GOLDEN DAWN CONNECTION CEREMONY

You should try and arrange your working space as far as possible as described here. If this is not possible, do what you can. Well enacted inner work and the right motivations are far more important than having the props in the correct spot.

Have a central altar draped in a black cloth with the cross and triangle in the centre, facing east. At the four edges of the altar should be the four symbols of the elements. Place your lamen on the altar also.

At the South quarter of the room place some incense. Be clear this incense does not represent elemental air or elemental fire. It represents and will be used to invoke fire derived from the white pillar of the Tree of Life.

At the north quarter of the room place a cup of water. This should be a different cup to your regular water cup. This water does not represent elemental Water. It represents and will be used to invoke water derived from the black pillar of the Tree of Life.

OPENING THE TEMPLE FOR GOLDEN DAWN CONNECTION CEREMONY

Please note that this may be your first full ceremony after several months of meditative and ritual practice. While the inner work here is important and should be conducted with care, please do not be unduly fazed by it. Your deep and altruistic aspiration will be the main driving force of this ceremony.

Lesser Banishing Ritual of the Pentagram.

Purification by Water. Go to the North and pick up the cup of water. Now cleanse the water using the technique for cleansing from the personal empowerment ritual in Chapter Three.

Now turn to face the East and close your eyes a little. Imagine before you very strongly the image of the Tree of Life, seeing it in the various colours. Now focus just upon the left hand pillar of severity. See only that pillar, large and strong. Allow your image now to change and see the pillar transform so it is a large black pillar before you; the black pillar of the temple. Despite seeing only a black pillar you are aware that it comprises the three Sephiroth of Binah, Geburah and Hod. The black pillar should fill your vision and seem alive to you. Now physically and inwardly hold out the cup of water towards the black pillar so that it actually merges with the power and blessings of the black pillar. See and direct the blessings of the black pillar into the visualised, astral, form of the cup and the water. Do this for about a minute so that the astral component of the water is now linked to and imbued with the blessings of the black pillar. Now simply open your eyes.

Proceed to the East moving sunwise. At the Eastern perimeter of the temple connect and draw up energy from your Malkuth and Kether. Merge the energy in your heart centre and direct it out to your hands and into the cup. Hold the cup up towards the East and inscribe an equal armed cross, about three feet in length, with the cup. Move from top to bottom and then from left to right. As you inscribe the cross; form it on the etheric level of the temple by directing out your merged energy in your heart through the cup. Form it on the astral level by seeing the cross formed very clearly in brilliant blue light. This is not the electric blue used for the Lesser Pentagrams, but the blue used for elemental Water. The water here however is the water derived from Hod, the receptacle of the energy of the black pillar.

Walk around the temple with the cup held high. As you walk visualise the power of the black pillar of the Tree of Life being formed around the temple. This has been connected to the water in the cup and it is best to see the energy as black, warm and alive light moving out of the cup and forming around the edge of the temple as you walk. The presence of the charged astral component of the cup as it moves through the astral sphere of the temple will help achieve the results required. At the South, West and North, perform the same inscription of the equal armed cross. Continue to perform the same inner work as you walk around to complete the circle back at the East of the temple.

Hold the cup on high and inwardly visualise and see the astral form you have created: the outside of the temple space filled with the power of the black pillar and the four blue crosses at the quarters. Once you see this clearly say outwardly: 'I Purify with Water!'

Consecration By Fire. Place the water back at the North and return to the central altar and pause for a while. Now move to the South and consecrate the incense in the same manner as the water, but changing the symbols as appropriate.

Now turn to face the East and close your eyes a little. Connect the incense to the white pillar of the Tree of Life using the same form of visualisation as for the water cup above. Simply change the image to match the white pillar.

Proceed to the East moving sunwise and then an equal armed cross at the East with the incense. Use the same form for the inner work as you did with the cup of water. Change the colour of the cross to red and inscribe the cross from top to bottom and then from right to left, not left to right. Walk around the temple performing exactly the same outer movements as you did with the water cup. Change the inner work, along the same lines, to match the white pillar of the temple and the cross of red light at the quarters. Back at the East, hold the incense on high and inwardly visualise and see the astral form you have created: the outside of the temple space filled with the power of the white pillar and the four red crosses at the quarters. Once you see this clearly say outwardly: 'I Consecrate with Fire!'

Consecrating the Four Elemental Symbols. Place the incense back at the South and return to the central altar and pause for a while. Now take the rose from the altar and move directly to the East of the temple. There hold the rose before you to the East and inwardly visualise the great Archangel Raphael standing at the East, just as you called him there in the LBRP. See him clearly and hold the rose out towards him. Intone his name several times. See him inwardly bless the astral component of the rose and infuse it with the elemental blessings of Air. Once this is done, thank Raphael and return directly to the altar and place the rose down in its original position. Return to the central altar and repeat the process above but with each of the symbols of the four elements; Fire, Water and Earth, working with Archangels Michael, Gabriel and Auriel. At the end of this process you should have the consecrated symbols of the elements upon the altar.

The Mystic Circumambulation. Now move to the North-East of the temple facing towards the South, ready to circumambulate around the temple. When ready, proceed to walk around, giving the Sign of the Enterer each time you pass East, which is described later in this chapter. You should walk slowly and complete three full circles of the temple and then move to the central altar facing East. The inner work here is similar to that described in the Watchtower Ceremony in chapter five, so please refer to that chapter. Basically you are bringing down the light to fill the temple as you walk. It comes from your Kether centre and out through your Tiphareth centre as you give the Sign of the Enterer and as you walk.

Adoration to the Lord of the Universe. Standing at the West of the central altar, facing East, give the adoration to the Lord of the Universe, using the Neophyte Signs as follows

> *Holy art though Lord of the Universe* (Projecting)
> *Holy art thou whom nature hath not formed* (Projecting)
> *Holy art thou the vast and the mighty one* (Projecting)
> *Lord of the light and of the darkness* (Silence)

Again the inner work required here may be found in the Opening by Watchtower. The One Being is adored and called forth into the temple. The temple is now opened and we are ready to begin the process by which we may connect with the Golden Dawn. One of the key themes within the Golden Dawn is the balance of the triad: a force, an opposite force and a third, higher reconciling force. The opening just enacted does this with the three pillars of the Tree of Life, the third, balancing middle pillar, being invoked through the mystic circumambulation and utilisation of the Ketheric light. Having this formula within the subtle component of the temple will greatly enhance our attempts to connect with the Golden Dawn. This is why this form of opening is used and not another.

Connecting to the Golden Dawn Currents

Return to the West of the altar facing East. Perform a Qabalistic Cross and cleanse the lamen. Again use the method based on the LBRP described in the personal empowerment ritual in Chapter Three.

State the intention of the ceremony. I use the form given in Chapter Six as an example with the same preamble there, followed by these specific words of intention:

> "…Tonight I seek to connect myself to the Golden Dawn tradition of Western Magic, to open myself fully to its blessings and currents, so that with such a connection I may unfold and grow spiritually and personally and be of service to the One (or God or Goddess).

And to this end I seek the aid of the One Being, my Higher and Divine Genius, and the inner guardians of the Golden Dawn who have aided and linked themselves to open, sincere aspirants of the mysteries, down through the ages. **Amen.**'

Separating the Elements. Take the rose from the altar directly to the East of the temple and place it down on the floor or a side altar there. Return directly to the altar once more and repeat the process with the lamp, the cup and the plate. You have now symbolically and energetically opened your elemental sphere. This openness is useful to allow the currents of the Golden Dawn entrance into your subtle bodies.

Charging the Auric Sphere. Standing West of the altar facing East, perform a Middle Pillar exercise without circulating the light.

The Oath. Once complete, kneel before the altar and repeat the following oath. It is best to learn this by heart before the night of the ceremony.

'I (name) in the presence of the Lord of the Universe, my own higher and Undying Soul and in this sacred temple of the Golden Dawn tradition, do hereby of my own free will pledge myself to:

Use the magical and psychic powers I will obtain through my initiations and studies for the greatest good of all;

Honour and revere the sacredness of the symbols, tools and mysteries of the Golden Dawn tradition of Western Magic;

And if I should break this, my solemn oath, and use my magical or psychic powers to intentionally cause harm or violence to another person, then I freely and willingly open myself to the return of such negative energy into my own being. May all my Sacred Ones witness my oath. So Mote It Be !'

Formulating the Triangle of Light. Rise, pause and then say clearly:

'Inner Guardians of the Golden Dawn tradition of Western Magic, I ask you now to help me formulate the Triangle of White Light within my sphere so that I may connect to you and your tradition.'

Move to the North of the temple, facing to the East, ready for another circumambulation of the temple. As you stand in the North become aware of the symbolic and energetic nature of the position you are standing in. You are in the disincarnate Mystery station, the darkest place of the circle. Before you lies birth at the very East of the circle, but what is born at the East is seeded in the mystery of the North. Become aware of a vast sense of openness and vacuum in the crown centre above your physical head. There is an empty space here. You may like to visualise it as endless, black space. Once you have a strong sense of this, or can see it clearly, begin to circle.

With this circumambulation there is no need to give the Sign of the Enterer as you pass the East. You are not directing energy or blessings from your sphere. As soon as you pass East begin to strongly visualise the base of a large white triangle of light forming within the dark space of your crown centre. This is the base of the white triangle of the symbol of the Golden Dawn. Walk very slowly around the temple, all the while visualising the base of the triangle getting clearer and stronger. As you pass East again, maintain the image of the base of the triangle but add the left hand arm, seeing it strong and clear and connected to the base. Visualise and formulate this strongly as you walk slowly around for the second time. As you pass East once more, complete the triangle by seeing the right arm formulate. So for this final round you are visualising a complete triangle of white light which glows more and more as you walk. At the completion of the circle, turn and face the altar.

Recitation of the Mystic Words. Move directly down to the East of the altar and pause there a moment, all the time maintaining the images of the triangle of white light above you. Go to the West of the altar and face East. Pick up your lamen in your passive hand and get ready to knock upon the altar top with your active hand. Focusing intensely on the triangle of light above you and holding the lamen, say:

'I am (name), I link myself to the Golden Dawn —

Khabs! *(knock on the altar)*
Am! *(knock)*
Pehkt! *(knock)*

Konx! *(knock)*
Om! *(knock)*
Pax! *(knock)*

Light! *(knock)*
In! *(knock)*
Extension! *(knock)*

As you say the words and knock, see and open yourself to a stream of blessings from the Golden Dawn tradition that enters the triangle of light above you and awakens it to full life. The words here are known as the Mystic Words of the Neophyte grade and will connect you to the Golden Dawn currents, as they are links to its blessings within the mental realm. With each word and knock see the triangle enlivened more. At the final word and knock, see a duplicate of the white triangle move away from the triangle above you and down through your body to rest below your feet. Visualise it so it is flat and you are standing upon it. So now you will have two triangles of white light, one above you and one below you, both alive and glowing.

Put your Neophyte lamen on, and as you do so visualise strongly that its presence helps to Earth the blessings of the triune light of the triangle, and a shaft of white light connects the two triangles above and below you. Stand for several minutes seeing this image.

Formulation of the Red Cross. Now move to North of the temple once more, ready for another circumambulation. At the North connect with and inwardly intone the password you have chosen. Become strongly aware of the magical and spiritual meaning it holds for you. Once you are clear of this, begin to circle. As you pass the East give the Sign of the Enterer, which symbolically and energetically shows that you are allowing the spiritual meanings and blessings of the password to flow through you and affect the world. Walk slowly around the temple to make three complete circuits. As you walk visualise very strongly a red Calvary cross formed above the white triangle in your crown centre. As you see the cross, slowly and carefully keep inwardly intoning and repeating your password. With each repetition see the cross grow more solid and clear.

Upon completing the final circle, move back to the altar and face East. Pause and then say:

'I am (name), and I am linked to the Golden Dawn tradition of Western Magic. So Mote It Be!

Re-membering the Elements. Move to the East, pick up the rose and take it directly back to the altar, replacing it in its original position. Do the same with the symbols for Fire, Water and Earth. You have now symbolically and energetically closed your elemental sphere.

Mystic Repast. Facing East once more say:

'Nothing now remains but to partake in silence of the Mystic Repast, composed of the symbols of the Four Elements.

To inhale the perfume of this rose, as a symbol of Air *(pick up and smell the rose).*

To feel the warmth of this sacred Fire *(spread your hand over the flame).*

To eat this bread and salt as types of Earth *(dip the bread in the salt and eat).*

And finally to drink this wine, as consecrated emblem of Water *(pick up the cup, use it to make the form of a cross and drink the wine).*'

Pause and drink any remaining wine. Invert the cup and place it down upon the altar with the words 'It is finished'.

When inhaling the perfume and feeling the heat etc, consciously see and open your self to the influx of the elemental blessings bestowed upon the astral forms of these symbols by the Archangels.

CLOSING OF THE GOLDEN DAWN CONNECTION CEREMONY

At the West of the altar, facing East, pause and then perform a Qabalistic Cross.

Purification by Water and Consecration by Fire. These two actions are done in exactly the same manner as the Opening. This is not a banishment, but a re-establishment of the balance (and the cleansing that comes from balance) between the two pillars of the Tree and between Fire and Water.

Reverse Mystic Circumambulation. Move to the South-East and face anti-sunwise towards the East, ready to circle the temple three times anti-sunwise. The reverse circumambulation is performed exactly as the opening circumambulation but with the Sign of Silence being given in place of the Sign of the Enterer. The inner workings can be found in the closing of the Watchtower ceremony in Chapter Five. Basically, the light and energy given out through the opening is now withdrawn.

Adoration to the Lord of the Universe. This is performed exactly as in the opening.

Lesser Banishing Ritual of the Pentagram

Thanks. At the East of the altar facing West, say:

> 'To those who have aided my spiritual endeavours tonight I give you thanks and blessings: the One Being of All, the Land that sustains and supports us all, my Higher and Divine Genius, and above all the Inner Guardians of the Golden Dawn tradition. Thanks and blessings. **Amen.**'

Your lamen can now be worn whenever you perform any act within the Golden Dawn tradition. Ensure that you perform the password connection process described below within a day or two of this ceremony.

MAINTAINING AND STRENGTHENING THE LINK WITH THE GOLDEN DAWN

After linking to the Golden Dawn tradition through this ceremony the astral and mental realm link must be maintained or it will weaken and eventually fade. This is done is two ways: through the six monthly Equinox Ceremony given later and a simple practice which focuses on the password. This practice may be performed daily or frequently. As part of the practice you will again formulate the white triangle of the Golden Dawn in the crown centre space above your head. Unlike the connection ceremony however this will be created in a particular way based on the Tree of Life. Diagram 34 shows the Supernal Triad of the Tree together with the Mystic Words of the Neophyte Grade. Each triad of the mystic words begins at a different Sephira. The first, Khabs Am Pehkt, begins at Kether. The second, Konx Om Pax, at Binah and the third, Light in Extension, at Chokmah. This reflects the recitation of the words by particular officers in the Neophyte Grade who reflect the blessings of these Sephiroth.

When you recite the mystic words in this practice you will visualise an angle, not an arm of the triangle being formed with each word. With the word 'Khabs' the angle that centres on the Sephira of Kether and includes half of each of the Paths of Beth and Aleph is formed. With the word 'Am', the angle that centres on Binah and includes half the paths of Beth and Daleth is formed. At this stage the arm between Kether and Binah would be fully formed. Finally, with the word 'Pehkt', the angle that centres on Chokmah and includes half the paths of Daleth and Aleph is formed. This completes the two paths of Daleth and Aleph and the whole

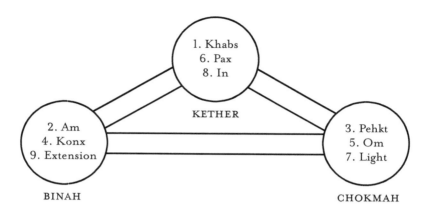

Diagram 34: Mystic Words Applied to the Supernal Sephiroth

white triangle is created. The second and third triad of words repeats the process but start from different Sephiroth. The whole image of the white triangle is maintained but at each word an angle of it becomes more solid, more alive and potent. By the end of all nine words the triangle will be very strong and formed via a balance of the Sephiroth.

Wearing your Lamen, perform the LBRP.

Pause. Now focus upon the crown centre above your head. Recite the Mystic Words Khabs Am Pehkt / Konx Om Pax / Light In Extension. With each word give a knock if possible or smartly stamp the heel of your right foot. As you recite, visualise the white triangle forming according to the description above.

Khabs – Top angle (Kether); **Am** – Left angle (Binah); **Pehkt** – Right angle (Chokmah).

Konx – Left angle (Binah); **Om** – Right angle (Chokmah); **Pax** – Top angle (Kether).

Light – Right angle (Chokmah); **In** – Top angle (Kether); **Extension** – Left angle (Binah).

At the final word and knock, see a duplicate of the white triangle move away from the triangle above you and down through your body to rest below your feet. So now you will have two triangles of white light, one above you and one below you, both alive and glowing.

Maintaining the awareness of the triangles connected by a shaft of light, visualise the red Calvary cross above the triangle above your head, forming the symbol of the Golden Dawn. When strongly visualised and clear, take a deep breath and outwardly intone the password once aloud, slowly and clearly, as if drawing into the Calvary cross the Solar force of the Golden Dawn tradition. The Calvary Cross has strong Solar and Tipharetic links and this process will be greatly aided by this symbol.

Now, just as you did with the white triangle, see a duplicate of the red cross slowly move away from the triangle above you and down through your body to rest below your feet, drawing with it the link with the Golden Dawn tradition. As you see the cross move down the length of your middle pillar intone the password outwardly once again. The password should be intoned throughout the full movement of the cross to Malkuth. That is, the intonation should begin upon the Cross leaving your Kether and not cease until it rests above the Triangle in your Malkuth. You now have two symbols of the Golden Dawn, one in your Kether centre and one in your Malkuth centre.

Pause a while feeling the link and blessings of the Golden Dawn entering your Kether and passing down into your Malkuth.

Finally, give the Sign of Silence to seal the link. Do not close with the Qabalistic Cross.

This simple procedure works by first maintaining and re-creating the symbol of the Golden Dawn within your astral body. This symbol is linked to the mental plane blessings of the tradition via the recitation of the mystic words. It is also linked to your own mental plane 'current' or 'push' toward spiritual unfoldment via the password. The symbol and the links are then earthed and grounded into your Malkuth centre so they will change and transform your life. Finally, the links and blessings are sealed within your sphere via the Sign of Silence.

THE EQUINOX CEREMONY

In the Golden Dawn tradition the initiate is linked to the Golden Dawn and the particular order via their Neophyte initiation. However, this link and the particular Order's own link to the broader Golden Dawn current require maintenance on a periodic basis. This is achieved via the Equinox Ceremony performed each March and September. This ceremony is an essential group ceremony within the Golden Dawn, for by it each Order and temple renew their connection to the inner realms that are the source of the magic and spiritual blessings of the tradition itself. Without the correct performance of the ceremony, this link is simply weakened or even lost. This is not a situation unique to the Golden Dawn, but follows the pattern of installation and re-consecration ceremonies within many Masonic and fraternal Orders in the West. Essentially what it is saying is that the spiritual blessings and currents of the Golden Dawn, like everything else within the manifest universe, are in a constant state of change and evolution. We need to reconnect with these sources from time to time to maintain our link in its most transformational and evolved form. To use a modern metaphor, we need to connect with the 'latest version' of the spiritual software.

This ceremony has been discussed in Pat and Chris Zalewski's *The Solstice and Equinox Ceremonies of the Golden Dawn* and in John Michael Greer's *Circles of Power*, which I highly recommend. The original Golden Dawn had a few notes on the inner workings of the Equinox, which may be found in Regardie's *The Golden Dawn*. Within many Western traditions deep magical work ceases in the days leading up to the Equinox. This is because at the Equinox the inner contacts of the magician and the Order, which are the source of any effective magic, are broken and must be picked up or renewed for the following six months. This is one of the functions of the ceremony. This may be understood by using the metaphor of surfing upon the Light. To surf we need a wave, a movement in the ocean, which in connection with the currents of Western magic is the movement of the Light from the highest point at Summer Solstice to the lowest at Winter Solstice and back again. As long as there is an imbalance between light and dark, there is a 'wave', a current of magic available. At the Equinoxes there is no imbalance – light are dark are equal and no current can be found.

As part of the Equinox we are required to embrace the stillness, the point of balance, and then to link ourselves to the first changes in the 'ocean', as they are the key to the growth of the light or dark, and the spiritual current for the next six months. In Golden Dawn terms, these first changes are expressed by the utterance of the new password, which embodies and grounds the currents into Assiah for the next six months. Within many Orders the password is obtained from the inner guardians who are beyond even the solar currents and Tiphareth and who therefore know, and in fact help gestate, the current for the forthcoming six months. Thus the password becomes a potent vehicle for the expression of the currents of the Order through its ceremonies and members.

As solo magicians, once we have connected to the Golden Dawn tradition through the connection ceremony described earlier, it is essential that we re-link and re-vitalise our connection every Equinox. To help solo magicians do this a modified solo Equinox ceremony is included here. There are a few other solo versions of the Equinox Ceremony extant but none that I feel explain the inner work adequately or avoid mixing the ceremony with Inner Order symbols and currents. I used solo versions of the Equinox to great effect for a number of years before the foundation of our current temple. The version here is very simple and is conducted within a temple that is also consecrated very simply. The reason for this is to allow newcomers to magic to start connecting to the tradition as early as possible. When you are more experienced and have other magical techniques clear and strong you may wish to enlarge this ceremony somewhat, based on the full ceremony itself. Suggestions for expansion are given throughout.

Preparation. As with the Connection Ceremony, a password will need to be chosen. Use exactly the same method as described earlier but focusing on your spiritual unfoldment over the next six months. You may choose this password during the weeks leading up to the ceremony; you certainly should know it a week beforehand. However it is important to continue to use your current password right up until the night of the Equinox and not to use the new password. Also when learning and practicing the ritual beforehand it is not a good idea to speak aloud the new password. Let it sit ready for the ritual itself. All ceremonies of the Equinox need to be performed on the day or within 48 hours of the Equinox. This is essential as we are working with real magical and seasonal energies and blessings linked to the physical Solar Cycle.

To gain the most out of the Equinox ceremony we need to be able to connect with the spiritual powers that infuse and are behind the complete solar cycle. For the newcomer to the ceremony an easy way to do this is to practice the following ritual several times a week in the period leading up to the Equinox. This little ritual is very useful for getting a clear understanding at a deep level of the cycle of various spiritual blessings and powers, and you may wish to practice it throughout the year.

MOVEMENTS WITH THE SUN

1. Lesser Banishing Ritual of Pentagram.
2. Ask your Higher and Divine Genius to aid you in this exercise to know fully in all of your being the four-fold cycle and power of the universe.
3. Take an empty chalice or cup and place within it a tea-light candle. A glass chalice is best or a votive candle holder, though they can get hot after a while. Place it at the East of your temple space.

4. Spend a few minutes consciously attuning yourself to the power of the Sun. Pay particular attention to the four phases of the Sun: Spring Equinox, Summer Solstice, Autumn Equinox and Winter Solstice. Do not worry if you do not have much ceremonial experience of these times of year, just open yourself to their energies by knowing them also as: Light Growing, Full Light, Dark Growing, Full Dark.

5. Go to the East. Light your candle. Extinguish any other lights in the room. With your right hand hold the chalice at the level of your heart. Know yourself to be at the East, and imagine yourself as the Spring Equinox; the light and dark equally balanced, though with the internal pressure for the light to grow. Feel what this is like.

6. Now slowly walk around the edge of your temple towards the South. As you walk, imagine yourself moving and changing through the season. As you walk slowly raise the chalice higher and higher, until by the time you reach South it is held as high as you can above your head.

7. Pause at the South for a while. Know yourself to be at the South, and imagine yourself as the Summer Solstice, the light in full expression, though at this exact moment of greatest light, the seed of the dark is reborn amidst the light, and from this moment on, the light will begin to lessen and the dark grow. Feel what this is like.

8. Now slowly walk around the edge of your temple towards the West. As you walk, imagine yourself moving and changing through the season. As you walk slowly lower the chalice lower and lower, until by the time you reach West it is held at the level of your heart.

9. Pause at the West for a while. Know yourself to be at the West, and imagine yourself as the Autumn Equinox; the light and dark equally balanced, though with the internal pressure for the dark to grow. Feel what this is like.

10. Now slowly walk around the edge of your temple towards the North. As you walk, imagine yourself moving and changing through the season. As you walk slowly lower the chalice lower and lower, until by the time you reach North it is held as low as you can towards the ground.

11. Pause at the North for a while. Know yourself to be at the North, and imagine yourself as the Winter Solstice, the dark in full expression, though at this exact moment of greatest darkness, the seed of the light is reborn amidst the dark, and from this moment on, the dark will begin to lessen and the light grow. Feel what this is like.

12. Now slowly walk around the edge of your temple, back towards the East. As you walk, imagine yourself moving and changing through

the season. As you walk slowly raise the chalice higher and higher, until by the time you reach East it is held level with your heart.

13. Pause at the East a while. Now repeat the cycle, this time shortening your pauses at the four directions, getting a sense of the continuous, unbroken cycle of the Sun and the four powers of the Universe. Keep repeating cycles until you can move without pausing, fully aware of the four-fold powers as part of an unbroken stream of life.

14. End by returning to the East, thanking your Higher and Divine Genius and performing any grounding you feel you may require.

As you develop ease and confidence with this exercise, add one correspondence from the table below to your journey, attuning to it at the four directions. So you may like to add the four elements, attuning to them at the quarters while you move as the Sun, until you get a sense of their connection and cycle. Then choose another correspondence until you have done several or all and you have experienced them interrelating as an unbroken cycle.

Table 8: Four-fold Correspondences

	Sunrise	Noon	Sunset	Midnight
Direction	East	South	West	North
Element	Air	Fire	Water	Earth
Power	Creation	Preservation	Destruction	Redemption
Colour	Yellow	Red	Blue	Green
Season	Spring	Summer	Autumn	Winter
Life Cycle	Birth	Maturity	Death	Mystery
Light	Light Growing	Full Light	Dark Growing	Full Dark
Moon	First Quarter	Full Moon	Last Quarter	New Moon
Archangel	Raphael	Michael	Gabriel	Auriel
Tool	Sword	Wand	Cup	Disk
Animal	Angel	Lion	Eagle	Bull
Power	Will	Daring	Knowledge	Silence
YHVH	Vau	Yod	Heh	Heh (final)

Solo Equinox Ceremony

Temple Layout: Lay out the temple and altar in the same way as the Golden Dawn Connection Ceremony above with the addition of a single, small white candle or lamp on the central altar. This should be placed directly East of the red cross.

Opening the Temple

Much of this is the same as the Connection Ceremony, so please refer to that ritual for further details. The temple may also be opened by the Watchtower Ceremony or simply include the Supreme Invoking Ritual of the Pentagram.

Lesser Banishing Ritual of the Pentagram.

Purification by Water. As in the Connection Ceremony.
Consecration By Fire. As in the Connection Ceremony.

Consecrating the Four Elemental Symbols. As in the Connection Ceremony. Take a minute or two to visualise the four Archangels around you also. If the temple was opened by Watchtower or in a more advanced ritual the four Kerubim would replace the four Archangels.

The Mystic Circumambulation. As in the Connection Ceremony.

Adoration to the Lord of the Universe. As in the Connection Ceremony.

Cleansing the Central Lamp. At the West of the altar facing East, pick up and cleanse the white candle or lamp using the method suggested for the incense in the Connection Ceremony.

Annoucing the Ceremony

Stand at the altar facing East. Knock once upon the altar. Pause and say clearly: 'I am (name) and I have come to celebrate the festival of the Vernal/Autumnal Equinox within the Golden Dawn tradition.'

Inner Work: As you stand facing East inwardly connect with the spiritual focus embodied by the new password. Remember the choosing of the word and the impetus of spiritual unfoldment it represents for you. Once you have this strongly in your consciousness, give the knock, which as the Golden Dawn text states symbolically and energetically 'heralds the initiation of a fresh current' and links it to the temple. By performing this simple action you make a link with the new spiritual current before you let go of the old. This ensures continuity across the still void of the Equinox. It is similar to taking hold of the rung of a ladder above you before letting go of the one in front of you. The statement of intention uses the form of the traditional Equinox ceremony and helps to form a link to it, however small.

Pause and then knock once on the altar. Say clearly: 'In the name of the Lord of the Universe, who works in silence and whom naught but silence can express, I acknowledge the Vernal/Autumnal Equinox is upon me and that the password (old password) is abrogated.'

Inner Work: Inwardly connect with the spiritual focus embodied by the old password. See the word in front of you and then quickly allow the image to fade, sensing and letting go of the spiritual impetus and meaning behind the word. Once you have done this, give the knock which grounds this process of surrendering into Assiah. The letting go of the meaning behind the word accomplishes the surrender on the mental level. The fading of the image of the word does the same on the astral level and the knock works upon the etheric level. The form of the words are from the original Equinox ceremony.

Say clearly: 'Let me consecrate according to ancient custom, the return of the Equinox.

Move to the East of the altar facing West. Stand in the form of a cross and say slowly, pausing between the words:

Light
Darkness
East
West
Air
Water

Inner Work: A this point in the ceremony you are preparing to bring the various forces within the subtle realms of temple into balance above the altar. At the end of this process all the forces will be balanced and unified in the temple, mirroring the balance of light and dark and the magical currents at the Equinox. Standing in the form of a cross helps to bring balance within your physical and etheric bodies. The position East of the altar mirrors the placement of the officer performing the balancing role within the traditional Equinox ceremony. While in the form of the cross imagine and see clearly your entire auric sphere glowing with white light.

Inwardly intone the names **AHIH** and **AGLA** several times and with each intonation see your sphere glow brighter. Through your visualisation and the sacred names you are charging your sphere with the Quintessence, the power and blessings of Spirit that will help reconcile and balance the elements.

Next there are three sets of polarities to be invoked. The first, light and dark, are brought about by simple visualisation; visualise strongly golden light from the sun at the East. Once you have this powerfully, say 'light' and see the light move from the East towards you, entering your astral sphere through your back and passing through you into the West. Now imagine darkness in the West and say the word, seeing the darkness move toward you and enter your sphere, passing through you into the West. Do the same with the words, East and West. With the elements, imagine strongly and call forth the blessings of Air from Raphael and Water from Gabriel as you say the words 'Air' and 'Water'. Again these should move into your sphere and from there through to the opposite end of the temple. There is now an energetic polarity from East to West running between the two opposite powers.

Knock once on the altar and say clearly: 'I am the reconciler between them'.

Inner Work: Inwardly now imagine the six currents of astral energy invoked by the words are now drawn into your sphere where they are balanced. This is done via your charged auric sphere, your will, visualisation and the placement of yourself towards the centre of the temple. The knock then links and grounds this balances into the subtle form of the altar.

Give the Sign of the Enterer directly towards the altar top. Follow it immediately with the Sign of Silence.

Inner Work: These signs will link your own personal sphere with the balance being established within the subtle components of the altar. The Sign of the Enterer sends out your will and Ruach to the altar to make the connection. The Sign of Silence withdraws the link and brings back the reconciliation into your sphere.

Pause. Now return to standing in the form of a cross and say slowly, pausing between the words:

Heat
Cold
South
North
Fire
Earth

Inner Work: The inner work here is very similar to that done between East and West but with a change in symbols and powers. After standing once more in the form of the cross, again see clearly your entire auric sphere glowing with white light. The three sets of polarities are formed from South to North and North to South passing through the left and right sides of your sphere respectively.

Knock once on the altar and say clearly: 'I am the reconciler between them'.

Inner Work: Inwardly now imagine the six currents of astral energy (invoked by the words) are now drawn into your sphere where they are balanced, as in the polarity between East and West.

Give the Sign of the Enterer directly towards the altar top. Follow it immediately with the Sign of Silence.

Inner Work: The same inner work occurs here as in the Signs given following the balance between East and West. The inner action up to now has created an astral form of an equal armed cross within the temple, running from the quarters and centring on the altar. This is the symbol of the reconciled four-fold powers of the elements and also a symbol of balance. The Neophyte Signs have linked your own personal sphere to this symbol and reservoir of balanced astral light.

Stand once more in the form of a cross and say clearly:

One Creator
One Preserver
One Destroyer
One Redeemer

Knock once on the altar and say clearly: 'One reconciler between them'.

Give the Sign of the Enterer directly towards the altar top. Follow it immediately with the Sign of Silence.

Inner Work: At the end of the balancing between North and South, the realms of the elemental powers and the powers of nature have been balanced. We now move to the balancing of the power of the Sun and also the spiritual powers of the Sun as expressed through the single word associated with the four directions. As you say 'one creator' visualise strongly the sun rising at the East of the temple and feel its creative, birthing power. After you have spoken, quickly visualise this power move around the temple towards the South. As you say 'one preserver' visualise strongly the sun high in the sky at the South and feel its preserving and growing powers. After you have spoken, quickly visualise this power move around the temple towards the West. As you say 'one destroyer' visualise the sun sinking into the Western ocean at the West and feel its destructive powers and sense its death. After you have spoken, quickly visualise this power move around the temple towards the North As you say 'one redeemer' visualise intense darkness alive with hidden powers at the North and sense the power of redemption and mystery. After you have spoken, quickly visualise this power move around the temple towards the East and complete the circle at the East.

If you have worked with the exercise described previously, 'Movements with the Sun', this process will be very easy to achieve. As you knock, draw this energetic circle of spiritual blessings inward towards the altar. This is not simply a process of drawing in from each direction but rather, the complete circle that is formed around the temple. It can be best visualised as a reverse ripple moving into and concentrating upon the altar. The knock earths and grounds this reconciliation and balance into the altar which you link to via the Neophyte signs once again. At this stage there is a complete equilibrium and balance of the various powers. Within this still void, a reflection of the macrocosmic stillness of the Equinox, you are ready to let go of the old impetus of your spiritual unfoldment symbolised by the password.

Move to the West of the altar. Take off your Neophyte lamen and lay it on the altar atop the cross and triangle. As you do so say: 'With the password (old password) I lay down my lamen.'

Pick up the rose and take it directly to the East of the temple and place it there. Return to the West of the altar and do the same with the lamp. Then the cup and finally the plate.

Inner Work It is here that you fully surrender the spiritual impetus or current symbolised by the old password. This current, through your magical work and previous Equinox Ceremony or Connection Ceremony, has been linked to your lamen. As you place the lamen on the altar, above the energised symbol of the reconciling spirit (the Cross and Triangle on the altar) you symbolically and energetically place the lamen and current into the sphere of reconciliation and balance, the still void. The current of the old password is then surrendered and disperses into this void. In a more advanced solo ceremony the magician's personal tools of the four elements (and any other tools) would be surrendered and placed within the sphere of reconciliation in a similar manner.

With the movement of the symbols of the elements to the perimeters of the circle you are in one sense opening your elemental and astral spheres. This will allow the influx of the new current to enter you and the lamen deeply later on. Another way of looking at this is to say that you have expanded your own elemental sphere to incorporate the entire temple and the powers invoked within it.

Move to the North-East and face the East, ready for a circumambulation around the temple. When ready, circle to the East. Stop and pick up the rose. Face East and hold the rose up towards the East. Say: 'Let us adore the Lord of the Universe. Holy art thou, Lord of the Air, who hast made the firmament.' With the rose inscribe an equal armed cross in the air, about three feet in length and width. Still holding the rose, carefully give the Sign of the Enterer towards the East followed immediately by the Sign of Silence.

Place the rose down and circle to the South. Pick up the lamp, face South and say: ' Let us adore the Lord of the Universe. Holy art thou, Lord of Fire, wherein thou hast shown forth the throne of glory.' With the lamp inscribe another equal armed cross. Still holding the lamp, carefully give the Sign of the Enterer towards the South followed immediately by the Sign of Silence.

Place the lamp down and circle to the West. Pick up the cup, face West and say: 'Let us adore the Lord of the Universe. Holy art thou, Lord of Water, whereon the spirit moved at the beginning.' With the cup inscribe another equal armed cross. Still holding the cup, carefully give the Sign of the Enterer towards the West followed immediately by the Sign of Silence.

Place the cup down and circle to the North. Pick up the plate, face North and say: 'Let us adore the Lord of the Universe. Holy art thou, Lord of the Earth, which thou hast made for thy footstool.' With the plate inscribe another equal armed cross. Still holding the plate, carefully give the Sign of the Enterer towards the North followed immediately by the Sign of Silence.

Place the plate down and continue to circle and complete the circle in
the East.

Inner Work: The circling around the temple is to link the invocations
of the macrocosmic elemental powers in one continuous stream, rather
than have them as four distinct invocations. Your repeated practice of
the exercise 'Movements with the Sun' is of help here. The rose and other
elemental symbols can be seen as the separated elemental principles of
your own sphere. During the invocation you are offering these aspects
of yourself to the Lords of the elements as a vehicle for their adoration.
The Macrocosmic powers of the Lord of the Air are now brought into
the sphere of the temple. As you say the words, try and connect with the
deepest sense you have of the elemental realm of Air. Aspiration alone
here is often enough to bring forth mental realm energies through the
Archangel already invoked during the opening. The cross is formed on
the inner levels in the same manner as the pentagrams; draw energy
from Kether and Malkuth and mix them in Tiphareth before directing
the combined energy out through the arms. The energy then enters the
vase and rose which modifies it further as you draw the cross. The cross
is visualised and formed in bright yellow light.

As you give the Sign of the Enterer, project your will through the
cross, sending it out to the ends of the Universe at the East to connect
with the full blessings of the Lord of Air. As you give the Sign of Silence
draw all the blessings of macrocosmic Air, mediated through the balance
of the cross, into your subtle bodies. The process of adoration, inscription
of cross and use of the Neophyte Signs is repeated in exactly the same
manner at each of the quarters. The only difference is the element, words
of adoration, tool and colour of the cross inscribed. The colours follow
the standard elemental colours. The final circling from North to East
completes the circle and links all four elemental powers and invocations.
In one sense this is the spirit active, the power that connects and links
the elements while each remain separate. The spirit passive, where the
elements unify and combine in the centre of the circle, is worked with
during the next invocation.

Move directly to the East of the altar facing West. Pick up the white
candle or lamp, hold it on high and say:

'Let us adore the Lord of the Universe. Holy art thou who art in all
things, and in whom all things art. If I climb up to heaven, thou art
there and if I go down unto Hell thou art there also! If I take the
wings of the morning and flee unto the uttermost parts of the sea,

even there thy hand shall lead me and thy right hand shall hold me. If I say, peradventure darkness cover me, even the night shall be made light unto thee! Thine is the Air with its movement! Thine is the Fire with its flashing flame! Thine is the Water with its ebb and flow! Thine is the Earth with its enduring stability!''

As you speak the final words 'thine is the Air...' onwards, inscribe in the air above the altar a Calvary cross so that its very base rests directly above your lamen and cross and triangle. Place the candle down and give the Sign of the Enterer towards and into the cross you have just inscribed, immediately followed by the Sign of Silence.

Inner Work: This is the most potent and beautiful part of the entire ceremony. This wonderful passage, based on part of Psalm 139, adores the ever present immanence of the Lord of the Universe, which relates to the Spirit within the elemental schema. During this adoration it is controlled but intense aspiration and worship that will help you to connect deeply at the mental realm. The form of Calvary cross is created in the same manner as the other crosses and is visualised in intense white light. Visualise the very base of the cross entering into your lamen and the cross and triangle. With the words describing the elements and at the name of the element themselves, visualise a beam of light in the colour of the element coming from the quarter into the white cross. So at the end of this adoration, inwardly and upon the astral level there would be four streams of light coming from the quarters and linking themselves to the central Calvary cross of white that hangs above the altar. All the blessings of the four elements, the active and passive spirit are being directed, through the base of the Calvary cross, into the subtle components of your lamen as well as the cross and triangle. This in effect consecrates your lamen.

Move to the East of the temple. Facing West and looking towards the altar, knock or stamp your right foot and say: 'I now declare the new password. It is _____.'

Move directly to the West of the altar, face East, pick up your lamen and say: 'With the power of the password _____ I claim my lamen.'

Inner Work: At the East, inwardly connect with the meaning behind the password and the spiritual impetus it represents for you. Once this is really clear and you can sense it well, say the words and give the knock.

As you speak the word for the first time, visualise it filling the temple space. See it in flashing gold light. Remembering the meaning the word holds for you will help you connect with the word on the mental realm, the visualisation on the astral realm and the knock will earth it into the etheric realm. As you pick up your lamen and speak, see the word enter the lamen, again in gold flashing light. This will link the balanced and consecrated lamen to your password.

Move to the East, pick up the rose and take it directly back to the altar, replacing it in its original position. Do the same with the symbols for Fire, Water and Earth.

Inner Work: You have now symbolically and energetically closed your elemental sphere. Within your sphere is the new password, the new spiritual connection to the Golden Dawn and the charged lamen.

CLOSING

The closing is essentially that of the Connection Ceremony but with the Mystic Repast being taken as part of the closing itself. If you have opened differently you will need to reverse all invocations and pentagrams who have invoked in the opening.

At the West of the altar, pause and then perform a Qabalistic Cross.

Purification by Water and Consecration by Fire. These two actions are done in exactly the same manner as the Opening.

Reverse Mystic Circumambulation. As in the Connection Ceremony.

Adoration to the Lord of the Universe. This is performed exactly as in the opening.

Mystic Repast. As in the Connection Ceremony.

When inhaling the perfume and feeling the heat etc, consciously see and open yourself to the influx of the elemental blessings bestowed upon the astral forms of these symbols by the Lord of the Universe and the greater Macrocosmic powers.

Lesser Banishing Ritual of the Pentagram.

Magical Use of the Neophyte Signs

Like all Western lodge traditions the Golden Dawn has a series of signs, grips and gestures that function as keys or secrets of particular grades. Unlike most traditions, within the Golden Dawn these signs have several layers of meaning and direct, practical application within magical ritual. The two signs taught as part of the Neophyte initiation, the Sign of the Enterer and the Sign of Silence, are the most flexible signs and may be utilised to help achieve a range of magical and spiritual actions. When used in conjunction with each other, the formula of the two signs is one of flux (the Sign of the Enterer) and reflux (the Sign of Silence). The Sign of the Enterer sends out a current of force which, after it acts upon something, or is itself acted upon, is drawn back in via the Sign of Silence. For particular reasons either sign may be used alone. The brief notes here show why these signs are used within the various ceremonies and rituals of the Golden Dawn and within this book.

Practical Uses of the Neophyte Signs

As a salute to the East or the Altar. The Sign of the Enterer is given to the East which is then immediately followed by the Sign of Silence. Traditionally this is done when entering or leaving a temple. The magician sends out a ray from her own will and energy to the East, which is then linked to the blessings of the East, as the place of spiritual re-birth, and then returned to the magician, via the Sign of Silence.

Opening and closing during group ceremony. Here the first sign is given to the East before an action by an officer, and the second at the conclusion of that action. This places that action under the presidency of the spirit of the East, and also makes the ritual more precise, marking off individual segments clearly.

Creation of a channel. Here a particular type of spiritual force is invoked and continually projected (even after the first sign is completed in some cases) until the Sign of Silence is given.

Projecting force from the aura. The particular spiritual force to be projected may be brought into the auric sphere of the magician as she projects it outwards. In this case the sign helps to channel the force. Or the spiritual force may have been previously invoked into the aura, at a different stage of the ritual, or may be from within the being of the magician herself.

Charging Items with Astral and Etheric Force. This is done normally for talismans or Eucharists. Often the signs are employed at the end of an invocation to project the last bit of the invoked force into the object, thus leaving the aura pure and sealed by the Sign of Silence.

The projection of an obsessing thought or negative part of the self. Here the area of the self (pattern of behaviour) to be removed is forcibly projected out and away from the aura, links cut and the Sign of Silence used to seal the aura. The obsessing thought is then banished by the LBRP. The ritual in Chapter Eight on evocation uses the signs in this manner.

An aid to Invocation. A divine power is first awakened within the sphere of the magician. This can be achieved via a number of means, some of which are discussed in Chapter Four. This microcosmic force is then projected out to the universe to awaken a corresponding macrocosmic force, which is then absorbed via the Sign of Silence. The classic example of this process occurs during the Adoration to the Lord of the Universe used within the Connection and Equinox ceremonies. The aspiration and yearning towards the One awakened by the words and adoration is projected out to awaken the powers of the One in the Universe. These are then drawn into the temple and magician at the final line via the Sign of Silence.

Transferring one's consciousness into different realms of being. This has been well discussed within Chapter Seven when discussing Travelling in the Spirit Vision.

Sealing the Aura. Here the Sign of Silence is employed alone. It is especially useful to return to a normal state of consciousness without banishing any spiritual blessings within in the aura that you wish to be retained. We described the use of the sign in this way at the conclusion the Magical Use of the Password process.

AN INVITATION TO SHARE YOUR SPIRITUAL BLESSINGS

THIS is a book about magic and as such the central theme is the transformation of consciousness through active partnership with the Divine. It is my profound wish and hope that any assistance or benefit stemming from this book will not rest with the individual magician, but spread out from them and cause direct and positive changes in the world. Indeed this is the only reason that this book has been written and one of the few valid reasons I can see for the ongoing practice of any form of magic or deep spirituality. In many ways this motivation and rationale counters the contemporary approach to Western magic and spirituality which can be seen in many books, courses and teachers. This approach is by and large concerned with the spiritual advancement of the individual magician and finds its ultimate expression in the striving toward that state of spiritual advancement, symbolised in Western Magic by the grade of Adept Exempt, where the magician no longer needs to re-incarnate after her death.

This individualist approach to the mysteries reflects the dominant Western ideology and is hardly surprising. It also rests upon a number of unconscious assumptions, not the least of which being that it is better 'to get off' the world rather than to heal and transform it. In my understanding however, deep spiritual transformation shatters the core of this 'me' approach and leads to a more compassionate and inclusive practice of spirituality, one that is concerned with community, society and the world.

This is part of a slow but ongoing unfoldment of consciousness, detailed with great excitement and skill by such scholars as Joanna Macy and which I think is best summed up in the phrase: 'moving away from individual salvation and toward communal transformation'. Such an ethic reflects the understanding that as a species, as a society, as a community and even as families, we find ourselves today in a situation where there is so much damage, so much pain and dysfunction, that we either all swim together or sink into oblivion individually.

Once we realize this within the deepest layers of our being, which is at some point *inevitable* if we follow such deep spiritual practices as those offered by the Golden Dawn *and remain fully open to change*, then we are moved to act to heal the world. Our spirituality then becomes a vehicle by which we and those spiritual presences we work with can affect this healing. Our spirituality is no longer cut off from others and concerned solely or mostly with our own 'advancement' but is a powerful force for change and healing of the whole world.

This way of looking at spirituality has always been present within many of the Eastern religions, particularly some Buddhist traditions. It finds its logical and compassionate expression in a tradition where the new monk or nun vows, upon beginning their spiritual path, to work for the liberation and happiness of all sentient Beings for the remainder of her current life and all future lives. This work only ends when all Beings attain Nirvana or the cessation of the causes of suffering – that is, when we all swim together. There are few Western equivalents of this vow, though I am convinced that the same consciousness and approach can be found in the core of the historical Western mysteries.

The germ of this same consciousness, the understanding of the need for societal transformation rather than individual advancement, may also be found hidden within many contemporary Western Magical traditions, including the Golden Dawn. Sadly however the Golden Dawn did not, and does not currently appear to be influenced to any degree by this inner core. Its active expression is found more in the work of Dion Fortune and her Fraternity (now Society) of the Inner Light and magical groups and teachers stemming from her spiritual impetus. It is also to be found in the political Neo-Pagan traditions and is given beautiful and poetic expression through such powerful figures as Starhawk, author, Witch and activist. I see these political-spiritual manifestations of the Goddess revival as continuing the work started by adepts such as Dion Fortune in the last century. I have no idea if Starhawk or her collective, Reclaiming, would agree with such a statement.

In some Buddhist traditions every individual spiritual act is also dedicated to liberation of all Beings by means of a prefacing statement which shares all spiritual benefit gained by the meditation or ritual with all Beings. The statement is accompanied by a profound intention, wish or visualisation, which is what accomplishes this sharing in the inner realms, the theory of which has been described throughout this book.

Once more there are few Western equivalents popular in today's magical community.

I would like therefore invite you to preface each and every spiritual act, meditation, ritual or pathworking, with a small statement to share any benefits you may obtain with others throughout the world. In this way we can all begin the movement away from the focus on personal advancement and move towards communal transformation.

These prefacing statements have been seen by some as silly and sentimental. Nothing could be further from the truth. Performed with a sincere intention they will actually increase the restoration of balance in the world. Further, on an individual level they begin to affect and change us in subtle but powerful ways. By dedicating our energies and awareness, our realizations and our spiritual bliss to help others, we set in motion a powerful force within ourselves. This force will begin to open our hearts more deeply, and make it easier to act within the material world to end injustice, to restore the balance. Our whole lives will become empowered with the energy of compassion and we may find ourselves doing things we never thought we would dare do before – writing letters of protest, making larger donations to charities or attending rallies that seek justice.

Remember, this is just an invitation, but one I ask you to seriously consider.

EXAMPLES OF PREFACING STATEMENTS

Here are a few different versions of Prefacing Statements you may like to consider using, or adapting to suit your own purposes. Writing your own would be even better. Remember it is the intention and sincerity behind the words that count, so do not be concerned with any lack of poetry or beauty you perceive in your own creations. For all of them, a simple visualisation of seeing the energy and insights gained spreading throughout the world will be just fine. You may see this as a light moving from you and expanding to fill the world, or you may see it as a drop of water entering the Sea of Consciousness and Peace where all Beings may drink. Or you may create your own visualisation.

From **Compassion and the Individual**, (1991) Gyatso, Tenzin the 14th Dalai Lama. Wisdom Publications, Boston.

> May all beings everywhere
> Plagued by sufferings of body and mind,
> Obtain an ocean of happiness and joy
> *By virtue of these merits.*
>
> May no living creature suffer,
> Commit evil or ever fall ill.
> May no one be afraid or belittled,
> With a mind weighed down by depression.
>
> May the blind see forms,
> And the deaf hear sounds.
> May those whose bodies are worn with toil
> Be restored on finding repose.
>
> May the naked find clothing,
> The hungry find food;
> May the thirsty find water
> And delicious drinks.
>
> May the poor find wealth,
> Those weak with sorrow find joy;
> May the forlorn find hope,
> Constant happiness and prosperity.
>
> May there be timely rains
> And bountiful harvests;
> May all medicines be effective
> And wholesome prayers bear fruit.
>
> May all who are sick and ill
> Quickly be freed from their ailments.
> Whatever diseases there are in the world,
> May they never occur again.
>
> May the frightened cease to be afraid
> And those bound be freed;
> May the powerless find power
> And may people think of benefiting each other.

From **The Tibetan Book of Living and Dying** (1992) Rinpoche, Sogyal, p.60. Rider, London.

'By the power and the truth of this practice:
May all Beings have happiness, and the causes of happiness;
May all be free from sorrow and the causes of sorrow;
May all never be separated from the sacred happiness which is sorrowless;
And may all live in equanimity without too much attachment and too much aversion,
And live believing in the equality of all that lives.'

Sogyal Rinpoche also gives the following statement that comes at the end of a practice, to 'seal' its energies into usefulness.

'May whatever merit that comes from this practice go toward the enlightenment of all Beings; may it become a drop in the ocean of the activity of all the Buddhas in their tireless work for the liberation of all Beings.'

Adapted from **The Rosy Dawn of the Emerging Goddess Tradition**:

'May all the energies and juices awakened by the virtues of the practices to follow be spread out to all Beings. In the name of She who is One, **Amenti**.'

Another Example:

'May all the powers, energies and consciousness I obtain through these practices be shared with all Beings, in all the worlds and may all come to find eternal peace and happiness. May there be peace, and peace and peace profound. **Amen**.'

SELECT BIBLIOGRAPHY

◆ Ayton, W. A., *The Alchemist of the Golden Dawn: The Letters of the Revd W. A. Ayton to F. L. Gardner and others, 1886-1905.* Wellingborough, Northamptonshire, Aquarian Press, 1985.

◆ Bonewits, Isaac, *Real Magic.* York Beach: Samuel Weiser Incorporated, 1989.

◆ Cicero, Chic & Sandra Tabatha Cicero, *The Essential Golden Dawn: An Introduction to High Magic.* MN: Llewellyn Publications, 2003.

◆ Cicero, Chic & Sandra Tabatha Cicero, *Experiencing the Kabbalah: A Simple Guide to Spiritual Wholeness.* St. Paul, MN: Llewellyn Publications, 1997.

◆ Cicero, Chic & Sandra Tabatha Cicero, eds., *The Golden Dawn Journal, Book I: Divination.* St. Paul, MN: Llewellyn Publications, 1994.

◆ Cicero, Chic & Sandra Tabatha Cicero, eds., *The Golden Dawn Journal, Book II: Qabalah: Theory and Magic.* St. Paul, MN: Llewellyn Publications, 1994.

◆ Cicero, Chic & Sandra Tabatha Cicero, eds., *The Golden Dawn Journal, Book III: The Art of Hermes.* St. Paul, MN: Llewellyn Publications, 1995.

◆ Cicero, Chic & Sandra Tabatha Cicero, *Secrets of a Golden Dawn Temple: The Alchemy and Crafting of Magickal Implements.* St. Paul, MN: Llewellyn Publications, 1992.

◆ Cicero, Chic & Sandra Tabatha Cicero, *Self-Initiation into the Golden Dawn Tradition: A Complete Curriculum of Study for both the Solitary Magician and the Working Magical Group.* St. Paul, MN: Llewellyn Publications, 1995.

◆ Cicero, Chic & Sandra Tabatha Cicero, *The New Golden Dawn Ritual Tarot.* St. Paul, MN: Llewellyn Publications, 1991.

◆ Colquhoun, Ithell, *Sword of Wisdom: MacGregor Mathers and the Golden Dawn.* London: Neville Spearman, 1975.

◆ Crowley, Aleister, *Magick* (book four parts I-IV). London, Routledge and Kegan Paul, 1973.

◆ Crowley, Aleister, *The Book of the Law.* York Beach: Weiser, 1976.

◆ Crowley, Aleister, *777 and Other Qabalistic Writings of Aleister Crowley.* York Beach: Samuel Weiser, 1955.

◆ Douglas-Klotz, Neil, *Desert Wisdom.* San Francisco, Harper, 1994.

◆ Douglas-Klotz, Neil, *Prayers of the Cosmos: Meditations on the Aramaic Words of Jesus.* San Francisco, Harper, 1990.

◆ Farrell, Nick, *Gathering the Magic: Creating 21st Century Esoteric Groups.* London, Immanion Press/Megalithica Books, 2007.

◆ Farrell, Nick, *Magical Pathworking: Techniques of Active Imagination*. St. Paul, MN, Llewellyn Publications, 2004.
◆ Farrell, Nick, *Making Talismans: Living Entities of Power*. St. Paul, MN, Llewellyn Publications, 2001.
◆ Fortune, Dion, *The Mystical Qabalah*. York Beach, ME: Samuel Weiser. 1985.
◆ Gilbert, R. A., *The Golden Dawn Companion*. Wellingborough: Aquarian Press, 1986.
◆ Gilbert, R.A., *The Golden Dawn Scrapbook*. York Beach, ME: Samuel Weiser, Inc., 1997.
◆ Gilbert, R.A., *The Golden Dawn: Twilight of the Magicians*. Wellingborough, Northamptonshire, UK: The Aquarian Press, 1983.
◆ Godwin, David, *Godwin's Qabalistic Encyclopedia*. 2nd Ed. St. Paul, MN, Llewellyn, 1989.
◆ Gray, William G., *Western Inner Workings*. NY, Weiser, 1983.
◆ Greer, John Michael, *Circles of Power: Ritual Magic In The Western Tradition*. St. Paul, MN, Llewellyn Publications, 1997.
◆ Greer, John Michael, *Earth Divination Earth Magic: A Practical Guide to Geomancy*. St. Paul, MN, Llewellyn Publications, 1999.
◆ Greer, John Michael, *Learning Ritual Magic: Fundamental Theory and Practice for the Solitary Apprentice*. St. Paul, MN: Llewellyn Publications, 2011.
◆ Greer, John Michael, *Paths of Wisdom: The Magical Cabala in the Western Tradition*. St. Paul, MN: Llewellyn Publications, 1996.
◆ Greer, John Michael, *Inside a Magical Lodge*. St. Paul, MN, Llewellyn Publications, 1998.
◆ Greer, Mary K., *Women of the Golden Dawn: Rebels and Priestesses*. Rochester, VT: Park Street Press, 1995.
◆ Griffin, David, *The Ritual Magic Manual*. s.l, Golden Dawn Publications, 1999.
◆ Howe, Ellic, *The Magicians of the Golden Dawn: A Documentary History of a Magical Order, 1887-1923*. London: Routledge and Kegan Paul, 1972.
◆ King, Francis and Skinner, Stephen, *Techniques of High Magic*. New York, Destiny Books, 1976.
◆ King, Francis, *Ritual Magic in England: 1887 to the Present Day*. London: Spearman, 1970.
◆ Knight, Gareth, *A Practical Guide to Qabalistic Symbolism*. NY, Weiser, 1975.
◆ Knight, Gareth, and Fortune, Dion, *The Circuit of Force: Occult Dynamics of the Etheric Vehicle*. Loughborough, Thoth, 1998.
◆ Knight, Gareth, *Experience of the Inner Worlds*. Cheltenham, Skylight Press, 2010.

- Knight, Gareth, *Magic and the Western Mind: Ancient Knowledge and the Transformation of Consciousness.* St. Paul, MN, Llewellyn, 1991.
- Knight, Gareth, *The Practice of Ritual Magic.* Cheltenham, Helios, 1969.
- Knight, Gareth, *The Rose Cross and the Goddess: the Quest for the Eternal Feminine Principle.* Northamptonshire, Aquarian Press, 1985.
- Knight, Gareth, *The Treasure House of Images: an Introduction to the Magical Dynamics of the Tarot.* Northamptonshire, Aquarian Press, 1986.
- Kraig, Donald Michael, *Modern Magick: Eleven Lessons in the High Magickal Arts.* St. Paul, MN, Llewellyn, 1988.
- Kuntz, Darcy, *The Complete Golden Dawn Cipher Manuscript.* Edmonds, WA: Holmes Publishing Group, 1996.
- Mathers, S. L. MacGregor & J.W. Brodie-Innes, *The Sorcerer and His Apprentice: Unknown Hermetic Writings of S.L. MacGregor Mathers and J.W. Brodie-Innes.* Aquarian Press, 1983.
- Mathers, S. L. MacGregor et al., *Astral Projection, Ritual Magic and Alchemy.* Ed. by Francis King; Rochester, VT: Destiny Books, 1987.
- Parfitt, Will, *The Living Qabalah: a Practical and Experiential Guide to Understanding the Tree of Life.* Dorset, Element, 1988.
- Regardie, Israel, *Foundations of Practical Magic,* Northamptonshire, Aquarian Press, 1979.
- Regardie, Israel, *The Complete Golden Dawn System of Magic.* Phoenix, AZ: Falcon Press, 1984.
- Regardie, Israel, *The Golden Dawn: A Complete Course in Practical Ceremonial Magic.* St. Paul, MN: Llewellyn Publications, 1989. 6th ed.
- Regardie, Israel, *What You Should Know about the Golden Dawn.* Phoenix, AZ: Falcon Press, 1983. 3rd ed.
- Regardie, Israel. *A Garden of Pomegranates: Skrying on the Tree of Life.* 3rd ed., St Paul, MN: Llewellyn Publications, 1999.
- Regardie, Israel. *Foundations of Practical Magic.* Wellingborough, Northamptonshire, The Aquarian Press, 1979.
- Regardie, Israel. *The Middle Pillar: The Balance Between Mind and Magic.* 3th ed., St Paul, MN: Llewellyn Publications, 1998.
- Regardie, Israel. *The Tree of Life: An Illustrated Study in Magic.* St. Paul, MN: Llewellyn Publications, 2000.
- Richardson, Alan, *An Introduction to the Mystical Qabala,* Northamptonshire, Aquarian Press, 1981.
- Stewart, R.J. (ed.), *Psychology and the Spiritual Traditions.* Dorset, Element, 1990.
- Stewart, R.J., *The Underworld Initiation.* Northamptonshire, Aquarian, 1985.
- Suster, Gerald, *Crowley's Apprentice: the Life and Ideas of Israel Regardie.* York Beach, ME: Samuel Weiser, 1990.

- Torrens, R.G., *The Inner Teachings of the Golden Dawn*. London: Spearman, 1969.
- Torrens, R.G., *The Secret Rituals of the Golden Dawn*. Wellingborough, Northamptonshire. Aquarian Press, 1973.
- Wang, Robert, *An Introduction to the Golden Dawn Tarot*. NY: Samuel Weiser, 1978.
- Wang, Robert, *The Qabalistic Tarot*, York Beach: Samuel Weiser, Inc. 1983.
- Wang, Robert, *The Secret Temple*. NY: Samuel Weiser, 1980.
- Westcott, William Wynn, *The Magical Mason: Forgotten Hermetic Writings of William Wynn Westcott, Physician and Magus*. Wellingborough, Northamptonshire: Aquarian Press, 1985.
- Zalewski, Chris, *Enochian Chess of the Golden Dawn*. St. Paul, MN: Llewellyn Publications, 1994.
- Zalewski, Pat & Chris, *Z-5 Secret Teachings of the Golden Dawn, Book 2: The Zelator Ritual 1=10*. St. Paul, MN: Llewellyn Publications, 1992.
- Zalewski, Pat, *Golden Dawn Enochian Magic*. St. Paul, MN: Llewellyn Publications, 1990.
- Zalewski, Pat, *Golden Dawn Rituals and Commentaries*. Rosicrucian Order of the Golden Dawn, 2010.
- Zalewski, Pat, *The Kabbalah of the Golden Dawn*. St. Paul, MN: Llewellyn Publications, 1993.
- Zalewski, Pat, *Z-5 Secret Teachings of the Golden Dawn, Book 1: The Neophyte Ritual 0=0*. St. Paul, MN: Llewellyn Publications, 1991.
- Zalewski, Patrick & Chris, *The Equinox and Solstice Rituals of the Golden Dawn*. St. Paul, MN, Llewellyn Publications, 1992.
- Zalewski, Patrick J., *The Secret Inner Order Rituals of the Golden Dawn*. Ed. by Joseph Lisiewski. Phoenix, AZ: Falcon Press, 1988.

Lightning Source UK Ltd.
Milton Keynes UK
UKHW010742050821
388357UK00001B/18